KIDS, COPS, AND CONFESSIONS

Kids, Cops, and Confessions

Inside the Interrogation Room

Barry C. Feld

NEW YORK UNIVERSITY PRESS

New York and London

NEW YORK UNIVERSITY PRESS
New York and London
www.nyupress.org

References to Internet websites (URLs) were accurate at the time of writing.
Neither the author nor New York University Press is responsible for URLs
that may have expired or changed since the manuscript was prepared.

Library of Congress Cataloging-in-Publication Data
Feld, Barry C.
Kids, cops, and confessions : inside the interrogation room / Barry C. Feld.
p.   cm.
Includes bibliographical references and index.
ISBN 978-0-8147-2777-5 (cl : alk. paper) — ISBN 978-0-8147-7046-7 (ebook) —
ISBN 978-0-8147-7067-2 (ebook)
1. Juvenile justice, Administration of—United States. 2. Police questioning—
United States. 3. Juvenile delinquents—United States.   I. Title.
HV9104.F443 2012
363.25´40830973—dc23   2012024948

New York University Press books are printed on acid-free paper,
and their binding materials are chosen for strength and durability.
We strive to use environmentally responsible suppliers and materials
to the greatest extent possible in publishing our books.

Manufactured in the United States of America

10 9 8 7 6 5 4 3 2 1

For Patricia

CONTENTS

ACKNOWLEDGMENTS

I have accumulated many debts and received assistance from many people to write this book. Support from the National Science Foundation #0813807 enabled me to code and analyze the data. I am grateful to Dr. Susan Brodie Haire, Program Director, Law and Social Science, who shepherded this naïf through the NSF bureaucracy. I received generous supplemental support from the University of Minnesota during my 2009–2010 sabbatical, when I began to write this book in earnest. The University of Minnesota Law School provided additional support during several summers of writing. Several deans at the University of Minnesota Law School—Alex Johnson, Fred Morrison, Guy Charles, and especially David Wippman—supported and encouraged this project.

Four county attorneys and their deputies cooperated and provided unrestricted access to their files without knowing what I might find. I am grateful for the access and assistance I received from Anoka County Attorney Robert Johnson, Jr., and head of juvenile division Mick Chmiel; Dakota County Attorney James Backstrom and head of the juvenile division Don Bruce; Hennepin County Attorney Michael Freeman and first deputy Pat Diamond; and Ramsey County Attorneys Susan Gaertner and John Choi and head of juvenile division Kathryn Santelmann Richtman. Commander Neil Nelson, St. Paul Police Department (ret.), trained Minnesota police to conduct recorded interviews, shared his expertise and experience, and facilitated my access to several departments and officers. Thirty-nine police officers, prosecutors, public defenders, and judges shared their insights. These busy professionals helped me to understand their work and appreciate its complexities.

The Robina Foundation sponsored a conference at the University of Minnesota Law School in May 2011 to review an earlier draft of this book. Donna Bishop, Susanna Blumenthal, Brad Colbert, Steve Drizin, Richard Frase, Bert Kritzer, Richard Leo, Robert Levy, Perry Moriearty, Josh Page, Allison Redlich, Kevin Reitz, Christopher Slobogin, Joshua Tepfer, Charles Weisselberg, and Jennifer Woolard read the entire manuscript, provided detailed critiques, and suggested many ways to improve the book. They brainstormed the title of this book— *Kids, Cops, and Confessions: Inside the Interrogation Room*—a vast improvement on my working title. Jack Greene and Ray Bull read chapters and provided additional insights. Patricia Feld read the final manuscript and provided editorial insights.

Despite their wise counsel, I alone am responsible for the contents of this book.

The University of Minnesota Law School is a marvelous place to work and provides terrific support for the scholarly enterprise. The Law School provided funding for initial data collection and ongoing research assistance. Several research assistants provided exceptional help with this project. Christina Wild, class of 2008, spent many hours culling and copying interrogation files in two counties. Joe Windler, class of 2007; Ben Kaplan, 2010; Julia Norsetter, 2012; and Jamie Buskirk, 2013, provided prompt and cheerful legal research on many topics. Sarah Lageson, Ph.D. candidate, Department of Sociology, provided statistical and analytical assistance far beyond my limited capabilities. The University of Minnesota Law School Library provides prompt and excellent support for faculty. David Zopfi-Jordan retrieved resources with speed and efficiency. I am grateful to all of these kind and generous people.

This book culminates a research project that began years ago. I published two articles based on initial research in Ramsey County. I am grateful to the *Minnesota Law Review* for permission to use "Juveniles' Competence to Exercise Miranda Rights: An Empirical Study of Policy and Practice," *Minnesota Law Review* 91:26–100 (2006), and to Northwestern University School of Law for permission to use "Police Interrogation of Juveniles: An Empirical Study of Policy and Practice," *Journal of Criminal Law & Criminology* 97:219–316 (2006).

As always, my wife, Patricia Feld, provides the foundation of all I do. Her unconditional love and unstinting support bring meaning, joy, and purpose to my life. More than many projects, she shared this study with me tape by tape as each story unfolded, and tolerated my distraction during the writing and revising of this book. There are no words adequate to express my gratitude to her for the life we share.

Introduction

Much of what passes for knowledge about police interviewing practices is no more than assumption and conjecture. Such knowledge probably owes more to television, films, or novels than to any informed understanding of what happens in police interview rooms. Because of the secrecy that has always surrounded police-suspect interviews and the traditional reluctance of police officers to allow outsiders access to the interview room, debates on the crucial questions of interview procedures had to be conducted in something of an information vacuum.[1]

Police interrogation raises complex legal, normative, and policy questions about justice administration and the relationship between the individual and the state. A fundamental tension exists between interests of law enforcement and protecting citizens. How should we structure the criminal process to maintain fair procedures, to process cases efficiently, to assure accurate fact-finding, to prevent police misconduct, and to protect the community from criminals? What practices should a democratic society allow police to use when they question citizens?

These questions become even more problematic when police question juveniles. For more than a century, juvenile and criminal justice policies have reflected two competing images of youth. On one hand, policymakers describe children as immature and vulnerable. On the other hand, they depict youths as mature, responsible, and adultlike. These competing constructs of youth implicate substantive policies (culpability and criminal responsibility) and procedural policies (competence to exercise legal rights) in the justice system.

At the beginning of the twentieth century, Progressive Era reformers emphasized youths' immaturity and vulnerability and created a separate juvenile court to shield children from criminal trials and punishment in adult prisons. They characterized children as irresponsible and incompetent, rejected claims for procedural protections, and created a civil, rehabilitative system for young people in lieu of punitive criminal justice.[2] By the end of the twentieth century, lawmakers adopted harsh, get-tough policies that equated adolescents' culpability with that of adults. In the 1980s and 1990s, states revised laws to prosecute more and younger juveniles in criminal court and to punish delinquents more severely.[3] The imagery of youth shifted from vulnerable children to mature, responsible offenders. The increased legal complexity and consequences of delinquency proceedings make greater demands on youth who may lack the ability or judgment to exercise rights effectively.

Over the past three decades, a procedural and substantive convergence has transformed the juvenile court from a nominally rehabilitative, social welfare agency into a second-class criminal court for young people.[4] While the sanctions of juvenile courts may be less harsh than criminal sentences, the direct penalties (institutional confinement) and collateral consequences (transfer to criminal court, use of delinquency convictions to enhance sentences, sex offender registration, and the like) share similar penal elements.[5] The Supreme Court recognized that "the State intended to punish its juvenile offenders," and *In re Gault* adopted the Fifth Amendment privilege against self-incrimination to bolster the adversarial model in juvenile courts.[6] *Breed v. Jones* applied the Fifth Amendment prohibition on double jeopardy to delinquency adjudications.

> We believe it is simply too late in the day to conclude . . . that a juvenile is not put in jeopardy at a proceeding whose object is to determine whether he has committed acts that violate a criminal law and whose potential consequences include both the stigma inherent in such a determination and the deprivation of liberty for many years. . . . [T]here is little to distinguish an adjudicatory hearing . . . from a traditional criminal prosecution.[7]

Accordingly, one cannot justify a less protective legal framework to interrogate juveniles than for adults because of juvenile courts' rehabilitative claims. On the other hand, adolescents' developmental differences may warrant different procedural safeguards during interrogations.

Obtaining information from suspects is a critical part of any criminal investigation. Offenders' confessions and admissions may be keys to successful criminal and delinquency prosecutions because they lead almost ineluctably to a plea or conviction. Despite the crucial role of interrogation in criminal and juvenile justice, we know remarkably little about what happens when police question suspects, what the outcomes of interviews are, or how they affect justice administration.[8]

Police, prosecutors, defense lawyers, and trial judges who deal regularly with the fruits of interrogation—confessions, admissions, denials, and leads to corroborating evidence—do not have the luxury to systematically analyze the process. Police have resisted incursions into interrogation rooms by social scientists, whom they suspiciously regard as outsiders and potential critics.[9] Law professors, psychologists, and criminologists who write about interrogation lack access to the places where police question criminal suspects. Appellate courts frame rules of interrogation based on a narrow and biased sample of cases. To obtain appellate review, a defendant must move to suppress a confession, receive an adverse ruling, plead guilty and preserve the right to appeal, or take the case to trial.

Most of what appellate judges, criminologists, legal scholars, and the public think we know about interrogation derives from aberrational cases of egregious abuses, false confessions and wrongful convictions, or television drama programs, "reality" shows, and movies that misleadingly depict how police question suspects. In the four decades since *Miranda*, we have few empirical studies about what actually occurs inside an interrogation room and no observational studies of how police question juveniles.[10]

At first blush, the Fifth Amendment privilege against self-incrimination is an anomalous constitutional provision. Other testimonial privileges—for example, doctor-patient, priest-penitent, or attorney-client—promote important relationships and serve social values in contexts where candor is paramount: health, salvation, or effective representation. By contrast, only people who believe they are guilty of a crime may invoke the Fifth Amendment to withhold information. Unlike the Fourth Amendment, which protects only "reasonable expectations of privacy" and even then only conditionally, the Fifth Amendment applies increasingly as the state's belief in a suspect's guilt rises. The protections of the Fifth Amendment are contrary to common sense, common morality, and decent conduct outside the courtroom. Every parent teaches a misbehaving child that the most important thing is to "tell the truth." The privilege functions as an impediment to finding the truth because in most instances, an accused person will be the best source of information about what happened. Rather than to protect the innocent, it may make it more difficult for a blameless person to establish the truth because it prevents police from questioning the guilty one. Western European democracies have no similar absolute prohibition; some allow judges or prosecutors to question defendants in court, and others draw negative inferences from a person's refusal to answer police questions.

With so little to commend the privilege against self-incrimination, why is it enshrined in the Constitution and popular culture—"I plead the Fifth"? Perhaps it protects an inarticulate innocent person from a bad trial performance if compelled to answer. Perhaps it encourages police to conduct better investigations if they have to work independently. Perhaps it allows a guilty person to avoid the "cruel trilemma" of self-incrimination, contempt for refusal to answer, or perjury conviction for answering falsely. Perhaps it protects personal dignity by not requiring a person to condemn him- or herself.

While the Fifth Amendment serves those functions incidentally, it serves as a bulwark of the adversarial process. The adversarial model envisions a passive umpire who adjudicates a dispute between two equal parties—the state and defendant.[11] Although the truth may emerge in a partisan battle in which each side presents its version, ascertaining the truth is not the only goal of the adversary system. Rather, the Fifth Amendment privilege, like other constitutional procedural protections, furthers three interrelated values. One, of course, is to promote factual accuracy —to ensure the reliability of the process and to reduce the possibility that the state will punish an innocent person. Second, the adversarial process makes the individual unavailable to the state as a source of evidence and thereby limits the pressure the state can bring to bear in pursuit of its own goals. Protecting citizens from government coercion is a value in itself and reduces the risk of errors that could systematically favor the state. Third, the adversarial process promotes respect for individual dignity and autonomy. It posits equality between the individual and the state and recognizes that allowing one side to use the other as a source of evidence could subvert that balance.

For more than a century, the Court's interrogation decisions have attempted to balance between the state's need for information that an individual possesses with protection of personal autonomy and freedom from police coercion. If the privilege functions to preserve the adversary process, then the state only threatens that balance when it seeks potentially incriminating disclosures from the individual. Because the person questioned usually knows whether the information sought will incriminate, he or she bears the burden to assert the privilege and preserve the adversarial balance. The privilege is not self-invoking and requires affirmative action by a suspect to secure its protections.

The Court has recognized that certain compulsive pressures may impair or prevent a person from asserting the privilege—that is, may overbear his or her free will. The Court has used three constitutional strategies —Fourteenth Amendment due process voluntariness, Sixth Amendment right to counsel, and Fifth Amendment privilege against self-incrimination

—to regulate interrogation, to restrict coercive pressures, and to preserve the adversarial process. The Court's Fourteenth Amendment decisions focus on whether a suspect's statement was voluntary under the totality of the circumstances—that is, whether the state used fundamentally unfair or coercive tactics to obtain a statement. The Court excluded involuntary statements that police elicited by psychological or physical coercion because they were unreliable, overwhelmed a person's free will, and used tactics a free society cannot condone.[12] The Court's Sixth Amendment decisions recognized that interrogation constitutes a critical stage in the criminal process because a confession effectively determines the outcome of a defendant's trial. Suspects need tactical and strategic advice of counsel to decide whether to confess, and the Court excluded confessions in which the state deprived them of legal assistance.[13] The Court used the Fifth Amendment privilege against self-incrimination to protect suspects from the compulsive pressures of custodial interrogation. The Court extended the Fifth Amendment privilege to the most inquisitorial stage of the adversarial process (the interrogation room), required police to advise suspects of the rights to remain silent and to assistance of counsel (the *Miranda* warning), and empowered them to terminate questioning.[14] Crucially, suspects' burden to assert the privilege arises when they are least able to do so—alone, isolated, and subject to the compelling pressures of custodial interrogation.

The Court's struggle and ultimate failure to adequately regulate interrogation practices reflects the constraints of constitutional adjudication and fundamental tensions in justice administration. Herbert Packer's "Two Models of the Criminal Process"—the Due Process model and the Crime Control model—identifies the inherent contradiction that interrogation poses for an adversarial justice system.[15] The Due Process model reflects a commitment to an adversarial process, whereas the Crime Control model envisions a more inquisitorial justice system. The Due Process model relies on formal fact-finding at trial, buttressed by procedural safeguards to assure reliable findings of legal guilt. The Crime Control model relies on informal, administrative procedures to separate innocent from probably guilty suspects. This inquisitorial stage views the accused as a primary source of evidence and relies heavily on confessions to screen suspects and fuel guilty pleas.

Suspects must assert their privilege against self-incrimination when they are most vulnerable—after arrest and prior to formal initiation of the judicial proceedings. During this narrow window of opportunity—typically

36 to 48 hours—the juvenile and criminal justice process more closely resembles an inquisitorial Crime Control system than an adversarial Due Process system. A person isolated in a police-dominated environment must courageously confront his or her interrogators and clearly invoke the right to remain silent or the right to counsel to preserve the adversarial balance.

The organization of this book reflects three analytic goals. First, it uses Packer's Crime Control and Due Process models to highlight the inquisitorial heart of our nominally adversarial process and the central role that interrogation plays. Constitutional theory notwithstanding, juvenile and criminal justice is an inquisitorial system for nearly all offenders. Police establish most offenders' guilt through informal, administrative fact-finding —interrogation—that leads to guilty pleas. A guilty plea in court ratifies the real trial that occurred when police questioned the suspect. Most jurisdictions do not create a complete record of what transpired during that critical stage of the process. Mandatory recording provides an objective basis for courts to review what happened inside the interrogation room that determined most defendants' guilt.

Second, the book empirically analyzes routine interrogation of older delinquents charged with felonies. Unlike most states, Minnesota has required police to record interrogations of criminal suspects for nearly two decades. Analyses of 307 tapes and transcripts describe in rich detail what actually happens when police interrogate serious young offenders. They begin to fill many gaps in knowledge about what happens and provide a framework for replication in other states as access to recordings increases.

Third, the book compares and contrasts these routine felony interrogations with those that elicited false confessions. While false confessions rightly garner legal and media scrutiny, policymakers require a baseline of everyday felony interrogations to determine whether and how these are aberrant outliers. Contrasting routine questioning with false confessions enables police, lawyers, and judges to identify interrogations that require enhanced scrutiny, to adopt policies to protect citizens, and to assure the reliability and integrity of the justice system.

Packer's Due Process and Crime Control models contrast the theory and practice of criminal justice administration. The vast majority of defendants plead guilty, and their cases receive no adversarial testing. They plead because they already confessed at the station house. The Court's three constitutional strategies to regulate interrogation all failed for the same reason—trial judges had no record of what happened during informal administrative fact-finding. Under the Fourteenth Amendment, trial judges admit only voluntary confessions, but without an independent record, they cannot assess the coerciveness of tactics, their impact on a suspect, or the reliability of a statement. Similarly, *Miranda* required the state to meet a heavy burden to prove a knowing, intelligent, and voluntary waiver of rights but did not require police to record warnings, waivers, or statements. Without an objective record, police almost invariably prevail in the swearing contest with defendants at the suppression hearing. Although the Due Process model envisions a formal adversarial proceeding to establish legal guilt, in reality few defendants receive a trial. The interrogation room is the trial—confessions determine guilt, and defendants have no record on which to appeal for judicial review.

Miranda provided judges with an objective alternative to a subjective inquiry about the voluntariness of a confession. It represented a symbolic expression of Packer's Due Process model—a per se rule to regulate police conduct, a mechanism to inform defendants of their rights, and a strategy to maintain the individual and state balance in an adversarial process.[16] *Miranda* erroneously assumed that a police-administered warning could offset the compulsive pressures of custodial interrogation and empower a suspect to assert the rights. Over three decades, *Miranda* has transmogrified from a protection for suspects to a safe harbor for police. The vast majority of suspects waive their rights despite a warning. Trial judges focus narrowly on whether police gave and suspects waived their rights, rather than on the voluntariness and reliability of confessions. If a suspect waives his or her rights, then police interrogate him or her as they did previously, and courts admit virtually any statement. *Miranda* simplified judicial review and enabled judges to avoid scrutiny of the subsequent statements.

This book begins to fill the empirical void about what happens in the interrogation room. It analyzes quantitative and qualitative data—tapes and transcripts, police reports, juvenile court files, and sentence reports—of routine interrogations of 307 sixteen- and seventeen-year-old youths whom prosecutors charged with a felony offense. Interviews with more than three dozen police, prosecutors, defense lawyers, and judges supplement these analyses. The book examines how police secured *Miranda* waivers, elicited information, and built the files that justice-system personnel used. It explores how youths' prior record and responses influence interrogations and how waivers of *Miranda* affect case processing.

Over the past three decades, developmental psychologists have examined juveniles' ability to exercise *Miranda* rights. The research questions whether youths possess competence, judgment, and understanding to employ legal rights. It indicates that young and mid-adolescents do *not* possess the competence of adults to exercise *Miranda*. Developmental psychologists argue that younger juveniles' limited competence warrants greater procedural safeguards. While most sixteen- and seventeen-year-old youths can understand *Miranda*, their performance remains problematic. I situate these interrogations of delinquents in the broader *Miranda* framework. Are the Court's surmises about young people's ability to exercise *Miranda* realistic? What types of pressures do police use when they question youths? How do juveniles perform when measured against the legal standard developed for adults?

Contrary to the popular view of interrogation as a rigorous and grueling inquisition, I find, as have other researchers, that routine questioning "involve[s] relatively simple and straightforward interchanges with reasonably compliant suspects."[17] Although false confessions almost invariably involve lengthy, coercive questioning, police conclude routine felony interviews quickly and with few psychological manipulations. This study provides an empirical baseline of routine felony interrogations. When corroborated by research in other jurisdictions, police, lawyers, judges, and policymakers will be better able to distinguish routine questioning from that which may produce false confessions.

Chapter 1 briefly reviews the three constitutional strategies the Court uses to regulate interrogation. They all failed because the Court had no way to determine what actually happened when police questioned suspects. The *Miranda* Court had no empirical evidence of the way police questioned suspects and instead used interrogation training manuals and programs as a proxy for real interrogation. The Court described the Reid Method—a technique of interrogation used then and now. The Reid manuals and training programs teach police to isolate suspects and to use psychological tactics—maximization and minimization strategies—to heighten their stress and anxiety and to manipulate their vulnerabilities to obtain confessions.[18] Although developmental psychologists question whether youths possess the cognitive ability or judgment to function on par with adults, interrogation manuals instruct police to use the same techniques with children as with adults. Post-*Miranda* research focused primarily on the impact of warnings on confessions. There is limited empirical research on what happens when police question suspects. The chapter contrasts the confrontational Reid Method employed in the

United States with investigative interview techniques developed in the United Kingdom.

Chapter 2 analyzes the law that governs interrogating juveniles. The Court has emphasized that youthfulness heightens vulnerability and has directed close scrutiny of juveniles' confessions. Despite concerns about youthfulness, the Court applies the legal standard for adults to evaluate juveniles' waivers of rights—"knowing, intelligent, and voluntary under the totality of the circumstances."[19] Most states require juveniles to understand the words and concepts the *Miranda* warning and to assert their rights as clearly as adults. While the law posits the same standard for children and adults, developmental psychologists question adolescents' competence to exercise rights and highlight their special vulnerabilities. Many juveniles—especially those fifteen years of age and younger—do not understand the words or rights contained in a *Miranda* warning. With impaired understanding, juveniles are at a comparative disadvantage and cannot meet adult performance standards. A disjuncture exists between legal expectations and developmental psychologists' research on adolescents' competence.

Chapters 3, 4, 5, and 6 present the empirical core of the study. Chapter 3 analyzes juveniles' exercise of *Miranda* rights—whether they make a knowing, intelligent, and voluntary waiver. It examines how and when police administer *Miranda* warnings, where and when they question suspects, who is present at the interrogation, and how police predispose youths to waive. Developmental psychologists report that most sixteen- and seventeen-year-olds can understand the words of a *Miranda* warning, even if they do not fully understand the concepts or appreciate the consequences of waiving.

Chapter 4 empirically analyzes how police interrogate the vast majority of youths who waive *Miranda*. It examines how police initiate an interview and frame their questions. It describes the psychological maximization and minimization techniques they use. It examines how police conclude an interview and demonstrate a voluntary waiver and statement.

Chapter 5 describes how juveniles respond to these tactics and their attitudes in the interrogation room. It examines how often police obtain confessions, admissions or denials, and leads to other evidence. It examines the length of interrogations and factors associated with longer questioning. It examines how juveniles' decision to waive or invoke *Miranda* affects case processing—offense level at conviction, charge reduction, and sentence. It depicts the Crime Control model in practice—confessions lead to guilty pleas.

Chapter 6 examines how interrogation practices vary with geographic context and produce "justice by geography."[20] Juvenile justice administration varies in urban, suburban, and rural counties and affects how judges adjudicate and sentence youths. Youths' race and crimes vary with geographic locale and affect interrogation practices. Urban police question a larger proportion of minority juveniles and youths charged with more serious offenses than do suburban officers and use somewhat different strategies to question them. Suburban police contact juveniles' parents more frequently than urban officers do, and suburban parents attend interrogations more frequently than do urban parents. Parents' presence provides an opportunity to assess their role when police question their children. Juveniles' race affects juvenile justice administration.[21] At every stage—arrest, intake, referral, petition, detention, trial, and disposition—youths of color fare less well than do their white counterparts, and disparate responses contribute to disproportionate minority confinement.[22] Because geography and race overlap—urban minority and suburban white—the chapter examines whether youths of different races waive *Miranda* differently and whether police question and they respond differently.

Chapter 7 reviews research on false confessions and contrasts them with routine felony interrogations. Studies of false confessions identify recurring elements: poor investigations that misclassify innocent people as guilty, confrontational questioning, use of false evidence, lengthy interrogations, and vulnerable populations.[23] False-confession research identifies youths—such as the sixteen- and seventeen-year-olds in this study—as among vulnerable populations.

Chapter 8 concludes with recommendations to reform the way police question suspects. Some focus on general interrogation practices—for example, mandatory recording of all interviews, prompt determination of probable cause, time limits on interrogation, and more use of investigative interview techniques rather than the confrontational Reid Method. Others focus on juvenile-specific reforms—mandatory assistance of counsel when police question delinquents fifteen years of age or younger. These reform proposals address the fundamental conundrum of interrogation in an adversarial process. *Miranda* failed to resolve its own internal contradiction—how can people subjected to the compulsive pressures of custodial interrogation make voluntary waiver decisions? Despite our nominally adversarial system, police interrogation is an inquisitorial process and exemplifies the Crime Control model of criminal and juvenile justice. Only mandatory recording of interrogations can make visible that which takes place in secret, provide suspects with an objective record on which to appeal inquisitorial fact-finding, and enable trial judges to assess *Miranda* waivers and voluntariness and reliability of confessions. It enhances factual accuracy, limits government overreaching, and maintains a proper balance between the individual and the state.

Appendix 1 describes the study's data and methodology. The Minnesota Supreme Court in *State v. Scales*[24] required police to record custodial interrogations of criminal suspects, including juveniles. County attorneys in four counties—two urban and two suburban—provided unrestricted accesses to cull files of sixteen- and seventeen-year-old youths charged with a felony. The four counties represent half the population and half the delinquency filings in the state. We searched for and identified 307 files in which juveniles either invoked or waived *Miranda* and police questioned them. I copied and coded tapes or transcripts, police reports, juvenile court records, and sentence reports for those interrogations. I interviewed more than three dozen police, prosecutors, defense lawyers, and judges to learn about interrogation practices and to corroborate my findings with their experience.

Historically and currently, juvenile courts treat male and female delinquents differently.[25] Appendix 2 compares and contrasts how police interrogated boys and girls—whether they questioned them differently, whether they responded differently, and whether their responses affected how courts disposed of their cases.

Interrogating Criminal Suspects

Law on the Books and Law in Action

Ours is the accusatorial as opposed to the inquisitorial system. Such has been the characteristics of Anglo-American criminal justice since it freed itself from the practices borrowed by the Star Chamber from the Continent whereby an accused was interrogated in secret for hours on end. Under our system, society carries the burden of proving its charges against the accused not out of his own mouth. It must establish its case, not by interrogation of the accused even under judicial safeguards, but by evidence independently secured through skillful investigation.[1]

For three-quarters of a century, the Supreme Court has struggled to find the right balance between needs of law enforcement and protection of individuals during interrogation. The state wants reliable statements that will lead to successful plea, prosecution, and conviction. Citizens have a right to be free from coercive tactics and practices likely to elicit unreliable statements. Court decisions accommodate legitimate police practices and suspects' rights.

An adversarial system of criminal justice presumes equality between the individual and the state. The parties—prosecution and defense—control the contest, and the judge functions as an umpire to enforce procedural rules.[2] The prosecutor seeks to obtain convictions and the defense to prevent them. In theory, partisan self-interest will promote a better-informed fact-finder. The state may ask suspects questions, but it may not compel them to answer or draw negative inferences from their silence. If the state can use persons as a source of evidence in their own prosecution, then it would convert the adversarial process into an inquisitorial one.[3]

Despite the value of independent investigation, suspects often are important sources of evidence—confessions, admissions, leads to witnesses, or the location of physical evidence—and questioning them contributes to successful prosecutions. When the state questions a person, the person usually will know whether the information sought could incriminate, and he or she must assert the privilege against self-incrimination.[4] However, police actions may impair suspects' ability to freely choose, for example, if they use threats or force. The Constitution limits the state's power to force answers and protects individual autonomy. Since the 1930s, the Court has used three strategies—Fourteenth Amendment due process voluntariness, Sixth Amendment right to counsel, and Fifth Amendment privilege against self-incrimination—to regulate interrogation, to balance individual and state interests, and to maintain a properly functioning adversarial system.

This chapter analyzes the Court's constitutional interrogation doctrines and their impact on justice administration. Part I briefly reviews the Court's three theories and their limitations. The Fourteenth Amendment voluntariness test posited limits on police interrogation tactics but did not identify prohibited practices in advance or provide guidance for police and courts. The Sixth Amendment right to counsel gave suspects access to a lawyer, threatening the state's ability to question suspects at all, and the Court quickly limited its applicability to interrogations conducted after the state has filed formal charges. *Miranda* recognized that the compulsive pressures of custodial interrogation threatened suspects' Fifth Amendment privilege against self-incrimination. The Court required a *Miranda* warning to empower suspects, to preserve the balance of equals in an adversarial system, and to regulate most interrogations. Part II analyzes how the *Miranda* Court viewed interrogation and how the Court's subsequent decisions have restricted and narrowed its meager protections. Part III reviews empirical research on interrogation. *Miranda* prescribed a protective warning in an empirical vacuum. The Court had little evidence about what actually happened when police interrogated suspects or how its ruling might affect interrogation practices.[5] It relied on interrogation training manuals and programs.[6] *Miranda*, subsequent rulings, and those manuals provide the framework for current interrogation practices.

I. The Court, the Constitution, and Confessions

The Constitution provides the theoretical framework for an adversary system of criminal and juvenile justice. In reality, states administer a plea-bargain justice system in which 90–95% of defendants admit their guilt for sentencing concessions rather than contest their innocence.[7] "The American system of plea bargaining is fundamentally a system of deal-making in exchange for self-incrimination—a process that begins during the investigative stage of detective work, well before the filing of any charges by the prosecutor, the negotiation of any reduction by defense counsel, or the ratification of any two-party deals by the judge."[8] The initial decision to confess determines subsequent stages of the process—whether a defendant has any plea-bargaining advantage or goes to trial—and converts the adversarial process into an inquisitorial one. Moreover, it occurs in secret, which limits the Court's ability to regulate police tactics. The Court developed three constitutional strategies to regulate interrogation without knowing what actually happens or how its rulings would affect justice administration.

A. Fourteenth Amendment Voluntariness

Until the mid-1960s, the Supreme Court regulated police interrogation in the states through the Fourteenth Amendment due process clause. To assure a fundamentally fair trial, the Court required a confession to be voluntary under the "totality of the circumstances."[9] Coercive practices rendered a confession involuntary and inadmissible in a criminal prosecution. Prior to World War II, police sometimes used harsh third-degree practices—for example, physical beatings amounting to torture, exposure to heat or cold, water-boarding, isolation, sleep deprivation, prolonged questioning, and the like—to elicit confessions.[10]

These tactics posed three constitutional concerns. Physical or psychological coercion could produce unreliable statements, undermine accurate fact-finding, and detract from the search for truth. Second, regardless of a statement's factual reliability in a particular case, coercive tactics create a substantial risk that innocent suspects will confess falsely—for example, succumb to threats, promises, or inducements. Third, tactics that impair peoples' autonomy fail to respect individual sovereignty and subvert equality.

The Court could more easily articulate constitutional values—assuring factual reliability, preventing governmental oppression, and respecting individual autonomy—than provide guidance for trial judges to apply them. The legal standard—voluntariness—lacks objective meaning and requires judges to assess suspects' subjective state of mind when they confessed. The due process approach focused on a person's "free will" decision to make a statement. The Court used various formulae to evaluate voluntariness—for example, "whether the behavior of the State's law enforcement officials was such as to overbear [the suspect's] will to resist and bring about confessions not freely self-determined"[11] or whether the suspect's "will has been overborne and his capacity for self-determination critically impaired."[12]

Free will and voluntariness are elusive concepts, and judges find it difficult to discern why people do what they do. It is hard to understand why they act contrary to their own self-interest and confess to a crime that can lead to imprisonment. It is even more challenging to reconstruct why they decided to confess at a suppression hearing conducted months later without a record of what actually happened. Except in extreme cases of physical brutality,[13] judges faced a difficult task to distinguish voluntary from coerced confessions.

Judges must evaluate both characteristics of a suspect and circumstances of an interrogation, reconstruct a person's state of mind when he or she confessed, and pronounce the decision to speak as voluntary or coerced. "[A] Court making this judgment must address not only the empirical question relating to the extent to which the police pressure restricted the suspect's freedom of choice but also the normative question of how much freedom of choice should be afforded to the individual under interrogation."[14] The Court in *Schneckloth v. Bustamonte* summarized factors to evaluate voluntariness.

> In determining whether a defendant's will was overborne in a particular case, the Court has assessed the totality of all the surrounding circumstances—both the characteristics of the accused and the details of the interrogation. Some of the factors taken into account have included the youth of the accused, his lack of education, or his low intelligence, the lack of any advice to the accused of his constitutional rights, the length of detention, the repeated and prolonged nature of the questioning, and the use of physical punishment such as the deprivation of food or sleep.[15]

These factors included objective elements (what did police do) and subjective features (how would these tactics affect a person's ability to resist or decide to talk). The Court seldom identified any particular tactic standing alone that rendered a statement coerced or involuntary.

> The test requires a court to reconstruct minute details of an interrogation after the fact, usually with the police and the defendant offering wildly varying accounts of what took place. A court determining whether or not a confession was voluntary must consider any and all circumstances that could enter into this inquiry. This includes not only obvious objective factors, such as the length of the

interrogation and whether the interrogators used force of any kind or degree against the suspect, but also subjective characteristics unique to the particular suspect. . . . The court must then throw all of these factors into a hat, mix them up in a totality of the circumstances approach, reach in and attempt to pull out the answer to a question that can never be answered with confidence by a judge, psychiatrist, or magician.[16]

Judges pronounce whether a person with some of the suspect's characteristics could resist those pressures and choose freely to confess. "[T]he admission of a confession turns as much on whether the techniques for extracting the statements, as applied to this suspect, are compatible with a system that presumes innocence and assures that a conviction will not be secured by inquisitorial means as on whether the defendant's will was in fact overborne."[17] The Court's efforts to distinguish acceptable and unacceptable tactics identified a laundry list of factors, no one of which was necessarily determinative. The Court applied philosophical, psychological, and legal principles to the circumstances to assess voluntariness.

First, there is the business of finding the crude, historical facts, the external "phenomenological" occurrences, and events surrounding the confession. Second, because the concept of voluntariness is one which concerns a mental state, there is the imaginative recreation, largely inferential, of internal, "psychological" fact. Third, there is the application to this psychological fact of standards for judgment informed by the larger legal conceptions ordinarily characterized as rules of law but which, also, comprehend both induction from, and anticipation of, factual circumstances.[18]

Police, trial, and appellate court judges encounter factual, legal, and administrative difficulty to apply an amorphous, multifactor test to a subjective state of mind.[19] The totality approach provides no advance guidance to police about permitted or prohibited tactics. Interrogating officers may not know features of a suspect—for example, education, IQ, or psychological vulnerability—that a court later may deem relevant to voluntariness. The voluntariness approach allows police to bring substantial pressures to bear on vulnerable or unsophisticated suspects.

The voluntariness of a confession posed a mixed question of fact and law for trial judges at a suppression hearing and appellate courts on review. Factually, trial judges first decide what actually happened. If police do not record an interrogation, then a judge must resolve a factual dispute in which police and suspects present dramatically different versions. Without a record, police almost invariably prevail in these biased and conflicting swearing contests. "To the extent that lower courts refused to accept suspects' truthful testimony relating to abusive interrogation practices, the fact-finding process presented an impenetrable barrier to the goal of regulating such practices."[20] Trial judges applied constitutional values to the facts and characterized a confession as voluntary or coerced—that is, a legal conclusion. The amorphousness of voluntariness impaired the legitimacy of trial court decisions and the effectiveness of appellate review. Once trial judges found facts and made a ruling, appellate courts lacked authority to reexamine facts independently to determine what happened or to control finding that a statement was voluntary. Tactics that rendered one suspect's confession involuntary might not produce a similar outcome in another case with somewhat different facts. High-profile crimes create political pressures for police to solve a crime and for judges to find confessions voluntary despite strenuous interrogation tactics.[21]

B. Sixth Amendment Right to Counsel

By the early-1960s, subtle psychological manipulations supplanted physical coercion and further complicated the Court's ability to distinguish voluntary from involuntary confessions.[22] The Court used the Sixth Amendment right to counsel as a second constitutional strategy to regulate interrogation.[23] The Court characterized a decision to waive the privilege against self-incrimination as a critical stage in the criminal process because pretrial interrogation could render trial safeguards a nullity. Suspects needed advice of counsel to make such critical decisions. The Court decided *Escobedo v. Illinois* the year before *Miranda* and expressed concern that pretrial interrogation could render other procedural safeguards irrelevant.

> The rule sought by the State . . . would make the trial no more than an appeal from the interrogation; and the "right to use counsel at the formal trial [would be] a very hollow thing [if], for all practical purposes, the conviction is already assured by pretrial examination." . . .
>
> It is argued that if the right to counsel is afforded prior to indictment, the number of confessions obtained by the police will diminish significantly. . . . This argument, of course, cuts two ways. The fact

that many confessions are obtained . . . points up its critical nature as a "stage when legal aid and advice" are surely needed. . . .

We have learned the lessons of history, . . . that a system of criminal law enforcement which comes to depend on the "confession" will, in the long run, be less reliable and more subject to abuses than a system which depends on extrinsic evidence independently secured through skillful investigation.[24]

Miranda supplanted *Escobedo* the following year, and the Court has limited Sixth Amendment protections to questioning that occurs after formal initiation of the criminal process. However, *Escobedo* recognized suspects' need for legal advice at the initial confrontation to avoid "making the trial no more than an appeal from the interrogation."

C. Fifth Amendment Privilege against Self-Incrimination

Miranda v. Arizona relied on the Fifth Amendment privilege against self-incrimination to resolve the conflict between the state's need for evidence and preserving individual autonomy.[25] *Miranda* characterized custodial interrogation as inherently coercive—a police-dominated environment that impaired a suspect's ability to choose whether to cooperate voluntarily. The compulsive pressures overwhelmed suspects' ability to waive without clear awareness of the right to refuse. The *Miranda* warning—an advisory of the rights to remain silent and to counsel—informed ignorant and naïve suspects of their rights to enable them to make knowing and intelligent decisions.

II. *Miranda* and the Conundrum of Confessions

The Fifth Amendment privilege against self-incrimination furthers several goals of the adversary process. These include

[1] our unwillingness to subject those suspect of crimes to the cruel trilemma of self-accusation, perjury or contempt; [2] our preference for an accusatorial rather than an inquisitorial system of criminal justice; [3] our fear that self-incriminating statements will be elicited by inhumane treatment and abuses; [4] our sense of fair play which dictates "a fair state-individual balance by requiring the government to leave the individual alone until good cause is shown for disturbing him and by requiring the government in its contest with the individual to shoulder the entire load," . . . ; [5] our respect for the

inviolability of the human personality and of the right of each individual "to a private enclave where he may lead a private life," . . . ; [6] our distrust of self-deprecatory statements; and [7] our realization that the privilege, while sometimes "a shelter to the guilty," is often "a protection of the innocent."[26]

These policies promote accurate fact-finding, prevent government oppression, and enhance individual autonomy. By potentially making a suspect off-limits, it reinforces the adversary system as a contest between equals—the citizen and the state—before a neutral fact-finder. Nevertheless, the Fifth Amendment embodies a contradiction. On the one hand, to successfully prosecute an offender, the state needs evidence, some of which only the suspect possesses. In most instances, a person will know whether a disclosure will incriminate and must assert the privilege when that danger looms.[27] Respect for personal autonomy allows people to make decisions that may not ultimately serve their own best interests.

Police typically question suspects at the earliest stage of the process, and the outcome of interrogation strongly influences subsequent stages. Herbert Packer's "Two Models of the Criminal Process" reflect the contradictions that interrogation poses in an adversarial system.[28] The two models—the Due Process model and the Crime Control model—describe tensions between the law on the books and the law in action, between legality and efficiency, between procedural formality and administrative regularity, and between per se rules and discretion.

The Due Process model represents a commitment to an adversarial model, whereas the Crime Control model envisions a more inquisitorial system. The Due Process model relies on formal fact-finding buttressed by procedural safeguards to assure reliable findings of legal guilt. It prefers per se rules (e.g., a *Miranda* warning) to discretion (e.g., voluntariness under the totality of circumstances) and favors judicial fact-finding to police administrative information gathering. In the adversarial contest, defense lawyers maintain the balance, foster equality, and monitor police and prosecutorial adherence to procedural rules.

The Crime Control model emphasizes efficient processing of large numbers of offenders in a system with limited resources. Efficient screening requires informal, discretionary procedures quickly to exonerate innocent suspects or to produce pleas from guilty ones. The Crime Control model resembles an administrative process—an assembly line—rather than a judicial proceeding. It seeks dispositive facts early in investigations to screen cases efficiently and, based on those facts, presumes that remaining suspects are guilty. The inquisitorial Crime Control model sees the accused as a primary source of evidence and seeks confessions to fuel a high rate of guilty pleas and final judgments.

Of criminal and delinquency cases, 95% or more end with guilty pleas rather than trials. In practice, both justice systems more closely resemble a Crime Control model (an inquisitorial system) rather than a Due Process model (adversarial testing). Theoretically, suspects can invoke due process procedural safeguards and put the state to its proof. In reality, the earliest stages when most interrogations occur are more inquisitorial and outcome determinative—once suspects confess, they are much less able or likely to contest their guilt. Police interrogation during these preliminary stages is not a dispassionate search for truth or an investigation by a neutral fact-finder. Rather, police seek confessions that lead to guilty pleas and enable the state to avoid the later adversarial stages. "The entire process of interrogation is structured to advance the penal interests of the state and secure a conviction."[29]

Most interrogations occur during a narrow thirty-six- to forty-eight-hour window of opportunity after police take a suspect into custody and before prosecutors file formal charges to initiate the adversarial process.[30] During this period, *Miranda* constitutes suspects' primary constitutional protection, but they must affirmatively invoke it. During this critical window, the Crime Control model prevails. "The police must have a reasonable opportunity to interrogate the suspect in private before he has a chance to fabricate a story or to decide that he will not cooperate. The psychologically optimal time for getting this kind of cooperation from the suspect is immediately after his arrest, before he has had a chance to rally his forces."[31]

By contrast, interrogation plays a relatively minor role in the Due Process model. "[I]f proper arrest standards have been employed, there is no necessity to get additional evidence out of the mouth of the defendant. He is to be arrested so that he may be held to answer the case against him, not so that a case against him that does not exist at the time of his arrest can be developed."[32] The Due Process model relies on judicial fact-finding with procedural safeguards to assure trustworthiness and to promote equality between the individual and the state. It places a higher premium on reliability than on efficient case processing because of the devastating consequences of wrongful conviction.

Interrogation is critical because of the power of confessions to convict. *Miranda* posited that the coercive pressures of custodial interrogation threatened a person's ability to resist self-incrimination. The Court extended the privilege against self-incrimination from compelled courtroom testimony to interrogation in the station house. It concluded that without adequate protective mechanisms, the inherent coercion of custodial interrogation would compel statements in violation of the privilege. It required police to warn a suspect of the right to remain silent and the right to counsel to neutralize the coercive pressures of custodial interrogation.

[T]he Court held that informal pressure to speak—that is, pressure not backed by the legal process or any formal sanction—can constitute "compulsion" within the meaning of the Fifth Amendment. Second, it held that this element of informal compulsion is present in *any* questioning of a suspect in custody, no matter how short the period of questioning may be. Third, the Court held that precisely specified warnings are required to dispel the compelling pressure of custodial interrogation.[33]

Miranda reflected a commitment to the values of the Due Process model.[34] The Court decided cases such as *Miranda* against the backdrop of the civil rights movement, urban race riots, and southern Jim Crow police abuse of black suspects.[35] Commentators have described *Miranda* both as the "high-water mark of the due process revolution" and as a self-inflicted wound of judicial activism that soon ended it.[36] *Miranda*, like other Warren Court due process decisions during the 1960s, exhibited certain general features: "(1) the substitution of broad, quasi-legislative rules of administration for the more traditional case-by-case adjudication; (2) reliance on the equality norm to reduce or eliminate disparities in treatment resulting from disparate financial means; (3) restriction of law enforcement discretion."[37]

The Court relied on per se rules (the *Miranda* warning) rather than post hoc discretionary evaluations (voluntariness under the totality of the circumstances) to assure that defendants made knowing and intelligent waivers of rights. It enabled suspects to request counsel to offset the state's inherent advantage during interrogation. The Court erroneously assumed that informing suspects of their rights would empower them to exercise them and reduce courts' burdens to assess voluntariness of confessions.[38]

The Court's post-*Miranda* decisions have recalibrated the balance between the individual and the state, strongly tilted the advantage toward police, and weakened the limited protection a warning afforded. In *Harris v. New York*, the Court allowed the state to use statements obtained in violation of *Miranda* to impeach credibility and gave police an incentive to question people after they invoked their rights.[39] In *Moran v. Burbine*, the Court upheld a *Miranda* waiver despite the failure of police to inform the suspect that a lawyer retained by his sister sought access.[40] "No doubt, the additional information would have been useful to [the suspect]; perhaps even it might have affected his decision to confess. But we have never read the Constitution to require the police supply a suspect with a flow of information to help him calibrate his self-interest in deciding whether to speak or stand by his rights."[41]

The Court subsequently insisted that the "primary protection afforded suspects subjected to custodial interrogation is the *Miranda* warnings themselves" and asserted that "full comprehension of the right to remain silent and request an attorney [is] sufficient to dispel whatever coercion is inherent in the interrogation process."[42] Moreover, "full comprehension" requires only an understanding of the warning, rather than an appreciation of the charges or the consequences of waiving.[43] Suspects must invoke their rights clearly to terminate interrogation, and police need not clarify whether an ambiguous request constitutes an invocation.[44] The Court will find an "implied waiver" if a properly warned suspect makes incriminating responses, even after hours of silence.[45] *Berghuis v. Thompkins* concluded, "The *Miranda* rule and its requirements are met if a suspect receives adequate *Miranda* warnings, understands them, and has an opportunity to invoke the rights before giving any answers or admissions."[46] The Court in *Dickerson v. United States* opined, "[O]ur subsequent cases have reduced the impact of the *Miranda* rule on legitimate law enforcement while reaffirming the decision's core ruling that unwarned statements may not be used as evidence in the prosecution's case in chief."[47]

Although *Miranda* insisted that the state bears a "heavy burden" to show a valid waiver, it did not require police to record it or corroborate it. Police testimony that they warned a suspect who then waived will suffice.

In weighing the credibility of police officers' and suspects' conflicting versions as to what transpired during an interrogation, moreover, judges are as inclined to credit the police today as they were in the pre-*Miranda* era. Thus, when police willing to engage in abusive interrogation practices are also willing to deny using them in court, *Miranda*'s safeguards provide no protection against the likelihood that the police testimony will be accepted.[48]

Miranda expected that warning suspects would embolden them to invoke their rights. Instead, it has provided police with a safe harbor to interrogate suspects. "*Miranda* turns out to be the police officer's friend. The *Miranda* warning has become, in the main, a benediction at the outset of every interrogation, sanctifying the very practices it was meant to end."[49] Courts focus on whether police gave a proper *Miranda* warning rather than whether a suspect made a voluntary statement.[50] After a suspect waives, *Miranda* imposes few restraints on interrogation practices,[51] and analysts conclude that "*Miranda* has had little effect on police behavior during interrogation."[52] Police use the same tactics today that *Miranda* reviewed four decades ago.

III. *Miranda* and Interrogation: Then and Now

The *Miranda* Court could not determine how police questioned suspects: "Interrogation still takes place in privacy. Privacy results in secrecy and this in turn results in a gap in our knowledge as to what in fact goes on in the interrogation rooms."[53] Police used incommunicado interrogation to make people admit what they did not want to tell, and the Court had no way to assess how they accomplished that task.[54] Moreover, interrogation evolved from physical coercion to psychological manipulation: "the modern practice of in-custody interrogation is psychologically rather than physically oriented."[55] Psychological manipulations—isolation, confrontation, and minimization—impaired the Court's ability to evaluate a person's subjective state of mind or willingness to provide information.[56]

Police then and now controlled access to interrogation rooms, and *Miranda* had no direct evidence of police practices. The Court used interrogation manuals and training programs as a proxy for the tactics police used.[57] The techniques recommended by Fred Inbau and John Reid, in *Criminal Interrogation and Confession*—the leading training manual—served as a surrogate for actual practices. The Court characterized the Reid Method as "the most enlightened and effective means presently used to obtain statements through custodial interrogation."[58] Inbau and Reid remains the leading interrogation manual and the Reid Method the most widely used training program. Its prominence provides a framework to analyze contemporary practices.[59]

Miranda summarized the Reid Method's tactics—physical isolation and psychological manipulation:

> The officers are told by the manuals that the "principal psychological factor contributing to a successful interrogation is privacy— being alone with the person under interrogation." . . .
>
> To highlight the isolation and unfamiliar surroundings, the manuals instruct the police to display an air of confidence in the suspect's guilt and from outward appearance to maintain only an interest in confirming certain details. The guilt of the subject is to be posited as a fact. . . . The officers are instructed to minimize the moral seriousness of the offense, to cast blame on the victim or on society. These tactics are designed to put the subject in a psychological state where his story is but an elaboration of what the police purport to know already—that he is guilty. Explanations to the contrary are dismissed and discouraged. . . .
>
> [T]he setting prescribed by the manuals and observed in practice becomes clear. In essence, it is this: To be alone with the subject is essential to prevent distraction and to deprive him of any outside support. The aura of confidence in his guilt undermines his will to resist. He merely confirms the preconceived story the police seek to have him describe. Patience and persistence, at times relentless questioning, are employed. To obtain a confession, the interrogator must "patiently maneuver himself or his quarry into a position from which the desired objective may be attained." When normal procedures fail to produce the needed result, the police may resort to deceptive stratagems such as giving false legal advice. It is important to keep the subject off balance, for example, by trading on his insecurity about himself or his surroundings. The police then persuade, trick, or cajole him out of exercising his constitutional rights.[60]

All psychological interrogations rely on processes of social influence and persuasion to elicit information.[61] Police isolate a suspect to eliminate psychological supports, to overcome resistance, and to increase willingness to confess. The Reid Method manipulates the suspect by "reducing the perceived negative consequences of confessing while increasing the anxiety associated with deception."[62] Because people are social beings, interrogation tactics seek to influence their perceptions of the situation and to emphasize short-term relief over long-term consequences. "[T]he goal of interrogation is to alter a suspect's decision making by increasing the anxiety associated with denial and reducing the anxiety associated with confession."[63]

A. The Reid Method

Police question suspects to elicit information about an earlier event. The person questioned initially must encode the incident in memory, store that memory, and later retrieve it.[64] The three stages—encoding, storage, and retrieval—involve complex psychological processes susceptible to social influences. "Each participant and his or her behavior, both verbal and non-verbal, can and will affect the behavior of the other(s) within the conversational situation."[65] The interviewer can affect a suspect's answers, and a suspect learns what responses the questioner expects and may adjust his or her responses accordingly.[66] Interrogators can manage these interactions to elicit truthful information, to gather evidence, or to secure a confession.

Police interrogators do not dispassionately seek the truth or objectively collect information but act as partisans to gather inculpatory evidence to assist prosecutors to convict suspects.[67] As partisans, police are one-sided skeptics who assume that most suspects lie, who believe that they can distinguish between truth tellers and liars, and who doubt that innocent people confess falsely in response to the techniques they use. Once police have decided that a suspect is probably guilty, they build the strongest case for the prosecution. They use social influences—interrogation tactics—aimed at "outsmarting the suspect, overcoming his resistance, obtaining compliance, and eliciting an admission or confession."[68]

Miranda repeatedly emphasized that the inherent coercion of custodial interrogation stemmed from interaction of physical isolation and psychological manipulations.[69] Despite the Court's concern that custodial interrogation created compulsive pressures that threaten the privilege against self-incrimination, after police warn suspects of their rights, they use the same interrogation practices they used prior to *Miranda*. Using the Reid Method, police isolate suspects and use tactics to overcome their reluctance to admit responsibility, to neutralize feelings of guilt, and to increase their desire to confess.[70]

Social psychologists describe these manipulations as maximization and minimization techniques. Maximization tactics "convey the interrogator's rock-solid belief that the suspect is guilty and that all denials will fail. Such tactics include making an accusation, over-riding objections, and citing evidence real or manufactured, to shift the suspect's mental statement from confident to hopeless."[71] Minimization techniques "provide the suspect with moral justification and face-saving excuses for having committed the crime in question. Using this approach, the interrogator offers sympathy and understanding; normalizes and minimizes the crime."[72] *Miranda* recognized and social psychologists argue that many of the Reid Method's techniques implicitly communicate threats and promises.[73]

The Reid Method remains the leading interrogation-training program in the United States, and its protocols dominate contemporary practice.[74] Reid instructors have trained more than three hundred thousand investigators, and it is the most widely used method in North America.[75] Its ubiquity provides the framework by which researchers analyze interrogation practices.[76]

Interrogators trained in the Reid Method rely on verbal and nonverbal cues—Behavioral Symptom Analysis—to distinguish between guilty and innocent suspects and to question them accordingly.[77] By contrast, psychologists dispute the theoretical underpinnings and scientific validity of the Reid Method. They criticize its claims and note that its advocates "have not published any data or studies on their observations. In other words, they have not collected any empirical data to scientifically validate their theory and techniques."[78] Laboratory research on the Reid methods —minimization and implied leniency—reports that they increased the rate of confessions by guilty people *and* innocent people. "[M]inimization, a common and legal interrogation technique, provided an effective means of obtaining true confessions; however, this technique also put innocent participants at risk for false confessions."[79]

The Reid Method prescribes a nine-step sequence of psychological pressures to weaken suspects' resistance, to provide face-saving rationales, and to encourage them to confess.[80] "Police interviews are tension-filled matters under the best of circumstances. Interviews in the absence of counsel, in the police-dominated custodial environment, are filled with tension in spades. And the tensions are created for the very purpose of overcoming the suspect's unwillingness to talk."[81] At the start of an interrogation, the officer confidently confronts a suspect with a direct and positive assertion of guilt. The officer offers neutralizing rationales or psychological themes to justify or excuse the crime. Reid training advises police to interrupt a suspect's denials and to rebuff explanations or assertions of innocence. It explains how to engage suspects if they become passive or tune out the questioner. It encourages police to show sympathy and urge the suspect to tell the truth. The questioner offers a face-saving, albeit incriminating, alternative explanation for why the person committed the crime. After obtaining an oral admission about some detail of the crime, the officer converts it into a fuller, written confession that the suspect signs.[82] The successive stages of the Reid Method are a "goal-directed, stress-driven exercise in persuasion and decision, one designed to produce a very specific set of psychological effects and reactions in order to move the suspect from denial to admission."[83]

The Reid Method's nine-step protocol uses three interrelated psychological processes:

> *Custody and isolation*, which increases stress and the incentive to extricate oneself from the situation; *confrontation*, in which the interrogator accuses the suspect of the crime, expresses certainty in that opinion, cites real or manufactured evidence, and blocks the suspect from denials; and *minimization*, in which the sympathetic interrogator morally justifies the crime, leading the suspect to infer he or she will be treated leniently and to see confession as the best possible means of "escape."[84]

The cumulative process increases anxiety, creates a state of despair, and offers surcease by minimizing the adverse consequences of confessing. Police manipulate a suspect to elicit a statement that courts later will characterize as voluntary and reliable.[85]

The Reid Method does not acknowledge juveniles' heightened vulnerability during interrogation or modify tactics to account for developmental differences between adolescents and adults.[86] It asserts that the same "principles discussed with respect to adult suspects are just as applicable for use with younger ones."[87] Police trained in the Reid Method view adolescents as just as competent as adults and use the same tactics with both.[88] Reid-trained officers are less sensitive to developmental differences than are non-Reid-trained officers and use the same techniques— isolation, psychological manipulation, and deceit—with both.[89] Another survey found that police "use the same interrogation techniques with juveniles as they do with adults, suggesting that they do not account for the influence of young age as a personal risk factor for false confessions in their practices during interrogation."[90] Reid training teaches officers to question juveniles and adults the same way.

The Reid Method dominates interrogation training in the United States. By contrast, practices in some other countries—for example, the United Kingdom, Norway, New Zealand, and Australia—tend to be less accusatory or confrontational, designed to allow suspects to give a free-narrative account, and aimed to elicit facts rather than to obtain a confession.[91] Several high-profile wrongful convictions impelled the United Kingdom to pass the Police and Criminal Evidence Act (PACE 1984), which required police to record interrogations and to modify practices.[92]

In the United Kingdom, police, psychologists, and lawyers collaborated to develop a method of interviewing that avoids the accusatory and confrontational excesses of the Reid approach.[93] The interviewer attempts to gather as much information as possible to create an accurate factual picture, rather than simply to elicit a confession. Rebecca Milne and Ray Bull examine the psychological research and theory that undergirds this alternative approach.[94] One earlier version of the investigative interview —Cognitive Interview (CI)—attempts to elicit a free report followed by questions and techniques to enhance memory retrieval.[95] The CI uses four strategies to increase the quantity and quality of information elicited, rather than just to obtain a statement that confirms preexisting hypotheses. A second approach—Conversational Management (CM)—includes preinterview preparation, within-interview interaction, and postinterview assessment. UK investigative interview training incorporates the strengths of the CI and CM approaches.

The mnemonic PEACE describes the five components of the British interview approach: "Planning and Preparation," "Engage and Explain," "Account," "Closure," and "Evaluate."[96] The PEACE approach encourages officers to establish positive rapport, to obtain a free narrative from the suspect, to use open rather than leading questions, and to provide meaningful closure by summarizing information and answering any questions.[97] Architects of the PEACE approach criticize the Reid Method as "contrary to the principles of good investigative interviewing."[98]

The Reid Method seeks to manipulate the suspect to extract a confession. It is accusatorial and guilt presumptive and uses tactics to elicit statements that confirm police hypotheses about the suspect's guilt. By contrast, the investigative interview seeks the suspect's version of events. It uses open-ended methods to gather information, rather than simply to confirm a preexisting assumption. Police encourage the suspect to speak freely without interruption and listen actively before asking clarifying questions. The goal is fact-finding rather than securing a confession.[99]

The Reid Method and officers trained in its protocols regard juveniles as the functional equals of adults. By contrast, PACE recognizes youths' special vulnerabilities and recommends additional precautions at their interviews.

> It is important to bear in mind that, although juveniles or persons who are mentally disordered or mentally handicapped are often capable of providing reliable evidence, they may, without knowing or wishing to do so, be particularly prone in certain circumstances to provide information which is unreliable, misleading or self-incriminating. Special care should therefore always be exercised in questioning such a person, and the appropriate adult should be involved. . . . Because of the risk of unreliable evidence it is also important to obtain corroboration of any facts admitted whenever possible.[100]

PACE requires the presence of an "appropriate adult" when police interview juveniles—a policy similar to those states that demand the presence of a parent during questioning.

Interrogation practices in Minnesota reflect elements of both the Reid Method and PEACE approaches. The Minnesota Supreme Court in *State v. Scales* required police to record all custodial interrogations of suspects.[101] Because of *Scales*, police had interrogated suspects "on the record" for more than a decade and developed less confrontational strategies for the recorded interview.[102] "[T]he interview is used to gather information, not look for a confession. . . . Your goal is to remove the adversarial nature of the interview."[103] Police trainers teach interrogators to avoid maximization and minimization tactics because fact-finders find such tactics distasteful.

> Remember that traditional "minimizing" technique does not translate well to the electronically recorded environment (e.g., it can lead to false confessions). Before *Scales*, minimizing was a standard technique, part of your work product; cops used it as a tactic to get bad guys to confess; since *Scales*, a defense attorney can attack every misleading thing you say to the suspect because it has been recorded.[104]

The purpose of the interview is "[t]o gather information (not to get a confession) as part of a thorough and exhaustive investigation."[105] The training protocol advocates use of open-ended questions to elicit a free narrative and instructs officers not to conduct the "recorded interview with the goal of getting a confession."[106] Neutral, open-ended questions and a free narrative enable suspects to provide information without putting them on the defensive. "Be polite and respectful; doing so will help enforce the non-adversarial atmosphere and will demonstrate that you expect politeness and respect in return."[107] The training protocol emphasizes a "partnership" between the officer and the suspect. "[S]et yourself up as the simple and impartial carrier of facts. You are the vehicle that takes the story to the higher power—the people who decide the suspect's fate (e.g., charging attorney, judge, jury)....Say that you are not the person who decides that the suspect's story is unworthy. Continually reinforce your role as partner and messenger, rather than decision-maker."[108]

As we will see later, many of the police I interviewed described their role as neutral fact-finders who convey juveniles' "story" to prosecutors and judges. Interrogators' use of less confrontational tactics, however, still produced high rates of *Miranda* waivers and confessions.

IV. Empirical Research on Police Interrogation

More than four decades after *Miranda* decried the empirical void, we still know remarkably little about what actually happens when police question suspects.[109] Psychologists, legal scholars, and criminologists have conducted few naturalistic or empirical studies of interrogations. Research in the late 1960s evaluated the impact of *Miranda*—whether police warned suspects and how warnings affected rates of confessions. Apart from empirical studies in the United States by Richard Leo[110] and Barry Feld,[111] "we know scant more about actual police interrogation practices today than we did in 1966 when Justice Earl Warren lamented the gap problem in *Miranda v. Arizona*."[112] Many analysts decry the dearth of research on interrogation.[113] By contrast, PACE recording has generated a substantial body of empirical research in the United Kingdom.[114]

Immediately after *Miranda*, several studies measured police compliance and the impact of warnings on confession rates.[115] The post-*Miranda* studies reported that police routinely warned suspects, and thereafter the vast majority waived their rights. *Miranda* warnings did not empower suspects to assert their rights. The early studies used different outcome measures—for example, whether the suspect signed a waiver form,[116] expressed a willingness to talk,[117] gave statements,[118] produced a written confession,[119] or gave oral or written admissions[120]—which made comparisons of *Miranda's* impact in different settings difficult. However, the research concluded that *Miranda* warnings had minimal effect on rates of waivers, confessions, and conviction or on interrogation tactics.[121] Police complied with *Miranda* and gave the required warnings, following which most suspects waived their rights. After police obtained a waiver, interrogation techniques did not change significantly. "*Miranda* did not appear to undermine the effectiveness of criminal investigation in the way that the law enforcement community had initially feared."[122] A reanalysis of post-*Miranda* impact studies concluded, "*Miranda's* detectable net impact on conviction rates shrinks virtually to zero."[123] Despite assertions that *Miranda* adversely affected police,[124] most research concludes that *Miranda* had no negative effect on confession or conviction rates.[125] However, only a 1967 New Haven study actually observed police question suspects.[126]

Nearly three decades after *Miranda*, criminologists ventured into the interrogation room to report what actually occurred. In 1992–1993, Richard Leo observed 122 interrogations in an Oakland, California, police department and reviewed sixty audio- and videotapes of interrogations performed in two other California departments.[127] He analyzed how police induced suspects to waive *Miranda*, how they interrogated them following a waiver, and how *Miranda* waivers or invocations affected case processing. Leo reported that police regularly used Reid Method tactics, but they did not use coercion, physical threats, or explicit promises of lenience. His mid-1990s research represents the only in vivo field study of interrogation in the United States.

In addition to Leo's field observations, criminologists and legal scholars have used indirect methods to study interrogation. This study expands on my earlier research that analyzed sixty-six tapes and transcripts of interrogation of sixteen- and seventeen-year-old felony delinquents in one county in Minnesota.[128] Lesley King and Brent Snook analyzed forty-four video-recorded criminal interrogations in eastern Canada to assess the prevalence of Reid tactics.[129] Paul Cassell and Bret Hayman attended screening sessions at which prosecutors and police reviewed the sufficiency of evidence to charge suspects. They interviewed police about whether interrogations occurred, whether they elicited a statement, and how suspects' responses affected case outcomes.[130] Charles Weisselberg used *Miranda's* methodology and analyzed interrogation manuals and training programs.[131] Training protocols encouraged police to continue to question suspects after they invoked *Miranda* to obtain statements with which to impeach them or leads to witnesses and evidence.[132] Training programs taught police to avoid *Miranda*'s applicability, for example, by obscuring whether a suspect was in custody.

In the wake of several high-profile false confessions, Great Britain enacted the Police and Criminal Evidence Act (PACE), proscribed psychologically manipulative tactics, and required police to record station-house interrogation of suspects arrested for indictable offenses.[133] PACE requires an "appropriate adult" to attend interrogations of vulnerable suspects, such as juveniles or persons with mental illness or mental retardation.[134] In 1993, the Royal Commission on Criminal Justice further reformed British interrogation methods and introduced the PEACE model of questioning.[135] PEACE techniques differ substantially from the more confrontational Reid Method; interviews are conducted as a search for truth rather than a quest for a confession, and the use of trickery is prohibited.[136]

Gisli Gudjonsson and associates developed sophisticated quantitative and qualitative methods to code and analyze PACE tapes and transcripts.[137] Their access to police and to suspects before, during, and after interrogation enabled them to document interview techniques, to assess their effectiveness, and to measure their impact on vulnerable suspects. Another UK researcher analyzed PACE transcripts of police interviews of juveniles.[138] British psychologist Ray Bull studied the development and implementation of the PEACE approach and police interviews with vulnerable suspects.[139]

In addition to direct or indirect field studies, psychologist Saul Kassin and his associates have conducted extensive laboratory studies of interrogation for more than two decades.[140] Their research attempts to replicate in a laboratory setting the psychological processes associated with custodial interrogation. They analyzed the dynamics of social influence, the accuracy with which police and naïve observers distinguish between truthful and deceptive subjects,[141] personal characteristics that increase suspects' likelihood to give false confessions, and police practices likely to elicit false confessions.[142]

Studies of false confessions and wrongful convictions provide another insight into how police interrogate suspects.[143] False confessions occurred in 15–25% of cases of wrongful convictions and DNA exonerations, and police elicited a disproportionate number from younger offenders.[144] An analysis of 340 cases of criminal exonerations between 1989 and 2003 reported that 42% of juveniles gave false confessions, compared with 13% of adults, and that among juveniles fifteen years of age and younger, 75% gave false confessions.[145] An analysis of the trials and postconviction records of 250 wrongfully convicted people whom DNA exonerated reported that 16% included false confessions.[146] In chapter 7, I contrast the routine questioning in this study with interrogations that elicited false confessions.

Summary and Conclusion

The Court's efforts to regulate interrogation foundered on its lack of knowledge about what actually happens during interrogations. Trial judges lacked an audio or video record of interrogations, and at suppression hearings, they attempted to reconstruct what transpired based on conflicting testimony. Police possess inherently greater credibility than criminal defendants do, and this disparity creates a systematic bias in judges' assessments of *Miranda* waivers and voluntariness of confessions. The complexity of a multifactor, quasi-subjective voluntariness standard impelled the Court to find an administratively easier, objective test to regulate interrogation. The *Miranda* warning provided an easily administered method to assure suspects made knowing, intelligent, and voluntary waivers of rights. Judges focused on when, whether, and how police administered the *Miranda* warning, rather than how they interrogated the vast majority of suspects who waived their rights.

Interrogation is a critical stage in an investigation because after a suspect confesses, other procedural safeguards are of relatively little avail. Interrogation occurs during the most inquisitorial stage of our adversary process. Prior to the filing of formal charges, investigators enjoy a narrow window of opportunity in which to question suspects in a police-dominated environment that creates compelling pressures. *Miranda* theoretically enables suspects to assert their privilege against self-incrimination, to invoke assistance of counsel, and to preserve the adversarial process and the balance of equality. In reality, virtually all people waive their rights, submit to questioning, and make incriminating statements which lead to guilty pleas.[147] The criminal justice system in practice more closely resembles a Crime Control model than a Due Process model. Police determine guilt informally, in an administrative setting—the interrogation room. Judicial review—the suppression hearing—provides defendants with limited recourse because judges have no record of what happened during interrogation.

Despite the critical role of interrogation in the justice system, we know remarkably little about what happens when police question suspects, what the outcomes of those interviews are, or how they affect justice administration.[148] *Miranda* described the Reid Method as the most sophisticated version of psychological manipulations that police used at that time.[149] The few empirical field studies and extensive psychological research document that it remains the predominant training method and technique used today in the United States.[150] By contrast, analyses of interrogations in the United Kingdom report that officers use less confrontational interviewing styles.[151] Moreover, officers' strategies vary with their experience, on-the-job learning, and personalities and styles.[152] Chapters 3 through 6 describe and analyze the strategies police use to question juvenile felony suspects.

Questioning Juveniles

Law and Developmental Psychology

The Supreme Court has decided more juvenile interrogation cases than any other aspect of juvenile justice administration. Although the Court repeatedly has cautioned trial judges that youthfulness could adversely affect young suspects' ability to exercise *Miranda* or to make voluntary statements, it has not mandated special procedures to protect them. *Fare v. Michael C.* endorsed the adult waiver standard—"knowing, intelligent, and voluntary" under the "totality of the circumstances"—to gauge juveniles' waiver of *Miranda* rights.[1]

Developmental psychologists have examined adolescents' decision-making capability, ability to exercise *Miranda* rights, and adjudicative competence. Their research questions whether juveniles possess the cognitive ability and judgment necessary to exercise legal rights. To meet *Fare's* "knowing and intelligent" requirements, youths must be able to understand the words and concepts of the *Miranda* warning. Many youths fifteen years of age and younger do not understand *Miranda's* words or concepts, nor do they function as well as adults. Accordingly, they may need additional safeguards to protect them in the interrogation room. Developmental psychologists report that the cognitive abilities of sixteen- and seventeen-year-old youths begin to approximate those of adults— they understand the words of the warning as well as adults do. However, *Fare's* "voluntariness" requirement focuses on how immature judgment and susceptibility to authority heighten youths' vulnerability.

This chapter reviews the legal framework and competence of juveniles to exercise rights. Part I reviews the law governing interrogation of youths. Although *Fare* and post-*Miranda* decisions hold juveniles and adults to the same standard, the Court's earlier solicitude about adolescents' immaturity and vulnerability persists. If a valid *Miranda* waiver must be "knowing, intelligent, and voluntary," then do juveniles understand the warning ("knowing and intelligent"), and can they exercise their rights ("voluntary")? Decisions about adolescents' culpability—*Roper* and *Graham*—also inform assessments of their competence and judgment. Part II reviews developmental psychology research that examines juveniles' capacity to understand words and concepts (cognitive abilities) and competence to make legal decisions (judgment). Part III applies the developmental research findings to the legal standards and concludes that many juveniles—especially those fifteen years of age and younger—lack sufficient understanding or maturity of judgment to make a "knowing, intelligent and voluntary" waiver of *Miranda* rights.

I. Questioning Juveniles: The Legal Framework

Juvenile rights decisions reflect cultural ambivalence about adolescents. They strike an uneasy balance between dependency and autonomy, vulnerability and responsibility, and incapacity and presumed competency. A protectionist stance shelters children from their immature judgment, provides them additional safeguards, and denies rights because of their presumed inability to exercise them responsibly. A liberationist model portrays youths as autonomous and adultlike and treats them as it does other responsible actors.[2] Court decisions reflect a constitutional ambivalence between competing liberationist and protectionist policies.[3] On the one hand, the Court extended to young people some legal rights of adults. On the other, it subordinated children's assertions of rights or claims to autonomy to other interests. Decisions about young people's legal status and rights reflect a judgment based on prudential and policy considerations, rather than on an empirical assessment of cognitive abilities or maturity of judgment.[4] Lawmakers' demarcations between childhood and adulthood reflect judgments about children's needs, risks they pose to themselves or others, and competing interests of parents, community, and state. The Court's juvenile interrogation decisions reflect the competing constructs—protectionist and liberationist—and contradictory views of adolescents' competence.

A. Voluntariness, Vulnerability, and Youth

Long before *Miranda*, the Court cautioned trial judges to examine closely how youthfulness affected the voluntariness of juveniles' confessions and adopted a protectionist stance. In *Haley v. Ohio*, police questioned a fifteen-year-old in relays beginning at midnight, denied him access to counsel, and confronted him with codefendants' statements until he confessed five hours later.[5] The Court decided the case under the Fourteen Amendment voluntariness standard, ruled that his confession was involuntary, and reversed his conviction: "The age of petitioner, the hours when he was grilled, the duration of his quizzing, the fact that he had no friend or counsel to advise him, the callous attitude of the police toward his rights combine to convince us that this was a confession wrung from a child by means which the law should not sanction."[6] The Court emphasized that youthfulness and inexperience increased Haley's vulnerability to interrogation techniques:

> What transpired would make us pause for careful inquiry if a mature man was involved. And when, as here, a mere child—an easy victim of the law—is before us, special care in scrutinizing the record must be used. Age 15 is a tender and difficult age for a boy. . . . He cannot be judged by the more exacting standards of maturity. That which would leave a man cold and unimpressed can overawe and overwhelm a lad in his early teens. This is the period of great instability which the crisis of adolescence produces. . . . [W]e cannot believe that a lad of tender years is a match for the police in such a contest. He needs counsel and support if he is not to become the victim first of fear, then of panic.[7]

In *Gallegos v. Colorado*,[8] the Court applied the Fourteenth Amendment voluntariness standard and identified youthfulness, prolonged questioning, and denial of access to parents as features that rendered a fourteen-year-old juvenile's confession involuntary: "The youth of the petitioner, the long detention, the failure to send for his parents, the failure immediately to bring him before the judge of the Juvenile Court, the failure to see to it that he had the advice of a lawyer or a friend—all these combine to make us conclude that the formal confession on which this conviction may have rested was obtained in violation of due process."[9] The Court emphasized youths' vulnerability to detention and isolation and cited age as a special circumstance that undermined a confession's voluntariness:

> [A] 14-year-old boy, no matter how sophisticated . . . is not equal to the police in knowledge and understanding . . . and is unable to know how to protect his own interests or how to get the benefits of his constitutional rights. . . . A lawyer or an adult relative or friend could have given the petitioner the protection which his own immaturity could not. . . . Without some adult protection against this inequality, a 14-year-old boy would not be able to know, let alone assert, such constitutional rights as he had.[10]

Both *Haley* and *Gallegos* found that youthfulness, lengthy questioning, and the absence of a lawyer or parent rendered the confessions involuntary. Children are not equals of adults and require additional safeguards —an attorney or parent—to compensate for their vulnerability.

In re Gault reiterated the Court's concern that youthfulness adversely affects the voluntariness of juveniles' statements.[11] "[A]uthoritative opinion has cast formidable doubt upon the reliability and trustworthiness of 'confessions' by children."[12] The Court repeated that "admissions and confessions of juveniles require special caution" and suggested that "[e]ven greater protection might be required where juveniles are involved, since their immaturity and greater vulnerability place them at a greater disadvantage in their dealings with police."[13] Gault cautioned that juveniles' admissions could be "the product of ignorance of rights or of adolescent fantasy, fright, or despair," rather than of considered judgments.[14]

Gault relied on the Fourteenth Amendment due process clause to grant delinquents most procedural rights—notice, hearing, counsel, and cross-examination. However, it applied the Fifth Amendment privilege against self-incrimination to delinquency proceedings.

> It would be entirely unrealistic to carve out of the Fifth Amendment all statements by juveniles on the ground that these cannot lead to "criminal" involvement. In the first place, juvenile proceedings to determine "delinquency," which may lead to commitment to a state institution, must be regarded as "criminal" for purposes of the privilege against self-incrimination. . . . [C]ommitment is a deprivation of liberty. It is incarceration against one's will, whether it is called "criminal" or "civil."[15]

The privilege against self-incrimination embodies the dual functions of procedural safeguards—assure accurate fact-finding and protect against government oppression—and the Court's commitment to an adversarial process. If Gault were concerned solely with the reliability of confessions and accurate fact-finding, then Haley and Gallegos's emphasis on voluntariness would have sufficed. However, Gault recognized that the Fifth Amendment functions to prevent governmental overreaching and to maintain equality between individual and the state:

> The privilege against self-incrimination is, of course, related to the question of the safeguards necessary to assure that admissions or confessions are reasonably trustworthy, that they are not mere fruits of fear or coercion, but are reliable expressions of the truth. The roots of the privilege are, however, far deeper. They tap the basic

stream of religious and political principle because the privilege reflects the limits of the individual's attornment to the state and—in
a philosophical sense—insists upon the equality of the individual
and the state. In other words, the privilege has a broader and deeper
thrust than the rule which prevents the use of confessions which are
the product of coercion because coercion is thought to carry with
it the danger of unreliability. One of its purposes is to prevent the
state, whether by force or by psychological domination, from overcoming the mind and will of the person under investigation and de-
priving him of the freedom to decide whether to assist the state in
securing his convictions.[16]

Thus, *Gault* articulated the Fifth Amendment's critical role to buttress the
adversary system and to foster equality between prosecution and defense.

Gault reflected a different vision of the juvenile court than that of its
Progressive founders. Progressive Era reformers created the juvenile court
to separate children from adults and to provide a less punitive system of
social control.[17] They described children as immature and irresponsible.
Court proceedings focused on a child's background and welfare and es-
chewed criminal procedural safeguards.[18]

During the 1960s, social structural and racial demographic changes
propelled the Warren Court's civil rights decisions, criminal procedure
rulings such as *Miranda*, and juvenile court judgments such as *Gault*.[19]
Gault began to transform the juvenile court into a very different institu-
tion from the one contemplated by the Progressives. *Gault* highlighted
the disjunction between rehabilitative rhetoric and institutional reality
and required juvenile courts to use fundamentally fair procedures.[20] On
the one hand, the Court required procedural safeguards to protect against
youths' immaturity and vulnerability. On the other hand, *Gault* assumed
that youths were competent to exercise legal rights and to participate in
an adversarial process.

Subsequent Court decisions further criminalized delinquency proceedings. *In re Winship* required states to prove delinquents' guilt by the
criminal law standard of proof beyond a reasonable doubt.[21] *Breed v. Jones*
posited a functional equivalence of criminal and delinquency trials and
applied the constitutional ban on double jeopardy.[22] *McKeiver v. Pennsylvania* denied delinquents the right to a jury trial because the Court feared
that a jury would impair the informality, flexibility, and confidentiality of

juvenile court proceedings.[23] However, *Gault* and *Winship* provided impetus to transform the juvenile court from a social welfare agency into a scaled-down criminal court.[24]

Macro-structural, economic, and racial demographic changes in American cities during the 1970s and 1980s and escalation in black youth homicide rates at the end of the 1980s provided the backdrop for states to adopt get-tough juvenile justice policies in the early 1990s.[25] The introduction of crack cocaine and the proliferation of guns in the inner city led to a sharp increase in black youth homicide.[26] Conservative politicians and the mass media pushed crime to the top of the political agenda and promoted get-tough policies.[27] The public and politicians no longer viewed young offenders as innocent and dependent children but as responsible and adult-like offenders—for example, the slogan "adult crime, adult time."[28]

Juvenile justice policy shifted markedly from its original mission to nurture youths toward a criminal justice purpose to punish young offenders—from protectionist to liberationist.[29] By the early twenty-first century, states embraced punitive policies, expanded the numbers of youths transferred to criminal court, and increased powers of juvenile courts to punish.[30] States' get-tough policies increased the direct and collateral consequences of delinquency adjudications—for example, sentence enhancements, sex-offender registration, and other disabilities.[31] Contemporary delinquency proceedings are more formal and complex than those envisioned a century ago and make greater demands on children's ability to participate.

Gault and *Winship* fostered a procedural and substantive convergence and unintentionally transformed the juvenile court from a social welfare agency into a scaled-down criminal court.[32] Emphasizing procedural regularity to determine delinquency shifted courts' initial focus from assessing youths' needs to proving they committed a crime. Granting delinquents the Fifth Amendment privilege against self-incrimination foreclosed the warm, informal talks between judges, children, and parents that the Progressives envisioned. More than any other procedural protection that *Gault* granted, the Fifth Amendment highlighted the adversarial aspects of delinquency proceedings. Professors Elizabeth Scott and Thomas Grisso, and Christopher Slobogin and Mark Fondacaro advocate more relaxed due process safeguards in juvenile courts to foster a rehabilitative or preventive mission.[33] "Permitting a juvenile to remain silent during interrogation or trial could easily reduce reliability and efficiency in the typical case, concerns that arguably trump the lesser autonomy interests at stake in the juvenile context. . . . [M]any technical rules that have developed around

Miranda would not need to be followed by law enforcement officials."[34] However, the conclusion in *Gault, Winship,* and *Breed* that delinquency proceedings are criminal-like in procedure and substance precludes a lower Fifth Amendment standard for delinquents than for adults.

B. Juveniles' Miranda Waiver—Knowing, Intelligent, and Voluntary

Fare v. Michael C. considered whether a sixteen-year-old with prior arrests and experience with police and who had "served time" in a youth camp made a valid *Miranda* waiver.[35] Although the juvenile in *Fare* repeatedly asked to talk with his probation officer before police interrogated him, the Court ruled that he did not invoke either the right to silence or counsel. The Court decided *Fare* as a *Miranda* case (whether a request for nonlegal assistance invoked *Miranda* safeguards) rather than as a juvenile interrogation case (whether youth required additional protections during interrogation).[36] *Fare* held that the "totality of the circumstances" test used to evaluate adults' *Miranda* waivers would govern juveniles' waivers as well. While *Haley* cautioned that "[t]hat which would leave a man cold and unimpressed can overawe and overwhelm a lad in his early tends,"[37] *Fare* declined to provide children with more procedural protections than those afforded adults.[38] *Fare* reasoned that *Miranda* provided an objective basis to evaluate waivers of rights and denied that developmental differences between juveniles and adults required special procedures.[39] *Fare* rebuffed claims that judges could not appraise youths' waivers against an adult standard and required them to assert rights clearly and unambiguously.

The Court in *J.D.B. v. North Carolina* examined another aspect of the *Miranda* framework and emphasized that youthfulness is an objective factor that warrants special consideration.[40] *Miranda* held that if police question a suspect who is in custody—that is, arrested or "deprived of his freedom of action in any significant way"—they must administer the cautionary warning.[41] In *J.D.B.*, a uniformed officer removed the thirteen-year-old youth from class and escorted him to a closed school conference room, where two police and two school administrators questioned him for thirty to forty-five minutes without administering a *Miranda* warning. *J.D.B.* posed the issue of "whether the *Miranda* custody analysis includes consideration of a juvenile suspect's age."[42] The Court concluded that age was an objective factor that affected how a person would feel restrained. "[A] child's age 'would have affected how a reasonable person' in the suspect's position 'would perceive his or her freedom to leave.' That is, a reasonable child subjected to police questioning will sometimes feel pressured to submit when a reasonable adult would feel free to go."[43] The Court noted that it treated features of childhood as objective facts—"children are most susceptible to influence" and "outside pressures"—when it ruled about youths in other contexts.[44] An officer who knew or should have known a youth's age could properly decide how that would affect the youth's feeling of custody. "[O]fficers and judges need no imaginative powers, knowledge of developmental psychology, training in cognitive science, or expertise in social and cultural anthropology to account for a child's age. They simply need the common sense to know that a 7-year-old is not a 13-year-old and neither is an adult."[45] *J.D.B.* recognized that juveniles could feel compelled in circumstances in which an adult might not—that is, youthfulness heightens vulnerability. Although *Fare* endorsed the adult standard to gauge waivers, youths' vulnerability renders their voluntariness more problematic.[46]

C. Waiving Miranda: *Knowing, Intelligent, and Voluntary under the Totality of the Circumstances*

The *Miranda* warning tells suspects of their right to remain silent and to counsel to enable them to make an informed and intelligent waiver decision. *Miranda* does not require suspects to appreciate the legal consequences of waiver or to know the offenses for which police question them.[47] *Miranda* does not require police to inform suspects that an attorney is outside the interrogation room and wants to consult with them.[48] A waiver is valid when "made with a full awareness of both the nature of the right being abandoned and the consequences of the decision to abandon it."[49] A voluntary waiver includes the factors described in *Haley, Gallegos,* and *J.D.B.*—youthfulness, lengthy interrogation, and absence of counsel or a parent.

Most states use the same *Miranda* waiver framework for juveniles and adults. They require only understanding the rights themselves and not collateral consequences, and they do not require a parent or lawyer to assist juveniles.[50] When trial judges evaluate waivers of *Miranda* rights, they consider characteristics of the offender (e.g., age, education, IQ, and prior police contacts) and the context of the interrogation (i.e., the location, methods, and length of interrogation). The leading cases provide extensive lists of factors for trial judges to consider:

1) age of the accused; 2) education of the accused; 3) knowledge of the accused as to both the substance of the charge, if any has been

filed, and the nature of his rights to consult with an attorney and remain silent; 4) whether the accused is held incommunicado or allowed to consult with relatives, friends or an attorney; 5) whether the accused was interrogated before or after formal charges had been filed; 6) methods used in interrogation; 7) length of interrogation; 8) whether vel non the accused refused to voluntarily give statements on prior occasions; and 9) whether the accused has repudiated an extra judicial statement at a later date. Although the age of the accused is one factor that is taken into account, no court, so far as we have been able to learn, has utilized age alone as the controlling factor and ignored the totality of circumstances in determining whether or not a juvenile has intelligently waived his rights against self-incrimination and to counsel.[51]

Appellate courts identify many factors but do not assign controlling weight to any. Instead, they defer to trial judges' decisions regarding whether a juvenile made a valid waiver.[52] Without bright-line rules or decisive factors such as young age, *Fare* provides no meaningful check on trial judges' decisions that youths waived their rights.[53] Many youths may claim to understand to avoid the embarrassment of conceding that they do not. However, if they say they understand the warning, then judges do not probe further to determine whether they actually comprehend it.[54] Once a judge finds a valid waiver, appellate courts may overrule it only if the decision was clearly erroneous or an abuse of discretion. Trial judges have failed to recognize juveniles' claims that waivers were involuntary or confessions coerced even when DNA evidence subsequently exonerated them.[55] In practice, judges invalidate waivers or exclude confessions only under the most egregious circumstances. They regularly find that children as young as ten or eleven years of age, with no prior law enforcement contact, with limited intelligence or significant mental disorders, and without parental assistance made valid waivers.[56]

About ten states assume that most juveniles lack the ability to make a valid *Miranda* waiver unaided and require a parent or other interested adult to assist them.[57] The Vermont court in *In re E.T.C.* held as a matter of state constitutional law that a youth

> must be given the opportunity to consult with an adult; ... that adult must be one who is not only generally interested in the welfare of the juvenile but completely independent from and disassociated

with the prosecution, e.g., a parent, legal guardian, or attorney representing the juvenile; and . . . the interested adult must be informed and aware of the rights guaranteed to the juvenile.[58]

Some states employ two-tiered rules that require parental presence for juveniles younger than fourteen years of age but create only a presumption of incompetence to waive by those fourteen or sixteen years of age or older.[59] Others require younger juveniles to consult with a parent, but only oblige police to offer older youths an opportunity to consult.[60] These states assume that most juveniles require an adult's assistance to decide whether to waive *Miranda*.[61] Adopting a categorical rule—parental presence—to prevent invalid waivers avoids after-the-fact review of how a youth's immaturity affected his or her waiver. Most commentators endorse parental presence safeguards, even though some question the policy assumptions or utility of their participation.[62]

States that require parental presence at juveniles' interrogations make several questionable assumptions. They posit an identity of interests between parent and child. They assume that parents possess greater abilities to make legal decisions that children lack. They believe that a parent's presence will enhance a child's understanding of rights, provide legal advice, mitigate danger of unreliable statements, reduce feelings of isolation, and lessen coercive influences.[63] Because most states do not record interviews, a parent can witness and assure the accuracy of any statement obtained.[64] A parent's presence may relieve police of the burden to assess a youth's cognitive ability and competency.[65] As juvenile justice policies have become more punitive, courts acknowledge that youths need additional safeguards to secure functional parity with adults.[66] More practically, parents provide the means through which some youths can obtain the assistance of counsel.

Despite these protectionist policy goals, these states' assumptions may not be valid. The interests of parent and child may conflict, for example, if the juvenile has assaulted or stolen from his or her parent or has victimized another sibling or if the parent also is a suspect.[67] Parents may have a financial conflict if they have to pay for their child's attorney. They may have an emotional reaction to their child's current arrest or chronic trouble.[68] Parental expectation that children should tell the truth perversely may increase pressures to confess.[69] Cases abound in which parents urged their child to stop lying or to tell the truth or physically threatened the child if he or she refused.[70] Finally, a parent may not understand legal rights or appreciate the consequences of waiver any better than the child does.[71]

Surveys of parents of high school students found that more than half disagreed with the idea that juveniles should withhold information to avoid self-incrimination.[72] A survey of middle-class parents reported that most would provide little or no advice and that the majority would tell their child to waive rights, as contrasted with only 4% who would advise against waiver.[73] Parents attended twenty-five interrogations (8.7%) in this study, and their performance provides an opportunity to test some assumptions about their role.

Minnesota, like the majority of states, follows *Fare* to gauge juveniles' *Miranda* waivers.[74] The Minnesota Supreme Court has rejected juveniles' claims that a parent should be present as a prerequisite to a valid waiver.

> Although we recognize that the presence of parents and their guidance during interrogation of a juvenile is desirable, we reject the absolute rule that every minor is incapable and incompetent as a matter of law to waive his constitutional rights. In determining whether a juvenile has voluntarily and intelligently waived his constitutional rights, parental presence is only one factor to consider and is not an absolute prerequisite.[75]

However, juveniles' repeated requests for a parent before and after a *Miranda* warning might render a waiver or statement involuntary.[76] *Fare* and Minnesota treat juveniles and adults as equals in the interrogation room, and youthfulness, inexperience, or a parent's exclusion are factors that affect the validity of a waiver.

D. Adolescents' Diminished Responsibility and Competence

Concerns about adolescents' competence arise in contexts other than interrogation. The Court in *Roper v. Simmons* barred states from executing offenders for murder they committed when younger than eighteen years of age.[77] *Roper* concluded that juveniles' immature judgment, susceptibility to negative peer influences, and transitory personality reduced their criminal responsibility compared with adults. *Roper* attributed diminished culpability to three factors:

> [1] [A] lack of maturity and an underdeveloped sense of responsibility are found in youth more often than in adults.... [T]hese qualities

often result in impetuous and ill-considered actions and decisions. [2] [J]uveniles are more vulnerable or susceptible to negative influences and outside pressures, including peer pressure. . . . [3] [T]he character of a juvenile is not as well formed as that of an adult. The personality traits of juveniles are more transitory, less fixed.[78]

The Court in *Graham v. Florida* relied on *Roper*'s categorical diminished-responsibility rationale and banned sentences of life without parole for youths convicted of nonhomicide crimes.[79] *Graham* reiterated the characteristics that *Roper* found to diminish juveniles' criminal responsibility and then asserted,

Developments in psychology and brain science continue to show fundamental differences between juvenile and adult minds. For example, parts of the brain involved in behavior control continue to mature through late adolescence. Juveniles are more capable of change than are adults, and their actions are less likely to be evidence of "irretrievably depraved character" than are the actions of adults.[80]

Roper and *Graham* offered three reasons why states could not punish youths as severely as they do adults. First, juveniles' immature judgment and limited self-control cause them to act impulsively without full appreciation of consequences. Second, juveniles' greater susceptibility than adults to negative peer influences diminishes their criminal responsibility. Third, juveniles' personalities are more transitory and less fully formed, and their crimes provide less reliable evidence of "depraved character" than do those of adults.

II. Developmental Psychology: Adolescent Competence

Roper and *Graham* concluded that immature judgment and susceptibility to outside influences reduce youths' criminal responsibility. Immaturity, impulsivity, and sensitivity to social influences heighten their vulnerability to coercive pressures and compromise their competence to exercise rights in the interrogation room. Developmental psychologists have studied how children's thinking and behavior change as they mature, have focused on youths' judgment and suggestibility, and have questioned their ability to make competent decisions or exercise rights. Research distinguishes between cognitive ability and maturity of judgment. The former bears on youths' ability to make a knowing and intelligent waiver, and the latter bears on heightened vulnerability to compulsive pressures—the concerns expressed in *Haley, Gallegos,* and *J.D.B.*

By midadolescence, most youth exhibit cognitive abilities comparable with adults. They can distinguish right from wrong—the minimum threshold for criminal liability—and reason similarly as their elders.[81] For example, youths and adults use comparable risk-benefit calculations to make informed-consent medical decisions.[82] These studies present research subjects with hypothetical scenarios, provide them with complete information in a relaxed setting, and compare reasoning processes that adolescents and adults use. The American Psychological Association affirmed the maturity of adolescent girls to make abortion decisions without parental assistance. "[B]y the middle adolescence (age 14–15) young people develop abilities similar to adults in reasoning about moral dilemmas, understanding social rules and laws, [and] reasoning about interpersonal relationships and interpersonal problems."[83] However, the ability to make good choices with complete information under laboratory conditions differs from the ability to make adultlike decisions under stressful conditions with incomplete information.[84] "[W]hereas adolescents and adults perform comparably on cognitive tests measuring the sorts of cognitive abilities . . . that permit logical reasoning about moral, social, and interpersonal matters—adolescents and adults are not of equal maturity with respect to the psychosocial capacities . . . such as impulse control and resistance to peer influence."[85] The latter require cognitive ability *and* risk assessment, maturity of judgment, and self-control.

Since the mid-1990s, the MacArthur Foundation Network on Adolescent Development and Juvenile Justice (ADJJ) has studied adolescents' decision-making and judgment, adjudicative competence, and criminal culpability.[86] The research distinguishes between cognitive ability and psychosocial maturity of judgment. The latter involves risk assessment, temporal orientation, capacity for self-regulation, and susceptibility to external influences.[87]

The ADJJ research reports a disjunction between youths' cognitive abilities and maturity of judgment. Adolescents by about sixteen years of age exhibit cognitive abilities comparable with adults. However, they do not develop psychosocial maturity, self-control, and competence to make adult-quality decisions until their twenties.[88] The ADJJ described the cleavage between cognitive development (nearly adultlike by midadolescence) and maturity of judgment (a work-in-progress for another decade) as the "Immaturity Gap." The disjunction between cognitive understanding (e.g., ability to distinguish right from wrong) and judgment and self-control (immaturity and vulnerability) provided bases on which *Roper* and *Graham* found youths' culpability diminished.[89]

A. Immature Judgment and Risk Perception

Youths differ from adults in perceptions of risk, time perspective, and appreciation of future consequences.[90] These differences affect their capacity for self-management and ability to make autonomous decisions. They have not fully learned to subordinate emotion to intellect, to control behavior, and adequately to consider long-term consequences.[91] Youths' poorer decisions reflect differences in knowledge and experience, short-term versus long-term time perspectives, attitude toward risk, and impulsivity.[92]

Good judgment and self-control require a person to think ahead, to delay gratification, and to restrain impulses. Emotions play an important role in decision-making, and psychologists distinguish between choices made under conditions of "cold" and "hot" cognition or states of arousal.[93] Mood volatility, an appetite for excitement, and stress adversely affect adolescents' decisions to a greater degree than they do adults'.[94]

Higher incidences of accidents, suicides, unsafe sexual practices, and criminal activity reflect adolescents' inclination to engage in riskier behavior than do adults.[95] Compared with adults, adolescents underestimate the amount and likelihood of risks, use a shorter time frame, and focus on gains rather than losses.[96] They possess less information and consider fewer options when they make decisions.[97] Youths and adults take about the same amount of time to solve simple problems, but the time used to solve complex problems increases with age.

Juveniles' risk perception actually *declines* during midadolescence and then increases gradually in the early twenties. Sixteen- and seventeen-year-olds are the most present oriented of all age groups and see fewer risks than do either younger or older research subjects.[98] Youths differ in their ability to delay gratification and more often opt for an immediate but smaller reward than adults do.[99]

Youth regard *not* engaging in risky behaviors differently than do adults.[100] Risky behavior provides excitement and an adrenaline rush. People's appetite for risk and sensation seeking peaks at ages sixteen or seventeen and then declines into adulthood.[101] The widest divergence between juveniles' and adults' perception of and preference for risk occurs during midteens, when youths' criminal activity increases.[102] Feelings of invulnerability and immortality heighten youths' risk proclivities.[103] Juveniles may possess adultlike cognitive abilities, but they are less able to make adult-quality decisions.

B. Neuroscience: Judgment and Impulsivity

The differences between adolescents' and adults' thinking and behaving correspond with development in the human brain, which does not mature until the early twenties.[104] The prefrontal cortex (PFC) of the frontal lobe of the brain operates as chief executive officer and controls executive functions.[105] Executive functions include abstract thinking, strategic planning, and impulse control. During adolescence and into the early twenties, increased myelination of the PFC improves cognitive function, reasoning ability, and response time.[106] The increase in white matter speeds transmission of neural signals and produces more efficient processing.[107]

The amygdala—the limbic system located at the base of the brain—controls emotional and instinctual behavior, for example, fight-or-flight response. In stressful situations, adolescents rely more heavily on the amygdala and less heavily on the PFC than do adults.[108] Their impulsive behavior reflects a gut reaction rather than sober reflection.[109] "For reasons undoubtedly related in part to limbic system arousal, they experience emotional urges more intensely, and the underdevelopment of the frontal lobes means that they have lesser capacity to hold these urges in check, or channel them into more appropriate outlets."[110] Novel circumstances and emotional arousal challenge youths' ability to resist impulses and exercise self-control. The interaction between the PFC (the executive functions) and the limbic system (associated with impulsive or instinctual behavior) contributes to adolescents' poorer decisions.

> [R]egions of the brain implicated in processes of long-term planning, regulation of emotion, impulse control, and the evaluation of risk and reward continue to mature over the course of adolescence, and perhaps well into young adulthood. At puberty, changes in the limbic system—a part of the brain that is central in the processing and regulation of emotion—may stimulate adolescents to seek higher levels of novelty and to take more risks; these changes also may contribute to increased emotionality and vulnerability to stress. At the same time, patterns of development in the prefrontal cortex, which is active during the performance of complicated tasks involving planning and decision-making, suggest that these

higher-order cognitive capacities may be immature well into middle adolescence.[111]

Adolescents do not have the neuroanatomical or physiological capacity of adults to make mature decisions or control impulses.[112] The neuroscience bolsters the developmental psychology research on adolescents' ability to exercise *Miranda* or to participate in legal proceedings.[113]

Developmental features—impaired judgment, risk calculus, short-term perspective, and the like—reduce youths' competence and contribute to immature decisions. As *Graham* noted, they adversely affect youths' ability to exercise rights and to cooperate with defense counsel.

[T]he features that distinguish juveniles from adults also put them at a significant disadvantage in criminal proceedings. Juveniles mistrust adults and have limited understandings of the criminal justice system and the roles of the institutional actors within it. They are less likely than adults to work with their lawyers to aid in their defense. Difficulty in weighing long-term consequences; a corresponding impulsiveness; and reluctance to trust defense counsel seen as part of the adult world a rebellious youth rejects, all can lead to poor decisions by one charged with a juvenile offense. These factors are likely to impair the quality of a juvenile defendant's representation.[114]

The Court long has recognized that children differ from adults and that this difference affects how they respond to interrogation.[115] *Fare* requires a knowing, intelligent, and voluntary *Miranda* waiver. A youth must be able to understand the warning to make a knowing and intelligent waiver. A youth must be able to exercise judgment and self-control to make a voluntary waiver and not to succumb to compulsive pressures. Developmental research reports that youth sixteen years of age or older exhibit cognitive abilities comparable to adults, although stress or emotional arousal may impair those abilities. Adolescents' immaturity, impulsivity, and risk perception affect their judgment, self-control, and vulnerability to compulsion. These features have a neurobiological basis and affect youths' waiver decisions and vulnerability to pressure.

III. Developmental Psychology Encounters Legal Expectations
Despite the Court's repeated references to developmental differences, youthful immaturity, and heightened vulnerability, most states do not

provide extra procedural safeguards for juveniles. Instead, they use adult standards to gauge juveniles' competence to stand trial and to waive rights. If youths differ from adults in understanding *Miranda*, conceiving of or exercising rights, or succumbing to pressure, then the law holds them to a standard that few can meet.

Developmental psychologists question whether juveniles can meet an adult waiver standard. Although *Miranda* requires police to advise suspects of their rights, some juveniles simply may not understand the words or concepts. *Miranda* did not require police to use specific language as long as a warning conveyed the substance of the rights.[116] Surveys of law enforcement agencies report that police around the country use more than five hundred different versions of the *Miranda* warning.[117] Psychologists have studied the vocabulary, concepts, and reading levels required to understand those warnings and have concluded that they exceed the intellectual ability of many adolescents.[118] Key words and concepts of a warning require at least an eighth-grade level of education to understand, and most juveniles thirteen years of age or younger cannot grasp their meaning.[119] Some concepts and words—for example, the meaning of the word *right*, the term *appointed* to secure counsel, and *waive*—require at least a high school education, which renders *Miranda* incomprehensible to many juveniles. Many juveniles cannot define critical words used in the *Miranda* warning.[120] Moreover, special "dumbed-down" juvenile *Miranda* warnings are often twice as long as those used for adults and further impede understanding.[121] If a demanding reading level or verbal complexity makes a warning unintelligible, then it cannot serve a protective function.[122]

A. Juveniles' Understanding of Miranda

Thomas Grisso has studied juveniles' ability to exercise *Miranda* rights for more than three decades. He reports that many youths do not understand the warning adequately to make a valid waiver.[123] Grisso conducted his pioneering research on adolescents' understanding of *Miranda* under relatively benign conditions—a researcher in a laboratory rather than an officer in an interrogation room—and used warnings that only required a sixth- or seventh-grade reading level. Under these favorable conditions, most adults exhibited adequate understanding of the warnings. By contrast, the majority of juveniles did not understand a *Miranda* warning well enough to make a knowing and intelligent waiver. Although age, intelligence, and prior arrests correlated with *Miranda* comprehension, more than half (55.3%) of juveniles, as compared with less than one-quarter (23.1%) of adults, had no understanding of at least one of the four warnings, and only one-fifth (20.9%) of juveniles, as compared with almost half (42.3%) of adults, grasped all four components of the warning.[124]

Grisso has developed and validated instruments to measure adolescents' understanding of *Miranda*.[125] These instruments test youths' understanding by asking them to paraphrase the four warnings, to define six key words in the warning—for example, *right, attorney, consult, appoint, interrogation, entitle*—and to interpret differently phrased sentences that have the same meaning as those contained in the warning.[126] Juveniles consistently underperformed when compared with adults and most frequently misunderstood the right to consult with counsel and to have one present.[127]

As a class, juveniles younger than fifteen years of age failed to meet both the absolute and relative (adult norm) standards for comprehension. . . . The vast majority of these juveniles misunderstood at least one of the four standard *Miranda* statements, and compared with adults, demonstrated significantly poorer comprehension of the nature and significance of the *Miranda* rights.[128]

Sixteen- and seventeen-year-olds understood *Miranda* about as well as did adults, although substantial minorities of both groups misunderstood some components.[129]

Age-related improvements in cognitive ability and *Miranda* comprehension appear in other studies. "Youths' general intellectual ability, verbal ability, attention, and executive functioning increased with age. This indicates that young adolescents may not yet have acquired the cognitive abilities necessary to adequately understand and participate in legal proceedings."[130] A review of research reported "the understanding of adolescents ages 15–17 with near-average levels of verbal intelligences tends not to have been inferior to that of adults. But youths of that age with IQ scores below 85, and average youth below age 14, performed much poorer, often misunderstanding two or more of the warnings."[131] Competence consistently correlated with age—younger juveniles understood *Miranda* warnings even less well than did midadolescents. One study found impaired *Miranda* comprehension by 58% of eleven- to thirteen-year-olds, 33.3% of fourteen- and fifteen-year-olds, and 7.8% of sixteen- and seventeen-year-olds.[132] Research that used broader measures to assess understanding of rights found more misunderstanding by youths—78.0% of eleven- to thirteen-year-olds, 62.7% of fourteen- and fifteen-year-olds, and 35.3% of sixteen- and seventeen-year-olds—than adults exhibited.[133]

Adolescents with low IQs perform more poorly than do adults with low IQs, and delinquent youths have lower IQs than does the general population.[134] "[A]ge and IQ are still the primary predictors of Miranda comprehension; older youths were generally better able to understand the Miranda warnings than were younger youths, and juveniles with higher IQ scores demonstrated better comprehension than those with lower IQs."[135] A study of detained delinquents reported that they had an average IQ of 82,[136] and larger proportions of delinquents than youths in the general population have lower IQs and mental disorders, which interact with and impede understanding.[137] Analyses of linguistic complexity conclude that the reading level required to grasp Miranda's meaning is beyond the ability of most sixteen-year-old delinquents.[138] "The synergistic effects of poor reading comprehension, low intelligence, and comorbid mental disorders are likely to have catastrophic effects on Miranda comprehension and subsequent reasoning. Reading comprehension alone may render most Miranda warnings ineffective for the majority of juvenile offenders."[139] Other research consistently reports that older youths understand Miranda about as well—or badly—as do adults, but many younger juveniles do not understand the words or concepts contained in the warning.[140] Youths fifteen years of age and younger had poorer understanding of legal proceedings, waived rights more readily, and confessed more frequently than youths sixteen years of age or older.[141]

Even youths who understand Miranda's words may be unable to exercise their rights as effectively as adults are able.[142] Juveniles do not appreciate the function or importance of rights as well as do adults,[143] which confirms Graham's observation that they are less competent defendants. They have greater difficulty conceiving of a right as an absolute entitlement that they can exercise without adverse consequences.[144] "[A] larger proportion of delinquent youths bring to the defendant role an incomplete comprehension of the concept and meaning of a right as it applies to adversarial legal proceedings."[145] Juveniles view a right as something that authorities allow them to do but that they may unilaterally retract or withhold.[146] They misconceive the attorney role and client confidentiality. Youths from impoverished backgrounds exhibit poorer understanding than do middle-class youths, "because children from lower socioeconomic backgrounds are less likely to grow up believing they are entitled to rights and may have fewer opportunities to try out social roles in which they are able to assert their rights."[147] Youths with a poorer appreciation of rights waive them at significantly higher rates than do youths with better comprehension.[148]

Psychologists who study juveniles' ability to exercise rights conduct research under laboratory conditions approved by institutional review boards (IRBs). IRB restrictions on experimentation on human subjects—especially vulnerable populations such as juveniles—prevent researchers from creating the stressful conditions that routinely occur during interrogation.[149] "Because human subject review boards balk at allowing researchers to replicate the pressures of the interrogation process in laboratory experiments, it has been difficult to design studies that directly test the effect of suggestive interviewing techniques on the likelihood that someone will take responsibility for committing a crime that she or he did not commit."[150] Laboratory research cannot ethically create the stress that a suspect experiences during interrogation—nervousness, criminal involvement, and threat of confinement.[151] Because psychologists cannot replicate the anxiety of arrest and interrogation, laboratory research likely overstates youths' understanding of and competence to exercise *Miranda* rights.[152]

The cognitive ability and competence of public school youths who participate in social psychologists' studies do not directly equate with delinquent populations, which tend to be poorer, to possess less verbal facility, and to have less understanding of legal abstractions.[153] "[D]elinquents with lower intelligence test scores, lower scores on a verbal ability test, remedial or problematic educational histories, and learning disabilities" exhibit poorer understanding of legal concepts.[154] As a result, laboratory research likely has overstated adolescents' competence because it "did not examine delinquent youths who are most likely to become defendants"; research that did, however, "usually found levels of performance that were no better (and often poorer) than the performance found in studies using non-delinquents samples."[155]

B. Adjudicative Competence

The Court long has held that a defendant must be competent to stand trial for a hearing to be fundamentally fair. *Dusky v. United States* held that a defendant must possess "sufficient present ability to consult with his lawyer with a reasonable degree of rational understanding . . . [and have] a rational as well as factual understanding of proceedings against him."[156] *Drope v. Missouri* held that "[i]t has long been accepted that a person whose mental condition is such that he lacks the capacity to understand the nature and object of the proceedings against him, to consult with counsel, and to assist in preparing his defense may not be subjected to a trial."[157] Mental illness or retardation typically impairs defendants' ability to understand the legal process, to make rational decisions, and to assist counsel.

Studies of adolescents' adjudicative competence bear on youths' ability to exercise *Miranda* rights.[158] Adjudicative competence requires "a basic comprehension of the purpose and nature of the trial process (Understanding), the capacity to provide relevant information to counsel and to process information (Reasoning), and the ability to apply information to one's own situation in a manner that is neither distorted nor irrational (Appreciation)."[159] Youths' development limitations impair their ability to understand, to make rational decisions, and to assist counsel in the same ways that mental illness or retardation render adults incompetent.[160] Significant age-related differences appear between adolescents' and young adults' competence, quality of judgment, and legal decisions.[161] Many juveniles younger than fourteen years of age are as severely impaired as adults found incompetent to stand trial.[162] In one study, 30% of eleven- to thirteen-year-olds and 19% of fourteen- to fifteen-year-olds exhibited deficits of reasoning and understanding comparable to that of incompetent adults,[163] and many older youths exhibited substantial impairments.[164] Age and intelligence interact and produce higher levels of incompetence among adolescents with low IQs than among adults with low IQs.

[Approximately] one fifth of 14- to 15-year-olds are as impaired in capacities relevant to adjudicative competence as are seriously mentally ill adults who would likely be considered incompetent to stand trial by clinicians who perform evaluations for courts. . . . Not surprisingly, juveniles of below-average intelligence are more likely than juveniles of average intelligence to be impaired in abilities relevant for competence to stand trial. Because a greater proportion of youths in the juvenile justice system than in the community are of below-average intelligence, the risk for incompetence to stand trial is therefore even greater among adolescents who are in the justice system than it is among adolescents in the community.[165]

Even nominally competent adolescents often make poorer decisions than do young adults because of differences in maturity and judgment.[166]

C. Suggestibility, Vulnerability, and Voluntariness

Roper and *Graham* emphasized youths' susceptibility to social influences as a factor that reduced culpability and diminished competence. Interrogative suggestibility is the "extent to which, within a closed social interaction, people come to accept messages communicated to them during formal questioning and as a result, their behavioral response is affected in such a way as to either accept or resist the suggestion."[167] People's susceptibility to external influences and pressures affects how they remember or report past events.[168]

Miranda characterized custodial interrogation as inherently compelling because police dominate the setting, control the flow of information, and create psychological pressures to comply.[169] Research on child-victims' ability to provide reliable accounts of past events highlights their susceptibility to social influences. Juveniles are more vulnerable to suggestion during questioning than are adults.[170] The form of the question, time delay between event and interview, and investigator's authority affect their responses.[171] People who have experienced negative life-events—for example, delinquent populations—more readily yield to negative feedback and change responses to conform to interviewer expectations.[172]

The legal and social status of youths and adults differ and render children questioned by authority figures more suggestible. We expect youths to answer questions posed by police, teachers, parents, and other adults; social expectations and children's lower status increase their vulnerability in an interrogation.[173] Younger adolescents waive rights and admit responsibility "because they are still young enough to believe that they should never disobey authority."[174] They are more likely to acquiesce to negative pressure or critical feedback.[175] They more readily accede to suggestions during questioning.[176] They weigh more heavily the approval of an interviewer than they do the negative consequences of falsely admitting responsibility.[177] "Psychologically coercive strategies that contribute to interrogative suggestibility play on young suspects' eagerness to please, firm trust of people in authority, lack of self-confidence, increased desire to protect friends/relatives and to impress peers, and increased desire to leave the interrogation sooner."[178] Adolescents with low IQs are more suggestible than are adults with limited intellect.[179] Adolescents' impulsivity and immaturity may cause them to confess in order to end an interrogation, rather than to consider the long-term consequences.[180]

[A]lthough the stereotypic rebellious adolescent might not be associated with an increased tendency to comply with authority, within the legal context, adolescent suspects, like child witnesses, often demonstrate such a tendency and differ in their susceptibility to adult deception as a function of the adult's perceived power. . . . [T]hey are more susceptible than adult offenders to negative feedback from authority figures, because they demonstrate an increased tendency to change their previous answers in response to negative feedback.[181]

The Court requires suspects to invoke *Miranda* rights clearly and unambiguously.[182] However, some groups of people—for example, juveniles, females, and racial minorities—speak indirectly or tentatively to avoid conflict with those who are in power.[183] If a suspect thinks he or she has invoked *Miranda* rights, but police disregard the request as ambiguous, then the suspect may feel overwhelmed by their indifference and succumb to further questioning. *Davis v. United States* recognized that to require suspects to invoke rights clearly and unambiguously could prove problematic for some. "We recognize that requiring a clear assertion of the right to counsel might disadvantage some suspects who—because of fear, intimidation, lack of linguistic skills, or a variety of other reasons—will not clearly articulate their right to counsel although they actually want to have a lawyer present."[184] The Court demands a level of assertiveness that runs contrary to how most delinquents respond when confronted by police.

Conclusion

A person must understand the words and concepts of *Miranda* to make a "knowing, intelligent, and voluntary" waiver. The warning provides knowledge of rights and empowers people to act on that information. However, many juveniles do not understand *Miranda*'s words or the concepts it conveys. Many youths lack a mature concept of a legal right as an entitlement. Youthfulness, linguistic complexity, educational deficits, and low IQs prevent many juveniles from grasping the information the warning contains. Youths fifteen years of age or younger exhibit clear lack of understanding. Juveniles sixteen years of age and older appear to possess the cognitive ability to understand the words, although many show deficits that increase their vulnerability during interrogation. "[J]uvenile suspects share many of the same characteristics as the developmentally disabled, notably their eagerness to comply with adult authority figures, impulsivity, immature judgment, and inability to recognize and weigh risks in decision-making, and appear to be at greater risk of falsely confessing when subjected to psychological interrogation techniques."[185] Thus, many juveniles—especially younger ones—may not be capable of a "knowing and intelligent" waiver.

A suspect must also give a voluntary waiver of *Miranda* rights. The Court long has recognized that children are more vulnerable to coercion than are adults. Socialization to obey authority and status differences between police and youths heighten suggestibility and susceptibility to social influences. Differences in risk appraisal, time perspective, and appreciation of consequences cause juveniles to make poorer decisions than do adults. Adolescents' immature and impulsive decisions reflect fundamental differences in neurobiology. Their brains have less developed executive functions and a more active limbic system that render them less able to make legal decisions with the same facility as adults. The Court long has recognized the unique vulnerability of youths during questioning and has found their acts coerced under conditions in which an adult could act voluntarily.

The Court decided *Miranda* to provide a simple, objective alternative to complex analyses of the voluntariness of confessions. Despite social, developmental, and biological differences, the Court treats juveniles and adult as equals. *Fare, Davis*, and *Berghuis* require juveniles to invoke *Miranda* rights clearly and unambiguously. However, to require youths to explicitly invoke *Miranda* contradicts the social and developmental reality that they cannot perform as well as adults. Many younger juveniles do not understand the warning or legal concepts. Older youths who understand the words may feel more constrained, more susceptible to the power differential in the interrogation room, and less able voluntarily to relinquish their rights. Apart from the few states that require a parent's presence, the legal framework of interrogation does not distinguish between juveniles and adults.

Against the contradictory backdrop of legal expectations and developmental realities, this study examines what actually happens when police question youthful suspects. It provides a thickly detailed empirical case study of routine felony interrogation. It provides an opportunity to test the hypotheses of developmental psychologists about the competence of older adolescents in the interrogation room. Do these near-adults understand *Miranda*? How do police document their comprehension? How do police question youths who waive *Miranda*? How do youths' decisions to waive *Miranda* affect how the justice system processes their cases?

The next four chapters take us inside the interrogation room. Chapter 3 examines where interrogations occur, who is present, and how police administer *Miranda* warnings and elicit waivers. Chapter 4 analyzes how police interrogate the vast majority of youths who waive their rights. Chapter 5 explores how juveniles respond to their interrogators and the impact of waiving *Miranda* on case processing and sentencing outcomes. Chapter 6 analyzes how interrogation practices vary in urban and suburban locales, how parental presence affects interviews, and whether interrogation practices vary with youths' race. These chapters begin to fill the knowledge gap that *Miranda* decried more than four decades ago.

To Waive or Not to Waive

That Is the Question

More than four decades ago, *Miranda* stressed that police secrecy produced a "gap in our knowledge as to what in fact goes on in the interrogation rooms." That gap persists. We do *not* know many things about routine felony interrogation. How soon after suspects commit a crime do police question them? Where do police interview offenders? Who is present when they question a suspect? How and when do police administer a *Miranda* warning? How do they predispose suspects to waive their rights? How many youths waive? How do police document a knowing, intelligent, and voluntary waiver? How do youths who waive differ from those who invoke their rights? How do police question the vast majority of youths who waive their rights? How do youths respond? How long do interrogations take? What evidence do police derive from questioning? How does waiving or invoking affect case processing and sentencing outcomes? Chapters 3, 4, and 5 begin to answer these questions about what happens inside the interrogation room.

This chapter analyzes interrogations of 307 youths aged sixteen and seventeen charged with felony offenses. Interviews with juvenile justice personnel supplement and aid interpreting the data. Part I describes the youth whom police questioned. Part II examines the context of interrogations—arrest and detention status, locations of questioning, and people present. Part III examines how police administer *Miranda* warnings—the delivery and timing of the warning. It describes how police establish that juveniles understand their rights and waive them voluntarily. *Miranda* requires a "knowing, intelligent, and voluntary" waiver of rights, but the Court distinguishes between understanding rights and appreciating the consequences of waiving them. I examine how justice system personnel perceive the relative competence of older adolescents, young adults, and younger offenders to exercise *Miranda* rights. Part IV analyzes how youths who waive their rights differ from those who invoke them.

Chapter 4 analyzes how police questioned the vast majority of the youths in this study who waived *Miranda*. It examines the process of interrogations—the types of tactics and Reid Method techniques police used. Chapter 5 analyzes how the youths responded. It evaluates the evidentiary value of statements and the impact of waiving or invoking *Miranda* on case-processing and sentencing outcomes. These three chapters provide the empirical core of what happens in the interrogation room. I compare and contrast these findings with those reported in studies of adults,[1] juveniles,[2] and in the United Kingdom.[3]

I. Characteristics of Juveniles Whom Police Interrogated

Table 3.1 summarizes characteristics of the 307 juveniles in this study whom police questioned and county attorneys charged with felony-level offenses. Males constituted the vast majority (89.3%) of youths whom police questioned. Somewhat more than half (55.7%) of the juveniles were sixteen years old at the time of questioning. Prosecutors charged more than half (55.0%) with felony property offenses—for example, burglary, larceny, and auto theft. They charged nearly one-third (31.6%) of the youths with crimes against the person—for example, murder, armed robbery, aggravated assault, and criminal sexual conduct. They charged the remaining youths with drug crimes (6.2%), firearm offenses (5.5%), and other felonies (1.6%)—for example, fleeing a police officer. Some youths charged with the most serious crimes are missing from this group because prosecutors filed certification motions, and juvenile court judges transferred them to criminal court.

Nearly one-third (30.6%) of the juveniles had no prior arrests. Police previously had taken into custody more than one-third of these youths for noncriminal status offenses (15.3%) or misdemeanors (22.8%). About one-third of these youths (35.1%) had one or more prior felony arrests. More than half (57%) had prior juvenile court referrals. Nearly one-third (29.9%) were under current juvenile court supervision—probation, placement, or parole status—when police questioned them. About half were white (52.1%), and the remainder (47.9%) were members of ethnic and racial minority groups—black, Hispanic, Native American, and Asian. Black juveniles accounted for more than one-third (34.9%) of the sample. Chapter 6 examines how police questioned youths of different racial backgrounds.

The youths in this study differ somewhat from the counties' ordinary sixteen- and seventeen-year-old felony caseloads.[4] This group includes a larger proportion of males, larger proportions of youths charged with property and violent crimes and substantially fewer youths charged with drug offenses. It includes a larger proportion of youths with prior court referrals. Overall, these interrogated youths constitute a more serious group of delinquents than counties' delinquent felony caseloads. It corroborates justice personnel's expectations that felony cases with interrogations would be more serious and contested (see appendix 1).

Table 3.1

Characteristics of Juveniles Interrogated

	N	%
Gender		
Male	274	89.3
Female	33	10.7
Age		
16	171	55.7
17	132	43.0
18	4	1.3
Race		
White	160	52.1
Black	107	34.9
Asian	17	5.5
Hispanic	15	4.9
Native American	5	1.6
Offense		
Property[a]	169	55.0
Person[b]	97	31.6
Drugs[c]	19	6.2
Firearms[d]	17	5.5
Other[e]	5	1.6
Prior arrests		
None	94	30.6
Status	47	15.3
Misdemeanor	70	22.8
One felony	43	14.0
Two or more felonies	37	21.1
Prior juvenile court referrals		
None	126	43.0
One or more	167	57.0
Court status at time of interrogation		
None	142	46.3
Prior supervision	61	19.9
Current probation/parole	75	24.4
Current placement	17	5.5

[a] Crimes against property include burglary, theft of a motor vehicle, arson, receiving stolen property, possession of stolen property, possession of burglary tools, criminal damage to property, theft, forgery, theft by swindle, and credit card fraud.

[b] Crimes against the person include aggravated and simple robbery, aggravated assault, murder and attempted murder, criminal vehicular homicide, criminal sexual conduct, and terroristic threats.

[c] Drug crimes include sale or possession of a controlled substance—crack, methamphetamine, marijuana, codeine, ecstasy, heroin—possession of a forged prescription, and tampering with anhydrous ammonia equipment (methamphetamine).

[d] Firearm crimes include possession of a firearm, discharge of a firearm, theft of a firearm, possession of an explosive device, and drive-by shooting.

[e] Other offenses are fleeing a police officer.

II. *Miranda* Framework: Custody + Interrogation = Warning

When police take suspects into custody *and* interrogate them, *Miranda* requires officers to warn suspects of their rights to dispel the inherent coercion of custodial interrogation. This section describes juveniles' arrest and detention status when police questioned them, where interrogations took place, how quickly police questioned youths after an offense occurred, and who was present.

A. *Where Police Interrogate Suspects*

Miranda assumed that the coercive pressures of interrogation arise when a person is in custody: "deprived of his freedom of action in any significant way."[5] The test for custody is objective—whether a reasonable person in the suspect's position would feel restraints to the degree associated with formal arrest—and *J.D.B.* held that a suspect's age can affect feelings of detention.[6] Analysts describe how some police manipulate the concept of custody to avoid giving a *Miranda* warning.[7] However, youths' custody status in these interrogations was unambiguous.

Police had arrested the vast majority (86.6%) of juveniles prior to questioning. They administered *Miranda* and made a *Scales* recording in all of these interviews, regardless of whether they formally arrested or later released a youth. They often told youths their custody status—"Because you're under arrest, I have to read you your *Miranda*" or "Before I get started here today, I want to tell you right off that I will not be placing you under arrest today, all right?" Police detained nearly two-thirds (61.7%) of the youths whom they interrogated and released the others to their parents after they questioned them.

Thomas Grisso found that police question the largest pluralities of juveniles either at a police station or at juveniles' homes.[8] These venues provide police with tactical advantages—interviews at the station increase coercive pressures, while questions at home lull juveniles to let down their defenses. More than half (55.7%) of all interrogations in this study took place in police stations or sheriff's departments. Another quarter (23.1%) occurred at detention centers or correctional facilities. Thus, police questioned more than three-quarters (78.8%) of youths in custodial settings.

Nearly one-tenth (8.1%) of interrogations in this study took place in a police car at the place of arrest. Squad cars are equipped with recording devices, and officers told youths how to speak for the recorder. "Why don't you just sit up close to the screen here, so you can hear me, Jonathan, and so that you can speak loudly into the tape recorder." Interrogations in squad cars may give police a tactical advantage. A public defender I interviewed suggested,

> Now they're doing a lot of interrogations in the squad car, when emotions are high and the kid really feels compelled to tell their side of the story to get out of the squad car, which I think is a new more aggressive technique that I haven't seen in previous years. Usually they'd process them first and then question them at the detention center after they've had some time to kind of think through things. They're removed from the situation, so they're a bit calmer and have more grasp of the seriousness of the situation. But I think when you question a kid in the squad car, there's this sense that "maybe I can get out of this if I just talk to the cops; they'll let me go home or let me out of the squad car."

Police conducted 6.2% of these interrogations at juveniles' homes. Officers described the tactical advantages of noncustodial home interviews, especially when they assured youths they would not take them into custody at that time: "It's much easier to do a noncustodial interview at their home or with their parent present. It takes some of that burden off of them if they know they're not going to be arrested on the spot or taken to jail for what they've done. I think there's always a sense of relief if they know they're not going to jail for something." The Reid Method recommends sequestering suspects, and other officers preferred not to question youths at home because juveniles feel more comfortable in familiar surroundings: "I feel you're not going to get the truth as easily as you would if you can isolate the individual and get them in a place that's unfamiliar to them."

Police interrogated 6.2% of these juveniles in schools. Officers described the psychological advantage of school interviews: "Because you have two forms of authority there. You've got the cops and the school. The school is the best form of authority because they are swift and fast for punishment or consequences." School resource officers (SROs) whom I interviewed suggested that school-based interviews differ somewhat from other interrogations because school personnel complement their role: "It's a different animal in a school setting because you're dealing with kids that already probably have spoken with their dean and probably already confessed to their dean. Then they're coming to my office, there's not whole a lot they feel they need to hide. They've already told the truth, they've already admitted to that. It's a really unique dynamic in the school." School staff attended a small proportion of these school interviews. If a youth already had confessed to the school official, then that official's presence increased the youth's pressure to ratify the earlier statement. Unlike the other interrogations, police did *not* arrest or detain the majority of youths whom they questioned in less custodial settings—school (84.9%) or home (57.9%).

Police described the types of officers who conducted interviews: "If it's an arrest on the street, it will probably be a street cop [patrol]. If it is a custodial situation where they've been put in jail, it's going to be rank—it's going to be a sergeant or detective." Suburban officers said that patrol officers often conduct interrogations for routine felony arrests:

> That's where we differ from a lot of agencies. We definitely have our patrol folks that are doing these interviews. And if investigations chooses to follow up the following day—obviously, if it was a homicide or something really big, we would at that point page in our investigators, and they very likely conduct the interview. But most of your run-of-the-mill robberies, assaults, things of that sort, we're doing on patrol.

Police reports only indicate the last name and badge number of the officer who questioned a youth. The place of interrogation provides a proxy for whether a patrol officer or a sergeant, detective, investigator, or SRO conducted it.

Table 3.2
Custody Status, Detention Status, and Location of Interrogation

	N	%
Custody status		
Arrested	266	86.6
Not arrested	41	13.4
Detention status		
Detained	184	61.7
Not detained	114	38.3
Location of interrogation		
Police/sheriff's department	171	55.7
Detention-correction	71	23.1
Place of arrest	25	8.1
School	19	6.2
Home	19	6.2
Hospital	2	0.7

Some variations in where police questioned youths reflect departmental policies. In some suburban departments, the patrol officer who arrested a youth might question him or her in the squad car or at the police station. In larger, metropolitan departments, an arresting officer would transport a youth to the police juvenile division or detention center, and a detective, sergeant, or juvenile officer would conduct the interrogation there.

Limitations on how long police can hold juveniles in adult jails provide one impetus to question them quickly. State law and juvenile court rules require prosecutors to charge youths held in detention within thirty-six hours of taking them into custody. Depending on when police arrest a juvenile and whether detectives or investigators are available, some interrogations occur after an overnight detention.

Interrogation Rooms. More than three-quarters (78.8%) of these interrogations took place in secure settings—police stations or detention centers—in specially designed interrogation rooms. Inbau and Reid describe features of interrogation rooms—small, private, quiet, bare, free of distractions or reminders that the setting is a police station, and minimally furnished with straight-backed chairs: "The room should be quiet, with none of the usual 'police' surroundings and with no distractions within the suspect's view.... [T]he less the surroundings suggest a police detention facility, the less difficult it will be for the suspect or arrestee who is really guilty to implicate himself."[9]

The police officers whom I interviewed distinguished between questioning conducted in "hard" and "soft" rooms or "cold" and "warm" rooms. The former resemble the stark, bare rooms that Inbau and Reid describe and that are depicted in movies and television—chairs, plain walls, audio- and video-recording equipment that activate on entry, and one-way viewing panels. Police described these rooms as "very bland, probably ten feet by ten feet, a table, two or three chairs, nothing on the walls, some Kleenex, a hidden camera, and that's it." Police furnished "soft" or "warm" rooms with carpets or rugs, sofas, and comfortable chairs to provide a more relaxed setting in which to interview victims, witnesses, and rarely a suspect. Police confirmed that custodial interrogation of suspects occurs in "hard" settings.

B. When Do Police Interview Suspects? From Offense to Interrogation

How quickly after a youth commits a crime do police question him or her? How does closeness in time between an offense and interrogation affect

Table 3.3

Time from Offense to Interrogation and Strength of Evidence

	N	%
Length		
Same day	214	69.7
Same week	39	12.7
Same month	30	9.8
More than one month	24	7.8
Strength of evidence		
Moderate	111	36.2
Strong	194	63.2

Relationship between Variables*

Length	Moderate evidence	Strong evidence
Same day or week	33.1% (83)	66.9% (168)
More than one week between offense and interrogation	51.9% (28)	48.1% (26)

* Statistically significant at $\chi^2(1, N = 305) = 6.774, p < .05$

the interview? I subtracted the date of offense from the date of interrogation to calculate how quickly police questioned juveniles—within one day, one week, one month, or longer. For example, if a juvenile committed an offense at ten at night, police arrested him shortly thereafter, and detectives questioned him at nine the following morning, I coded it as an interrogation that occurred within one day.

Police arrested and questioned more than two-thirds (69.7%) of these youths within less than one day of the offense, often within a matter of a few hours. They interrogated the vast majority (82.4%) within a week of the crime. Only one-sixth (17.6%) of crimes required extended investigation—one week or longer—before an interrogation occurred. No significant relationship appeared between type of crime and length of time to the interrogation.

Interviews with police confirmed that they conducted most interrogations shortly after arrest—whenever that occurred—and either at the station or a detention facility. The timing depended on the time of arrest, availability of investigators, and progress of the investigation.

If they're brought in while people are working, the interview is done almost immediately before they're actually placed in juvenile detention center or released to their parents. So ideally it would be within half-hour to hour-and-half of when they were taken into custody. If there isn't a juvenile investigator on [duty], if it's an arrest on the midnight shift, then they'd be placed in the juvenile detention center so somebody would get there about seven or eight in the morning.

After officers completed their initial investigation, they wanted to question a suspect promptly, because, as one said, "the more time the guy has, the more time he has to figure out not to talk." Whether or not juveniles told the truth, officers wanted to pin down their story—what Inbau and Reid describe as "locking in a lie." "We like to interview them as soon as we can to get them locked into a story, whether it's accurate or fictional. If you can lock in your main suspect or suspects into a story, you can really start picking it apart." When officers interrogated a suspect depended on the investigation's progress and the amount of evidence they possessed. Police described when they question a suspect: "as soon as you feel you've gathered as much information as you need to approach a suspect. Usually, the suspect is the last person you're going to interview." Victims, witnesses, and other investigations gave police the evidence they needed to control and confront a suspect's responses.

After police arrested juveniles and transported them to the station, they notified the juvenile division, sergeant, or investigator who conducted the interview. If police arrested a juvenile at night, then a detective might not conduct the interview until the next morning. Police detained youths arrested for serious offenses overnight to allow experienced investigators to conduct the interview. The time juveniles spend handcuffed, waiting in a holding cell, or placed in detention increases their nervousness and anxiety.

Minnesota's detention statute prohibits police from holding juveniles in an adult jail for more than six hours, after which officers either place them in a juvenile detention facility or release them to a parent.[10] Some county detention facilities use restrictive offense criteria to reduce the numbers of youths detained. Investigators said they feel some time pressure to interview youths quickly after patrol brings them to the station.

> For an arrest, if we have a juvenile in custody, the interview occurs within six hours. Say we arrest a kid driving a stolen car, we will call the detective in, and that interview occurs immediately. And that has to do with—there's a state law says that municipal lockups can only hold juveniles no longer than six hours. If we want a detective

to talk to a kid, we need to get them in immediately, because most of the kids that we arrest, particularly for property crimes and other lower-level felonies, the Hennepin County juvenile detention center will not accept them. So if we don't interview that kid when we've got them, then you might as well count on never getting one, because to follow up on it later is next to impossible sometimes.

Another officer confirmed that many interrogations take place immediately, but it varies depending on "what the case is, the person you're going to interview, and where you're at in your investigation. You may not have enough to do an interview right away. You may have to go out and gather some more facts and information before you're ready to do an interrogation. It could be anywhere from fairly immediate to within thirty-six hours."

Strength of Evidence. Police apprehended many of these youths at the scene of the crime—for example, responding to a burglar alarm or a neighbor's call or stopping a stolen car—or shortly thereafter and in close proximity. As a result, they often had strong evidence against a suspect even without a successful interrogation. Several decades ago, I worked as a prosecutor and charged and tried criminal felony and delinquency cases. Based on my experience, I evaluated the strength of the evidence police had when they conducted an interview in these cases. In about two-thirds of the cases (63.6%), they had strong evidence—beyond a reasonable doubt—that could have led to a conviction or plea even without an interrogation. In about one-third of the cases (36.4%), police had moderately strong cases—more than sufficient for probable cause to arrest and charge but not necessarily strong enough to convict without an admission to bolster a missing element, for example, intent. The strength of evidence affects how police conduct an interview and its outcome.[11]

A significant relationship existed in these cases between the strength of evidence and the time within which police questioned youths. Police were more likely to have strong evidence in cases in which they apprehended youths quickly. Evidence was less strong in cases in which one week or more elapsed between offense and interrogation. Police had strong evidence in two-thirds (66.9%) of cases in which they questioned youths within a week, as contrasted with less than half of cases (48.1%) in which they interrogated them one week or more later. Police can question suspects more effectively—confront with evidence, contradict denials, and the like—when they have strong evidence.

C. People Present at the Interrogation

More-experienced officers—sergeants, detectives, and investigators—conducted the vast majority of these interrogations. I asked the nineteen veteran officers whom I interviewed whether they received any specialized training to question juveniles. A majority had received Reid training at some point in their careers. They also received interrogation training in police academy, in-service departmental instruction, and other programs. Several of them also trained other police as interrogators. Regardless of background, their training did not differentiate between questioning older juveniles and adults, although one recalled instruction about questioning younger juveniles—"little kids, thirteen, fourteen, and under." One experienced officer noted, "I've never seen a Reid training that separates juveniles and adults." Officers' comments corroborate surveys of police that report that Reid Method training does not incorporate developmental differences between juveniles and adults.[12]

Inbau and Reid emphasize that a suspect is "much more apt to reveal secrets in the privacy of a room occupied only by himself and the investigator rather than in the presence of an additional person or persons."[13] Police trainers in the United Kingdom agree that the presence of more than one interviewer may disrupt the rhythm of questions or alter memories.[14] Table 3.4 reports that a single officer conducted the vast majority of interviews in this study (86%). Except for two "good-cop, bad-cop" interrogations, if a second officer was present, he or she played a minor role during questioning.

Police expressed a strong preference to question a suspect alone. They had confidence in their skills and felt that a second officer could disrupt or impede their inquiry: "you really have to be on the same page." Several

Table 3.4
People Present at Interrogation

	N	%
Police interrogators		
One	264	86.0
Two	43	14.0
Others		
Parent	25	8.1
Other[a]	5	1.6
None	277	90.2

[a] Probation officer or school official

commented that a second officer could upset the rhythm of questioning: "If you're on a roll and doing your questioning, sometimes it gets very frustrating if somebody else changes the course of the ship and starts asking different questions." The presence of a second officer also could change the dynamic in the room: "Our discussion would be completely different; we'd have a different tenor to this if there was another person sitting here. You get to sit there, and this person confides in you, and it's hard to get them to confide in two people." Another officer observed, "Right away the chemistry tips; it's two against one." A second officer could intimidate or distract a suspect, and another officer observed that with multiple police present, "You can get attacked in court by outnumbering the suspect. If you have two or three or four police officers—adults—in a room with one juvenile, he's going to admit anything you want."

Workload pressures also militated against more than one officer conducting interviews. "If you're an investigator, [excluding homicide] in most other cases, you get assigned that case in the morning; that's a single investigator. I mean you're not going to ask your partner that also got two cases assigned to him, 'Hey, come and sit with me during this interview.'" Several officers noted that *Scales* recordings eliminate the need for a second police officer to witness an interrogation and to corroborate a statement. "Now in the early days, when you needed that corroboration, when it was going to be our word against whatever, before recording, then almost everything was two officers. But now, there's no need for two officers. Recording takes the place of a witness officer."

Police said that two officers more often participated in interrogations about serious crimes—for example, homicide, criminal sexual conduct—or as a matter of departmental policy. Two officers might question a youth if each was investigating separate crimes in which the youth was a suspect or if the youth committed offenses in different police jurisdictions. A second officer might assist an investigating officer if he or she had previous experience with or special knowledge about a suspect. Even with *Scales* recordings, a second officer might listen and take notes. Some urban police speculated that suburban officers might not be as experienced interrogators as urban police and might feel more secure with backup assistance.

Police questioned the vast majority (89.8%) of these juveniles only once. They reinterrogated a few youths a second time to clarify an earlier statement—after they questioned a codefendant or to resolve discrepancies after further investigation—or if the juvenile asked to speak with them. Officers attributed a second interrogation to discovery of new information from other witnesses or the availability of forensic evidence — "pieces of the puzzle falling together." Research in the United Kingdom also reports that police interviewed the vast majority (92.7%) of suspects in that study only once.[15] In Minnesota, restrictions on how long police can hold youths in jail or in detention oblige prosecutors to file charges within thirty-six hours and juvenile court judges to appoint defense counsel, which limits opportunities to question juveniles thereafter.

Police interrogated a juvenile alone in the vast majority of these cases (90.2%). A parent attended questioning in less than one-tenth (8.1%) of cases, and school officials or probation officers joined a small fraction (1.7%) of cases. Minnesota does not require a youth's parent to be notified or present at an interrogation. However, if a juvenile repeatedly requests a parent, then the parent's absence or exclusion may undermine the voluntariness of a waiver or statement.[16] Police interrogated 6.2% of these juveniles at home, and parents sat in on nearly half (42.1%) of those interviews. Suburban police contacted juveniles' parents more often than did those in urban counties, and suburban parents attended interviews more frequently. Chapter 6 describes how police enlisted parents' assistance and neutralized their presence and the role parents played.

III. The *Miranda* Warning

Decades of experience and court-approved formulae have reduced the *Miranda* warning to a litany that officers read to a suspect from a card or waiver form. *Miranda* formalized interrogation practices, gave police a bright-line rule, allowed courts to use an objective standard to gauge waivers, and enabled judges to avoid subjective evaluations of a confession's voluntariness.[17] The Court in *Duckworth v. Eagan* disavowed any rigid verbal formula as long as a warning conveyed the substance of the rights.[18]

Researchers report many versions of *Miranda* warnings. Although these different versions convey the basic constitutional information, one survey of 560 *Miranda* warnings reported 532 unique wordings,[19] and a second survey of 385 warnings reported 356 unique versions.[20] The length, complexity, and reading grade level necessary to understand warnings varied considerably.[21] Advice about the right to appointed counsel required a higher reading ability—above a tenth-grade level—than did advice about the right to remain silent. Although some jurisdictions use a different *Miranda* warning for juveniles, paradoxically these warnings may be twice as long and require higher-level reading ability than do adult versions.[22] For example, youths' understanding of the legal concept of a right and the meaning of appointed counsel required a high school education. Despite efforts to create "dumbed-down" versions of *Miranda*, "[t]hese findings are especially problematic for younger adolescents, ages 13 to 15, who lack sufficient reading comprehension even when their academic attainment is at the expected levels."[23] Youth have more difficulty understanding an oral warning than a written one because of sentence complexity, vocabulary, and concepts.[24] An assessment of *Miranda* comprehension in a delinquent population reported that the majority of younger juveniles and more than one-third of sixteen- and seventeen-year-olds exhibited significant lack of understanding.[25]

How police administer a warning may affect adolescents' ability to understand it. Police may warn by "reciting it carefully and slowly, delivering it in a rapid and rote fashion, giving a verbal and then a written form, giving a written version with no verbal version, asking the suspect to read the warning (silently or aloud), giving an explanation of the warning, and asking the suspect to explain or paraphrase it."[26] We do not know how the way police warn suspects affects their understanding.

The post-*Miranda* impact studies reported a high level of police compliance: "[P]olice almost always followed the *Miranda* requirements. It appeared that officers generally read *Miranda* warnings and waivers from a card."[27] Unlike some jurisdictions that use standard, state-issued *Miranda* advisories,[28] Minnesota police use *Miranda* cards provided by their county attorneys, the Bureau of Criminal Apprehension, or their respective departments. In addition to *Scales* recordings, police document that they gave the warning in their written reports. A typical report entry noted, "I read [juvenile] the *Miranda* warning from the card I carry with me supplied by the Bureau of Criminal Apprehension."

"On the Record." Prior to and during interrogations, police sometimes reminded juveniles that they were recording the conservation. Officers asked juveniles to move closer to the recorder and to speak up, reminded them to answer aloud rather than to nod their heads, and told them not to cover their mouths.

Try to speak clearly enough, loudly enough, that it can be understood. And also keep in mind that it doesn't pick up on nonverbal gestures. You have to say "yes" or "no."

When I'm talking to you and taking a statement from you, it's very important that you speak loudly and clearly and that you don't have your hands or your fingers in your mouth. That way the machine will pick up all your answers.

Some officers explained the rationale of *Scales* to juveniles at the start of questioning.

This is a digital recorder. The reason I got that playing is because anytime a police officer in the state talks to somebody that's in custody it has to be recorded. It's as much for your protection as anything. I can't allege that you said this or whatever. This all becomes a court record. It has to be typed. Keep in mind if you decided to talk to me, speak clearly and loudly enough so the poor secretary can understand it when it's typed.

Some officers noted that before the advent of digital recording, they used a handheld microcassette recorder and that suspects occasionally objected to recording. One youth in this study invoked *Miranda* because he objected to recording his statement. Officers in several departments described how they finessed that potential problem. Some reported that automated interrogation rooms made a record without their intervention —the recording equipment activated when they entered the room. One officer said, "We were under no obligation to tell them they were being taped, either audio or video. So we didn't. Our tape-recording equipment was remote from the room." Another officer explained, "Once we go into the room, everything is recorded. We don't have the ability to turn it off or on. As soon as kids saw a [handheld] recorder—and they saw it—they'd stop talking. They may not object, because they don't see it happening." Other officers described ploys in which they turned off a visible hand recorder, even though the interrogation room also was equipped with unobtrusive automated video- and audio-recording devices.

Officers praised recordings because they obviated the need to take notes during questioning, which might chill a suspect's willingness to talk. "Writing is the last thing you want to do when you go into an interview, because it says 'document' to them. It says, 'This is being recorded; this is being written down.' You might as well just tell them to keep their mouth shut. It's just another signal saying, 'Be quiet.'"

Every juvenile in this study received a proper *Miranda* warning, and one-fifth (19.5%) of the files contained an initialed and signed warning form. Departmental policy determined whether officers supplemented *Scales* tapes with waiver forms, and most did not. The initialed and signed forms provide prosecutors another way to prove that police warned and juveniles purported to understand *Miranda*. The St. Paul police department warning and waiver form (figure 3.1) represents typical advisories.

CN _____

SAINT PAUL POLICE DEPARTMENT
_____

DATE _____ TIME OF INTERVIEW _____

NAME _____ AGE _____ DOB _____

ADDRESS _____ MARITAL STATUS _____ PHONE _____

EMPLOYED BY _____ ADDRESS _____ PHONE _____

EDUCATION: LAST GRADE COMPLETED _____ SCHOOL _____

You have the rights to protection against self-incrimination listed below. Please read along with the Officer, and initial each statement if you understand it.

1. You have the right to remain silent and refuse at any time to answer any questions asked by a police officer. _____

2. Anything you do or say can be used against you. _____

3. You have the right to talk to a lawyer and to have the lawyer with you during any questioning. _____

4. If you cannot afford a lawyer, one will be appointed for you, and you may remain silent until you have talked to the lawyer. _____

The above rights have been read to me. I have initialed each paragraph to show that I understand each of my rights. I have received a copy of this form.

_____
SIGNATURE OF RECEIPT

OFFICER _____ DATE _____ TIME COMPLETED _____

PM 247.1-954

Fig. 3.1. The St. Paul police department *Miranda* warning and waiver form

Although *Miranda* requires police to warn suspects, officers' objective to solve crimes provides no incentive for them to encourage offenders to invoke their rights. One of *Miranda*'s root contradictions is that "it assumes that these suspects can receive adequate advice and counseling about their constitutional rights from adversaries who would like nothing more than to see those rights surrendered."[29] This inherent contradiction requires officers to engage in a quasi-confidence game—"systematic use of deception, manipulation, and the betrayal of trust in the process of eliciting a suspect's confession."[30] Richard Leo likens an officer eliciting a *Miranda* waiver and confession to a confidence man manipulating his victim's vulnerability "through false representations, artifice, and subterfuge."[31]

Officers must give a *Miranda* warning and elicit a waiver without alerting the suspect to its significance or consequences. Leo described several ploys officers use to predispose suspects to waive—admonishing them of the importance of telling the truth, minimizing the significance of the warning, or telling suspects that this is their only opportunity to tell their side of the story.[32] The law of interrogation treats juveniles as the equals of adults, and officers use similar techniques to persuade both to waive *Miranda* rights. When asked how police initiated an interview, a judge commented on the similarities of strategies with juveniles and adults. He saw police "trying to make the kid comfortable, like they do with adults": "I don't see a whole lot of difference in terms of how they treat sixteen- and seventeen-year-olds and how they treat adults."

A. The Timing of the Miranda Warning

An interrogator must establish rapport, develop a level of comfort and trust, and maintain a positive relationship with a suspect to obtain a waiver and elicit a statement.[33] The initial stages of an interrogation provide an opportunity to soften up a suspect and allay his or her fears. "They must first establish a rapport with him. The interrogator asks background questions, engages in small talk, and may even flatter or ingratiate the suspect to create the illusion of a non-threatening, non-adversarial encounter."[34] Several officers described their initial approach:

Sit down, introduce myself. Kind of go over a few things. I don't ask them any questions. Go over a few things. Tell them what I'm up do, and I'd like to hear what they have to say because it's very important. Kind of lay a little foundation, but before they have a chance to tell me or do that, I have to read them their rights. It's not the first thing I do—sit down and read them their rights—kind of lay a little ground work, soften them up.

Introduce myself, take into account that the kid is nervous and insecure, try to lighten things, try to talk about neutral things. Explain the *Miranda* form. Make sure they don't see it as threatening. And then, depending on how the kid feels, if the kid is still uncomfortable, a lot of times, I'll go to talking small talk about sports or anything to kind of get them to relax and get them a little bit more comfortable.

A public defender described these rapport-building strategies as efforts to "portray themselves as an ally or someone there to help the kid."

The timing of the warning gives police opportunities to build rapport with suspects and predispose them to waive rights. The Court in *Missouri v. Seibert* prohibited police from using a two-step process—interrogation followed by a midstream warning and then more questioning to elicit a statement or to ratify the earlier one—to circumvent *Miranda*.[35] However, the Court allows police to talk with suspects before they issue a warning, during which time they may build a relationship and create a favorable climate to confess.[36] The Court in *Rhode Island v. Innis* and *Pennsylvania v. Muniz* allowed police to ask routine booking questions before they gave a *Miranda* warning.[37]

In about half of the cases in my study (52.8%), police gave the *Miranda* warning immediately after identifying the suspect. Police said they gave the warning immediately to assure admissibility of any statements. "You read it to them almost right away. You have to because anything they say before you read them their rights, they're not going to let you keep it. Give it right away, get it out in the open, and be done with it."

In the other half of cases (47.2%), police asked juveniles booking questions—name, age, and date of birth, address and telephone number, grade in school, and the like—before they gave the *Miranda* warning. Officers

Table 3.5
Timing of the *Miranda* Warning

	N	%
Immediately	162	52.8
During booking questions	128	41.7
Longer preliminary conversation	17	5.5

made small talk with suspects as they asked booking questions "to disarm the suspect, to lower his anxiety levels, to improve his opinion of the detective and to create a social psychological setting conducive both to a *Miranda* waiver as well as to subsequent admissions."[38] Officers used juveniles' responses to engage in conversations, to put youths at their ease, and to accustom them to answering. For example, a question about a youth's grade in school might lead to a side conversation about favorite subjects or academic progress.

Police explained that at the start of an interview, most juveniles are frightened. A number of officers used the same expression—"deer in the headlights"—to describe many juveniles' initial emotional state. They use the initial process to allay anxiety and build rapport. A juvenile court judge observed that police deemphasize the significance of the warning:

> They tend to be much more casual and much more conversational in dealing with kids. I mean, it's kind of a minefield for a police officer because you never quite know what you're going to get when you're talking to a sixteen-year-old. I think it's generally conversational. The *Miranda* warning is given, but it's given in a much more—I don't want to say relaxed—but in a much more informal [manner].

In addition to using booking questions to build rapport, in a small fraction of cases (5%), officers asked juveniles if they wanted food or a drink or needed to use the bathroom. Another apologized for the temperature in the interrogation room: "It is a little chilly in here. I apologize for that, but that's just the way this building is." At the start of a homicide interrogation, a detective reminded the juvenile that he was being treated respectfully. "I want you to realize, you're sitting here right now. You're not in handcuffs, right? And I brought you a can of pop, right?" Police use these preliminary contacts to develop a positive relationship.

B. Negotiating the Miranda *Warning*

Miranda requires police to warn suspects of their rights. Police can comply *and* predispose suspects to perceive waiver as the normal and expected response. "Officers sometimes use 'softening up' tactics—such as conditioning suspects to waive their rights or describing the evidence against them and making their situation appear hopeless—before giving warnings or obtaining waivers."[39] Richard Leo and Welsh White describe three ways police administer *Miranda* warnings to obtain waivers:

First, the police may deliver the warnings in a neutral manner; second, they may de-emphasize the warnings' significance by delivering them in a manner that is designed to obscure the adversarial relationship between the interrogator and the suspect; and third, they may deliver the warnings in a way that communicates to the suspect that waiving his rights will result in some immediate or future benefit for him.[40]

Police may predispose youths to waive their rights by emphasizing the importance of telling the truth, by nodding their head while reading the warning to cue suspects to agree, or by telling suspects that the interview constitutes their only opportunity to tell their story.[41] Training manuals instruct police to blend the warning into the conversation, to describe it as a formality that understates its importance, to tell suspects that this is their opportunity to tell their story, or to summarize the evidence and tell suspects that they can only explain it if they waive their rights.[42] One judge described administration of *Miranda* this way: "In terms of the intro, police try to make them feel comfortable and make it sound like the *Miranda* is just routine. Just trying to get everybody calm. 'Don't pay a lot of attention to what I'm about to say.'" Police officers described strategies to embed *Miranda* in other preliminary conversations with suspects to avoid drawing attention to it: "It was better if you didn't just dive right into the water like that. Generally speaking, start out with asking questions about their well-being, in terms of 'Do you need a restroom? Would you like coffee, soda? Are you feeling all right?' Then later, when we get to *Miranda*, it looks like *Miranda* is just one of several things we're concerned about."

Police can influence suspects' disposition to waive rights by using a neutral or indifferent voice to give the warning. Leo described officers who "delivered the *Miranda* warnings without any build-up and in a seemingly neutral tone, without any apparent strategy, as if they were indifferent to the suspect's response."[43] Others report that police deemphasize *Miranda* by "becoming less animated while reading the warnings" or giving them "in a perfunctory tone of voice, suggesting that the warnings are a bureaucratic form that do not merit the suspect's concern."[44] Similarly, a British researcher observed, "The police caution (like, say, the wording of an oath in court or the Lord's Prayer) can easily take on the form of an empty ritual or an unthinking recitation."[45] In the vast majority of cases in this study (92.8%), officers delivered the *Miranda* warning to juveniles in a neutral manner.

Police in these interrogations sometimes framed a *Miranda* waiver as the prerequisite to juveniles' opportunity to tell their side of the story. "If the suspect wants to tell the interrogator his side of the story, he will first need to waive his rights."[46] Police regularly conveyed to juveniles the value of talking—"telling their story"—and telling the truth before they gave a *Miranda* warning:

> I just started investigating [your case] yesterday, and what I've learned over the years is there's always two sides to every story, and this is your opportunity to give your side of the story. Under law, I have to advise you of your *Miranda*—your legal rights, per *Miranda*, and I'll read those now.

> I appreciate your cooperation so far. I think you're being somewhat honest with me. And I'd kind of like to get your side of the story tonight on what went on: what part you had and what part your friends had and that type of thing. Help yourself out a little bit. Before I do that, though, since you were arrested, I have to read you the *Miranda*, okay?

Officers depicted the warning as an administrative formality to complete before they can talk with the suspect: "Okay, due to the fact that you are in custody, I have to advise you of your *Miranda* rights before I do any questioning. I'm gonna read this to you real quick. I need your initials and a signature."

Police deemphasize *Miranda* by portraying the warning as "an unimportant bureaucratic ritual [that] communicates, implicitly or explicitly," that the officer "anticipates that the suspect will waive his rights and make a statement."[47] Officers sometimes referred to the warning as "paperwork" to lessen its significance and to stress its bureaucratic quality. "We can go through a little bit of paperwork. Um, let me explain a few things to you, and then if you want to, you can sign right there." A mechanical tone of voice suggests that the warning is an unimportant formality. Particularly for juveniles whom police have questioned in the past, officers may present *Miranda* as a ritual with which to comply: "You've been down here before, right? Have you ever had these statements read to you before? I gotta go through these again."

A public defender confirmed the conversational tone and approach police use to secure juveniles' waivers. "They tend to start out pretty buddy-buddy. It tends to be very conversational. 'So here we're going to do the waiver now.' Especially with the older kids, it's usually, 'You've probably heard this before.' It is very conversational, it's very fast, almost kind of like it's a throwaway. 'We have to get through this so we can get to the good stuff.'"

The Court in *Dickerson* noted that *Miranda* is "embedded in routine police practice to the point where the warnings have become part of our national culture."[48] Interrogators invoke that cultural pervasiveness and minimize the warnings by "referring to their dissemination in popular American television shows and cinema, perhaps joking that the suspect is already well aware of his rights and probably can recite them from memory."[49] Officers emphasized the routine nature of warnings by referring to suspects' familiarity with them from television and movies: "I'll read it out loud to you, and then I'll let you read it through if you want. It's a Warning and Consent to Speak. Basically you've heard the *Miranda* warning on *Cops* and TV and stuff. I'm gonna read you your rights like you see on TV." A public defender observed that cultural exposure to *Miranda* does not translate into understanding its meaning or consequences: "*Miranda* continues to exist because it's a TV right. The fact that it's a TV right, kids just kind of know it exists, but they don't really know what it means."

A *Miranda* waiver form provides another opportunity to convert its delivery into a bureaucratic exercise. "I'm going to read these rights to you. I need you to initial down the side, and when I'm all done reading them to you, sign your full name at the bottom. And that's just for your rights. That's just all this covers right here is your *Miranda* advisory, okay?"

In addition to the strategies Leo and White described to elicit a *Miranda* waiver—neutral delivery, deemphasis of significance, and implied benefit—officers in this study sometimes preceded the warning with a brief summary of their case against the youth. The summary of incriminating facts created a pressure for suspects to waive *Miranda* to provide an explanation—to tell their story. In one interview, the officer prefaced *Miranda* with some circumstantial evidence:

Let me just explain a few things to you, okay? The CDs you had, the victim identified them as stolen. My partner just went down to the underground garage where the car was broken into. Your shoe prints matched exactly with the prints on the ground. I have a witness that saw you in the underground garage, okay? Let me just explain some things to you. My whole thing is, obviously, you're in possession of stolen property. I wanna know the whole story. If you know some stuff, that's what I wanna know. I want the truth, that's what I want. Let me read something to you real quick, okay? [Officer reads *Miranda* warning.]

Other officers provided similar factual preambles before they gave the *Miranda* warning.

C. Understanding the Warning versus Appreciating the Consequences of Waiver

Miranda's cultural ubiquity may detract from youths' understanding its protections. The warning becomes part of the background noise of an interrogation—a ritual without meaning. "[D]espite increased exposure to the *Miranda* warnings from depictions in television and movies, juvenile offenders today understand their rights in much the same way adolescents did generations ago."[50] Police have no obligation to emphasize the warning's significance or to encourage suspects to invoke their rights. As members of the prosecution's crime-control team, they have contrary incentive to embed the warning in a preamble that discourages invocations.

Fare v. Michael C. requires a knowing, intelligent, and voluntary waiver. *Miranda* focuses narrowly on suspects' ability to understand the words and opportunity to exercise rights. Police satisfy those requirements if they advise juveniles of *Miranda*, they say they understand, and they voluntarily relinquish their rights. Police do not need to tell suspects about the seriousness of the crime or that a family member has retained counsel who seeks access to them.[51] Understanding the warning does not require appreciating the consequences of waiver—the tactical and strategic ramifications of relinquishing rights.[52]

Developmental psychologists report that the cognitive ability of sixteen- and seventeen-year-old youths begins to approximate that of adults. However, their ability to make adultlike decisions, to control impulses, and to exercise judgment remains a work-in-progress. By contrast, the ability of many juveniles fifteen years of age or younger to understand *Miranda* or to exercise rights becomes increasingly problematic. Delinquent youth share many characteristics—lower IQ, poorer school performance, and lower reading skills, compared to the general population—that impair *Miranda* understanding.

1. UNDERSTANDING *MIRANDA*: SIXTEEN- AND SEVENTEEN-YEAR-OLD YOUTHS

I asked justice system personnel to reflect on the ability of sixteen- and seventeen-year-old juveniles like those in this study to understand *Miranda*. One judge suggested that delinquents' intellectual limitations and the stress of interrogation impaired their ability to understand the warning:

> Unfortunately, I don't think a lot of them do. A lot of these kids that are in serious troubles have very little education, and frankly sometimes they're not all that bright to begin with. So when they don't have an adult representative or a parent or an attorney, I don't think they get it. They know they're in trouble, and they know that they need to somehow get out of trouble. That's how they think. I think kids are pretty simple that way. When they hear the *Miranda* warning, and they hear the rights that they have, some of the brighter ones will understand what it means. But I don't think most of them do. I think most of them think it's just a protocol. It doesn't mean much, and "if I tell you what happened, if I blame my buddies, can I go home?" So I think they're in a hurry to speak.

Another judge agreed that for many delinquents, the *Miranda* warning is background noise:

> I don't know how much they understand. I don't know how much adults understand it. *Miranda* in some ways has become a mantra, like kids singing the words to the "Star Spangled Banner" and don't have any idea what the words are even and get them confused with other words. I'm not sure there's a huge amount of tracking for adults or juveniles, but my gut tells me it's a higher level of not tracking for juveniles.

Several public defenders pointed out that most delinquents suffer from educational deficits, learning disabilities, and other limitations that compromise their understanding:

> Kids who come into juvenile court are not frequently the high-performance students. They're not the ones who're doing well in school. Most of them are not doing particularly well in school, and so when an adult authority figure says, "You have the right to remain silent and to refuse to answer any questions asked by a police officer,"

do you understand that? It's familiar, it's familiar, they've heard it before, they've seen it on a bazillion cop shows, they've seen Court TV, it's familiar. So they say, "I understand it." Which is how they're getting through school. "Yeah, I heard this before." Do they appreciate it, do they know that at that moment they can say, "I'm not talking to you anymore"? No, I don't think they make that connection.

Despite these reservations, justice system personnel felt that most juveniles understand the *Miranda* warning. Many cited its cultural ubiquity and pervasiveness. An urban prosecutor commented, "It's just part of popular culture these days. If you've watched enough TV, you probably understand the *Miranda* warning. I'm amazed at how everyone seems to know it because it's such a part of culture—TV culture, movie culture—half of PG-13 movies probably have a *Miranda* warning in there."

Police believed that adolescents understand *Miranda* "to the extent that any criminal understands it. It's pretty simple language. I don't think there's really anything complicated about it, and most kids have heard it." Another officer observed, "*Miranda* has become so much the norm. Kids watch it on just about every cop show. They're at an age when they're sixteen or seventeen years old, they have the competency to sit there and listen and understand it. They fully understand it. Most people completely understand *Miranda* now." Officers strongly felt that youths with prior justice system experience—"frequent fliers"—understand *Miranda*:

> The kids that you're typically dealing with are familiar with the law enforcement system. They've been in contact with law enforcement. Unless you just have a random case, I think these kids are familiar with it and understand it. They may not fully understand the predicament and the ramifications of waiving their rights and what they're going to tell you, but I think they do understand the basic premise of it.

A "knowing" waiver may not be an "intelligent" one. A juvenile who understands the words of a warning may not be able to act on the information provided. Several interviewees described juveniles' practical perplexity when advised, for example, of the right to counsel: "They don't have any idea when that lawyer will be available. They don't have any idea of what happens if I say, 'I want a lawyer,' and they don't have the sophistication to understand that it won't be three weeks or a month or even a week, that if you ask for a lawyer, it will happen relatively quickly, and this part will end."

Interviewees distinguished between juveniles' ability to understand *Miranda* and to appreciate the concepts of rights or the consequences of waiver. One judge said, "I think they understand the words. I'm not sure that they understand the concepts." Another judge distinguished between understanding the words and appreciating the consequences of waiver. He attributed it to "their lack of sophistication, their lack of understanding of how the process works": "I think it works against them in terms of having a really deep-down understanding of what trouble they can be creating for themselves." Police also distinguished between youths' understanding *Miranda* and appreciating the consequences of waiving:

> I don't think they quite understand all the pieces afterwards of if they talk or not talk. What can happen next, if they talk to the police and are forthcoming and honest about what happened? How that reflects on them later on. Or whether they know it can hurt them if they don't talk and they take the blame—especially in some of the gang stuff—and everything goes onto them. I don't think they quite understand all the ramifications of admittance or not admittance.

Public defenders most strongly emphasized the distinction between "understanding what's said to you and understanding what rights you're giving up." They attributed delinquents' failure to appreciate the consequences of waiver to immaturity, a deficient understanding of the justice process, and an urgent desire to get out of custody.

> I don't think kids have the faculties to appreciate the long-term consequences of what they're doing. "I'll just tell them what happened, and maybe they'll let me go home." I don't think they realize they're in as big a mess as they really are, because the *Miranda* warning really doesn't convey that. I don't think kids overall, even kids with some experience with the criminal justice system, have the maturity to really appreciate the magnitude of that decision.

> I think they're under the perception that things are going to go better for them if they cooperate, that they're probably going to get out of jail. I don't think they realize how serious giving a statement is and the consequences it has behind them and how that's going to get turned around and used against them.

As we will see in chapter 5, delinquents' waivers of *Miranda* and admissions limit public defenders' ability to plea-bargain on their behalf.

2. UNDERSTANDING *MIRANDA*: OLDER ADOLESCENTS AND YOUNG ADULTS

I asked justice system personnel to compare and contrast older adolescents' and young adults' ability to understand *Miranda*. Most did not distinguish between their competences to understand the warning. One officer asserted, "There isn't any difference." Another said, "I don't see a huge difference in understanding *Miranda* between adults and juveniles." Another reported, "No difference. By the time they're all in high school, they all know what it means. They know that if they don't want to talk to you, they don't have to. Kids know what it means." Another officer compared midadolescents with young adults and conceded that "their understanding of the system may be more limited, but at sixteen or seventeen years old, they're pretty much just in the same area as eighteen-, nineteen-, twenty-year-olds. They know what's going on." Public defenders did not distinguish between the ability of older adolescents and young adults to understand *Miranda*, although they felt that both performed inadequately. "I'd put [older adolescents] on par with the young adults, and they are equally ignorant. I give a lot of credence to the brain-development theories going around that it's not fully developed."

Justice system personnel did distinguish the ability of older adolescents and of young adults to appreciate the consequences of waiver. They attributed young adults' greater appreciation of the consequences to experience and familiarity with the justice system—*Miranda* as a learning experience. One police officer observed, "I don't think there is a big difference as far as the *Miranda* warning. Sometimes, once they're a little bit older, they understand the ramifications and seriousness of the situation more, but not necessarily the *Miranda*." Another officer said, "An adult that's been Mirandized before will realize the consequences of making statements that can be used against him, whereas a juvenile wouldn't understand that or see that as much just because of their age." One judge opined,

> It's all a matter of experience. By the time you get to be a young adult—say you're twenty, twenty-one—you've been through the system more. You understand more. You've been arrested more. You've heard *Miranda* more, and so you're getting there. For most of them [midadolescents], it's still a pretty new experience to be in a room

and to be questioned about a felony and realize how much trouble they're in.

A public defender concurred that young adults have learned from the prior consequences of waiving *Miranda*. "They [juveniles] don't seem to understand that they are creating evidence by making a statement. Adults seem to have a better grasp of what the long-term consequences are of making a statement. 'If I make this statement, then I am giving the police the ammunition they need to charge me, whereas if I keep my mouth shut, that ammunition may not be created down the road.'"

3. UNDERSTANDING *MIRANDA*: OLDER AND YOUNGER JUVENILES

Developmental psychologists report a significant drop-off in the cognitive and judgment abilities of youths fifteen years of age and younger. They note that many younger juveniles exhibit impairments comparable to adults who have been found incompetent to stand trial.[53] Despite this research, some officers regarded younger juveniles as equally capable as their midadolescent peers to understand *Miranda*. They felt that even a "twelve-year-old has heard it": "They understand it. Do they get the point that they don't have to talk to me? They get it." Another officer felt that younger juveniles grasp *Miranda* as well as older youths do but insisted that he was obliged only to read their rights, rather than to probe their subjective understanding. "If they're telling me they understand, it's not my job to really determine did they understand or did they not understand. I just read it to them." A public defender felt that younger juveniles understand *Miranda* about as well as midadolescents do. "They [younger adolescents] understand *Miranda* at about the same level [as older ones], if you factor out how many times they've heard it and been interrogated. Twelve-, thirteen-, fourteen- are as able to understand the words as well as sixteen- or seventeen-year-olds."

Most juvenile justice personnel perceived differences between the ability of sixteen- and seventeen-year-old delinquents and younger juveniles to understand and appreciate *Miranda*. One judge observed that younger adolescents have a poorer grasp of *Miranda* or of the consequences of waiver than do their older peers:

They just have a lower level of understanding of everything. I don't know that they have any meaningful understanding of *Miranda*. I don't think they have a meaningful understanding. They are competent from a psychologist's point of view of the rules of juvenile court standard for competency, but understanding the role of the system and the judge and the adversarial system and all of those kinds of things, a lot of kids don't have a clue about the overall court system, let alone things like *Miranda*.

Another judge observed that young juveniles suffer from educational deficits that impair their understanding and increase their likelihood to waive and confess. The judge described them as

> kids often that are truant, broken educations and broken home, so their education level is not the average thirteen- and fourteen-year-old's. They may not have great reading skills, although it's being read to them. The whole comprehension issue is high. They understand they're in trouble. They understand there's going to be further repercussions. Do they understand all of that, that every word is going to be used against them? I don't know that they totally grasp it. They're more apt to be scared. Fear plays a big role. If you're afraid, you're really thinking, "How do I get out of this?"

If youths understand *Miranda* and appreciate the consequences of waiver, then they must also be able to invoke those rights clearly and unambiguously. A public defender questioned whether younger juveniles had the ability to invoke rights:

> I don't think it's so much understanding [*Miranda*] as a willingness to stand up to an officer—not physically stand up but verbally sit there and say, "No, I'm not going to talk to you. I want my lawyer." I think that is more difficult for them. For twelve-, thirteen-, fourteen-year-olds—"You don't have to talk. You can have a lawyer present" —I think they all understand that. Do they have the emotional and mental capacity to say that to an authority figure? Because their whole life, everywhere they go—home, school, wherever you go— you don't talk back to authority figures.

A valid *Miranda* waiver must be "knowing, intelligent, and voluntary." Developmental psychologists observe that most youths sixteen years of age or older have the cognitive ability to understand the warning and to meet the threshold of a "knowing" waiver. Some justice system personnel questioned youths' understanding because of intellectual limitations. Others felt that *Miranda* has a ritualistic, background-noise quality that does not penetrate the stress of interrogation. Justice system personnel agreed that juveniles do not appreciate the consequences of waiver. They did not distinguish between the understanding of older adolescents and of young adults, but they recognized that prior exposures to *Miranda* and greater experience with the justice system better enables young adults to exercise their rights. Most personnel confirmed psychologists' concerns that younger juveniles have less ability to understand or exercise rights.

IV. Waiving or Invoking *Miranda* Rights

After police advise suspects of their rights, they may either waive or invoke them. *Fare v. Michael C.*, *Davis v. United States*, and *Berghuis v. Thompkins* require suspects to invoke the right to silence and to counsel clearly and unambiguously.[54] The Court does not require police to clarify any ambiguous invocations. The privilege against self-incrimination is the foundation of the adversary system, but the burden to invoke it rests with a suspect to resist compulsive pressures and to do so explicitly. Juveniles' legal obligation to clearly invoke their rights conflicts with research that finds that many youths do not understand *Miranda*, do not appreciate the function of rights, and lack the psychological fortitude to assert them effectively.

A. Juveniles' Miranda Waivers—Knowing, Intelligent, and Voluntary

Police establish objectively that juveniles understands their rights— "knowing and intelligent"—by reading the warning and eliciting an affirmative response. In the most direct version, the officer reads each of rights to the youth, followed by the question "Do you understand that?" One judge commented, "I've been pretty impressed by how they are very clear with the *Miranda* warning—'Do you understand?' It's given slowly and understandably, and they make sure the kid understands. They really bend over backwards to be fair." The juveniles in this study acknowledged receiving each warning on the record—the *Scales* tape—and, in some departments, signed a *Miranda* form. After police warned these youths and answered any questions, every juvenile claimed to understand *Miranda*, and those who waived their rights indicated a willingness to do so.

Despite youths' apparent understanding, Grisso and other researchers question whether juveniles grasp the warning.[55] Juveniles lack the competence of adults to understand *Miranda*, to waive the rights, or to understand legal consequences.[56] Juveniles' appearance of comprehension—an affirmation of understanding, a nod in agreement, absence of signs of confusion—may reflect compliance with authority or passive acquiescence rather than true understanding. "Vulnerable witnesses can spend much of their lives trying to appear competent and, therefore, may be especially unwilling to admit 'I don't know.'"[57] Juveniles may say they understand *Miranda* when they do not to avoid appearing ignorant or confused.[58] A public defender commented that youths' claim to understand does not mean that they actually do: "I see kids who say yes when they're reading the *Miranda* advisory. They're just saying yes to everything. And just by the tone of their voice, maybe by some of the questions they ask, I can tell they don't understand, and they're just saying yes to go along with the officer." Without clinical assessments of suspects' competence and understanding before or after interrogations, justice system personnel rely on *Scales* tapes, signed forms, and police testimony to establish comprehension.

Dumbed-down warnings. Some officers accompanied the *Miranda* warning with further explanation to clarify its meaning and to assure juveniles' understanding. Officers occasionally provided a simultaneous, dumbed-down paraphrase of the warning:

> One, you have the right to remain silent and refuse at any time to answer any questions asked by a police officer. Do you know what that means? It means you don't have to talk to me if you don't wanna. Two, anything you do or say can be used against you. That means if you make a statement, I've got to put it in a report. Three, you have the right to talk to a lawyer and to have the lawyer with you during any questioning. That means if you wanted to have a lawyer, you could. Four, if you cannot afford a lawyer, if you don't have the money, or your dad, if he didn't have the money for a lawyer, the court would give you one, and you could remain silent until you had a chance to talk to that lawyer.

Repeat-back warning. Many juveniles, especially those with learning disabilities, may claim to understand even if they do not. If youths state that they understand their rights—whether or not they actually do—then judges will find a knowing and intelligent waiver. Analysts propose that police ask juveniles to explain *Miranda* in their own words to clarify their understanding, or lack thereof.[59] A few officers asked juveniles to repeat back the warning in their own words, and some of the juveniles displayed surprising sophistication:

Q: You have the right to remain silent. Can you explain what that means to you?

A: That I can just shut up and tell you guys that I ain't talking to anybody until I speak to my lawyer. And then we can just go to court from there.

Q: Anything you say is evidence and will be used against you in court. Do you understand what that means?

A: Everything here is being tape-recorded. If there's evidence that certainly proves that I did that thing, you guys can bring me to court and play it.

Q: Right. You're entitled to talk to a lawyer now and have him present now or anytime during the questioning. Do you know what —can you explain that one to me?

A: I could ask to call my lawyer and that I could be silent until my lawyer comes. And I could talk to him in a room that ain't got no tape recorder or anything, and then he could talk to you guys, and I could talk to you, but he does most of the talking.

Some justice system personnel agreed that a repeat-back warning strategy would better reveal whether a juvenile understands the *Miranda* warning. Several said that if a juvenile struggles with preliminary questions—for example, where he or she goes to school or a parent's name and address—then it would be desirable further to clarify a juvenile's understanding. One prosecutor said, "If they are struggling to get that information, I think it is appropriate for them to be checking it out a little further to explain back in their own words."

Others observed that youths in a high-stress situation might not actually hear or heed the warning because of their psychic turmoil: "You have to slow down and not use legalese and make sure kids know what's going on, because they just don't really pay attention very well." A prosecutor opined that repeating back the warning might better focus juveniles' attention: "I would recommend that officers do that as a general practice because it can just sound to a kid like a bunch of legal mumbo jumbo." A judge agreed: "Based on what I've learned about teenagers and how they listen and how they attend to things, that's a good way to find out the degree to which they've heard what they've been told." Investigators acknowledged that repeating back could better reveal whether a youth understands the warning, and a few endorsed the practice: "It's like when kids memorize words to songs. They know every damn hip-hop word of it, but do they know the meaning of it? People have heard the *Miranda* warning so many times that every Joe Citizen, including kids, can repeat it. But I don't know if they ever thought about it."

Despite the potential value of repeating back the warning, police and prosecutors viewed the practice as problematic. Most officers reasoned that *Miranda* and *Fare* did not require a more elaborate warning for youths. To do so only would provide defense counsel with additional issues at a suppression hearing.

> Our attorneys and the judges here in the state don't allow us to play around with *Miranda* at all. It is designed to be read the way it is read. I'm not able to interpret it for people, because if you start going down that road, you're really opening yourself in court for some defense attorney to say I interpreted it incorrectly. I'm somebody who just reads it as it is. If you tell me you understand it, you understand it. If you tell me you don't, I'll read it again.

Officers feared that if they were to use protocols beyond those required by *Miranda* and approved by courts, then "you open doors that it could be challenged." A prosecutor opined,

> I don't think it's the function of the law enforcement to, because then there could be questions, and then they're almost advising, almost acting like a lawyer. If the kid says, "Then do you think I should have a lawyer?" what does the cop say? I think it's better to ask, "Do you have any questions about these rights? Do you understand this?" I've seen cops, I'm surprised how often, just terminate questioning because the kid just couldn't understand the *Miranda* warning. I've seen them write in the reports that "this child didn't understand the *Miranda*, so I terminated the interview."

Defense lawyers agreed that a repeat-back policy would increase the number of suppression hearings, because it would clearly demonstrate that most youths do not understand their rights: "It would make a number of statements inadmissible because it would be pretty clear that the kid doesn't get it. It would certainly be a better guarantor that the child actually understands the process, what their rights are."

B. Juveniles Who Waive Miranda Rights

After suspects have been warned by police, they must either waive or invoke their *Miranda* rights. *Berghuis v. Thompkins* found an implied waiver after a suspect sat mute for two and a half hours before making an incriminating admission. By contrast, police in this study consistently obtained express waivers. After police warned one youth, the waiver process concluded with an officer saying, "Bearing in mind that I'm a police officer and I've just read your rights, are you willing to talk to me about this matter?" Another version of the waiver formula ended with an officer saying, "Having these rights in mind, do you wish to talk to us now?"

Justice White's dissent in *Miranda* identified one of the decision's internal contradictions. *Miranda* required police to warn a suspect to dispel the inherent coercion of custodial interrogation. White asked why those same compulsive pressures do not coerce a waiver as readily as they do an unwarned statement. "The court apparently realizes its dilemma of foreclosing questioning without the necessary warnings but at the same time permitting the accused, sitting in the same chair in front of the same policemen, to waive his right to consult an attorney."[60] If the compulsive pressures taint any response given without a warning, then why do they not also compel a person's waiver of counsel or silence? Legal analysts concur with Justice White's intuition that a warning cannot adequately empower suspects after police isolate and subject them to a police-dominated environment.[61]

Criminologists buttress Justice White's suspicion that a warning provides limited protection against those compulsive pressures. Post-*Miranda* impact studies reported that most criminal suspects waived their rights, agreed to talk with the police, and confessed. A summary of those studies concluded that "after initially adjusting to the new rules propounded in the *Miranda* decision, police have complied with the letter, but not the spirit, of the required fourfold warnings; [and] that despite these standard warnings most criminal suspects routinely waive their constitutional rights."[62] Studies in several jurisdictions and spanning decades consistently report high waiver rates. The *Yale Law Journal*–New Haven Study reported, "Warnings had little impact on suspects' behavior."[63] An observer in California reported that more than three-quarters (78%) of suspects waived *Miranda*, and three-quarters of them made incriminating statements.[64] Observers at police-prosecutor charging conferences reported that 83.7% of adult suspects waived *Miranda* rights.[65] A survey of 631 police investigators estimated that 81% of adult suspects waived their rights.[66] Research in England reported that between half and two-thirds of people confessed, a more stringent criterion than waiving rights.[67]

Juveniles waive *Miranda* rights at somewhat higher rates than do adults. Grisso reported that 90.6% of juveniles waived *Miranda* and agreed to talk with police.[68] A retrospective study of delinquents in detention reported that 87% waived their right to silence.[69] Three decades of research on juveniles' *Miranda* waivers reports that the vast majority waive their rights:

> [I]n two studies from the 1970s, over 90% of juveniles waived their *Miranda* rights. In [one] . . . about 70% of the total number of juvenile felony arrests examined, involved police interrogation, and, in those cases, only 6.5% of youthful suspects refused to talk to police; the other suspects offered statements that contained some level of admission (approximately 85–90%) or denial (approximately 10%) of involvement in the offense (approximately 10%).[70]

Juveniles' somewhat higher rates of *Miranda* waivers may indicate that they are less able than adults effectively to invoke their rights. Equally plausibly, waiver rates may reflect prior experience, and juveniles will have had fewer experiences with police and interrogation than older offenders have.[71] Earlier in this chapter, interviewees distinguished between the ability of adolescents and young adults to appreciate the consequences of a *Miranda* waiver, based on their prior experience.

The vast majority of juveniles (92.8%) in this study waived their *Miranda* rights. This high waiver rate is consistent with other studies of juveniles' waivers[72] and about 10% higher than rates reported for adults.[73] The waiver rate may be inflated somewhat because this sample includes only youths whom police questioned *and* prosecutors charged with a felony. Some justice system personnel I interviewed thought the waiver rate would be somewhat lower if the study included youths who invoked *Miranda* and were *not* charged by prosecutors (see appendix 1). They reasoned that prosecutors charge suspects more readily when suspects waive and confess than when they invoke *Miranda*. One judge cautioned, "There may be a higher portion of those denials in the police interviews that are either declined by the county attorney or aren't submitted to the county attorney where police have a pretty good idea that the kid is involved, but the kid denies it, and they don't have enough case without the kid admitting it, and the kid doesn't admit it."

Despite those cautions and the potential sample-selection bias, justice system personnel confirmed the accuracy of my findings—that the vast majority of delinquents waive *Miranda*. When asked how many juveniles waive *Miranda*, one officer said, "Almost all of them. I couldn't even tell you the last time a kid told me he didn't want to talk." Another estimated 90%: "not very many kids that don't talk to you." Other police officer said, "I haven't had very many not speak to me. I would have to say 95% of them or more talk." A second confirmed, "I'd say better than 95%," and a third said, "Vast majority, I'd say high 90s." A suburban prosecutor observed, "We don't have very sophisticated criminals. Maybe 10% refuse to talk." Almost all personnel thought that 90% or more of youths waive *Miranda*, and none estimated that fewer than 80% waive.

People waive their *Miranda* rights and talk with police for several reasons. The *Miranda* decision recognized the psychological compulsion of the interrogation room—isolation-amplified social pressure to speak when spoken to and to defer to authority.

> Beyond the ubiquitous social pressure to confess, psychological factors make silence virtually impossible for many people when they are interrogated. A universal rule of social discourse is to speak when spoken to. Silence conveys arrogance, hostility, rudeness, and, most of all guilt. Police interrogators are taught to be careful not to provide an excuse for silence by violating the rules of etiquette. At the same time, they are taught to orchestrate environmental cues with stratagems designed both to lull and to intimidate the suspect into talking.[74]

Police, prosecutors, and defense lawyers I interviewed offered several reasons why so many juveniles waive their rights. Parents teach their children to tell the truth—a social duty and value in itself. Many juveniles waive to avoid appearing guilty, to tell their story, or to minimize their responsibility. One officer said, "They want to look cooperative. If they didn't do it, why would they invoke? Even those who've been in prison think they're going to outsmart us." Another officer explained, "Kids always talk.

Whether they think they can outtalk you or outsmart you, most of them realize they got to talk. When it comes to kids, they talk." Another officer said, "Some kids just can't wait to tell you exactly their side of the story. They're used to telling teachers and parents their side of the story, and they want their side heard." A prosecutor concurred that juveniles waive "because it's their opportunity to either admit and mitigate any of the negative outcomes they see will happen, or to spin the story in a way that makes it appear that their role is less culpable."

Some justice personnel thought juveniles waive because they do not expect severe sanctions or they believe they can mitigate negative consequences. As one officer observed, "Most kids are generally honest, especially the ones that are new to the system. Most of them understand that they're not going to get thrown away for life. If they confess they took the car, they're going to be on probation. I think most of them understand that. They want to tell you, get it done, get it over with, and move on." A public defender agreed, "They are convinced that it will go better for them if they cooperate with the police. Some of them have the illusion that they can make it better by talking, by explaining things. They're accustomed to talking their way out of things, so they talk." Another defender attributed juveniles' waivers to naïve trust and lack of sophistication: "They're much more likely to talk because they think, 'I can get out of my situation if I just explain and I'm truthful. I'm going to get some help. They're not going to prosecute me. This is what my parents want me to do.' I mean their mind-set is much more trusting of adults, so they're not as aware of the sense of danger from talking." Some youths' prior experience may contribute to their waivers if they have talked to police previously and then returned home.

Some public defenders attributed juveniles' high waiver rate to fear and a desire to escape from the interrogation room—the compulsive pressures that *Miranda* purported to dispel. Even juveniles who understand the words may not feel empowered to act on them. One defender said, "I think they understand technically what it means, but I think they're personally afraid to say no. I think they're just afraid of law enforcement, and they don't want to upset them." Another defender thought that juveniles waive because the short-term desire to end the stress of interrogation trumps any rational, long-term calculus: "They're scared, and they want to go home. And the cops make it very clear to them that that's not going to happen unless they give a statement. They'll say what it takes to get out of here, and then we'll straighten it out later."

C. Juveniles Who Invoke Miranda Rights

Table 3.6 reports the number and proportion of juveniles in this study who invoked or waived their *Miranda* rights. More than nine out of ten (92.8%) juveniles waived their *Miranda* rights. Somewhat larger proportions of juveniles charged with drug (15.8%) and firearms (11.8%) crimes invoked rights than did youths charged with person, property, or other felonies, but the differences are not statistically significant.

Some juveniles invoked their *Miranda* rights immediately after the warning—"I don't want to talk" or "I want a lawyer." Other juveniles invoked their rights somewhat inarticulately but clearly enough to terminate the interview: "I already got nothing to say. I don't care if you want to ask me a question, ask me. But I already got nothing to say." Some juveniles invoked their right to remain silent by refusing to answer officers' questions. After a juvenile's persistent silence, one officer asked, "I'm sorry, are you waiting for me, or am I waiting for you?" and then terminated the interrogation. *Berghuis v. Thompkins* held that trial judges could find an implied waiver from silence, if a properly warned person spoke thereafter. Some juveniles in this study had brief conversations with police before they explicitly invoked. "How long, how hard would it be—I mean, how much time would it take for me to get a lawyer 'cause I want a lawyer, 'cause I don't wanna say—I got the right to remain silent I guess. I think I'd

Table 3.6

Juveniles Who Waived or Invoked Their *Miranda* Rights by Offense and Prior Arrests

	Total		Waived		Invoked	
	N	%	N	%	N	%
Offense						
Person	97	31.6	92	94.8	5	5.2
Property	169	55.0	157	92.9	12	7.1
Drugs	19	6.2	16	84.2	3	15.8
Firearm	17	5.5	15	88.2	2	11.8
Other	5	1.6	5	100.0	0	0.0
Total	307	100.0	285	92.8	22	7.2
Prior arrests*						
Nonfelony	216	72.0	205	94.9	11	5.1
One or more felony	84	28.0	73	86.9	11	13.1
Total	300[a]	100.0	278	92.7	22	7.3

[a] Seven juveniles (2.3%) initially waived their *Miranda* rights and subsequently invoked them during interrogation, at which point interrogation ceased. Because they were truncated interrogations, I exclude them from analyses of police interrogation tactics.

* Statistically significant at $\chi^2(1, N = 300) = 5.7, p < .05$

feel more comfortable talking with my lawyer first because I'm not good at things like this." While some youths invoked clearly and unambiguously, others expressed themselves ambivalently, and it sometimes took several exchanges to clarify a request for counsel.

Do you want to talk to us about what happened?
I need time to talk to myself about it first.
You need time to talk to yourself. It's fine. You want to talk to a lawyer.

We won't—
I don't need to talk to a lawyer, I just—
You don't want to talk to what? You don't need to talk to anybody else?
I'll do a lawyer.
You'll do a lawyer?
I'll ask for—I'm asking for a lawyer.
You're asking for a lawyer right now?
I request a lawyer.

Many jurisdictions follow *Davis v. United States* and do not require police to clarify ambiguous invocations. Because many juveniles speak indirectly or ambiguously to avoid conflict with authority figures, police may not recognize some youths' attempt to invoke their rights, whereas juveniles may perceive that police have ignored their request.

1. INVOKING RIGHTS AND PRIOR ARRESTS

The Court in *Fare v. Michael C.* cited the offender's prior experience with police as an important factor when it found a valid waiver. Trial judges consider "a juvenile's lack of prior contacts with police . . . as weighing against sufficient understanding of *Miranda* warnings, . . . [and] extensive prior experience has sometimes been cited by judges as suggesting greater understanding of *Miranda* warnings due to more frequent exposure to them and familiarity with court processes."[75] Criminologists consistently report a relationship between prior experience with police and *Miranda* invocations:

[T]he only variable that exercised a statistically significant effect on the suspect's likelihood to waive or invoke his *Miranda* rights was whether a suspect had a prior criminal record. . . . [W]hile 89% of the suspects with a misdemeanor record and 92% of the suspects without any record waived their *Miranda* rights, only 70% of the suspects with a felony record waived their *Miranda* rights. Put another way, a suspect with a felony record . . . was almost four times as likely to invoke his *Miranda* rights as a suspect with no prior record and almost three times as likely to invoke as a suspect with a misdemeanor record.[76]

Other research reports that suspects' prior police contacts influence their decision to invoke *Miranda*: "[I]individuals who have no prior felony record are more likely to waive their rights than are those with a history of criminal justice 'experience.'"[77] Post-*Miranda* impact research reported that defendants with more prior arrests and felony convictions gave fewer confessions than did those with fewer arrests or convictions.[78] Older juveniles and youths with prior felony referrals invoked their rights more frequently than did younger juveniles and those without prior police contacts.[79]

About one-third (35.1%) of juveniles in this study had one or more felony arrests before the offense for which police questioned them (see table 3.1). Table 3.6 reports that juveniles with one or more prior felony arrests waived their rights at significantly lower rates (86.9%) than did those with fewer or less serious police contacts (94.9%). Several factors likely contribute to higher rates of invocation by those with more extensive police contacts. Youths who waived during prior arrests may have learned from the negative consequences—confessing redounds to their disadvantage. The time juveniles spend with lawyers contributes to greater understanding of rights, and youths with prior felony arrests may have learned from their lawyers.[80] Prior experience may fortify youths to cope with and resist the pressures in the interrogation room.

Juvenile justice personnel confirmed that prior felony arrests serve as a reasonable proxy for justice system experience. The opportunities to learn from prior encounters are legion—experience with police, hearing the *Miranda* warning, experiencing interrogation, consulting with counsel, and learning the consequences of waiving. Justice system people in different roles described youths who invoke in similar terms—"sophisticated," "savvy," "streetwise," "gang involved," and the like. A public defender described the youths who invoke as

the ones who have been through the system before and are more savvy, are a little more streetwise. They've dealt with police officers before. Probably they've had either a lawyer or somebody give them advice that it's not a good idea to talk to police in previous cases. Or if they've given a statement before, and it's turned around and used against them actually. Savviness or experience with the criminal justice system. The kids who have experience tend not to give up their rights as easily as first-timers. Kids that have more gang ties, and I would attribute that to getting advice from other people.

A prosecutor gave a similar explanation of why youths invoke: "It tends to be largely prior exposure to the system. But I think there are other factors at play. How they're raised. Their attitude toward law enforcement. Their exposure to the system and the media. Certain juveniles develop street smarts, savvy about the system. Those are the juveniles—repeated customers—who develop resistance to talking to the police because they've learned." A judge described youths who invoke as "kids who've been through the system before, are more sophisticated. They're sometimes gang involved. They know more about the criminal justice system. It's not necessarily the severity of the crime; it's more their own level of sophistication." An officer described youths who invoke as "more streetwise. They've been in the system. They know that talking to us isn't going to help them; it's just going to help us get them convicted. They're more streetwise. They're tougher kids. They know the game."

Some justice system personnel attributed some youths' invocation to other family members' experiences with the justice system. One judge observed, "They may have older siblings who've had problems with the law." A prosecutor confirmed, "Dad's been in and out of prison, brother's been in and out of juvenile system. So there may have been family gatherings with discussion of 'you never talk with a cop.'" A public defender observed, "They have parents that have had police contacts that have made it clear to them that they don't talk to police."

2. QUESTIONING OUTSIDE OF *MIRANDA*

If a suspect invokes his or her *Miranda* rights, then interrogation must cease. Prosecutors may not use subsequent statements as part of their case in chief. However, the Court allows the state to use voluntary statements obtained in violation of *Miranda* to impeach a defendant who testifies,[81] as leads to other witnesses,[82] or as clues to physical evidence.[83] The collateral uses of statements obtained in violation of *Miranda* create incentives for police with a "nothing to lose" attitude to question suspects "outside of *Miranda*" after they invoke their rights.[84] An analysis of interrogation manuals and training materials found that they encouraged police to continue to question suspects after they invoked *Miranda* to obtain evidence for impeachment or leads to other evidence.[85] Confirming the real-world impact of these training protocols, Leo reported that about one-quarter of detectives questioned suspects after they invoked *Miranda*.[86] By contrast, in this study, only one officer questioned a juvenile after he invoked. In more than 95% of cases in which juveniles invoked, questioning ceased immediately, and no interrogation "outside of *Miranda*" occurred.

Conclusion

This chapter describes the context of routine felony interrogation—when it happened, where it occurred, who was present, and how police warned and elicited waivers of *Miranda* rights. Police conducted more than two-thirds of interrogations within less than a day of the crime. The vast majority of interrogations occurred in custodial settings—police stations and detention facilities—or squad cars. Police had arrested nearly all the youths whom they questioned and subsequently detained more than half of them. Typically, only one officer questioned a juvenile. Police follow a standard *Miranda* protocol but use several strategies to deemphasize its significance and to secure an express waiver. Youth with more extensive experience in the justice system appear better equipped to invoke their rights. The vast majority of delinquents waived them.

Developmental and social psychologists contend that many juveniles do not understand *Miranda* and lack the ability to exercise their rights. These concerns are heightened for youths fifteen years of age and younger. When trial judges conduct suppression hearings, they seldom receive clinical evidence of suspects' cognitive, emotional, or motivational characteristics. They rely instead on objective, external behavioral indicators. By those measures—verbal statements of understanding, *Scales* tapes, signed *Miranda* forms, and express agreements to waive rights—sixteen- and seventeen-year-old felony delinquents appear to understand *Miranda*. More experienced youths appear somewhat better able to exercise their rights.

The law of interrogation equates juveniles and adults, and police treat them similarly. Police use the same *Miranda* warning to interrogate all suspects—juveniles and adults. As a minor concession to youthfulness, a few officers in this study explained or clarified the warning or asked juveniles to repeat back its meaning in their own words. For the vast majority, however, police used the same tactics to elicit *Miranda* waivers from juveniles as from adults. As with adults, once police gave the warning, the vast majority of suspects waived and allowed police to question them. In short, juveniles and adults receive the same *Miranda* warning and waiver process.

As a protective device to offset the inherent coercion of custodial interrogation, as a legal tool to empower defendants, and as a procedural counterweight to maintain a balance of equality in the adversarial system, *Miranda* fails. *Miranda* provides a warning that few suspects heed, and it benefits primarily more sophisticated youths who do not need a warning to know that adverse consequences loom if they talk to police. The next chapter examines how police questioned the vast majority of youths who waived.

Police Interrogation

On the Record

Interrogation is an art, rather than a science. Interviews vary with the personality and style of each investigator and offender, the circumstances of the offense and the evidence available, and the ebb-and-flow of conversations. One officer explained, "You're taught a technique. And then you build on it. And then you end up developing what works best for you as a detective. Every detective interviews differently." Another officer used a terpsichorean metaphor and observed, "The biggest thing about an interview is it's like a dance. It's not a set thing. You've got to be able to dance and respond to what the kid needs in the room." How does a social scientist capture the common and recurring features from among the variability of hundreds of interrogations?

More than four decades ago, Aaron Cicourel described police interrogation of juveniles. First, police gather information from witnesses, victims, and other officers to understand what happened:

> The interrogation, therefore, is often based upon some fairly definite interpretations of "what happened" and a kind of plan of action for reaching a particular disposition. The alternatives that might emerge here are contingent upon the *suspect's demeanor*, the details he reveals about participation in activities under investigation, his past record, the kind of imputations the officer makes about his home situation, and the control the officer assumes can be exercised by the parents and police over his future conduct.[1]

I emphasize "demeanor," because chapter 5 reports how youths' attitude affects interrogation tactics and outcomes. The officer's interview strategy emerges through

> a variety of hunches, theories, rules of thumb, general procedures, and on the spot strategies for dealing with different juvenile suspects. The officer's past experience and the information available prior to the interview lead him to make quick evaluations of his client as soon as there is a confrontation. The interrogation, therefore, is *highly structured* in the sense that the information revealed by the juvenile is *evaluated quickly* in terms of a set of *categories* which

the officer invokes by means of questions posed for the suspect. The interrogation is designed to *confirm* the officer's suspicions or firm beliefs about "what happened" and how the particular suspect is implicated.[2]

Cicourel describes interrogation as a highly structured interaction in which officers make quick evaluations to classify a juvenile as probably innocent or guilty, use stereotypic categories to shape their approach to the interview, and elicit information to confirm their suspicion of "what happened." Cicourel's description shares features of the Crime Control model —informal administrative fact-finding—to efficiently screen cases and to gather information to reach a prompt disposition.[3] Accordingly, administrative regularities impose one structure on interrogations.

Miranda imposes another structure on interrogations: warning, waiver, interrogation and response, and closure. Police must build rapport, successfully negotiate a warning, and elicit a waiver before they begin questioning. The Reid Method provides another semistructured template to organize how police question offenders. The type of questions (maximization and minimization) and the psychological manipulations (themes and alternative questions) provide another framework with which to analyze the process. Despite the variability of police-offender dyads, offenses, and available evidence, interrogations follow a certain routine from which generalizations emerge.

This chapter analyzes how police questioned the 285 juveniles in this study who waived their *Miranda* rights. How did they begin an interview? How did they frame their questions? What types of maximization and minimization techniques did they use? How did they conclude an interview? I compare and contrast the results with those reported in studies of adults[4] and juveniles.[5] Interviews with juvenile justice personnel expand the interpretation of the data.

I. Police Interrogation Tactics

Police question suspects to obtain a confession or incriminating admission, which leads to a guilty plea. Statements may provide leads to other evidence—for example, physical evidence, identity of other participants, witnesses, or stolen property to recover—to strengthen the prosecutor's case. Police seek suspects' statements—true or false—to pin them down, to control changes they later make in their stories, and to impeach their credibility. One detective observed, "I have always thought that a lie is almost as good as a confession. If they want to lie and put themselves somewhere else that can be refuted, great."

A. A Beginning Is a Delicate Place

Interrogation training programs instruct officers to familiarize themselves with the case file, to gather information, and to learn about the suspect before questioning him or her.[6] Many officers described a similar process to prepare for an interview: "After I have a good understanding of the offense that was committed, I want to talk to victims and witnesses first before I talk to a suspect. I want to go into that interview with the most knowledge I can possibly get prior to it." The brief delay for investigation prior to the interview increases a suspect's anxiety and readiness to talk.

Many of the arrested youths in this study initially were upset, and most officers used a gentle approach to calm them down. They introduced themselves to youths in a holding cell, unfastened the handcuffs, and walked them to the interview room to build rapport and relax them.

> Try to do some background on people before interviewing them. Try to get a sense of them. Is it a good kid gone bad or just a bad kid? Where is their maturity level? Where are they at in the system? Have they been in the system before? My approach is always pretty laid-back. I try to be as calm and collected with them as I can. Because if you come in and you're too overbearing with them, you (a) may scare them, or (b) they'll clam up. That's when you're more apt to get someone to say, "I don't want to talk to you." You've really got to soft sell these people to get them to trust you to begin to talk. Everything with me is pretty soft sell to start with.

Officers recognized that two actors play roles in every interview, and their behavior and attitude affect a juvenile's response: "Whatever I have in my mind, whatever I feel in the room is going to have a significant impact on that kid. That's why mainly I want a neutral state of mind and stay in a more compassionate feeling, because I want the kid to respond to that."

Minnesota training for recorded interviews instructs officers to describe their role as neutral report writers who want to learn what happened and to put those details in a report for prosecutors and judges to evaluate.[7] Several officers described themselves to juveniles as dispassionate messengers who just want to present the facts to subsequent decision-makers:

You know, this is your show. You decide what happens here. What I do is, I don't charge you with any crime. I try to get the facts on what happens. I send it to the county attorney. They decide if you'd be petitioned into the juvenile court system for an offense, and then a judge would read the reports, the statements, anything else relevant to the offense, and then you would appear in front of him and answer to that, okay?

I always come in after the fact. So for me to write down something, for me to guess at something I think to be the truth and write it down, I can't do that. I don't take sides in this. I got no emotional involvement in this whatsoever. I'm just here as a detective taking down the facts. And that's all it is. The facts and everything else will speak for themselves.

Police frequently advised suspects that the interview provides their opportunity to tell their story.

B. Framing Questions

Police choreograph, orchestrate, or stage-manage how suspects tell their story.[8] The strategies array along a continuum spanning more confrontational, controlling tactics to elicit incriminating facts (e.g., the Reid Method) to more open-ended, nondirectional techniques to elicit a free narrative (e.g., the investigative interview). How officers frame their questions—open-ended, closed, echoing, leading, multiple questions, interruptions, and long pauses—affects the types of response they elicit. Inbau and Reid advise police to ask open-ended questions—who, what, when, where, and why—and to avoid leading questions, especially about crucial corroborating details.[9] Open-ended questions that construct a narrative without feeding suspects crucial facts enhance the credibility of a statement for judges and juries.[10]

1. FORM OF QUESTIONS

There are many ways to ask questions, and they are not mutually exclusive. Officers asked different forms of questions during an interview. Table 4.1 reports that officers asked some open-ended questions in every interrogation (99.6%) and invited juveniles to provide an account. A public defender described the process of asking open-ended questions: "They get the kids talking, and they leave it open-ended. And they get the kids

Table 4.1
Forms of Interrogation Questions

Interrogation strategy	N	%
Open-ended	284	99.6
Closed-ended	276	96.8
Echoing	102	35.8
Multiple	70	24.6
Leading	55	19.3
Interruption	20	7.0
Silence	15	5.3

Note: Based on juveniles (N = 285) who waived *Miranda* rights and whom police questioned

talking and then jump in as the kid is giving a statement, trying to pin down and clarify. They start out very open-ended. And then they turn around and go back over the statement with the kid, things that don't make sense, contradictory evidence. And they start pinpointing the kid down and nailing him down on stuff." A judge confirmed, "Officers are very open-ended—'what happened next'—only asking clarifying questions or repeating things to make sure that they understand it." A prosecutor agreed, "Over the course of an interrogation, it will go from open-ended to more suggestive, especially if a child isn't giving much." A public defender agreed that the form of questions depends in part on the youth's initial responses. "It depends on the first couple of responses they get from the kids, where either they're friends with them or they are not friends with them. If they're friends with them, then they let the kid lead what seems to be a discussion. If the kid seems hostile at all, then it is nothing but leading questions. They lie to the kids."

Police consistently expressed a strong preference for open-ended questions: "I want them to give me as much free-standing communication as they can do. So I ask them very open-ended questions to allow them to funnel a full paragraph into their statement. I don't want yes-nos. I want the story. I want the truth. I want an understanding of their perspective." Open-ended questions enable officers to get suspects talking more quickly and fully and enable them to elicit more details with which to evaluate and control subsequent statements. Officers recognized that open-ended questions avoid the dangers of contaminating a person's statement:

I don't want to plant. Kids can be really susceptible to planting ideas.
I don't want to give them—one of the things I've been really cautious

about is giving them a story, giving them ideas of a story. I just want them to tell the truth. Very open-ended and general, and then once I have an understanding—I'll read the reports or talk to the officers before about the details of the case—I'll have a sufficient working knowledge to know if they're being truthful or not. General and then they get more specific.

Officers said that most youths are anxious to tell their story. Police commenced interviews by giving youths the opportunity to explain themselves:

> Most of the time, that's all you've got to do, especially with kids. "I just want to get your side of the story. Just be honest. Just tell me the truth. Everything can be explained. Sometimes we screw up, and we make a mistake in life. It's not so much the mistakes that we make; it's what you do after you get caught with that mistake that matters more. So now is your opportunity to tell your story." And I would tell you, most of the time, kids just start talking.

Many interrogations began with an open-ended invitation to suspects to "tell their story."[11]

> What I've learned over the years is there's always two sides to every story, and this is your opportunity to give your side of the story.

> You just go in and tell them that this is your opportunity to tell me your side of the story. I've already got the other side of the story. I just want to hear what you say happened, and then I'm going to write it up and send it on. And they'll decide. But if you don't want to tell me your side of the story, then they're just going to believe what this guy is telling them.

Officers' invitation to suspects to tell their story sometimes emphasized discrepancies among witnesses' or codefendants' statements: "We have to investigate it. First we have to gather knowledge, talk to people, get witness statements, talk to maybe people that were involved with things. The thing is we're here to get your side of the story. We've already got the other side of the story. We want to get your side of the story."

Prosecutors said they prefer open-ended questions because the responses create a more compelling narrative: "The higher-quality investigators ask open-ended, nonleading questions because they're truly looking for information. And they use a variety. It's not one way or another; there may be a mix of open-ended and closed-ended questions."

A closed question offers an interviewee a relatively narrow range of responses.[12] In nearly every interview in this study (96.8%), police asked some closed-ended questions for clarification, typically as follow-ups to open-ended narratives. As interviewees noted, questioning proceeds from general to specific, and closed questions elicit more specific details.

Interrogators can demonstrate sincerity, maintain rapport, and encourage a free flow of information by active listening.[13] The interviewer concentrates on suspects' answers, mirrors or echoes back their previous responses, and reinforces additional disclosure. Interrogators "echoed" —repeated back a phrase or the last few words of the previous reply—in about one-third (35.8%) of cases to invite further responses. Officers asked inartful, multiple questions in about one-quarter (24.6%) of cases.

Leading questions suggest the desired response. They impose the questioner's viewpoint on the suspect's response and can cause a person to produce an inaccurate response.[14] Leading questions play a prominent role in studies of false confessions because they require suspects to adopt interrogators' incriminating premises or feed suspects information that only a guilty party would know.[15] Police asked juveniles leading questions in less than one-fifth (19.3%) of these interviews, and they did not feature prominently in any case. One public defender observed, "When they ask a lot of leading questions, it's a dead giveaway that they've talked to the kid prior to the formal interrogation starting."

The Reid Method instructs interrogators to cut off suspects' denials and to prevent them from solidifying their disclaimers.[16] In these interviews, police deliberately interrupted juveniles' answers very seldom (7%), although both talked simultaneously or overlapped in tapes and transcripts.

A long pause after a question or answer may increase social pressure on a person to respond.[17] Officers allowed a long pause to hang in the air in a few cases (5.3%), and the silence created a pressure to respond. One prosecutor observed that when confronted with a long pause, "the inexperienced delinquent will jump in." Although a few transcripts noted long pauses, I encountered them more frequently in the tapes I transcribed. This form of question probably occurs more frequently than the data indicate. A prosecutor agreed, "You're more aware of it [long pauses] if you're listening to the recording. It's not always translated in the transcript."

C. Maximization Techniques to Overcome Resistance

Police use maximization tactics to scare or intimidate a suspect by overstating the seriousness of the offense, exaggerating the strength of the evidence, confronting the suspect with evidence, and the like.[18] They use minimization techniques to induce a statement by offering sympathy, providing moral justifications, lessening the seriousness of the crime, blaming the victim or accomplices, and the like.[19] Police use these strategies in tandem "to persuade the suspect that he is trapped and powerless, to diminish his self-confidence to deny the detectives' accusations, and to offer him a way to seemingly minimize his culpability and mitigate his punishment if he provides a statement."[20] The double-barreled approach overwhelms resistance and enables suspects to admit responsibility.[21]

The law treats juveniles just like adults in the interrogation room. Police training does not distinguish between tactics used for youths and those employed with adults. Justice system professionals reported that police question delinquents just like adults. One defender noted, "They employ the same techniques that they use with adults. I think that they directly embrace Reid-type techniques for the purposes of interrogation. I see them employing the same techniques on juveniles as they do with adults." Similarly, a judge observed, "My experience in adult court and juvenile court—I wouldn't see a lot of difference between the two except that juveniles were more likely to talk."

Detectives have a variety of maximization tactics at their disposal. They may overstate the seriousness of the crime, confront suspects with real or false evidence, or accuse them of lying. They may challenge inconsistencies or contradictions, emphasize the implausibility of claims, and describe how false statements negatively affect prosecutors and judges.[22] The Reid Method teaches use of Behavioral Analysis Interview (BAI) questions early in an interview—"Did you do it?" "Why would people accuse you?" and the like.[23] Police ask these emotionally charged questions to provoke suspects' reactions as indicators of guilt or innocence. Although the Reid Method advises use of BAI questions during the preliminary interview to distinguish the likely innocent and probably guilty, few of these files indicated that police had any conversations, much less conducted interviews, prior to the *Scales* recordings.

Police interviewees acknowledged using many maximization techniques regularly, especially, as one officer said, "when I think I'm getting lied to and told false information that's not consistent with the case." Police initially encouraged a suspect to commit to a story—true or false—

and then used more confrontational tactics to challenge the suspect's version of events:

> I would get the information that I know isn't truthful into the statement, and then after they give me that information, then I will become a little more confrontational and start calling them out on things. But I've got that baseline through witness statements and physical evidence or whatever that I can poke holes through later. Because sometimes a lie is as good as a truth. So at the end of my interview, I will then start attacking holes that I can find and say, "Look, this didn't happen this way. I know this didn't happen this way," and I start getting more confrontational.

A public defender confirmed that police confront youths with evidence "if the kid doesn't give them the full story that they're looking for. That seems to come up when the kid deviates from the story they're trying to confirm." A prosecutor agreed that police use confrontational tactics more readily if juveniles are not forthcoming:

> Is the kid coming in, and is the kid forthright about what he did? Then it's a much more conversational interrogation or statement. Obviously, if he is denying everything straight out, but there's a ton of evidence or other witnesses to his behavior, I think it is more confrontational. I think the officers will confront him with the inconsistencies: "This person is saying this. This is not gelling with what you are saying."

One judge, who presided in both juvenile and criminal courts, felt police use maximization more extensively with delinquents than with criminal defendants: "I see that more in juvenile than I did in adult actually. I think kids are more malleable than adults, less experienced. The officers find it's more fruitful in the juvenile context, when the time comes, to come down hard on them and say, 'That's all bullshit. Let's get to the truth.' I see that a lot more in juvenile than I did in adult."

Table 4.2 summarizes maximization strategies police used during an interrogation. They confronted juveniles with evidence (54.4%), accused them of lying (32.6%), exhorted them to tell the truth (29.5%), asked BAI questions (28.8%), challenged inconsistencies (20.0%), emphasized the seriousness of the offense (14.4%), and accused them of other crimes (8.4%).

Table 4.2
Maximization Questions: Types and Frequency

	N	%
Interrogation strategy		
Confront with evidence	155	54.4
Accuse of lying	93	32.6
Urge to tell the truth	84	29.5
Ask BAI questions	82	28.8
Use confrontational tactics	57	20.0
Warn about causing trouble for others	41	14.4
Accuse of other crimes	24	8.4
Number of tactics per interrogation		
None	95	30.9
One	71	23.1
Two	44	14.3
Three	38	12.4
Four	24	7.8
Five	24	7.8
Six	9	2.9
Seven	2	.7

In nearly one-third (30.9%) of interviews, police did not use any maximization techniques at all. In another quarter (23.1%) of interrogations, they used only one. Thus, most juveniles did not require much intimidation or persuasion to cooperate. By contrast, police used three or more maximization tactics in less than one-third (31.6%) of cases. Several different tactics could occur even in the same question—for example, confronting a youth with another person's statement and appealing for the truth.

1. CONFRONT SUSPECTS WITH EVIDENCE

In more than half (54.4%) the interrogations, police confronted juveniles with evidence—witnesses' identification, codefendants' statements, physical evidence, or the like. "Evidence ploys are used to make a suspect perceive that the case against him is so overwhelming that he has no choice but to confess because no one will believe his assertions of innocence."[24] Research on interrogations with juveniles in the United Kingdom and with adults in the United States reports that detectives confront a suspect with some evidence initially or disclose it during questioning.[25] Police in the interviews in this study confronted juveniles with statements from witnesses or codefendants, physical evidence, and real or implied fingerprints or DNA evidence.

a. Witnesses

Crimes against the person include both victims and other potential witnesses. Officers regularly referred to eyewitnesses who identified juveniles as perpetrators. To emphasize the strength of the case, one officer pointed out to a suspect, "We got—I'm guessing we got one, two, three, four—four people saying you hit him." Another officer observed, "Eyewitnesses, that's the best evidence possible. I mean, you can't get better than witnesses, and I've got witnesses, neighbor witnesses that's sitting on the deck by the trailer." In other cases, friends, acquaintances, or accomplices furnished identification testimony.

Juveniles commit their crimes in groups to a greater extent than do adults.[26] Interrogators exploit juveniles' uncertainty about the reliability of their confederates. One judge observed this strategy regularly in juvenile courts: "You'll see them a lot more divide and conquer in juvenile than you do in adults, because so often these crimes are committed with two, three, four kids. Kids aren't that sophisticated." Police regularly confronted suspects with statements made by other participants that implicated them. At the start of a second interview, an officer confronted a youth with a co-offender's statement to overcome his denial: "You're going on it because I got a perfect statement from Gary. I'm going to get one from Ron. I got the gun. I know about the phone. The whole nine yards. Three burglaries that you did. You, Ron, and Gary."

The increased prevalence of surveillance cameras in public and private spaces such as parking garages enables officers to confront youths with video imagery to supplement witness testimony: "If you didn't know, there's cameras in the lobby, and there's cameras in the garage. And there's one actually right by where the vehicle that you guys went into. I just got done watching the tape. Let me tell you again, I watched the tape. I saw who broke the window. I saw who took the stereo. I saw who took the CD. I saw who took the other stuff."

b. Physical Evidence: Real, Implied, and False

Police regularly used physical evidence to confront suspects who deny involvement: "If a guy is being adamant in his denial, and we had the evidence to show that he was lying, then at some point, to call him a liar is important. You've got to get him off the 'No, it's not me.' And sometimes, confrontation is necessary to do that. There may come a time during the interrogation where you use it [evidence] for leverage, and that would be the confrontation." Police commonly confronted juveniles with direct and circumstantial evidence of criminal involvement. For example, while questioning a youth about an auto theft, an officer pointed out, "The problem is here that you were driving a stolen vehicle. It's got a smashed window. The ignition was all jacked up, punched out. There's no keys, there's no ignition keys in it, and you're driving it. And you get stopped, you lie about who you are, and you're driving a stolen vehicle."

After police arrested a youth near a strong-arm robbery, the officer asked the juvenile, "Then how did her [the victim's] credit card and her lipstick get in the house that you guys were found at?" In another robbery investigation, an officer marshaled direct and circumstantial evidence against the youth—witnesses, prior record for similar offenses, and lack of abili—to show the implausibility of his denials:

> The best evidence you can possible get is an eyewitness, an eyewitness that is unbiased—meaning someone that doesn't know you, that doesn't have a grudge against you. And that's what I've got. I've got physical evidence too. Plus there's a lot of circumstantial evidence there too: fingerprints, like you just said, footprints, all that kind of stuff if you want to go that route. And another thing is circumstantial evidence. You have no alibi. You can't tell us where you were that night. You've got a history like you would not believe, crimes related to the offenses we're accusing you of right now. We've got people that were involved in this offense, people who were involved in this offense. They're saying that you done it. They're making deals, because they're an adult.

Police sometimes referred to fingerprints or the possibility of obtaining fingerprint evidence to bolster their case. An officer who investigated a stolen car gave a suspect a minicourse on fingerprint evidence and how latent prints taken from the vehicle led to his arrest:

> I want to know how your fingerprints got on the car that had things taken out of it because your fingerprints were there. You know, the officer got a call that there was a car broken into. He goes there, and he fingerprints the car—you know, dusts for fingerprints. And lo and behold, he gets latent prints. Latent prints are fingerprints from a crime scene. You know, it could be a partial fingerprint, a whole fingerprint, no matter. You know what a fingerprint looks like? You leave a fingerprint on a glass or something? So he pulls the prints

off the car, he pulls them off, and he turns them into our crime lab. So two weeks later, I get a crime lab report, and what do you think it says? "Lee Richards [the suspect], date of birth 9/18/89." See, your prints are on file. Any time somebody gets arrested, you know, they take your fingerprints, and they're on file in a computer. They take those latent fingerprints, they put it into a machine, and the machine studies the latent fingerprints from the crime, and then they match it through the whole database of anybody arrested in the state of Minnesota. So I just want to know how your fingerprints—if you weren't there, don't know anything about the car—do you know how your fingerprints would have gotten in there?

c. *Implied and Hypothetical Evidence: "What If I Told You . . . ?" or "Is There Any Reason Why . . . ?"*

In most cases, DNA, fingerprint, or video-surveillance evidence will not be available or analyzed between the time of suspects' arrest and their interrogation. Sometimes, police described an investigation as if they already had obtained the evidence. Officers regularly referred to hypothetical or implied evidence or evidence that later investigations would reveal. Sometimes, they asked juveniles how they would respond to hypothetical evidence—for example, "What if I told you that someone identified you?" or "that police found your fingerprints?" In another version, an officer might ask a juvenile, "Is there any reason why your DNA might be on the gun?" or "why you would appear on surveillance video?" "Usually, when we're interviewing them, we won't have physical evidence yet. You can ask them, 'Is your DNA going to be on the gun? Because we're going to get it tested.'" Officers used implied evidence or hypothetical evidence regularly during interrogations—"What if I said we've got a witness that saw you take it [the car]?" or "Any idea why you might be on videotape doing this crime?"

Officers explained that they ask hypothetical questions because they do not possess the actual evidence with which to confront a suspect.

Say you go to a robbery you catch the kid, you arrest him for the robbery, and maybe he's got the gun on him or the money or something. But you can't verify on fingerprints. You won't know how good the video is. You won't know if the fingerprints, the DNA, are on the gun. So more than actually using the true evidence in interviews, I've tended to use the potential that there is evidence. "We're going to Buccal swab you and compare it to the DNA on the gun. Is it going to be a match?" "We've got the video. We're going to be comparing what you were wearing with what's on the video. Is it going to be a match?"

During a burglary interrogation, an officer explained how potential evidence would ripen into proof of guilt—fingerprints would be recovered: "You guys didn't wear gloves when you went inside that house, did you? Fingerprints can be recovered very quickly, and I have done enough checks to see you have quite a little history, so your prints are on file. So there were prints that were recovered from this house from the money jar that was full of money. And I've got a feeling that yours may be on that, or John's may be on that." Similarly, officers asked juveniles about the possibility of finding their DNA on evidence. An officer asked a youth arrested for possessing drugs and a crack pipe, "So if we wanted to get a DNA swab or something like that, would it come back to your mouth? Has you mouth been on that pipe?" Another officer asked a juvenile to consent to a DNA swab to compare with smoked cigarettes found at the scene of a burglary: "So when I fill out this—it's a form you have to complete to get saliva from the cigarette butts tested—and it comes back with your DNA, what are you going to tell me about that? You'd be willing to give me a swab test, like if I wanted to swab your cheek? You'd be willing to do that for me so I can run the DNA against the DNA on the cigarettes?"

Justice system personnel confirmed the regular use of hypothetical or implied evidence tactics—"what if"—during interrogations. A public defender described the prevalence of the technique:

In the more serious cases, the cop might say, "Well, am I going to find your fingerprint on that gun?" or "What's going to happen if I find your fingerprint on the knife or the door? Your DNA might be there." A lot of this "what if" stuff. But as far as actually telling the kid, "We got your fingerprint," I've had that happen, but that would be more the exception than the rule. A lot of speculation what's going to happen: "If I find your fingerprints on there—I shouldn't find your fingerprints on there if what you're telling me is true."

Officers distinguished between implied evidence and false evidence: "I never lie about something that can be proved differently. The closest I get to stretching the truth is 'Is there any reason . . .?': 'Is there any reason that a hidden camera that you weren't aware of saw somebody that matched your description?'"

d. False Evidence

Researchers focus primarily on the use of false evidence because of its role in eliciting false confessions and producing wrongful convictions.[27] Richard Leo reported that police confronted suspects with false evidence in nearly one-third (30%) of the interrogations he observed.[28] Unfortunately, he did not define false evidence (e.g., nonexistent or made-up evidence) as distinguished from embellished evidence (officers overstating confidence in a witness' identification) or implied or hypothetical evidence (things that police expect or hope to discover during the investigation). Leo observed detectives question suspects and then asked them afterward whether they had the evidence they claimed. Tapes and transcripts do not allow me independently to verify whether police possessed evidence to which they referred during interrogations.

In cases in which officers' references to witness statements or physical evidence aroused suspicion, I reexamined the police reports to see if the files contained that evidence. In some instances, they did not. These may be instances of false-evidence ploys or simply incomplete files. Other officers may have phrased their questions more artfully, and false-evidence ruses thus may occur more frequently. Legal scholars and social psychologists strongly condemn police use of false evidence during interrogation because it may elicit false confessions from innocent suspects who feel overwhelmed.[29] Not surprisingly, public defenders see false-evidence ploys used more frequently than do police or prosecutors: "I've seen a lot of lying, like 'we have fingerprints' when they really don't have fingerprints. 'We have a witness that says they saw you there,' when they really don't have a witness that saw him there. There's a lot of flexibility there, with lies unfortunately in the interrogation room. It really is a form of coercion, of psychological coercion, that's very effective with kids." We do not know how frequently police use false-evidence tactics, and tapes or transcripts of interrogations may not reveal them. As we will see in chapter 7, false-evidence ploys play a prominent role in cases in which police elicit false confessions.

Several police officers described the use of props during interrogations—for example, a thick file folder intended to create an impression that it contained evidence. One officer described using a blank videotape to masquerade as a surveillance tape: "The biggest stretch that I've ever done is to have a fake video that states the business that they burglarized and the time frames. And it's sitting there. I never even look at it, but I know they see it. I never talk about it." However, officers cautioned that false-evidence ploys are fraught with peril: "When you do that, you need to be very careful, because they can catch you lying too. And if you screw it up, then you've lost it. And they know they've got you then. It's very important, if you're going to do that, that you're able to back it up somehow or at least sell it somehow." Other officers acknowledged the hazards of false-evidence ploys and said they choose not to use them: "I'm very straightforward with evidence. If I have a print that was recovered, I will let them know that prints were recovered. I won't lie to a kid. I'm very honest and straightforward in my interviews."

2. ACCUSE SUSPECTS OF LYING

In about one-third (32.6%) of the cases in this study, officers accused juveniles of lying. Police typically allowed juveniles to commit themselves to a story and then confronted them regarding fabrications:

> As you're going through your interview with people, you just know we're not getting anywhere. He's lying about this. We need to start pointing things out to him. You start subtly pointing things out. And then you may get to the point where, "You know what? You're lying. We're not even going to go any further." That may come very quickly in the conversation; it may take a while to get to that point. It's just reading the people. I've cut people off after two sentences: "Stop, you're lying. If you're going to keep lying to me, I'm going to get up and get out of here, because I have other things to do." Because that may push them to get to the truth quicker, or it may get them to tell me to get the hell out of the room, and that's what I was looking for anyway.

When juveniles denied involvment, officers directly challenged their veracity: "You are lying to me, okay? I've been doing this a long time." Other officers were equally blunt stating their disbelief: "If you're saying you didn't, you're a liar. I'm telling you this as I look you in the eye: you're a liar." When juveniles protested their innocence, officers dismissed their claims: "Do you know how many times I've heard that [denial] over ten years of investigation? You wouldn't be here right now if you weren't involved, if we did not have evidence that you were involved."

Changes in a youth's story could lead to accusations of lying. Police told juveniles that internal inconsistencies in their story rendered all assertions unbelievable: "Yeah, but you tell me one thing, now you're telling me another not to get yourself in trouble. How can I believe you?" Officers regularly implored juveniles to stop lying and tell the truth: "Lying to me at this point is not gonna help you at all. So you need to be honest with me. It's as simple as that."

3. EXHORT SUSPECTS TO TELL THE TRUTH

Accusing youths of lying and encouraging them to tell the truth are opposite sides of the same coin. Police used both tactics in this study and in about the same proportion of cases. In nearly one-third of cases (29.5%), officers urged juveniles to be honest and tell the truth. Although no officer explicitly said, "The truth shall set you free," they all clearly implied that "honesty is the best policy." One officer advised a youth, "The best thing for you right now is to tell the truth about what happened up there. That's gonna help you the best in this mess, is to just tell the truth about what happened up there. Now, what I want you to do is don't bullshit me now on this. 'Cause if you lie, if you tell me one lie, then that makes everything you say a lie. The best thing to do is to just tell us the truth."

Officers regularly implored youths to tell the truth: "You gotta give up the truth, the whole thing. The only thing that can help you is the truth." Some police officers cautioned youths that they were "human lie detectors" and that their professional expertise enabled them to determine whether a suspect was telling the truth. "To be a good detective, I can damn near look at somebody and tell when they're not being completely truthful. Now, what I'm getting here from you is some truth. But sit here and fuckin' lie and not be truthful, that's gonna get more serious than what it already is." Officers assured juveniles that if they told the truth, then they would be able to receive the help they needed: "I would be much more appreciative and give you much more credit for telling me the truth and what's going on here so that we can spend more time deciding how we're going to handle getting you the help that you need, okay?"

In officers' quest for the truth, they reaffirmed their roles as neutral fact gatherers and conduits of information: "I don't want to put words in your mouth. I just want you to tell me the truth. I can't add anything to the tape." They assured juveniles that they would accurately convey their truthful statements to the decision-makers: "That's all I want is the truth. You tell me you're telling the truth, and I'll put that in the report. Because I can't add anything. It's on the recorder. So if you tell me what you're saying is the truth, then I'll put it in there. All I want to know is what happened." In their role as an information conduit, officers wanted to convey accurate information to justice system personnel: "I'll write down whatever you tell me, but I want to be able to write the truth. I don't want to be writing lies for a judge to see. I don't think you want that either. This is no cloak-and-dagger here; there's no mirrors or nothing else. This is just about getting the truth and putting this matter behind you."

Officers regularly cautioned juveniles that a prosecutor, judge, and even their own defense attorney would react negatively to an implausible story: "You can pretend you're a lawyer and you're listening to yourself talk. How would you feel if the person isn't being truthful? Because they're not trying to help their cause. It seems like they're lying or withholding information." Police told juveniles that judges respond more favorably to truthful defendants than to those who lie. "If that's your side of the story, it's not going to look too good when the judge hears this with all these other statements from all these other people." Finally, officers advised juveniles to tell the truth during the interview, rather than to wait until trial: "This is your opportunity to be truthful. This is going to court. It's gonna look a lot better for you if you're honest with us right now. Tell us the full story so that when it goes to court, you're not looking like a liar."

4. ASK BEHAVIORAL ANALYSIS INTERVIEW QUESTIONS

A criminal investigator initially must distinguish between probably innocent and probably guilty suspects. At the preliminary interview, Inbau and Reid advise interrogators to ask "behavior-provoking questions that are specifically designed to evoke behavioral responses."[30] They posit that innocent and guilty people respond differently to these emotionally provocative questions and thereby enable the investigator accurately to classify them.[31] Despite Inbau and Reid's claims of diagnosticity, police cannot distinguish any better than laypeople between truth tellers and liars; neither does so accurately, and BAI questions do not provoke responses that accurately separate them.[32]

Leo reported that officers asked BAI questions in 40% of the interrogations in his study.[33] In this study, police used BAI questions in more than one-quarter (28.8%) of interviews. Police most commonly asked, "Do you know why I have asked to talk to you here today?" They used versions of the BAI question "Why do you think the victim is saying you are the one who did this?" One officer asked a juvenile, "Why do you think she would have a reason to come here and make this statement—say that you sexually assaulted her? Why do you think that she would do that?" In the face of protestations of innocence, an officer asked a youth, "Why would people want to frame you? You said you don't have any enemies—why would people want to frame you?" In other interviews, officers lifted the BAI questions directly from the Inbau and Reid script: "Well, how do you feel about me being here and interviewing you about this?"; "Tell me why you would not do something like this'; and "What do you think should happen to someone who does something like this?"

5. CONFRONT SUSPECTS: CHALLENGE, DISPUTE, MAXIMIZE SERIOUSNESS, INCREASE ANXIETY

In one-fifth (20%) of the cases in this study, officers used confrontational techniques to challenge suspects' assertions. Pointing out inconsistencies, disputing claims, and questioning credibility increased youths' anxiety and undermined their confidence. Officers regularly responded to juveniles' protestations of innocence with a barnyard epithet: "Bullshit."

Many interviews began with an invitation to youths to tell their story. But police warned them that it was a time-limited opportunity—take it or leave it. If they did not take advantage of their only chance to explain, then they might regret it later:

> I'm not going to talk to you and come back next week and say, "Did you change your mind? Do you really want to talk to me now?" Now is your opportunity. Because once I leave this door, I'm just going to go back up and type up my petition, and I'll see you in court tomorrow morning and then set a court date. Then you go to court, and words will be words, and the cards will be stacked. What do you say?

Officers played on juveniles' uncertainty about how much information they already had. Several officers used poker analogies to describe the strategy of interrogation: "I'm not gonna lay my cards out in front of you and let you know exactly what I have in terms of cases that I'm working. But I'm going to find out how honest you are very quickly with some of these questions I'm gonna ask you." Another officer described interrogation as "kind of like the game of poker": "I'm not going to tell you what my hand is." Police withheld information from juveniles about the course of an investigation to increase uncertainty and anxiety:

> I'm not going to sit here and tell you what other people told me, because I don't play those games. That's kind of private. I'm not going to

tell you what he told me; I'm not going to tell him what you told me right now. I don't work that way. You'll find out in court, if it goes to that degree. I think there's something we can do now. That's why it's important for me to get your side of the story for the tape recorder.

Police occasionally warned a youth that silence could make the situation worse. Officers cautioned a reluctant youth that co-offenders might make a deal at his expense: "Where's it going to look better when it goes to court: if we have your story of what happened, or if we just have other people's story against you? We're trained to get all sides of this story before it goes to court. Otherwise, we would not be doing our jobs to the fullest." They played on juveniles' uncertainty about the reliability of confederates, urged them to tell their own story, and warned that without their version, others would shift responsibility to them:

Let's get to the truth and get on with this so we can figure out how to help you out and get through it. I don't want your buddies' stories to be the only thing to go off from here. Because you are getting the finger. The finger is being pointed at you. Do I believe that everything they are saying is true? No, I don't believe it. Do I want to get your side of the story? Heck yeah, I do. Because that is where the justice is going to come from. I don't want you to take the whole fall for this. I believe it should be split up evenly because that's the way it happened. I don't want you to take the whole thing.

Police referred to youths' physiological symptoms of nervousness further to increase their anxiety. They warned one suspect that his body language betrayed him even as he tried to dissemble: "Joe, your body language is telling me that you're not telling me the truth. This is what I do for a living. And so I want you to be truthful for me, and I'm sure it's very difficult to talk about this." Officers used juveniles' physiological symptoms to demonstrate that their demeanor revealed their dishonesty: "But I can see the way your body language is, the way you're talking to me, the influx, the way your eyes are, and everything else that you're not being honest with me about what happened." Officers regularly admonished youths to maintain eye contact and told them, "Your body is telling me one thing, while your mouth tells me another."

Another confrontational tactic officers used was to maximize the seriousness of the crime. In an interrogation about an aggravated assault with a knife, the officer described the fine line that separates an assault from murder:

> This is some serious stuff. This is not a fistfight in a parking lot or something like that. This kid actually went to the hospital. Fortunately for you, he's all right, or he's gonna be all right. He's got some recovering stuff to go through, from what I understand, according to the doctors. He was still stabbed with a knife. You didn't kill him, though, so this isn't a homicide investigation. If something happens, he gets an infection, that's some serious stuff, you know. And that would be an end result of you sticking him with that knife. It's a serious crime, though, this is: gets stuck with a deadly weapon—that's what a knife is.

Some officers maximized the seriousness of the offense by using its legal label. After learning that a youth previously had received a speeding ticket, the officer asked, "Do you know what a felony is? That's what you committed today. It's the most serious level of offense that we have." Others emphasized the seriousness of a youth's crime by distinguishing it from run-of-the-mill juvenile felonies: "Felony theft for a juvenile is nothing. That's a speeding ticket to an adult. Felony narcotics, that's a whole different thing. It's a much higher crime. That's not your run-of-the-mill theft. So, you know, we can't promise you anything, make deals with you, or anything like that. But you need to think about your case that you are being charged with this felony narcotics, intent to distribute."

Officers suggested that a refusal to cooperate could result in more punishment, whereas an admission might garner leniency. Two police officers questioned a juvenile about multiple burglaries committed in different counties and described the value of confessing to a package deal:

> We've got information on a lot of different burglaries here. It's probably in your best interest to share this information with us now so we can clear all this up. If you're keeping stuff from us, it's just a matter of time until we tie it to you guys. How many burglaries you've been involved in? This is all going to get lumped together. If other burglaries come up that you were involved in, that's gonna be all separate charges. You know, you can get more time with that than just by coming open and telling us everything you know about the burglaries.

Police raised the specter that juveniles could face waiver to criminal court, an adult criminal record, or a longer sentence if they failed to cooperate:

> The thing is that you're at that age where you're going to be adult. Don't screw this up for your adult record, because if they put this all together and they want to try you as an adult, if they find that you're not cooperative, they could technically do that. This happened last week with a kid that I had in custody, for a seventeen-year-old that had a history like you. They tried him as an adult. You know, that goes on your adult record, and I don't think you want that. Do you?

Police regularly portrayed themselves as report writers and information conduits to the prosecutor and judge. They warned juveniles that truthfulness with the officers and their recommendations could affect county attorneys' and judges' decisions: "You don't want to create an impression that you don't care. You don't want to create the impression that you're cold-blooded. You don't want to create an impression that you're a liar, okay?" Officers regularly asked juveniles to think how judges hearing their responses would view them:

> You have got to think about what the judge is going to say to you, because we're going to do a detailed report on what happened during this interview that is being taped. If I'm a judge and I'm listening to somebody that is cooperative with the police, willing to help them out, I'm going to be a little more lenient if I was a judge. If I'm a judge and I hear a guy doing what you're doing, saying you know what—"I'm not giving that up"—what do you think the judge is going to do? Do you think he's going to give you a harder punishment?

6. WARN SUSPECTS ABOUT CAUSING TROUBLE FOR OTHERS
Officers occasionally (14.4%) cautioned juveniles that their failure to cooperate could have serious repercussions for innocent third parties, such as a parent or sibling. In one interview, an officer advised a youth whose mother lived in public housing, "Your ma is involved now, too. Because she's looking at getting booted from her apartment because her son brought in some weed into the apartment." In another interview, the officer informed a juvenile who used his father's truck to commit the crime that the vehicle could be forfeited:

You were driving your father's vehicle while committing a felony. Do you realize that vehicle can be confiscated? Forfeiture means that the state or the government takes your property and claims that as their own. If a vehicle is used in a commission of felony, the state of Minnesota tells us that the vehicle has been subjected to forfeiture —meaning that your dad's vehicle would then be the city of Lino Lakes'. We would own it, sell it at auction, and make a profit—put it in our account. That's what you got your dad into by your actions.

An officer questioned a girl whom he suspected held a gun for her boyfriend and described a scenario in which lying to protect her boyfriend could endanger her mother: "Somebody's going to get hurt and killed. Could be you. Could be Raymond [the boyfriend]. Could be—I don't want to say this, but I'm gonna—it could be your mom. Because she could just be at the wrong place at the wrong time, and somebody could come by and does a drive-by shooting, and she could get hit too. Somebody's gonna get hurt here." Officers regularly reminded juveniles of their parents' love, concern, and hurt. Their parents did not want to see them continue in a life of crime:

She was pretty upset yesterday when we found that stuff [drugs]. She was scared. She's afraid too that you're going to go to prison for a long time. I know you don't treat your mom very well, but she's still your mom, and she still cares about you, and she's really afraid that you're going to go away for a long time, and she's very scared. But that's why we're here talking, so we can try to avoid that, so we can be up-front and help you out.

Police advised youths that their denials would force the police to continue their investigation, which could inconvenience innocent third parties and compound their difficulties. During a burglary investigation, an officer warned, "If I don't get the full truth here, we're going to have to bring your brother back from the military. He ain't gonna be happy, and neither is the military. I don't really want to have to do that, and I shouldn't have to." When police questioned a robbery suspect who drove a car in which his younger sister was a passenger, they warned him that if he did not cooperate, they would detain his sister to determine whether she was an innocent bystander or a participant: "I'm just trying to understand, 'cause do you want to see your sister go to the juvenile detention center? No, and I don't either. I don't want to see her go. When I get her side of the story, I wouldn't have a problem with your sister or your mother or somebody come and pick her up, you know? But I need to understand what her part was in this thing."

In another robbery investigation, police expressed uncertainty whether an adult girlfriend who drove the car in which police arrested the juvenile was an accomplice. If the juvenile failed to cooperate, then his silence could adversely affect how the girlfriend's case was handled:

> Now if you want to keep her out of it, I need the whole truth. She says she dropped you off with them. Now if she's lying, it means she's implicated, and if we get her charged, we'll get her charged with aggravated robbery, just like you, for driving the car. Now, if she truthfully didn't know exactly what was going down, we could probably take her out of it. I can't guarantee it, but there's probably a better chance that she can stay out of it if we get the entire truth.

7. ACCUSE SUSPECTS OF OTHER CRIMES

During interrogations, officers sometimes accused juveniles of other crimes to intimidate them and increase their anxiety. Accusations of other crimes included descriptions of a similar modus operandi (MO) or impaired credibility. An officer who questioned a juvenile about one robbery accused him of other robberies or referred to previous robbery convictions: "Then the next night were you involved in another robbery? Over on the East Side? Well, so far I think we've got at least one of the three of you identified as doing this other robbery. We're looking at you guys. We're looking hard at you guys for about a half a dozen of them—all the same MO. We're talking about some more robberies. We'll be liking you for those other robberies, too."

As the foregoing illustrates, officers used similar maximization strategies to manipulate and intimidate juveniles as they employ with adults.[34] Although police spoke firmly and directly with juveniles, they did not shout at or threaten them on the tapes to which I listened.

D. Minimization Techniques

Minimization tactics offer suspects face-saving excuses or moral justifications to reduce the crime's seriousness, to provide a less odious motivation, or to shift blame to a victim or accomplice.[35] Minimization themes suggest that suspects will feel better or imply they will benefit if they confess: "They work by shifting the blameworthiness of the act from the suspect to another person; by attributing the blameworthiness to the social circumstances that allegedly led to the act; or by redefining the act in a way that appears to minimize, reduce, or even eliminate the suspect's culpability because the act now seems less criminal or no longer criminal at all."[36] Themes that reduce suspects' culpability implicitly communicate that they may receive less punishment.[37] A judge observed that when police use minimizations tactics, juveniles "respond positively. It's human nature, but it's even more human nature when you're young, to think, 'Maybe I'm not in as much trouble as I thought.'"

Police used minimization tactics in one-sixth (17.3%) of the interrogations in this study. By contrast, they used maximization tactics in more than two-thirds (69.1%) of cases—about four times as frequently. One officer explained that even though prosecutors charged all of the youths in this study with felonies, "most of these are fairly minor, so you don't have to do a whole lot of minimizing."

Officers used scenarios or themes to reduce suspects' culpability in 15.4% of cases; appealed to self-interest in about one-tenth (11.9%) of cases; expressed empathy and a desire to help a youth in about one-tenth of cases (10.5%); and used other tactics in a few cases. The paucity of minimization tactics is consistent with research in the United Kingdom that reports that "[t]he tactics deemed by several psychologists to be the most

Table 4.3
Minimization Questions: Types and Frequency

	N	%
Interrogation strategy		
Neutralize guilt	44	15.4
Appeal to self-interest	34	11.9
Express empathy	30	10.5
Appeal to honor	25	8.8
Minimize seriousness	15	5.3
Blame third parties	10	3.5
Number of tactics per interrogation		
None	254	82.7
One	33	10.7
Two	14	4.6
Three	5	1.6
Four	1	.3

problematic (i.e., initimidation, minimisation, situational futility, and maximization) never or almost never occurred."[38]

1. NEUTRALIZATION: THEMES AND SCENARIOS

The Reid Method advises police to develop a theme or scenario to neutralize suspects' guilt to make it easier to confess. "[P]sychologists refer to this internal process as techniques of neutralization. Those classifications are remarkably similar to what we refer to as themes (for example, 'denial of responsibility,' 'denial of injury,' 'denial of victim,' and 'condemnation of the condemners')."[39] Developing a theme entails "presenting a 'moral excuse' for the suspect's commission of the offense or minimizing the moral implications of the conduct. Some themes may offer a 'crutch' for the suspect as he moves toward a confession. Most interrogation themes reinforce the guilty suspect's own rationalizations and justification for committing the crime."[40]

Criminologists use techniques of neutralization to explain how youths rationalize engaging in delinquency. Neutralizations defuse guilt and reduce culpability and allow youths to lessen responsibility, to blame the victim, or to provide mitigating justification.[41] Many themes are logical extensions of criminal law defenses—provocation, intoxication, or insanity—that provide rationales to reduce moral responsibility. David Matza's classic *Delinquency and Drift* contends that juveniles occasionally adopt rationales to sever the bonds of the conventional order and that these episodes of moral drift free them to engage in delinquency.[42] "The major bases of negation and irresponsibility in law rest on self-defense, insanity, and accident; so, too, in the subculture of delinquency. The restraint of law is episodically neutralized through an expansion of each extenuating circumstances beyond a point countenanced in law."[43] For example, delinquents may reject the suggestion that they are mentally ill but readily embrace the idea of "going crazy" or "being mad" to rationalize criminal conduct. Interrogation themes use similar rationale to minimize juveniles' responsibility or to explain their offense. Police regularly refer to a youth's crime as a "mistake" rather than deliberate wrongdoing, or venture that it was "out of character."

Police in this study suggested at times that madness or excitement of the moment accounted for youths' uncharacteristic behavior:

And you were so hyped up, I bet you don't even remember hitting him here. I do things in the heat of the moment. "Did I do that, or didn't I do that?" That's just a normal reaction. You get so freaked out because you're a decent person. You get overloaded, and you do things and you perceive things different than you react. So a witness who's standing here breathing normal sees what's really happening, versus what you think is going on because you have this massive adrenaline rush. I believe that's why you did what you did: you got caught up. You got caught up, and because you got caught up, you did things you don't normally do and you would never do intentionally. That's a good explanation, I think. You got caught up in something here.

I can understand you're whipped up. You're adrenalized. You've seen this going on. You're in a frenzy, that sometimes you just do stuff and you don't remember what happened. Could it have been that things just kind of got out of control and that you just got wrapped up in it and kicked him a couple of times?

Getting mad or losing control—insanity—can mitigate or minimize the seriousness of a crime. One officer inquired whether a youth charged with criminal sexual conduct experienced an "irresistible impulse": "Did you just get thoughts in your head? Were they thoughts that you had all day, or did they just come upon you really quick?"

Police suggested and juveniles readily invoked intoxication—drinking alcohol or using drugs—to diminish responsibility and to excuse behavior that they would not have engaged in while sober. While not a significant criminal defense, intoxication provides an acceptable explanation for uncharacteristic behavior: "Being under the influence of alcohol is likened to losing one's mind, going crazy."[44] If a juvenile is intoxicated, then he or she is not responsible. Officers regularly offered juveniles intoxication as a face-saving explanation for their misconduct: "There was probably a lot of people drinking down there. I'm not saying you were the only one, and I'm not trying—don't worry about minor consumption and that kind of stuff, because I'm not worried about that. I just wanna get your mind frame here when you picked up the knife. I'm not saying it was right if you were drinking, but what I'm saying is, was alcohol a factor?"

Police provided juveniles with opportunities to diffuse responsibility by suggesting that they succumbed to negative peer influences. Because juveniles often commit their crimes in groups,[45] police blame other group members and allow juveniles to shift the blame to others:

Rick [the suspect] knew he made a mistake. Maybe Rick was forced to do it. I know how peer pressure goes. You know, I went along to be with the crowd, because I thought it was cool at the time. I've been there. I know how it is. "Come on, let's be cool and do it. Come on, let's do it. Let's do it for the dare." Right? That kind of thing. I've heard that before. This is reality. And the reality is, Rick, we want your side of the story. How did you do it? Why did you do it? Did someone make you do it? Did someone bully you into doing it or dare you to do it?

Police took advantage of group criminality to allow juveniles to claim a minor, albeit incriminating, role in the offense. One officer said, "Crimes with juveniles, oftentimes there are numerous people involved. It's easier to get someone to say they were involved in a smaller part of the crime."

Police commonly minimized a youth's offense by describing it as a mistake. Parents regularly refer to errant children's behavior as a mistake, and children learn to claim mistakes as a way to mitigate responsibility. Officers regularly enabled juveniles to attribute their delinquency to a mistake or youthful indiscretion:

You and Miguel ended up making a mistake. You know, no one got hurt here: no one was shot or stabbed or anything. I'm sure it was an opportunistic thing because this lady was at the bottom of the stairs and coming down the stairs. You made a mistake and taking some things from her.

Now I can understand that at your age, you don't think about the future too much; you think about today. Because of that, you're young and you make mistakes. I can understand because you're human and you're young and you make mistakes. But you have to be man enough to face up to it here and tell the system that "Yeah, I made a mistake and I'm sorry for it, and I'm going to change."

If a juvenile's crime was a mistake, then it does not indicate he or she has "bad character." A public defender described how police use this ploy to help to facilitate a youth's admission: "You know, son, I've been doing this along time. I know the difference between a kid who wants to do wrong and a kid who just fell into doing wrong. And I know the judge. You just tell me what happened, and I'll make sure the judge knows you're just a kid who fell into doing wrong or who just made a mistake. Let me help you help yourself, because I know you're not a bad kid."

Officers sometimes blamed the victim to reduce juveniles' guilt or to excuse their conduct. An officer suggested to a girl who burglarized a former boyfriend's home,

> What it looks like is that you had a bad relationship which you were getting out of and that you were mad and you were upset, and probably rightly so from what little I know of Carson [former boyfriend-victim]. I know he can be a pain in the butt. And I can probably understand where you're coming from if you were mad at him and wanted to get back at him. And, yes, I know you're human and that when your relationship and stuff like that happens, it's a hard thing to deal with, especially when people aren't very nice to you.

Police questioned a suspect about criminal sexual conduct and employed the classic "blame the victim" scenario. This blame-shifting theme fits readily with denial of responsibility and loss of self-control attributable to raging adolescent hormones:

> I'm waiting for the truth. You had sex with this girl. Something happened in the laundry room, then got out of hand? Understand, I'm a guy too. You know, I understand this stuff. Things happen. Been with a girl before, want a little action, and get 'em over there, try to get frisky with her and stuff. Things get a little further than you want to be. Things like that happen. Told her you wanted to talk to her alone. Escorted her back down the hallway. Took her back in the laundry room. Acting a little frisky. Kissing. Caressing. Kiss her on the breast in there. Get all worked up. And you get all worked up, get all hot and heavy. Decide to go take it a little further. You're thinking, "Ah, heck, this girl's down with it, man. She'll give me some sex when I need it." Right? You're a seventeen-year-old guy. You get horny, right?

Because of youths' discomfort with sexual matters, officers explained that sex crimes particularly lend themselves to minimization or blame-the-victim tactics. One officer explained,

> I minimize the crime. Because I'm dealing unfortunately with a lot of sex-related cases, I'll get to their level, and say, "I can understand why you did what you did with your sister. She's really attractive, and

I can understand what you're saying," if that's what he's saying. I'll try to bond with him in that way, because a lot of times, they'll start thinking they're talking to someone who's like them. And they'll start to spill their guts to you and completely forgetting that you're the officer. You're just somebody that's talking to them about things they understand.

Some officers expressed discomfort with using neutralization tactics such as blaming the victim. One officer observed, "I kind of do have a problem with some of that. Say it's a sex-abuse case: 'Well, you know, she was curious,' that sort of thing. I just personally—I feel dirty about that. I don't like it. With the violent crimes, I don't like putting myself in that spot on tape minimizing robbery or sex abuse."

Another officer said that he eschews minimization tactics because he does not "want a person of that age to be under the impression they're not in trouble, and then they're in a lot of trouble." Minnesota's training manual for the recorded interview discourages minimization tactics.[46]

Self-defense is another well-recognized criminal excuse, and officers offered a youth involved in a gang shooting this less serious explanation for his behavior: "You know who pulled the gun. If you pull the gun because you're afraid of getting stabbed, then that's a whole different ball game, isn't it?" Several officers reported they use neutralization techniques routinely and gave thematic examples: "The stuff with property crimes or theft, that's a lot easier to do, especially if it's like, 'Hey, you took the car. You weren't going to keep it or strip it. You just needed to get a ride. It was cold out. We can understand that.'"

The Reid Method recommends use of an "alternative question" when interrogators develop a theme. An alternative question is one that offers a "guilty suspect the opportunity to start telling the truth by making a single admission. The alternative question is one that presents to the suspect a choice between two explanations for possible commission of the crime."[47] An alternative question elicits an incriminating admission by enabling the person to adopt a less reprehensible reason for his or her behavior: "And what I guess I'm wondering, Patrick, is are you kind of a habitual thief who it's just in your blood and you steal just because you enjoy stealing, or am I looking at a kid here who was having some tough times, has been in and out of some foster homes, and was on the run this summer and needed some money?"

2. APPEAL TO SELF-INTEREST

Police appealed to juveniles' self-interest in about one-tenth (11.9%) of cases and identified benefits they might derive from confessing their crime. Police suggested that juveniles would experience immediate emotional relief and feel better after they confessed. They opined that prosecutors and judges view more favorably youths who confess than those who lie or deny involvement. And they intimated that if a judge has a more favorable impression of a youth, then the judge might be inclined to deal with the youth more leniently. Psychologists describe these types of tactics as implied promises of leniency that might induce an innocent person to confess falsely.[48]

Interrogators referred to the burden of emotional guilt—a weight on a juvenile's heart or shoulders. If a youth admitted responsibility, then it would help him or her set the burden down—an emotional expiation. Officers assured juveniles that they would convey their feelings of remorse to the authorities:

> I know from my heart that you got a boulder on your shoulder about the size of Mount Everest. I mean, you gotta feel like the whole weight is on your shoulders. I know you do. I've been here before with people. I know how you feel. But you gotta trust me when I tell you I need the truth, and I don't mean part of the truth. I need the whole truth, and I'll write the truth as you give it. And if after you tell me the truth, you tell me you're sorry, I'm gonna write down that you said you're sorry. That you never wished it would have happened.

Police told juveniles that the prosecutors who charge and recommend sentences react more favorably to youths who cooperate, tell the truth, or assist officers:

> I know all the prosecuting attorneys up there, all the juvenile attorneys. I could say, "Hey, you're cooperative. You're helping us get stuff back. You're showing us something. You're showing us something. You're making a step in the right direction." How do you think that looks? Rather than sitting there like a hard-ass: "No, I didn't do it." And then you wait to be convicted. You wait to be found guilty of something with a bad attitude. You know, that doesn't look good.

They advised juveniles that judges view suspects who assume responsibility in a more positive light:

> If you did something that you know you shouldn't have, and you 'fess up to it and tell me everything that happened, and you express remorse, and you acknowledge that it was a stupid kid thing to do, a mistake, that is going to be seen way more favorably than sticking with this story that you have come up with and making me put that down on the report and presenting it to a judge. Put yourself in the judge's shoes. If you were going to give leniency, do you think that you would give it to the guy who is obviously lying through his teeth and all of the evidence speaks 180 degrees opposite of what he was saying, or would you rather give a little leniency to the guy who is stepping up to the plate, acknowledging the stupid kid mistake that he did, and is willing to acknowledge that he screwed up?

If judges view juveniles who assume responsibility more favorably, then they might treat them more leniently:

> I'll tell you though, if the judge thinks you're lying, the consequences are much more severe than if the judge thinks you're telling him the truth. There's a big difference going in there in front of a guy and trying to cop the bad-boy attitude, thinking that this is not big thing, than it is going in there a humbled man, ready to accept the consequences for his actions, and taking it like a man and moving on, and making it a mistake so you can gain some life experience out of it. That's the difference.

Police intimated that they had direct access and could convey information about the youth to the judge: "I can't say how many times I've talked to judges and can say, 'Yeah, Tom seemed remorseful' or 'Tom was cooperative. Tom gave me his side.' And I can't say how many times I've talked to judges: 'This kid is an asshole.' I've said that too."

Officers' implications that personnel in the system view those who confess more favorably have some basis in reality. In chapter 5, I examine how juveniles' decisions to waive or invoke *Miranda* rights affected case processing. Prosecutors and judges felt that youths who assume responsibility and confess exhibit amenability to treatment and said that juveniles' cooperation garnered them some benefit on the margin in charging or sentencing.

3. EMPATHY AND UNDERSTANDING

Officers regularly expressed empathy and understanding for a youth's plight. An officer expressed concern about a juvenile's well-being and analogized his role to a counselor's rather than a criminal investigator's:

> You know, what we're trying to do here is to help you guys out. You're young, you're sixteen, you got your whole life ahead of you. I'm just trying to find out who was there so we can talk to them, so we can tell them, "You have to stop doing this because somebody's gonna get hurt." You know what counseling means? Okay, police do that too. We sometimes act as counselors, and we talk, like I'm here talking to you. I don't want to see this happen to you, because you know, at sixteen, you've got your whole life ahead of you.

A public defender corroborated the "counselor" role and described interrogators as comforting youths and reassuring them in a high-stress situation:

> The more serious the offense is, where the kid really knows they are in trouble, the cop will try to appeal to their need for comfort in that high-stress situation. They will say, "You know, I know you're a good guy. I know you are a good person in a bad situation. I know you want help. I know you never want to do this again." They kind of imply that they're not going to be going to prison for this; they're going to get some kind of help: "It's better to be honest about it so we can get you the help you need so you won't be in this situation again." One of the officers mentioned, "I have a kid your age. If you were my kid, this is what I'd want you to do." So they kind of use psychological tactics to tap into that insecurity of the kid or that need for comfort.

4. APPEAL TO HONOR: "IT TAKES A REAL MAN"

Officers frequently coupled appeals to tell the truth with offers to investigate further or work on behalf of a youth: "I'll respect you a lot more for telling me the truth than lying to me. We all make mistakes. I've made plenty over the years. But it takes a hell of a guy to admit to them and then get some help. And that what this is all about is getting some help." Officers used flattery and appeals to honor to induce admissions. Sometimes, flattery was as simple as "You're a good kid. You don't want to screw that up." In other cases, officers told juveniles that it takes "real guts" to admit guilt and urged them "to be a man":

> Time to stop acting like a child and take responsibility for the mistake that you guys made. Be a man. Tell me what happened. I am
> trying to help you here.

> So now's the time to be the man. And a real man can admit that he made mistakes. And this obviously is a big mistake that was made, right? And now's the time to start letting it out, figure things out. Let us take care of business. Let you take care of business so you can reconcile with this and carry on with your young life. Don't blame anybody else here but yourself. And that's what I'm trying to tell you is that now's the time for you to clear your conscience, clear your mind. Put it right down on the table. Tell me everything that happened from the start to the end, so we can take care of business.

5. MINIMIZE SERIOUSNESS

A person who aids, advises, conspires, or encourages another to commit a crime is liable as an accessory to the same extent as the perpetrator.[49] Despite accessorial liability, officers sometimes minimized juveniles' role or involvement to enable them to confess. While interviewing a youth who drove a getaway car, an officer suggested, "Your best chance right now is to be a witness to what happened" rather than a confederate. An officer questioned a youth, Jay-Jay, about a robbery and aggravated assault and suggested that if Jay-Jay beat the victim with a stick, then he could not be the person who shot him:

> So if I got a witness that says, "Jay-Jay hit him with a stick," and I say, "Jay-Jay, did you hit him with a stick?" [and] you say, "Yeah, I hit him with a stick," that means you can't be shooting him. That just proves that you didn't shoot the gun. Well, the only way we're gonna prove that is with your honesty, and you tell us the same story that corroborates with what the witnesses say. You're afraid to tell us that you hit him with the stick because you think that's a bad thing. The

bad thing here was shooting the man. There's a reason we brought you here first, right? Because you got the least to lose. You hit the man with a stick. That was it.

Minimizing seriousness emphasizes the relative triviality of youths' crime compared with the gravity of other delinquents' offenses:

> We've got your witnesses saying that "we see you coming out of the house with the stuff in your hands." We're not talking about your beating up anybody, okay? What we're talking about is you going into your neighbor's house, which you've already said that you went into your neighbor's house. All we need to know is your side of the story—I mean, error in judgment? People make it all the time. Now, it's not like you went in and robbed some old lady and beat her to death, okay? You went into someone house.

Even with a serious crime—a drive-by shooting—officers would suggest that it could have been worse if the shooter had hit the intended target. Officers minimized the seriousness of what happened—compared with what could have happened—and urged a youth to tell the truth: "All we want is the truth. The big thing is nobody got hurt here. I mean, this is a serious matter, but it could—it could be a lot worse. It really could. We just want the truth. Nobody, nobody got killed, nobody got hurt. I mean, this is still a serious thing. Everybody makes mistakes. But now is your time for you to tell your version of it. All we want is the truth."

The rationale of juvenile justice—treatment rather than punishment—provided officers with another theme to minimize seriousness. Both police and prosecutors reported that officers sometimes remind juveniles, "This is juvenile, not adult. You're not going to prison. The purpose of juvenile is rehabilitation, not punishment. We want to get you help." One officer told me,

> One of the tactics you use with sixteen- or seventeen-year-old kids is you can tell them, "Look, you're sixteen years old. You're not eighteen years old. We're not talking prison here. You need some help. You committed some serious offenses here, but we want to help you. We want to get you into a facility that's going to give you treatment, so you don't come back here as an eighteen-year-old and do this and end up in prison.

E. Multiple Interrogations

Police interviewed the vast majority (89.8%) of the juveniles in this study only once. They conducted a second interview if they talked with other suspects or obtained additional information and needed to clarify discrepancies. Supplemental interrogations occurred shortly after the initial interrogation because of time limits on how long police can hold youths in jail and how promptly prosecutors have to charge youths held in detention. Police attributed the infrequency of mutiple interrogations to time constraints and appointment of a public defender before they could question suspects again: "There's a small time window in there, because they're going to get counsel at a certain point, where you can't talk to them any longer, once the petitions get filed. So we've got that small window."

F. Closure

Toward the end of an interview, police asked youths whether they wanted to add to or clarify anything in their statement. More than three-quarters (75.1%) of interrogations ended with some type of closure question: "Is there anything else you would like to tell me?"; "Is there anything else you want to say?"; "Anything else you want on the record about this whole incident?" They told the juveniles, "It's just your opportunity to say whatever you want to say." Some officers asked juveniles to affirm the truthfulness of their statements: "Now is everything that you told me here today true?"

Officers also used closure questions to encourage juveniles to express sorrow or remorse. At the end of one interview, the officer reminded the juvenile, "You indicated to me ealier that you feel some remorse for what you've done. Do you want to tell me about that?" This prompted the juvenile to offer his appology: "I feel guilty for everything that I have done, and I am guilty for everything that I've done. And I feel ashamed of myself." Some juveniles combined their expressions of regret with rationalizations for their crime. UK training protocols recommend closure questions to maintain rapport with the suspect, to elicit complete information, and to create a positive impression on other justice system actors and fact-finders who subsequently review the interview.[50]

G. Free Will and Voluntary Statements

Any statement must be voluntary and not prompted by threats or promises. Some investigators concluded by asking a suspect whether the officer used any coercive influences to elicit the person's statement. "[T]he purpose of this postadmission influence technique is to create the appearance of a legally voluntary and factually reliable confession and thereby divert attention from the manipulative and potentially coercive interrogation methods that may have been used to elicit it."[51] After the closure question, more than one-third (37.5%) of officers asked whether the juvenile gave the statement of his or her own free will:

> Before we conclude this statement—I have made no threats, promises, anything like that for you to give me this statement, correct? And you've given this statement on your own free will?

> Has this been a true and accurate statement given of your own free will without any threats, promises, or inducements?

Officers attributed use of this closure to the *Miranda* cards and training provided by their departments or the county attorney. Several officers endorsed use of boilerplate voluntariness language to emphasize that they did not coerce a statement: "I do that to demonstrate that even though it's recorded, there is time when I'm with the child or with the suspect alone prior to the interviewing, and I want to make it clear to everybody that's listening to this tape that none of these threats took place. I don't threaten them, obviously, so I don't worry about that ending at all."

Other officers dismissed the voluntariness questions as surplussage. In their view, the tone and contents of the tape—the questions and answers—speak for themselves and demonstrate clearly that the statement was voluntary: "I think the interview itself will speak for itself." However, if officers stopped the tape during an interview—for example, to take a telephone call or to leave the interrogation room—when they resumed questioning, they would elicit a statement that no threats, promises, or inducements occurred while the recorder was turned off: "I just turned back on the tape recorder. When I turned off the recorder, did I promise you anything? [*No.*] Okay, did I have any conversation with you? [*No.*] And the reason why I shut off the tape recorder was to take a phone call? [*Yes.*]"

Conclusion

Police told the 285 youths in this study who waived *Miranda* that the interview was their opportunity to tell their story. Police described themselves as detached fact-finders who gather information and write reports. They encouraged youths to help create the record on which prosecutors and judges subsequently would rely.

Police questioned juveniles to elicit information. They used open-ended and closed-ended questions in every interview to give juveniles the chance to tell their story. They did not use leading questions frequently or extensively.

The Reid Method uses maxization and minimization techniques to weaken suspects' resistance and to encourage them to talk. Earlier research described the prevalence of both types of tactics in interrogations of adults,[52] and police used similar tactics with these older juveniles. In more than two-thirds (69.1%) of cases, they used one or more maximization tactic. In half the cases, they confronted youths with some type of evidence—eyewitness identification, physical evidence. In most cases, they possessed the evidence to which they referred. In others instance, they implied the existence of evidence—"What if I told you . . . ?" or "Would we find your DNA?" In about one-third of cases, officers confronted juveniles for lying (32.6%) and urged them to tell the truth (29.5%). The pervasiveness of Reid training was evident in more than one-quarter (28.8%) of cases in which officers used BAI questions to unsettle a suspect. In one-fifth of cases (20%), officers used confrontational tactics to increase a suspect's anxiety, and in one-seventh of cases (14.4%), they warned youths that their refusal to cooperate could adversely affect other people.

Officers used minimization tactics less frequently than they did maximization techniques. Police felt that minimizing seriousness or using blame-shifting themes did not play well on tape for fact-finders. They used techniques of neutralization (15.4%), appeals to self-interest (11.9%), empathy and understanding (10.5%), and appeals to honor (8.8%) only in a small proportion of cases. Officers questioned juveniles a second time in a small proportion of cases. Justice system time constraints somewhat limited opportunities for reinterrogation. Officers generally elicited incriminating information during the initial interview and did not require a second bite of the apple.

At the end of an interrogation, most police gave juveniles an open-ended opportunity to complete the record, to clarify any information, and to express remorse. More than one-third of officers concluded interrogations with boilerplate language to confirm that the youth's statement was voluntary. Chapter 5 analyzes how juveniles responded to these tactics.

Juveniles Respond to Interrogation

Outcomes and Consequences

This chapter examines how the 285 youths whom police questioned responded to their interrogators. Part I examines how they answered and how much information they provided. It analyzes their demeanor during questioning, how their attitude affected whether they cooperated or resisted, the evidentiary value of statements, and the length of interrogations. Part II focuses on how youths' decisions to waive or invoke *Miranda* affected outcomes and sentences. The criminal and juvenile justice systems rely heavily on plea bargains, and youths' admissions affect the balance of advantage between prosecutors and defense lawyers. The relationship between confessions and pleas highlights Packer's Crime Control model of justice with one critical difference. Although police interrogation involves an informal, administrative inquiry, in Minnesota it is a proceeding "on the record." *Scales* tapes enable prosecutors and defense lawyers to review and a judge at a suppression hearing to determine admissibility of a statement based on an objective record, rather than a swearing contest between police and youth.

CHAPTER FIVE

I. Juveniles' Responses to Interrogation

Chapter 4 examined how police questioned juveniles. Here, I assess how juveniles responded. First, I examine the forms of juveniles' responses—whether they gave positive or negative answers, whether they gave justifications or rationalizations for their behavior, and whether they sought information from police. I examine whether an interview produced a confession, admission, or denial. I assess how youths' attitudes influenced whether they confessed or denied and whether statements led police to new evidence—other offenders, witnesses, or physical evidence. Finally, I examine how long police questioned juveniles. One of the most important findings of this study is how brief routine felony interrogations are. I examine why police concluded most interrogations so quickly and identify factors associated with longer questioning.

A. Form of Responses

Juveniles responded to officers' questions in different ways. They did not give a single type of response, and their answers varied during an interview. I coded responses into five categories: short positive, extended positive, negative, rationalizing involvement, and seeking information.[1] The categories subsume both the length and content of responses. A juvenile's short positive response was agreeing with a question or making a brief factual statements. An extended positive response was a narrative that contained a juvenile's version of events—that is, they told their story —if the response was three sentences or longer. A rationalization could be contained in either a short or long response in which a juvenile provided an explanation or justification, minimized his or her role, minimized the seriousness of the offense, or apportioned responsibility to other parties. Juveniles' negative responses—short or extended—included denials, rejection of assertions, inability to remember, or claim of lack of knowledge. Finally, juveniles sought information from police about details of the investigation or what would happen to them.

Table 5.1 reports that in nearly every case (97.2%), juveniles gave at least some short positive responses to questions. They provided brief accounts or explanations or agreed with officers' assertions or statements. Short responses may or may not have contained incriminating admissions. In about two-thirds (65.6%) of cases, juveniles told their story or gave a version of events that rationalized or excused the crime or adopted themes suggested by interrogators. In such instances, juveniles minimized their role, offered a reason for their actions, played down the seriousness of the offense, blamed the victim, or decided to "do their time" without implicating others. Nearly two-thirds (64.6%) of juveniles gave extended narratives. An extended narrative often contained a rationlization. In more than one-third of cases (37.2%), juveniles gave negative responses to some or all the questions. Negative responses took several forms: disputing assertions, rejecting inferences, denying involvement, denying knowledge, being unable to remember, or selectively refusing to answer. Juveniles sought information from police in less than one-quarter of cases (22.8%). They asked about facts gleaned during the investigation, the likely disposition

Table 5.1
Form of Juveniles' Responses

Response	N	%
Short positive	277	97.2
Rationalization	187	65.6
Extended positive	184	64.6
Negative—denial	106	37.2
Seeking information	65	22.8

of their case, or the likelihood of release from custody. Different forms of responses were not mutually exclusive, and juveniles made several types during an interview.

Short positive. Juveniles gave several different types of positive responses, and those inclined to cooperate with police typically did so from the outset. For example, when an officer investigating criminal sexual conduct asked a juvenile why he was being questioned, the youth responded, "Because I sexually offended a foster kid at my foster home." One officer contrasted the lengths of juveniles' and adults' responses and hypothesized that the adolescent "brain isn't developed enough to go into long stories, and they can't think quick enough. So they do give shorter answers than adults."

Rationalization. Police sometimes used themes to neutralize offenders' guilt or to justify or excuse their conduct. Juveniles employed similar rationales to minimize responsibility, to minimize the seriousness of the offense, or to blame the victim. About two-thirds (65.6%) of juveniles used neutralizations to excuse or explain themselves. For example, a girl minimized her role in a burglary by suggesting that her confederate misunderstood her: "I was joking around at first, and I was like, 'Oh, yeah, whatever.' I was joking at first, you know." Juveniles minimized the seriousness of robberies by insisting that they did not use loaded weapons or took precautions not to hurt their victim: "Let's make an understanding of this. I didn't want no one to get hurt. In the first place, the safety was on the whole time. And it wasn't a gun; it was a BB gun." Juveniles involved in group crimes emphasized their minor role in the crime. For example, youths untutored in the law of accessorial liability more readily admitted to serving as a lookout rather than to participating in an armed robbery. A juvenile who committed a home burglary with other youths insisted that he did not personally remove any of the stolen items: "I didn't steal nothin'. I didn't take nothin' out of the house. So therefore I didn't rob the house. I was there, yeah." Because juveniles often commit their crimes in groups, they invoke peer pressure to excuse or explain their actions. During several interrogations, youths claimed to be victims of negative peers and bad influences: "They're just the wrong crowd to hang around with. Because they're always making me do the wrong—the wrong decisions."

Negative responses. In more than one-third (37.2%) of cases, juveniles disputed officers' assertions or rejected their claims. When an officer asked a youth the location of a stocking mask worn during an armed robbery, he vehemently denied involvement: "I don't have no stocking over my head. I keep telling you that. I did not have no stocking on my head." A girl whom police charged with assaulting a female officer claimed that the police attacked her: "She was grabbing on me, hitting me, and everything else, and I'm trying to get her off of me. Then they sprayed me with mace, and then they pinned me with bats and stuff. I didn't hit her. The police were fighting with me." Sometimes, juveniles responded to officers' questions with partial silence. Other juveniles' responded negatively to protect confederates—to "do their own time" without implicating others: "Do the time and get out. What's the point of havin' both of us in here. I'm gonna still be in here, so what's the point of having Brad in." Others did not want their confederates to know that they had implicated them: "I don't want any of my boys hearing this stuff, what you're going to tell them, like this tape." Police obtained incriminating admissions even when juveniles responded negatively. When one juvenile was questioned about his role in a robbery, he insisted, "I just acted as lookout. That's all. I did not go in the store."

Seeking information. Youths had many questions about the interrogation process. Some officers opened their interview with a question such as "Do you know why you're here?" to which a juvenile responded, "Yeah, that's what I want to know: why am I here?" Often youths feigned ignorance of the reasons for their arrest: "Do I have a right to know what kind of charges I'm being against or why I'm here? Nobody said anything to me when they picked me up off the street. They just kind of ran up, grabbed me, and threw me in the back of the cop car. I have no idea what's going on." Youths sought information about the progress of the investigation or their disposition. They asked about the status of their victims: "I just want [to] know, is Richie alive or not?" They wanted to know about the arrest status of other youths: "Was I the only one that was taken to jail?" They offered to cooperate with police to secure release from custody: "There wouldn't be any way I could get out of here fast if I helped you all out?" Some juveniles' inquiries resembled the reinitiation of interrogation described in *Oregon v. Bradshaw*: "What's going to happen to me now?"[2] At the end of an interrogation, juveniles asked how prosecutors or judges would view their cases: "So what's going to happen? What's the worst thing that can happen?" Juveniles expressed concern about how a judge would react: "When I ask you if I'm going to jail, I mean after all this."

B. Outcomes and Attitudes

The outcome of an interrogation is classified based on the evidentiary value of a statement.[3] I coded interrogation outcomes into three categories: confessions, admissions, and denials. Confessions were when juveniles admitted that they committed the crime and provided supporting details or when their cumulative responses satisfied the elements of the offense—that is, provided all the facts necessary to convict offenders. Admissions linked youths to a crime or provided direct or circumstantial evidence of an element of the offense. Admissions often occurred when a getaway driver, lookout, or codefendant admitted participating but minimized his or her role or responsibility. Denials were when juveniles disavowed knowledge or responsibility or gave an explanation that did not include any incriminating admissions. In addition to the evidentiary values of youths' statements, they sometimes provided leads to other corroborating evidence.

1. OUTCOMES

a. Confessions

Table 5.2 reports outcomes of interrogations: confessions, admissions, and denials. A majority (58.6%) of juveniles confessed and admitted their involvement in all of the elements of the offense. Most confessed at the outset or within a few minutes of waiving their *Miranda* rights. They did not require any prompting by police. As one officer said, "A lot of kids seem to admit right away. It seems like the majority of kids admit right away." Another officer confirmed, "I would say most people give it up within a minute or two." For example, one officer opened with "Do you know why you're here today?" and the girl replied, "I stole my grandpa's car without asking him."

Research in Britain confirms that the majority of suspects confess; in that study, "almost all did so near the beginning of the interviews."[4] UK

Table 5.2

Outcome of Interrogation, Corroborating Evidence, and Youths' Attitude*

	All youths		Cooperative youths		Resistant youths	
	N	%	N	%	N	%
Outcome						
Confession	167	58.6	162	71.4	5	8.6
Admission	85	29.8	57	25.1	28	48.3
Denial	33	11.6	8	3.5	25	43.1
Total	285	100.0	227	79.6	58	20.4
Corroborating evidence provided	52	18.2				

* Statistically significant at $\chi^2(1, N = 285) = 7.84, p < .001$

analysts suggest that "suspects enter a police interview having already decided whether to admit or deny the allegations against them," and interrogation tactics have little impact on whether they subsequently confess.[5] Police whom I interviewed corroborated the UK findings: "Most people when they come into the interrogation room, they want to tell you something. It's just a matter of getting them to tell you the truth. If you go into a room, they'll tell you something. It's what you believe when you leave the room that matters." An officer with more than two decades' experience said, "I have to strain to remember kids who didn't confess."

Police in this study sometimes used leading questions to complete a confession and to obtain legal closure. Legal closure entails a "question which seeks to ensure that the suspect provides verbal proof of one element of an offence in a single answer."[6] Closure questions typically elicited the intent element of an offense—for example, in an assault, "What was your intent with your knife [pressed against victim]?" and, in a burglary, "Did you have permission from the owner when you went into the building?" An officer investigating a youth for a burglary in which he stole guns asked a sequence of questions—each of which elicited an affirmative response—to establish the youth's intent and awarness of wrongfulness: "And you knew what you were doing was wrong? But you knew that when you agreed to take that gun home that day for him, that was wrong? You knew what you were doing was stealing? You work with guns, so you know that stealing a gun is a high-level crime?"

b. Admissions

An additional one-third (29.8%) of juveniles provided statements of some evidentiary value, for example, admitting that they served as a lookout during a robbery or participated with others during a burglary even if they did not personally steal property. Officers agreed that most juveniles give them at least some incriminating information: "Most of them will pretty much tell you the whole truth, but not necessarily all the truth. They may still want to hide a little bit of what they did because they know they were wrong. It could be very embarrassing for them." A judge observed that when police question juveniles, "they just talk. They just cough it up. Some of them are deceitful and more clever, but they still talk. Some of them think they can talk their way out of it, but they're dealing with a professional investigator, and that normally doesn't end well for them."

c. Denials

Only a small proportion (11.6%) of juveniles denied involvement or made no incriminating admissions. Without invoking *Miranda* outright, forms of resistance included juveniles' claiming lack of knowledge, denying culpability, lying, evading, or shifting blame. One prosecutor described these youths as "a stubborn subset that is conduct disordered." A police officer described them as "your hard-core kid. You can talk to them until you're blue in the face, but they have it set in their mind that they're not going to confess or admit what their involvement was." Another prosecutor attributed resistant youths' posture to criminal sophistication: "There's outright defiance, which is a small subset. That again is the repeat offenders—we call them 'frequent flyers' in the system."

d. Accounting for Success

Other studies corroborate the high rate of successful questioning reported here. Richard Leo observed successful outcomes in three-quarters (76%) of cases in which adult suspects waived *Miranda*.[7] The Yale–New Haven study reported that about two-thirds (64%) of interrogations produced incriminating evidence.[8] A survey of police investigators estimated that two-thirds (68%) of suspects made incriminating statements.[9] An analysis of 177 taped UK interrogations reported that police received confessions in 40% of cases and obtained admissions in another 25%.[10] Other research in the United Kingdom reports an interview success rate of 77%, ranging from 64% to 97% among various police stations.[11] A study of juvenile interrogations in England reported, "In 76.8 per cent of cases suspects readily confessed. . . . Indeed, this open admission usually occurred in the first sentence or so of the interview."[12] In a study of delinquents held in detention, more than half (55%) retrospectively reported that they had confessed.[13]

I had planned to analyze tactics police used to provoke changes during an interrogation—for example, from an initial denial to a subsequent admission. I could not do so because the majority of youths admitted some degree of involvement from the outset, and very few changed their stories under questioning. UK research reports only 3% of suspects changed from denial to admission during interrogation, and analysts attributed few of those changes to the effectiveness of the interviewer.[14] "The great majority of suspects stick to their starting position—whether admission, denial, or somewhere in between—regardless of how the interview is conducted."[15]

A review of six hundred recorded interviews found that only twenty suspects changed stories, and fewer than half those changes resulted from interviewers' tactics.[16]

Interviews with police corroborated a high level of successful interrogations: "I'm going to say 80%–90% give me something." Another officer agreed, "If a juvenile talks to you and you know what you're doing, you should be able to get full or at least partial confessions." Several police officers echoed the theme "a lie is as good as the truth" and felt that as long as a suspect talked, an interrogation could be successful: "A lying statement is just about as good as a confession. As long as they talk to you, you've got a case. If they confess, that's icing on the case, but if they lie, that's almost as good." One prosecutor described the majority of youths as "very cooperative, and [they] go along with and pretty much spill their guts and tell what happened." Another prosecutor attributed some of the police success to the inexperience of many young offenders: "Some of them will break down and just confess. Some of them, right from the beginning, they tend to be naïve, no experience with the system." Another prosecutor said that juveniles are not as adept liars as are adults: "Some of it has to do with kids probably can't keep their story straight as well as adults in general, and they may end up inadvertently making admissions."

Justice system professionals attributed juveniles' proclivity to confess fully to several factors: proper socialization, a desire to tell the truth, lack of appreciation of consequences, emotional needs, or the compulsive pressures of interrogation. Officers attributed some juveniles' willingness to confess to respect for authority: "Most kids are taught growing up, 'Respect authority, and if a cop asks you a question, you answer it.' So those kinds of kids, when the cop is asking a question, they've been trained to answer that question." Guilty youths confessed as a form of expiation. Several officers commented that juveniles confess readily because they think, "I really want to get this off my chest. I made a mistake. I screwed up, and I need to tell them, 'This is why I screwed up.' I want an honest representation of myself and why I did what I did."

Officers attributed juveniles' readiness to confess to differences in judgment between adolescents and adults. Youths lack a sense of self-preservation (long-term consequences) and respond more readily to their present situation (short-term consequences): "I don't think they're thinking, 'I need to protect myself. I need to make sure I don't go to jail.' They're in the here and now: 'It feels good to be talking to you,' or 'It feels good to brag about this now." Whereas adults often make tactical admissions to mitigate responsibility, police reported that juveniles confess more fully:

> I think juveniles when they finally accept responsibility, my experience is they're far more relieved when they can now start sharing openly, and they don't have to try to cover for what they done. When they finally say, "Oh, my God, I did it," when they go—when they finally admit, "I'm responsible for this," it's almost like they're in for a penny, in for a pound. They're far more forthright, far more cooperative showing me the gun, giving me the stuff. I think when someone says, "I done it," unlike adults, I think kids are far more forthright at that point.

Officers sometimes described their role as "counselors," and justice system personnel attributed their interrogative success to their ability to address youths' emotional needs. A public defender observed that officers' rapport with youths encourages them to confess more fully than adults do:

> You know, a lot of these kids are so damaged and estranged from their family of origin, it's almost like they're looking for anyone to stand in as a parental figure. I find that a lot of kids are much more forthcoming with information if the cop comes off as a nice guy that wants to help them, that sees the good in them, sees their potential —a lot of kids will disclose under those circumstances.

A judge concurred that juveniles respond to an empathetic officer more fully than do adults because of their emotional needs:

> A lot of these kids have no dads. And there's a lot of very tough love going on—the mothers who say, "I have to whup him so he won't be part of a gang." So these cop figures seem like teachers—kind, patient, gentle: "They're not going to hurt me if I tell them I did something bad." And these kids are emotionally needy, a lot of them, and that still plays in, because they're still at—if they were adults—the same person as an adult is now hardened and defiant and hates the system. These kids are still trying to do good, and the confession is a way to do good.

Miranda focused on the inherent coercion of custodial interrogation. Several officers attributed juveniles' haste to confess to those pressures: "They're usually itchy when they sit for that hour and half or two hours before you go to interview them. They're hot messes in the jail cell. They're so scary for a kid. They so desperately want to talk to someone. Nine out of ten of them are just spewing before you get an opportunity." Similarly, a judge attributed the fulsomeness of youths' statements to the inherent stress of interrogation: "I think people forget, because we've never been there, how intimidating it is to deal with law enforcement in a room: knowing you can't leave, knowing you're in trouble, serious trouble. Mostly, you're thinking, "How do you get out of here?" And most people want to talk." For whatever reasons—honesty, feelings of guilt, failure to appreciate consequences, emotional bonding, or compulsive pressures—justice personnel perceived that delinquents confess more readily and fully than adults do.

2. ATTITUDE

Criminologists have studied the interplay of juveniles' attitudes and police responses for decades. Police officers' discretion is greatest when they deal with less serious crimes and in low-visibility settings. In those situations, whether police arrest a person hinges, in part, on whether a person shows appropriate deference.[17] When police interact with citizens, they must establish immediate control of the situation, and they expect people to defer to their authority.[18] For less serious offenses, deferential offenders reduce their likelihood of arrest, while contumacious youths or adults increase it.[19] "Within a considerable range, police judgment of substantive misconduct will be mitigated by expressions of diffidence on the part of young people and aggravated by their arrogance."[20] In nonfelony encounters, police rely on behavioral cues such as juveniles' attitude as an indicator of their moral character—juveniles' demeanor substantially affects arrest decisions.[21] Ethnographic studies of police and probation officers' interactions with youths observed that their attitudes affected how officials perceived them, judged their moral character, and responded to them.[22] When decisions are contingent on attitude and demeanor, minority youths typically fare worse than their white counterparts do.[23]

Police reported that juveniles' attitudes range the gamut: "some are scared to death, and others, it's almost a joke." Many officers described youths as scared, especially "the kids that are new to the process." For youths with more experience, "a lot of them try to play tough; they're not going to show you anything." Another officer surmised that "adults go through the criminal justice system, and they've learned their role. Kids are still learning the ropes and are almost more confrontational, if they're going to be confrontational, more so than adults." One officer used the term "felony mouth" to describe "kids trying to be men who have no men in their lives." One consequence is that "cops take them to jail to teach them who is boss. Felony mouth will get you a ride to the jail."

Although officers described some youths as confrontational, they characterized most youths as compliant or submissive: "I would say that 90% or more would probably be cooperative, and the other percentage would be the frequent fliers, so to speak." One officer observed, "For the most part, most kids are pretty humble. They know they got caught. It's their opportunity to tell the truth. They just tell it. Most are humbled to a certain extent. They just want to get it over with, just tell what happened, and we can move on." One officer observed, "You can kind of tell the kids who are the first time in the interview room—just the look in their eyes, kind of deer in the headlights." Public defenders described most juveniles as defeated or beaten down when they confess:

> Most of the time, they're just sort of very monotone. I almost feel like I'm watching someone that's just given up. There's kind of a hopelessness to being interviewed by police. Occasionally, you get the really conduct-disordered kids who really cop an attitude, but they're the exception to the rule. Most of the kids are fighting off the tears, maybe trying to act tough, but very monotone. On the videos, their heads are down. They just feel like they've already been beat.

Attitude is a well-established criminological variable, and juveniles' demeanor affects the process and outcome of questioning. Ethnographers acknowledge the importance and difficulty of characterizing attitude: "rude or impolite, aggressive or passive, laughter or tears, and the like."[24] Juveniles in this study exhibited many attitudes during interrogation— for example, cooperative, polite, distressed, remorseful, frightened, sad, nonchalant, cocky, resistant, aggressive, and confrontational. Their demeanor fluctuated during questioning—defiant one minute and cooperative the next.

Characterizing a youth's attitude from a tape or transcript entails an impressionistic, subjective judgment. Fortunately, police reports frequently included comments about juveniles' demeanor and behavior during interrogation. Officers reported whether they believed suspects told the truth or lied and whether juveniles cooperated or resisted. One officer reported that the juvenile "was cooperative. He stated he was sorry he stole the items." Another described a youth as "cooperative and forthright throughout the interview." Another depicted a youth as "not very cooperative. He was kind of just sit there and stare down at his legs. Nathan was not very forthcoming with the information." Police told the youths that their attitude and responses could affect how the justice system treated them: "For what it's worth, two people were arrested. If that guy spills the beans, tell me everything I ask him—because you won't—if he does, he looks more cooperative than you. And you're okay with that? Because I'm going to mark you down as uncooperative."

Officers' reports described youths' emotional responses: "Marvin's demeanor during my interview showed no remorse. Marvin at times had a flat affect and at other times appeared to be slightly amused by my questions." Police reports detailed youths' behavior as well as demeanor. An officer depicted a juvenile as "increasingly agitated during the interview": "His demeanor varied between sarcastic and angry. [He] became increasingly hostile and asked for a lawyer, and I ended the interview. As he was leaving the room, he turned in the doorway and glared at me and was yelling obscenities."

Based on my impressions and officers' reports, I categorized youths' overall attitude as cooperative or resistant. Other research has used similar categories and has described 80% of suspects as cooperative:[25] "It may have been that many of these suspects were less than wholly open or truthful when being questioned, but in their general attitude and manner most were polite and pleasant enough."[26] Juveniles may cooperate for many reasons—a desire to act decently in social interactions, fear and anxiety, dependency on authority figures, or coercive pressures—but most exhibit positive attitudes. One public defender described youths' attitude as "trusting, which is kind of strange, but not so strange, when you think about how we generally raise children to believe they can trust a police officer."

Table 5.2 reports that the majority of juveniles (79.6%) in this study exhibited a cooperative demeanor, and only one-fifth (20.4%) appeared resistant—results identical to those reported in the United Kingdom.[27] Not surprisingly, the vast majority (96.5%) of cooperative juveniles confessed or made incriminating admissions. As one officer observed, "I would say most of them end up in some sort of confession at some point. It might not be the full-blown thing. They might minimize what their involvement [was]. But in reality, they're confessing." A judge described the relationship between youths' attitudes and admissions: "Some people think they can outsmart the cop and lie their way out of it. Some people feel bad and want to 'fess up. And some people are intimidated, I'm sure. But the sense I have is that a real significant number of the people who are choosing to talk to the cop are, by definition, going to be the cooperative group."

Officers recognized that some juveniles cooperate out of a desire to please: "You have to be on guard for them saying what they think you want to hear. They don't think of it as lying. They think of it as trying to please."

One-fifth (20.4%) of these juveniles resisted their interrogators. Of those, fewer than than one-tenth (8.5%) confessed, and almost half (43.1%) provided no useful admissions. One-tenth (11.6%) of youths denied involvement. However, three-quarters (75.8%) of those who did so exhibited resistant attitudes. The low proportion of deniers (11.6%) and resisters (20.4%) suggests that most youths who waive *Miranda* succomb to the compulsive pressures of interrogation.

3. CORROBORATING EVIDENCE

Police interrogate suspects to elicit confessions and admissions or to obtain stories that prosecutors later can use to impeach testimony. Suspects' answers may provide leads to other evidence, for example, witnesses, co-offenders' identity, or the like. Some analysts assert that "a principal purpose—if not the primary purpose—of interrogation is to obtain information such as the location of physical evidence."[28] By contrast, others have observed that "police rarely obtained incriminating fruits."[29]

Table 5.2 reports the proportion of cases in which interrogation yielded corroborating evidence. I defined corroborating evidence conservatively as information which police did not possess prior to questioning—for example, leads to physical evidence, a crime-scene diagram, or the identity of a co-offender. By this criterion, fewer than one-fifth (18.2%) of interviews yielded new information, and gathering collateral evidence appears to be a secondary goal of interrogators.

Most commonly, juveniles identified other participants in their offense. Police conducted photo lineups and asked juveniles to identify their confederates: "I want you to look at this and tell me if you recognize anybody in this photo lineup." Some juveniles drew diagrams of the crime scene and described where each participant stood. An officer showed a juvenile surveillance video and asked him to identify others present: "We're just walking across the hall to my office, and I'm gonna pull up these videos on my hard drive. Come around here and watch this. Who is that on the video? [*That's Adam.*] And who's that? [*That's me.*] That's you with the hat on, right? And who's that? [*That's Casey.*] Casey with the hat on? [*Yeah.*]" Juveniles sometimes provided officers with leads to physical evidence—for example, recovery of stolen property—and in a few cases, police accompanied them to recover guns.

Some police attributed the paucity of corroborating evidence to time pressure and the volume of cases. Police usually obtained a confession or admission quickly, and they did not press youths for more evidence in less serious cases: "They're used to, 'All right you gave it to me. I don't need anything else. We're out of this room.' If, had the cop asked one more question down the road—'Did you tell anyone else about that?'—that does not show up because it's not part of those cases."

Although prosecutors confirmed that interrogations do not often lead to corroborating evidence, they attributed the lack of productivity to good police work: "I don't see that very often. I don't know if that's because by the time the police talk to that suspect they have done such a good job with their investigation that they have everything else, but I don't see very often that it leads to other evidence." Both police and prosecutors said that statements often provide the basis to obtain search warrants, which produce additional corroborating evidence.

C. Constructing Culpability

Leo argues that after officers induce a suspect to admit or confess, they must then collaborate to "create a persuasive narrative of the suspect's culpability that transforms the fledgling admission into a full-formed confession."[30] The interrogator shapes suspects' version further to incriminate and strengthen the case against them. Investigators and suspects must incorporate five elements into an admission for it to appear genuine and compelling: "(1) a coherent, believable story line, (2) motives and explanations, (3) crime knowledge (both general and specific), (4) expressions of emotions, and (5) acknowledgment of voluntariness."[31]

Most of these elements emerged naturally during the interrogations in this study. For example, youths' extended narratives and rationalizations provided motives and explanations and typically included general and specific crime knowledge. Closure questions enabled juveniles to express emotions, for example, sorrow or remorse. About one-third of officers asked youths to acknowledge the voluntariness of their statements.

However, once investigators elicited a statement, they did not recapitulate or shape the story—the tapes spoke for themselves.

D. Length of Interrogation

False confessions arise almost invariably as the outcome of lengthy interrogations. It takes a long time and rigorous questioning to elicit a false confession—a minimum of six hours and more commonly twelve to eighteen hours.[32] Are lengthy interrogations common? Or are lengthy interrogations and the concommitant risk of false confessions outliers from routine questioning? If the latter, then time limits on interrogation length may be necessary to protect people from coerced confessions and to preserve the integrity of the justice process.

I directly timed the length of recorded interrogation in some cases. And in most of the interrogations for which I had transcripts, officers stated the start and stop times at the beginning and ending of questioning. For transcript interrogations without start-stop times, I estimated the duration of interrogation from the length of the transcript by cross-tabulating the number of transcript pages and length of interrogation of those for which I had both measures. I always rounded time estimates up to the longer interval. Table 5.3 reports the length of time that police questioned these juveniles, the duration by type of offense and by whether the offense involved a gun.

Table 5.3

Length of Interrogation by Type of Offense* and Weapon**

Time	Overall		Person		Property		Drug		Firearms		Other	
(minutes)	N	%	N	%	N	%	N	%	N	%	N	%
1–15	220	77.2	62	67.4	131	83.4	15	93.8	9	60	3	60
16–30	38	13.3	20	21.7	13	8.3	1	6.3	3	20	1	20
31+	27	9.5	10	10.9	13	8.3	0	0.0	3	20	1	20
Total	285		92		157		16		15		5	

All Cases Involving Guns

Time	Overall		Cases without guns		Cases with guns	
(minutes)	N	%	N	%	N	%
1–15	220	77.2	192	80.3	28	60.9
16–30	38	13.3	29	12.1	9	19.6
31+	27	9.5	18	7.5	9	19.6
Total	285		239		46	

* Statistically significant at $\chi^2(1, N = 285) = 32.3, p < .05$; ** statistically significant at $\chi^2(1, N = 285) = 9.4, p < .01$

Routine felony interrogations are brief. Police completed three-quarters (77.2%) of these interviews in less than fifteen minutes and concluded nine in ten (90.5%) in less than thirty minutes. Police questioned three youths (1.1%) for one and a half hours in the longest interviews. Even though prosecutors charged these youths with one or more felonies, police questioned the vast majority for short periods of time. Brief interrogations are unlikely to elicit false confessions. "[I]nterrogations conducted in low profile cases—the type of case likely to be collected in a random sample of interrogations—would be much less likely to produce a false confession. In low profile cases, interrogators are generally disinclined to expend the time or employ the range of tactics likely to produce an untrustworthy confession."[33]

Although the brevity of these interviews initially seemed surprising, other research confirms that interrogations of even two or three hours are exceptional and frequently problematic,[34] and Inbau and Reid warn against questioning suspects for more than four hours.[35] The 1967 Yale–New Haven study reported that police questioned suspects for fifteen minutes or less in 36% of cases, between sixteen and sixty minutes in 49% of cases, and for more than an hour in only 15% of cases.[36] Leo reported that police questioned one-third (34.6%) of suspects for less than thirty minutes, another one-third (36.6%) for one-half to one hour, and only one-quarter (28.7%) for more than one hour.[37] Paul Cassell and Bret Hayman reported that only 13% of interrogations took more than thirty minutes, and only one lasted longer than an hour.[38] "Observational studies have suggested that routine interrogations tend to be relatively brief encounters, with the modal duration ranging from 20 minutes to an hour."[39]

Research on interrogation of British juveniles reported that "[i]nterviews tended to be very brief with the majority taking less than fifteen minutes (71.4 per cent). Although the average length of interviews was around 14 minutes, the most frequent length was around 7 minutes."[40] Gisli Gudjonsson described several British studies which reported that police completed 80% of interviews in less than thirty minutes and 95% within one hour; they completed 99% of interviews within forty-five minutes; and they finished 93% within one hour.[41] An analysis of six hundred taped UK interrogations reported that "most were short and surprisingly amiable discussions" in which more than one-third of suspects confessed at the outset.[42] An analysis of forty adult interviews reported that police concluded all of them in between fifteen and sixty minutes.[43] A summary of studies reported that "[m]ost of the interviews were short (80% lasted less than 30 minutes; 95% were completed within 1 hour), the confession rate was 58%, little interrogative pressure was applied, and very few suspects who initially denied guilt eventually confessed."[44]

These brief interrogations seem far removed from popular perception of lengthy questioning depicted in television and movies. I asked justice professionals to estimate interrogation length, and they agreed: "They're actually very short." Their estimates confirm these findings: "I would think interviews are fifteen minutes"; "fifteen minutes"; "twenty or twenty-five minutes"; "ten to twenty minutes"; "maybe thirty minutes"; "less than fifteen minutes"; and "ten to fifteen minutes." One veteran officer reported, "My longest has maybe been an hour." Another officer confirmed, "Most of them are twenty minutes. With kids, seldom have I gone over an hour, most of them are ten, fifteen, twenty minutes." One judge opined, "fifteen or twenty minutes," a second judge confirmed, "usually ten to twenty minutes," and a third judge agreed, "It doesn't take very long to get them to 'fess up: twenty minutes." A prosecutor said interrogations are "very short, usually": "I would say under ten minutes, the vast majority under ten minutes." A public defender thought that "typical interrogations take thirty minutes," another confirmed, "twenty to thirty minutes," a third observed, "on average about twenty minutes," and a fourth agreed, "not more than twenty minutes." The longest estimate was that interrogations average "thirty to forty-five minutes." After eliciting these responses, I described my findings—three-quarters in fifteen minutes or less, 90% in half an hour or less—and they agreed that they are consistent with their experience.

Police and justice system personnel attributed the brevity of routine felony interrogations to several factors. Many professionals referred to workload pressures. One officer explained, "These guys are in the meat grinders. We got to get out of here. I got ten cases I got assigned today. Either you're going to give this up today—they don't ask the extra questions, once you told me you did it." Another officer suggested that police question suspects longer about serious cases but do not regard most juvenile felonies as serious crimes:

> When you get to a lot of the minor stuff—the shoplifting, the fights in school, and stuff like that—we get too many of them. The cops are trying to push through those. We've got two dozen cases sitting on our desk. You're not going to spend an hour or an hour and a half

with an assault in school. With an ag[gravated] robbery, you're going to take the time and effort—just more complexity to the crime. It doesn't take much time for Joe to tell me, "He said my girlfriend is ugly, so I punched him."

One prosecutor felt that police do not invest a lot of energy to questioning most juvenile suspects. Another prosecutor said that caseload volume and police staff reductions preclude extensive interviews with most juveniles: "It's a lack of resources now. They just don't have as much time to devote to juvenile cases unless they're really serious. I've kind of noticed that there isn't as much effort to try to—I'm not saying coerce a confession —but trying to get to the truth, not calling them on inconsistencies." Prosecutors agreed with *Hamlet*'s Polonius—"brevity is the soul of wit"—and felt that a shorter interview enhanced its credibility: "A good interrogation is a little bit on the shorter side, and it gets to the point. With a *Scales* tape, potentially you're going to be playing this tape for a judge or jury, and you want it to get to the point; you don't want to have a lot of extraneous stuff in there."

A juvenile court judge confirmed that workload pressures and the diminishing utility of longer interrogations contribute to their brevity: "Police are busy, and they're moving on with what they need to do. They're not there to socialize. They're there to get their job done and move on. They've got a ton of work to do in that case and lots of others. So they're trying to be efficient, and a longer interrogation probably wouldn't produce more than what they've already got." Another judge explained, "They're not going to do a two-hour interrogation in an auto theft. They do triage in terms of the level of time and energy they put into cases."

Several officers attributed brief interrogations to the relative simplicity of most youth crimes and their ability to elicit admissions quickly: "It's about a getting to the facts and walking out." They explained that most suspects confess without much prompting: "If you get them to tell you the truth, there ain't nothing else to talk about. Once you get the statement from them, once you get the story from them, that's all you need. You're not going to sit around and hold their hand all day. Here's the statement. Let's move on."

Some analysts attribute brevity of interrogations to premature closure.[45] Interrogators approach suspects with a predetermined theory or investigative hypothesis, and once they elicit facts that confirm their assumption, they conclude the interview. A public defender confirmed,

"They never ask more questions than they need to have the solution that they're looking for. I think they get what they're looking for, and they don't look for anything more than that, and they're very good at getting that." Similarly, a judge confirmed that "they're very successful in getting admissions from juveniles." Brevity and premature closure may pose a problem of confirmation bias—the tendency to seek out confirmatory facts and to disregard inconsistent or contradictory facts.

1. INTERROGATION AND GUNS

Detectives question suspects longer about more serious crimes. Leo reported that they were twice as likely to question suspects for more than one hour in high-seriousness crimes and three times as likely to conclude interviews in less than thirty minutes in low-seriousness crimes.[46]

In this study, statistically significant variations occurred in lengths of interrogation by type of offense. Police questioned larger proportions of youths charged with property and drug crimes for fifteen minutes or less than youths charged with other types of offenses. These crimes typically involve some physical evidence—drugs, stolen property, automobiles—which may provide police with more evidence with which to question juveniles.

Cases involving firearms resulted in significantly longer interrogations. Although police questioned only 9.5% of suspects for longer than thirty minutes, they interrogated twice as many (20%) juveniles charged with firearms offenses for longer than thirty minutes. Because of the small number of cases in which prosecutors charged youths only with a firearm crime (fifteen), I compared interrogation lengths in cases that involved guns—for example, armed robbery, aggravated assault, firearms possession, or burglary in which youths stole guns—with those that did not involve a gun. Some cases coded for guns included paintball guns (which put out a victim's eye) or pellet and replica BB guns (used in armed robberies) rather than real firearms. My earlier research only coded real firearms—handguns and rifles—and found a similar relationship between guns and interrogation length.[47]

Guns provide an indicator of an offense's seriousness.[48] A judge confirmed that by definition, a gun makes a crime serious: "Whenever there is a gun at large or a gun involved, particularly where there is a gun at large, everyone focuses in on that. That's kind of the cornerstone of what's a serious offense in this day and age." In the interrogations in this study, guns affected interrogation tactics as well as their length. Apart from the associated crime, police wanted to recover guns used or stolen by youths. They used aggressive maximization tactics (threats) and minimization techniqes (implied promises of lenience) to retrieve them:

> Well, I don't give a flying fuck about this morning [burglaries]. But I want that gun. I don't care who took it. I just want it. Or you're going to burn, I'm telling you. I will personally go to the judge with this and see that the court just—I want that gun off the street. I don't want it floating in your place. I don't want it floating with Bernard, Trey, or anybody else. So if you know where that piece is, now would be the real good time to tell me about it.

Officers referred to the benefits that would accrue to a youth who helped to recover a gun—implied promises or inducements: "Now if you made a goodwill effort and if I got the gun, certainly I would mention that to the county attorney that you helped out in retrieving that gun. Will that help you? I say that Sam helped me out getting the gun, and I don't think I could have found the gun without his help. You tell me, does that help you? Yeah, it would help you a lot."

In addition to threats or implied benefits, police described the dangers that guns pose to people who hold them, those around them, and other potential victims. Police used variations of the tactic in *Rhode Island v. Innis*, in which the officer expressed concen that "God forbid one of them [handicapped children] might find a weapon with shells and they might hurt themselves."[49] An officer warned a youth of the dangers the gun posed to innocent bystanders: "We know that that gun is out there. That gun hasn't been recovered. At least help me find where the gun is, so a young, innocent kid doesn't pick that up and hurt himself or someone else. Just imagine if that is your younger brother or sister. Just imagine if that was your brother or sister: how would you feel if that gun got into their hands?" Officers advised youths that they could be held responsible for crimes that other people committed with the guns they had stolen. An officer gave a gun-burglary suspect a *Miranda* warning and then delivered an extended monologue:

> The biggest thing that I don't want to see happen is to see you get in any worse trouble than you're in right now. Does that make sense? So it's sorta like you stole a car, and you got caught for it, and you're in trouble for that. But you're not in trouble for stealing a car, running

from police, plowing into someone at an intersection, and killing two people—that'd be a lot worse, correct? All right, well, what's going on here tonight is that you're in a stolen car, and you're still in it, and you're still running from the police going through intersections at a thousand miles an hour, hoping that you're not going to run into somebody and kill them because—and remember I'm not asking you to say anything here; I just want you to listen—because of that rifle that's out there, and if somebody uses that rifle now, a year from now, and kills somebody, that's coming right back to your mailbox. If we don't go and try and recover that rifle, and it gets used in a crime, it's coming back to your mailbox now, a year from now. Just the simple fact alone that you two guys broke into that trailer and did whatever you did in there that—that's like stealing a car and getting caught with the car. Well, now we've crossed a threshold, and now there's a weapon involved, and we've got to get that weapon back. That's my number-one objective, and my question obviously at this point is, is that something that you're gonna help us get done or not? Because I wouldn't want to see you end up spending the next— you know, God forbid that someone gets killed with that in the near future. I'd hate to see you end up in prison for thirty years. That's how serious this is.

Guns pose a threat to the public and to police. One officer described in an interview with a suspect how badly he would feel if he had to shoot an armed youth because of the stolen gun.

2. GUNS AND VOLUNTARINESS

Prior to *Miranda*, the Court used the Fourteenth Amendment due process clause to review the voluntariness of confessions in criminal cases.[50] The Court excluded confessions obtained by methods that raised doubts about their reliability and truthfulness, that created risks that an innocent person might confess falsely, or that overwhelmed suspects' free will.[51] In addition to youthfulnesss, several factors could render a confession involuntary: physical brutality;[52] threats of physical or psychological harm;[53] prolonged interrogation;[54] deprivation of food, water, or sleep;[55] or inducements or explicit promises of leniency in exchange for admissions of guilt.[56] Some interrogation techniques—for example, suggesting that judges view suspects who confess more favorably—implicitly promise leniency but fall within the ambit of judicially permitted practices.

Courts view explicit threats or quid pro quo promises of leniency as more problematic.[57] However, the Court's fractured opinion in *Chavez v. Martinez* concluded that coercive tactics do not violate suspects' Fifth or Fourteenth Amendment rights until the state offers a statement at trial, because until then, one cannot be "compelled to be a witness against himself in a criminal case."[58]

Two interrogations in this study raised issues of voluntariness, and both involved guns. Police questioned these juveniles for the longest period of time, used the most maximization techniques, and made explicit quid pro quo promises of leniency to enable police to recover guns. In one case, police questioned a juvenile about possessing and firing an AK-47 rifle at a house after residents ejected him from a party. Police arrested him a week after the incident, questioned him unsuccessfully for more than one hour, and then terminated the interrogation. The officer later returned, conducted a second short interview, and made an explicit quid pro quo offer. She threatened the juvenile that if he did not confess, cooperate, and recover the gun, then the prosecutor would file a motion to transfer him to criminal court, where, if convicted, he faced a mandatory minimum of five years in prison. If he cooperated and recovered the gun, then the state would prosecute him as a juvenile. The following quid pro quo offer occurred during the second interrogation:

> I talked to the county attorney this morning, and you're being charged with possession of a firearm by a minor, which is a felony. I'm just going to lay it out for you. What I have here is an offer for you—one time. You're being charged with possession of a firearm by an ineligible person because you're a juvenile. And you're being charged with reckless discharge of a firearm in the city. What is in question—and that won't be decided by the police, will be decided by the county attorney's office—is whether or not you will get certified as an adult or that they'll move to certify you as an adult. Like I say, that's what's still up in the air: certifying you as an adult. And here's your deal. As you know, we have not recovered the gun. I don't have much time to do this, and I'm not going to take much time to do this. The deal is, or the offer is, we can get our hands on that gun, get it off the street, then maybe there is a chance that you won't be certified as an adult. If you're certified as an adult, and you're convicted of possession of firearms, you'll get an adult sentence, and an adult sentence is five years. There's no possibility of it being any less. That's five years in

St. Cloud [Reformatory] or Stillwater [Prison]. Do you need time to think about it, or do you want to tell me to forget it, or what do you want to do?

The juvenile agreed to the deal, accompanied police to recover the gun, pled guilty, and received an Extended Jurisdiction Juvenile (EJJ) blended sentence rather than risk prosecution as an adult.[59]

In the second case, two officers questioned a juvenile about an armed robbery. One officer had investigated the youth a week earlier about a burglary in another county in which thieves stole guns that police believed he had used to commit the robbery. Police questioned him at length—more than one and a half hours—and used several maximization techniques. The two officers—a female and a male—used gender roles to conduct a "good cop, bad cop" interrogation. After the female officer initially questioned the juvenile unsuccessfully, the male officer intervened:

> You're in some serious trouble, my friend: agg [aggravated] robbery. Think about this. Seventeen-years-old, close to being an adult. You're damned lucky you're not an adult. Agg robbery out of Ramsey County. And guess what? It all comes back to the burglary, doesn't it? Guess where those guns came from? They came from your neighbor's house. Guess where the neighbor's house is? Two doors from where you live. So right now, my friend, you are sitting here in some real deep doo-doo. And this is your chance. She's giving you the opportunity to tell the truth. She's giving you the opportunity. And I'm not here to play games. You've got no friends. Right now you're on your own. You're out here dangling. You're going to be in the system before long. But this is your chance. Instead of sitting here lying and insulting us, you start coming clean with some of the information. If you don't spill your beans, you're going down hard. You know that? You are. So this is time to come clean, and what I'm looking for is this: We got guns floating around out there. These cops are really nervous about that. The thing that police dislike the most is knowing that there are stolen guns out there that can potentially be used to kill somebody. Do you understand the seriousness of it?

The female officer then described the benefit of handling the burglary and robbery together and offered the juvenile a quid pro quo exchange of release from pretrial detention in return for assistance to recover the stolen guns:

> Are you going to stay in lockup? That's something we could talk about here. You know, we could talk about this deal. You got to work with us though. You got to show us something. You work with us, we'll work with you. We're looking for cooperation. We're looking for your help, and we can help you. This is a two-way street. Right now, you're scared, and that's understandable. Everybody makes mistakes. Everybody makes mistakes. You're just a kid. We can write this off to youthful stupidity, right, but gosh, I mean, when you get to be eighteen, nineteen, twenty years old, you're going through the adult system, you know, a little different ballgame. Right now, you're a juvenile. You're fortunate for that. What we're saying is that if you get the information, Richard, that I feel is genuine, and I think you know what that means, that I could make some phone calls today and get you out today.

After the juvenile confessed to the robbery, the officers released him from custody and he assisted them to retrieve the guns.

In both gun cases, police made explicit quid pro quo offers of leniency —trial as a juvenile or release from pretrial detention—in exchange for an admission and cooperation. In both cases, the juveniles confessed and assisted to recover the guns, pled guilty and received the proferred deals, and waived objection to the admissibility of the statements or evidence they provided.

3. LENGTH OF INTERROGATION AND SERIOUS CRIMES

Police and justice system personnel attributed longer interrogations to more serious crimes—for example, homicide or criminal sexual conduct —and those with multiple defendants, several witnesses, and deceptive suspects. As one officer observed, "more complex-type cases: a kid that's not telling the truth; they're either not talking at all, deflecting, trying to talk about something else, taking you longer to get to the story; someone that's lying to you." Public defenders confirmed the relationship between more serious crimes and lengthier interrogations, which they estimated could last from sixty to ninety minutes. "Seriousness of the offense, crimes of violence, obviously, homicides, rapes, just more the seriousness of it." A judge identified similar characteristics: "Those generally are either sexual assault cases or real serious aggravated robberies or homicides. They're the top of the heaps in terms of seriousness."

Justice system personnel confirmed the relationship between guns and interrogation length and agreed that guns provide a proxy for seriousness. One judge said, guns are "an indicator to almost everybody in the system that things are going to the serious level. So much of adult and juvenile criminal conduct is really chicken shit, but when a weapon shows up, that opens the door to much more serious conduct." Police associated guns with youths' gang involvement—another indicator of seriousness. One officer observed, "It's more than likely a gang member, so not only is their own offense history going to play into their sophistication, but they're around offenders all the time, sharing stories and teaching each other about how it works. Once you bring firearms into it, it jumps way up in sophistication."

Police viewed gun crimes as more serious because of the inherent dangers of guns in the hands of children. Adolescents' immature judgment and lack of appreciation of consequences increase the risks of guns. One officer said, "Guns related to anything are going to get a higher attention. They're focused on gun violence. Most cops are not gun-control people, but I am, just because I've seen what kids and guns do. These kids pull the trigger, and I don't believe they have any connection between what happens after they pull the trigger. So getting guns out of the hands of kids would be a focus of mine." Police conducted more probing interrogations for gun-related offenses in order to solve the crime, to recover the gun, and to learn what other youths had contact with it. Public defenders attributed lengthier interrogations about guns to the broader criminal context in which they appear: "There is a definite attitude of wanting to get guns off the street, wanting to track them down: where did they come from? who else had the gun? Tracking guns down and getting them off the street is a high priority for police, and I see their interrogations being focused on that."

Police expect gun-involved youths to be serious offenders with prior arrests, which contributes to lengthier interrogations. Youths know that gun crimes garner serious consequences and raise the stakes, which gives them greater incentive to resist their interrogators. One officer said, "You want to get the gun. Most of the time, you don't have the gun. So you have to get them to tell you where the gun is at, and that's where it gets hard. Because most of them know when you bring a gun into the game, they've increased the penalty. For the kids who are bringing the guns, they're a little more savvy. They've been in the system. So they know not to admit something." In addition to public safety concerns, officers garnered more prestige from colleagues for eliciting statements and recovering guns than they did for solving less serious felonies. Serious crimes are more likely to go to trial because of the higher stakes, and police invested more effort to elicit confessions to strengthen prosecutors' cases.

II. *Miranda* and Case Processing

How does a juvenile's decision to waive or invoke *Miranda* affect how a court handles his or her case? Theoretically, defendants enjoy the protections of the Due Process model—an adversarial system—in which they may invoke procedural safeguards and force the state to prove its case. In reality, the justice system much more closely resembles the Crime Control model, in which confessions lead to guilty pleas. A confession creates "a strong disincentive for the suspect—who has already incriminated himself in the most damning of ways—to take his case to trial and risk being convicted of the most serious possible charges and receiving the harshest possible punishment."[60] As one officer explained, "If you get a good solid statement from them, the likelihood of having to go to court and to take other people through that process, such as witnesses, is almost nonexistent. We don't go to court on juvenile cases. I think that is maybe a testament to the fact that 85% or more give confessions. That coupled with the physical evidence and witnesses' statements pretty much locks them in."

A confession greatly tilts the balance of advantage in favor of the state.[61] Defendants who confess have less plea-negotiation leverage than do those who remain silent. Research on adults indicates that suspects who confess seldom have a jury trial and receive fewer plea concessions than do suspects who do not make a statement.[62] Prosecutors charge offenders who confess with a greater number of and with more serious crimes, set higher bail, offer fewer charge reductions, and dismiss fewer charges than against those who remain silent.[63] One study reported that "[d]efendants who confessed were more likely to be convicted—and more likely to be convicted of more serious charges—than those who did not."[64] Defense attorneys may pressure a client who confesses to accept a guilty plea to avoid the risks of trial and a harsher sentence.[65]

A. Scales *Recordings Obviate Motions to Suppress Statements*

Research attributes the paucity of suppression motions to defense lawyers' heavy caseloads, lack of support resources, and juvenile court cultures hostile to adversarial litigation.[66] Even when defense counsel file motions to suppress confessions, judges rarely exclude statements.[67] "Thus, it appears that motions to suppress confessions under *Miranda* are rarely raised, rarely affect convictions, and rarely serve as the basis of successful appeals."[68]

More significantly than caseload pressures, *Scales* recording requirement has virtually eliminated motions to suppress juveniles' statements:

> Judges are not called on to spend time conducting pretrial hearings, listening to contradictory testimony from police and defendants, and attempting to determine where the truth lies. The use of recordings has proven to increase the number of guilty pleas, which in turn relieves trial judges from spending time presiding over contested bench or jury trials; hearing arguments and ruling on admissibility of evidence, and the many other issues presented in contested trials; and deciding the outcomes in bench trials.[69]

Only one file in this study of 307 cases contained a motion to suppress a statement—a private attorney filed what appeared to be a pro forma motion. Interviews with prosecutors, defense attorneys, and judges confirmed that defenders file very few motions to suppress for *Miranda* violations. A prosecutor estimated that she encountered "maybe one or two a year." Another prosecutor recalled "six omnibus [suppression] hearings which involved statements, none of which involved suppression, in two and a half years." One judge reported "maybe one in the last year," and another described them as "very infrequent, maybe a couple of times a year." One defense lawyer said she only filed "a couple a year," another said, "In this year, I filed about three of them," and a third said, "I've had years where I haven't done it at all, because I haven't had anything that's right for trial." Even when defense counsel file suppression motions, *Scales* recordings obviate hearings. As one prosecutor commented, "There are a number more motions made than actually end up in hearings, and that's typically because matters resolve or we get to the hearing and the issue is waived."

An urban judge attributed the paucity of *Miranda* suppression motions to *Scales* recording requirement. He contrasted his experience as a judge with his previous role as a defense lawyer: "We haven't had all that many cases involving full-scale trials that would involve *Scales* tapes. One little anecdotal observation: When I was a defense attorney, these cases went to trial regularly. Now that was pre-*Scales*. Since *Scales* tapes, I'm finding these cases settle more often than not, so I'm not seeing it very often. It's usually resolved, and I'm not getting those kinds of cases."

A public defender described the futility of raising even meritorious claims because juvenile courts' rehabilitative ideology lowers the likelihood of successful challenges to statements: "If I challenge a statement, I think the court still feels, 'We're trying to help the kid out, so if I let the statement in, the kid will get the help he needs.' It's still about rehabilitating the kid, so it's easier for the judge to err on the side of 'We'll let that statement in. It's still juvenile court. We're here to help the kid.'" Another defender noted that he rarely prevails on suppression motions, and clients prefer release from custody to legal vindication: "The rate of success is never high, and any time you start raising any issues as far as statements, they inevitably come back with offers that your client wants to consider because they're probably sitting in the JDC [juvenile detention center]. They're very adult in their processing, that they want to get out too."

Justice system personnel attributed *Scales*'s virtual elimination of suppression motions to several factors. First, *Scales* required police to act professionally and to comply with *Miranda*'s protocol. A prosecutor observed,

> When the issue regarding the *Scales* interview comes up, there isn't much to fight about. There is a protocol that the police follow, and they read it verbatim. The juvenile has it physically in front of them as it's being read to them. They're asked to follow along, and every step of the way, they're asked, "Do you understand that?" and it's recorded per case law and protocol. So there is generally not much discussion regarding whether the statement could come in. It's a standardized protocol. It's written, and they follow it fairly tightly. It's tight. We rely on it. They rely on it. The juvenile investigators are extremely careful.

Scales recordings eliminate any ambiguity about warnings and waivers. In addition, most juveniles confess, and tapes provide unimpeachable evidence of their statements. One public defender said, "I don't file them [suppression motions] very often, because our kids do such a good job at hanging themselves." Another defender agreed, "Most kids are bad criminals, and irrespective of the *Scales* tape, they are usually way caught, and usually it's more negotiation to save the damage or minimize the damage of what they've already done." A judge commiserated with the obstacles public defenders confront: "I think down here it's real hard being a public defender, because if your kid has been in custody, he's likely cooked his own goose by the time you get to him." Virtually all juveniles confess or make admissions, which limits defense attorneys' options. One judge observed, "I think juveniles tend to confess more and unequivocally. And as a result, there are fewer trials, and it's more about the disposition and what the disposition is going to be than guilt or innocence."

Juvenile court personnel acknowledged that the justice system resolves cases with plea bargains, rather than trials. As one judge observed, "Most of our young people are represented by public defenders who are real busy. I think that it's fair to say that the culture and process down here is sort of slanted toward making a deal. We don't litigate much. They're being settled. They don't get to trial, and so we don't have some of these pretrial issues." The crucial concern is to negotiate an appropriate disposition rather than to contest guilt or innocence. One judge observed that defense attorneys conduct a cost-benefit calculus and focus on dispositions:

> When the attorneys have met with their clients, they've decided to expend their energy focusing more on settlement and what's an appropriate disposition and how to best situate things for their clients. There are some cases where there are fights over who done it—is the person guilty or not—but in a very large portion of the cases, the focus of things is on can we work out a disposition that everyone can live with or that particularly the child and defense attorney can live with.

A public defender confirmed the vital role that confessions play in a plea-bargain system of juvenile justice:

> I think with the number of cases we have in the system, if we didn't have some cases that had an admission, I think the system would be deadlocked with litigation and cases that were contested. It's a bad thing that police officers take advantage of these kids, but it does resolve cases pretty quickly, when they've admitted to it. Usually a kid doesn't want to litigate a *Miranda* issue once they've admitted it.

In short, *Scales* recordings enhance police professionalism, document *Miranda* waivers and statements, obviate the need for suppression hearings, lead quickly to guilty pleas, and focus lawyers' attention on the appropriate sentence. *Scales* enables justice system professionals to administer a Crime Control model of justice "on the record," which expedites routine processing of cases and reserves the Due Process model for factually contested cases.

B. Impact of **Miranda** *Waivers on Sentences and Charge Reduction*

The vast majority (92.8%) of youths in this study waived their *Miranda* rights, confessed or made incriminating admissions (88.4%), and reduced defense counsels' ability to negotiate compared with those who invoked *Miranda*. Because few youths invoked their rights, analyses of the relationship between waivers and sentence measures are tentative. Table 5.4 reports how a juvenile's decision to waive or invoke *Miranda* affected offense level at conviction, charge reductions, and sentences.

Prosecutors initially charged all these juveniles with felonies. Youths who waived *Miranda* were somewhat more likely to be convicted of a felony (90.4%) than were those who invoked (81.0%). Conversely, juveniles who waived were less likely to have the charges dismissed (3.5%) than those who invoked (9.5%). However, the association of juveniles' waivers and prosecutors' ability to convict at the highest level may reflect a relationship between the strength of evidence available to police, the decision to waive, and prosecutors' decision to charge. A police officer observed, "What percentage of cases are there confessions without strong evidence? You have a solid witness or you have solid physical evidence—it probably lends itself more to a confession than others if you don't have solid witness." If the state has stronger evidence with which to charge, then it has less incentive to reduce charges.

Juveniles' waivers of rights affected charge reductions as well. No reductions in charges occurred for three-quarters (76.2%) of cases in which youths waived their rights, compared with two-thirds (66.7%) of those in which they invoked. Although not statistically significant, juveniles who invoked were more likely than those who waived to have felony charges reduced to misdemeanors (9.5% versus 5.7%) or dismissed (9.5% versus 3.5%).

Research reports that judges sentence youths who confess more severely than those who do not:

> If a juvenile denies the crime, given due process protections, the county must prove the case against the juvenile. In a system that is already overloaded, many counties, especially the urban ones, do

Table 5.4
Outcomes by Waiving or Invoking Rights

	Waive	Invoke	Total
Offense Level at Conviction			
Felony			
N	255	17	272
%	90.4	81.0	89.8
Misdemeanor			
N	17	2	19
%	6.0	9.5	6.3
None			
N	10	2	12
%	3.5	9.5	4.0
Reduction from Original Charges			
No charge reduction			
N	215	14	229
%	76.2	66.7	75.6
Felony to reduced felony			
N	41	3	44
%	14.5	14.3	14.5
Felony to misdemeanor			
N	16	2	18
%	5.7	9.5	75.6
Dismissed			
N	10	2	12
%	3.5	9.5	4.0
Sentence*			
Institution			
N	44	5	49
%	16.4	25.0	17.0
Out-of-home placement			
N	74	4	78
%	27.5	35.0	27.0
Probation			
N	141	7	148
%	52.4	35.0	51.2
None			
N	10	4	14
%	3.7	20.0	4.8

* Statistically significant at $\chi^2(1, N = 307) = 12.5, p < .1$

not have the resources to investigate the crime thoroughly, to sub-poena witnesses, and to hear testimony. Thus, if the urban courts have to rely on the juvenile's admission for evidence and if the juvenile denies committing the crime, then judges may have no recourse but to dismiss the charges.[70]

I found the opposite relationship between the severity of sentences that judges imposed on youths who waived or invoked their rights. Judges were more likely to commit to institutions (25.0% versus 16.4%) or to remove from home (35.0% versus 27.5%) youths who invoked their rights than those who waived. Conversely, about one-half (52.4%) of youths who waived received probation, compared with about one-third (35.0%) of those who invoked. Thus, judges appeared to sentence somewhat more harshly youths who invoked their rights than those who waived ($p < .1$). However, youths with prior felony arrests were significantly more likely to invoke than were those without prior arrests, and their harsher sentences may reflect prior justice system involvement rather than exercise of constitutional rights.[71]

Police, prosecutors, defense attorneys, and judges all described the impact of confessions on juvenile justice administration as "huge," "very significant," "the nail in the coffin," "extremely important," "a crucial piece of evidence," and "the heart of the case." Beyond universal agreement about the importance of confessions, perspectives varied with officials' roles. Police regarded a statement—true or false—as a crucial tool with which to control suspects: "Anytime you get a statement from someone, it's crucial because it locks them into a story then. You lock them into their story, and then when you go and prove all their story wrong, then you can go back at them." Similarly, a judge described the role of statements either to incriminate or to close off subsequent lines of defense:

Sometimes they get pieces of information that fit together or tie up their case. Other times, they've cut off avenues of defense. Sometimes the purpose of the interrogation isn't to get a confession, but if the kid isn't asserting self-defense at that point and had a chance to say it was self-defense, it's harder to bring up later. It cuts it off defenses or eliminates theories they have to investigate or run down. It narrows a defendant's options. Sometimes they get "I did it. I'll sign everything."

Analysts contend that confessions may be necessary to convict suspects in about one-fifth to one-quarter of cases.[72] Police strongly emphasized their importance, and several suggested that prosecutors are reluctant to charge cases in which they do not obtain a statement:

A lot of times, you have a good case without a statement, but even though there's a case there, the county attorney's office wants you to try to get a statement before they'll charge. I think there are plenty of good cases out there that can be charged without a statement, but we'll take a statement, try to get a statement basically to lock them in. Hopefully, they'll confess, put that final nail in the coffin, so to speak, to close the case. Because obviously, if you've got a confession, it just tightens it down—less likely to go to trial. That may be what the county attorney's office wants as well. If you don't have a confession, most cases—especially, burglaries, robberies, dope— without a confession, they don't get charged.

Prosecutors agreed that statements greatly strengthen their hand to deal with juveniles' attorneys: "It's usually the heart of the case, because there's usually always some lose ends where the cops didn't have enough physical evidence to put all the pieces together. Any gaps in the case are filled in by the respondent." The importance of statements as gap fillers varies with other evidence available, but they enable prosecutors better to control juveniles' testimony or to avoid trial.

A judge suggested that prosecutors may be more inclined to negotiate a better plea with a juvenile who does not confess: "I think it affects it at the charging stage and especially at the plea stage. More often, without a statement, the prosecutor is going to view it as a vulnerability in their case, and the plea offer is going to reflect that. A full admission is going to affect both charging and plea." Similarly, a public defender conceded that a juvenile's confession limited her options: "A statement makes our job incredibly difficult. So from that standpoint, I think it's almost everything. Even though in many situations they don't need the statement to make their case, it makes it very difficult to defend the case, and almost all of them settle that way."

The state adjudicated—convicted or pled—nearly every offender in this study of some offense, and the crucial issue in delinquency cases is the disposition rather than guilt or innocence. From the perspective of justice system personnel, plea bargains and admissions to lesser charges increase the likelihood that a juvenile will receive treatment, whereas a trial carries the risk of acquittal or dismissal. Earlier research reported that "juveniles who admitted committing the crime received more severe adjudications than did juveniles who denied committing the crime."[73] By contrast, I found that youths who confess may receive less severe sentences. "Given that the juvenile justice system is more focused on rehabilitation than the adult system, it is plausible that youth who confess to offenses may be seen as more remorseful and less deserving of punishment."[74] Admitting to a crime may indicate a juvenile's rehabilitative potential and greater likelihood to respond to intervention.[75]

Several police, lawyers, and judges spontaneously emphasized that the juvenile justice system attempts to rehabilitate youths. One prosecutor chided me, "The function of the juvenile justice system is rehabilitation. I don't know about you academics—I'm sure you probably think otherwise —but we really do. It's a great day when kids get off probation and do well, beat their addiction, whatever. We really do want the goal of rehabilitation." Another prosecutor said,

> I think what people outside of the juvenile justice system don't see is the sincere desire on police officers and prosecutors to divert as many cases as we can from the juvenile justice system while still maintaining our obligation to protect public safety. I think people outside of the system assume that what we really are doing is laying in wait for the kids, and what we're really trying to do is nail as many hides to the wall as we can, when nothing can be further from the truth. I think what we want is to take these as teachable moments and respond appropriately.

I asked justice system personnel whether youths' decision to waive *Miranda*, to confess, or to assume responsibility indicated amenability to treatment or influenced charges or dispositions. Prosecutor suggested that for less serious felonies, a juvenile's admission might garner some benefit at charging: "Frankly, if I see a kid who has confessed, and it is a crime against property—not a serious crime against the person— as a prosecutor, I would be more likely maybe even to cut him a deal because he seems like he has taken some sense of responsibility." Another said, "When a kid's confessing to what they did, they're remorseful, they're acknowledging their behavior, there's some sense of self-understanding, self-awareness that they have done something that's hurt someone, hurt their parents, hurt society. In the run-of-the-mill case, I do think it makes a difference." Another prosecutor agreed, "People would be surprised at how often that information usually is used for the kid's benefit. Because they talked, we charge it maybe a little bit different way or cut them a bit of slack when negotiating because it shows a willingness to cooperate and be amenable to programming, based on their willingness to take responsibility, especially for the lower level of offenses."

Some prosecutors expressed reservations about reducing the initial charge if a juvenile confesses because it misrepresents the criminal conduct and penalizes other youths for exercising constitutional rights. However, all agreed that a youth's decision to confess is relevant at sentencing:

> We don't punish them for exercising their right not to speak with police officers. So if they chose not to, that's fine; it doesn't impact them dispositionally at all at sentencing. But certainly, if they do choose to speak to police officers, that's something that is brought up at disposition, that they were cooperative and had a good attitude. It doesn't impact whether I charge it or not, because they don't have to talk to police, but public defenders or private attorneys will say they were cooperative.

Prosecutors noted that confessions positively influence judges: "If you get on board pretty quickly—'I did this. I assume responsibility'—the bench looks favorably upon that. I've seen them comment in cases in which kids plead pretty quickly and take responsibility."

Judges differed whether confessing affects dispositions. On the one hand, a judge observed, "I always consider it a good sign for somebody to take responsibility for what they do. When I'm dealing with kids from the bench, when I see that, I take that as being a very, very positive sign. And I think it's a very good sign when kids apologize for what they've done. And a lot of kids don't do that." On the other hand, a judge noted that because the vast majority of delinquents confess, a juvenile's cooperation does not distinguish him or her from other youths. By the time a judge considers a case at disposition, "you're moving on to the factors in the family and the type of offense and what programs the kid has been involved in."

Minnesota's adult sentencing guidelines allow judges to make downward departures from a sentence for defendants who cooperated, and that can affect juvenile court judges as well:

I think it is probably a safe assumption that kids that are confessing and owning up or taking responsibility for their actions get a better deal than those who are dug in and fighting it. I don't think it's a key factor or key variable how well a kid is going to respond to programming or other things, but I think it can play a role. Acceptance of responsibility on the adult side is an accepted reason for a downward departure under the sentencing guidelines and is one that's used quite frequently as the stated reason for the departure.

Defense lawyers questioned whether a youth's confession provides any charge or sentence benefits. Although they use the fact that a youth has confessed to argue for a more favorable disposition, they did not think it affects justice system decisions, because the vast majority of juveniles confess: "They definitely don't get a break for singing. They definitely don't seem to charge them any less than they could because they spoke. There's no benefit to them in talking. You might think that if a kid is willing to acknowledge they did something wrong and take responsibility for it, that there's some sort of reduction in how they're treated. But—but I don't see that at all." While defense attorneys did not see juveniles who confess garner any benefits, they agreed with other professionals that a youth has to move from denial to assuming responsibility for the system to treat him or her successfully.

Summary and Conclusion

Police in this study who questioned juveniles did not use maximization or minimization techniques extensively, and youths did not require much persuasion to talk. The vast majority (79.6%) cooperated; about two-thirds of them provided long responses to police questions and rationalized or explained their behavior. About one-third made some negative responses to police, but only about one in ten (11.6%) denied responsibility. More than half (58.6%) of juveniles gave full confessions, and another one-third (29.8%) made incriminating admissions. Virtually all youths who implicated themselves did so early in the interview, and very few changed from denial to admission in response to police questioning.

Police questioned youths briefly. They concluded more than three-quarters (77.2%) of interviews in fifteen minutes or less and 90.5% in half an hour or less. Police devoted the first few minutes of these brief interrogations to establishing rapport and completing *Miranda* formalities. Police conducted longer interrogations when a crime involved a firearm.

Police questioned about one-fifth (19.6%) of youths for half an hour or longer in cases involving guns, as contrasted with only 7.5% of youths whose cases did not involve a firearm. Guns provide a proxy for offense seriousness, and police question youths longer in more serious cases.

Juvenile courts rely on youths' pleas to efficiently process cases. The juvenile justice system more closely resembles the Crime Control model than the Due Process model of adversarial testing that *Gault* envisioned. The state of Minnesota convicted more juveniles who waived *Miranda* at the highest level, and they enjoyed fewer charge reductions or dismissals than did youths who invoked. However, youths who waived were significantly more likely to receive probationary dispositions and less likely to be confined than were youths who invoked. Police, prosecutors, and judges opined that youths who confess and assume responsibility exhibit greater amenability to treatment. However, neither they nor defense attorneys saw any appreciable benefit from confessing per se at charging or sentencing.

Justice by Geography

Context, Race, and Confessions

The same laws—statutes, procedural rules, and court decisions—apply throughout a state. But states decentralize justice administration, and courts function at a county or judicial district level. At the local level, judicial operations vary with social structure and community context and produce justice by geography.[1] For example, urban courts operate in a milieu that provides fewer mechanisms for informal social control than do suburban or rural courts. Urban courts are more due process oriented, place more youths in pretrial detention facilities, and sentence offenders more severely than do suburban or rural courts.[2] No reasons exist to believe that rural delinquents are more competent to waive rights than are urban juveniles, but rural judges appoint lawyers for them less often than do urban judges.[3] While the presence of a lawyer indicates a juvenile court's due process orientation, procedural formality is associated with sentencing severity.[4] Community context affects resources available and juvenile justice practices—where a youth lives determines, in part, how the system will handle him or her.

Community structure and racial demographics also affect characteristics of youths whom police and courts encounter and how the justice system responds.[5] Minority youths disproportionately live in urban settings, and youths' race influences justice administration.[6] Police arrest urban youths for more serious offenses, and urban youths accumulate more extensive records.[7] Thus, some geographic differences in justice administration reflect differences in the present offenses and the criminal histories of delinquent youths.[8] However, juvenile courts refer, detain, adjudicate, and sentence minority youths at higher rates than they do similarly situated white youths.[9] Juvenile justice administration reflects the interplay of geography and race, and this chapter examines the impact of these factors on interrogation practices.

Municipal police departments operate even more locally than county juvenile courts. Differences in delinquency and crime and in community and political expectations affect resources and police practices.[10] The four counties in this study differ in population, crime rates, and law enforcement resources. Anoka County has a population of about a third of a million people served by nine police departments and one county sheriff. Dakota County has a population of more than a third of a million people served by

CHAPTER SIX

178

eleven police department and a county sheriff. Ramsey County has a population of almost half a million residents served by eight police departments and a county sheriff. Hennepin County has more than one million residents served by thirty police departments and a county sheriff.[11]

Police departments' culture and practices vary with social structure and community context.[12] Analysts attribute elements of police culture to shared danger and group loyalty, an "us versus them" view of criminals, social isolation, and authority to use force.[13] Officers develop mechanisms to cope with the threat of danger in their environment: a suspicious outlook, a take-charge attitude, and an aggressive style.[14] Egon Bittner provides an outstanding analysis of how routine police practices interact with the social construction of adolescence to produce distinctive responses when police confront delinquents.[15]

James Q. Wilson's seminal *Varieties of Police Behavior* argued that different departments emphasize different aspects of police functions: order maintenance, law enforcement, and public service.[16] He related the different foci and practices to community characteristics and political expectations. At the community level, street-patrol officers provide correspondingly different types of policing—a watchman style, a legalistic style, and a service style—that reflect departmental orientation. Wilson attributed the varieties of police behavior to community characteristics—for example, high or low crime rates, racial diversity, affluence, public and political expectations—the structure of municipal government, and departmental organization: "[P]olice work is carried out under the influence of a political culture though not necessarily under day-to-day political direction. By political culture is meant those widely shared expectations as to how issues will be raised, governmental objectives determined, and power for their attainment assembled; it is an understanding of what makes a government legitimate."[17]

The crime problems that police encounter vary with community characteristics and affect their responses.[18] Changes in personnel recruitment and selection, community policing philosophies, and departmental structure further contribute to variations in police practices.[19] In the decades since Wilson's pioneering study, increased police professionalism may have reduced somewhat how much political climate or bureaucratic structure affect law enforcement styles, but community and organizational diversity remains.[20]

Community differences and departmental cultures affect police practices on the ground, for example, how aggressively officers use routine traffic stops to search vehicles or use force in their encounters.[21] Similarly, Wilson contrasted how professional and nonprofessional police departments in two structurally similar cities responded to juvenile criminality.[22] Officers in the professional department emphasized general rules, enforced laws evenhandedly, and arrested juveniles at twice the rate as did those in the nonprofessional department, where officers used a more flexible, informal response. In another study, families in an affluent suburb used their economic and political resources to protect their children, and police responded by minimizing use of formal arrests and keeping informal records to maintain social control.[23] External political pressures—for example, politicians' discovery of a gang problem—can induce police to manipulate internal statistics and records to bolster political claims-makers.[24] Police practices vary with and respond to social structure and community expectations.

In the decades since Wilson described variations in police orientation and practices, we have few studies that link community structure and police procedures. We have no analyses of how interrogation practices vary with department, community, or race of suspects. We do not know how differences in practices affect suspects' invocations of rights or rates of confessions. Roger Evans's research in the United Kingdom suggests how and why department interrogation practices might vary and produce different outcomes. He reports, for example, that

> there are significant differences in admission rates depending on the [police] subdivision in which the interview takes place. . . . Interview styles may vary from station to station and have an impact on outcomes. This would be consistent with the thesis that police stations have their own ethos and culture. It would also be consistent with the thesis that police interviewing techniques take place on the job. If individual police stations develop their own distinctive approaches then the dominance of on-the-job training might ensure that these are passed on to new recruits to the station.[25]

In addition to structural variations in departmental orientation and practice, urban and suburban police encounter delinquents with different racial demographics and offense types. Minority juveniles reside disproportionately in urban counties. Police arrest them for violent crimes at higher rates than they do white youths.[26] Historically, juvenile courts' rehabilitative ideology has emphasized intervention in a child's best interests. Individualization encourages decision-makers to treat offenders differently based on perceived needs and circumstances. From juvenile courts' inception, control of ethnic and racial minority youths was one of their most important functions.[27] Get-tough juvenile policies in the 1980s and 1990s amplified racial disparities and punished minority offenders more harshly than white youths.[28] Three decades of research consistently report that black juveniles are more likely to be referred, detained, and incarcerated in the juvenile system, more likely to be transferred to criminal courts, and more likely to be imprisoned as adults than are their white counterparts.[29]

The skewed ethnic composition of urban and suburban counties complicates my ability to attribute differences in interrogation practices to geography or racial demography. In these analyses, I first examine relationships between county variables and interrogation practices. I then examine the relationship between delinquents' race and interrogation practices. Part I explores how police practices vary with geographic context. Youths' offenses and prior records vary with community context. Do techniques police use to question them vary with community setting? Do youths in urban and suburban settings respond differently? How often do parents attend police interviews? What role do they play? Three times as many suburban parents as urban parents attended the interrogations of the juveniles in this study. How did police adapt, co-opt, or neutralize their presence? Part II reports some significant differences in how police questioned juveniles of different races and how the juveniles responded. Despite these differences, multivariate analyses attribute variations in police practices to geography—urban versus suburban context—rather than to juveniles' race.

I. Interrogation in Urban and Suburban Contexts:
Justice by Geography

This chapter explores how urban and suburban county characteristics affect police practices. The analyses combine the two urban and two suburban counties examined in this study and relate differences in community structure to variations in delinquency and interrogation strategies. For example, suburban police question youths who have fewer serious offenses and shorter prior records than urban officers do. Interrogation practices likely vary with the sophistication of delinquents whom police question. James Q. Wilson and Albert Meehan described relationships between community affluence, parental political influence, and policing style.[30]

Table 6.1

2005 County Demographics

	Urban		Suburban	
	Hennepin	Ramsey	Anoka	Dakota
Total population	1,089,910	476,715	320,803	381,267
% white	77.42	76.08	89.99	88.17
% black	10.07	9.50	3.07	3.90
% Asian	5.55	9.59	3.46	4.15
Median household income	$55,996	$49,898	$61,634	$66,467
% households with income < $15,000	11.41	13.24	6.38	6.80
% households headed by single female whose income is under the poverty line with children under 18	39.20	32.20	18.70	17.50

Source: U.S. Census American Community Survey 2005

For example, I would expect more affluent suburban police departments to place greater emphases on community relations, accountability, and transparency. And these policies should be associated with an increased presence of parents at interrogations.

Police in the two suburban counties in this study operated in different a milieu than did their urban counterparts. Anoka and Dakota Counties are suburban and rural, whereas Hennepin and Ramsey Counties are urban and suburban (see table A1.1). The counties' population and racial and economic characteristics differ considerably. Table 6.1 reports that the smaller suburban counties are predominantly white (89.0% and 88.27%), whereas the urban counties have larger minority populations (77.4% and 76.1%). African Americans constitute about 10% of the urban counties, as compared with 3% of the suburban counties.

Suburban-county residents are wealthier than their urban counterparts are. The suburban households' median income is about $10,000 higher than that of urban households. And one indicator of poverty—proportion of households with annual incomes of less than $15,000—is about twice as high in the urban counties (11.4% and 13.2%) as in the suburban counties (6.4% and 6.8%). In the urban counties, more than one-third (39.2% and 32.2%) of children are raised in a household headed by a single female with income below the poverty line, as contrasted with less than one-fifth (18.7% and 17.5%) of suburban children. These structural differences—urbanism, population density, racial diversity, family composition, income, and poverty—are associated with differences in crime rates and justice system responses.[31]

The offenses and prior records of delinquents whom urban and suburban police questioned differed significantly. Table 6.2 reports that police questioned fewer delinquent girls in suburban (8.4%) than in urban counties (12.8%). The race of youths whom police questioned reflected the

Table 6.2

Characteristics of Juveniles Interrogated: Urban and Suburban

	Urban		Suburban	
	N	%	N	%
Gender				
Male	143	87.2	131	91.6
Female	21	12.8	12	8.4
Age				
16	94	57.3	77	53.8
17	66	40.2	66	46.2
18	4	2.4	0	0.0
Race*				
White	54	33.5	106	74.1
Black	78	48.4	29	20.3
Other	29	18.0	8	5.6
Offense[a]**				
Property	78	47.6	91	63.6
Person	61	37.2	36	25.2
Drugs	11	6.7	8	5.6
Firearms	11	6.7	6	4.2
Other	3	1.8	2	1.4
Prior arrests***				
None	41	25.5	56	40.3
Status	23	14.3	24	17.3
Misdemeanor	40	24.8	32	23.0
One felony	27	16.8	18	12.9
Two or more felonies	30	18.6	9	6.5
Prior juvenile court referrals****				
None	59	36.9	67	50.4
One or more	101	63.1	66	49.6
Court status at time of interrogation				
None	69	43.4	73	53.7
Prior supervision	40	25.2	21	15.4
Current probation/parole	39	24.5	36	26.5
Current placement	11	6.9	6	4.4
Total	164	53.4	143	46.6

[a] For offense details, see table 4.1

* Statistically significant at $\chi^2(2, N = 304) = 50.369, p < .001$; ** statistically significant at $\chi^2(4, N = 307) = 8.2, p < .1$; *** statistically significant at $\chi^2(4, N = 300) = 14.8, p < .01$; **** statistically significant at $\chi^2(4, N = 293) = 8.498, p < .1$

population composition of the counties. Only one-third (33.5%) of youths whom urban police questioned were white, as contrasted with nearly three-quarters (74.1%) of suburban youths. Likewise, half (48.4%) of youths whom urban police questioned were black, as compared with one-fifth (20.3%) of suburban youths. The overlap of race and geography—that is, minority and urban, white and suburban—requires separate analysis of their impact on interrogation practices.

The crimes for which police questioned youths differed significantly by locale. Police questioned less than half (47.6%) of urban youths about property crimes, as compared with nearly two-thirds (63.6%) of suburban youths. Police questioned more than one-third (37.2%) of urban youths for crimes against the person, as compared with only one-quarter (25.2%) of suburban youths. Fortunately for these comparative analyses, about half the youths (53.4%) whom police questioned lived in urban counties, and the other half (46.6%) lived in suburban counties.

Juveniles' prior arrests, prior court referrals, and court status at the time police questioned them differed significantly by locale.[32] Two-fifths (40.3%) of suburban youths had no prior arrests when police questioned them, as compared with only one-quarter (25.5%) of urban youths. More than one-third (35.4%) of urban youths, as compared with less than one-fifth (19.4%) of suburban youths, had one or more prior felony arrests. Reflecting the differences in prior arrests, more than half (50.4%) of suburban youths had no prior juvenile court referrals, as compared with about one-third (36.9%) of urban youths. Fewer suburban youths had juvenile court supervision. Suburban police encountered and questioned a less serious or chronic delinquent population with fewer minority juveniles than did urban officers.

As in chapter 3, I compared the youths whom police questioned with other data on these counties' juvenile court dockets.[33] In both the urban and suburban counties, the youths whom police interrogated were more serious offenders than the counties' routine felony docket. The interrogated sample includes a larger proportion of youths charged with felonies against the person and property, fewer youths charged with drug offenses, more youths with prior records, and a larger proportion of minority youths.

A. Location, Timing, and People Present at Interrogation

The arrest and detention status of urban and suburban youths whom police interrogated differed significantly. Table 6.3 reports that suburban

Table 6.3

Custody Status, Detention Status, and Location of Interrogation: Urban and Suburban

	Urban		Suburban	
	N	%	N	%
Custody status*				
Arrested	147	89.6	119	83.2
Not arrested	17	10.4	24	16.8
Detention status**				
Detained	116	70.7	68	47.6
Not detained	42	25.6	72	50.3
Location of interrogation***				
Police/sheriff's department	86	52.4	85	59.4
Detention-correction	56	34.1	15	10.5
Place of arrest	7	4.3	18	12.6
School	6	3.7	13	9.1
Home	9	5.5	10	7.0
Hospital	0	0.0	2	1.4

* Statistically significant at $\chi^2(1, N = 307) = 2.719, p < .1$; ** statistically significant at $\chi^2(2, N = 307) = 20.074, p < .001$; *** statistically significant at $\chi^2(5, N = 307) = 31.866, p < .001$

police formally arrested a somewhat smaller proportion of youths than did urban police when they conducted a *Scales* interview (83.2% versus 89.6%). They detained a significantly smaller proportion of youths following questioning than did their urban counterparts. Urban police detained more than two-thirds (70.7%) of youths, as compared with less than half (47.6%) of suburban youths. Some of these differences reflect the crimes and prior records of youths whom urban and suburban police questioned.

Urban and suburban police questioned youths in significantly different locations. They interviewed about the same proportion of youths at police stations (52.4% versus 59.4%). However, urban police conducted about one-third (34.1%) of interrogations at detention facilities, as compared with only one-tenth (10.5%) of suburban interrogations. Urban counties detained more youths because prosecutors charged a larger proportion with more serious offenses. In urban counties, patrol or juvenile officers and court intake and detention personnel detained youths, and then urban detectives questioned the youths when they came on duty. Suburban police conducted more interrogations at the place of arrest (12.6% versus 4.3%) and at schools (9.1% versus 3.7%) than did their urban counterparts. In several suburban departments, patrol officers interviewed youths whom they arrested rather than pass them on to sergeants or detectives for questioning.

Table 6.4

Time from Offense to Interrogation and Strength of Evidence: Urban and Suburban

	Urban		Suburban	
	N	%	N	%
Length of time*				
Same day	105	64.0	109	76.2
Same week	26	15.9	13	9.1
Same month	15	9.1	15	10.5
More than one month	18	11.0	6	4.2
Strength of evidence				
Moderate	63	38.7	48	33.8
Strong	100	61.3	94	66.2

* Statistically significant at $\chi^2(3, N = 307) = 9.014, p < .05$

Suburban police conducted three-quarters (76.2%) of interviews within less than one day after the crime, as compared with less than two-thirds (64%) of urban interrogations. Suburban police had somewhat stronger cases at the time of interrogation than did urban officers (66.2% versus 61.3%). From the immediacy of interrogation and strength of evidence, I infer that suburban officers likely caught more youths in the act than did their urban counterparts. Corroborating that inference, suburban officers conducted proportionally three times as many interrogations at the place of arrest as did urban officers (12.6% versus 4.3%).

Beer Burglary, a.k.a. Garage Shopping. I attribute some of the immediacy, strength of evidence, and location of interrogations to a uniquely suburban crime: "beer burglary," stealing alcohol from private property. Prosecutors charged more than half (55.0%; see table 3.1) of all youths with property crimes. Sixty-five property felonies (21.2%) involved burglary—unlawful entry of an occupied or unoccupied dwelling or a commercial building with intent to commit a crime. Eleven burglaries were beer burglaries (16.9%), and ten of these (90.9%) occurred in the suburban counties.

Many suburban households have a second refrigerator in the garage to keep beer and wine cold. Groups of juveniles drive around the suburbs looking for targets of opportunity—"garage shopping." The youths enter garages to steal alcohol. In the beer burglaries in this study, when a resident or neighbor saw the youths remove the beer, he or she then called 911 to report the crime, followed the youths' car, and gave updates to police dispatch by cell phone. Police apprehended the youths near the scene, and within minutes, the trailing neighbor identified them, and police searched the car and recovered the beer. Police separated youths into different squads to question them. Interrogations were brief, juveniles admitted participation, and interviews focused on who instigated the thefts —each youth attributing responsibility to others involved. Although beer burglaries appear to be minor thefts, entry of a garage attached to a house constitutes a burglary, and if people are present in the dwelling, it technically constitutes a serious home invasion.

Some suburban prosecutors expressed reluctance to charge youths with a serious crime—burglary—for stealing alcohol without forcible entry: "If it's an open garage door, and they just walk in and leave, it's just theft. It bothers me when we're charging kids with a felony that can have so many negative repercussions, when they're just walking in and walking out." Despite the reservations, prosecutors charged eleven youths with felony beer burglary.

B. Parental Presence

About ten states require a parent to consult with his or her child before an interview and to be present during questioning. If police deny parents' access to their child, deprive them of an opportunity to confer, or rebuff their efforts to be present during questioning, judges exclude any subsequent statements. These states assume that a parent's presence will offset a child's lack of competence, avoid speculation about waivers, reduce coercion during questioning, increase the reliability of any statement, provide a mechanism through which to obtain counsel, and enable parents to participate in significant decisions that affect their child. However, to place parents in an advisory capacity forces them to choose between teaching their child a moral lesson (e.g., to respect authority or to tell the truth) and exercising the best legal option (to remain silent). "If a parent encourages the child to remain silent in the face of the police, what message is communicated to the child about obeying authority? If a parent encourages the child to 'tell the truth,' and the child subsequently confesses and is incarcerated, the parent may ultimately feel that she did not protect her child in the face of adversity."[34]

Although courts envision parents playing a protective and supportive role, parents raise children to tell the truth, and this expectation increases children's pressure to confess.[35] Cases abound in which parents urged their child to stop lying, instructed them to tell the truth, and ordered them to tell the police everything they know or threatened to "clobber" them if they refused.[36] Parents are not state actors, and courts find that parental urgings do not overbear a child's will, reject claims that parents acted as agents of police, and commend them for "motherly concern for the basic precepts of morality."[37]

Earlier research reported that parents did not provide children with useful legal advice, increased pressure to waive their rights, and urged them to make a statement.[38] In that study, only one-third of parents present at an interrogation gave their children any advice at all, and most advised their children to waive their rights. A survey of parents of high school students reported that the majority believed that their children should not withhold information from police to avoid self-incrimination.[39] A study of detained youths reported that most parents provided their children either no guidance (55.6%) or urged them to "tell the truth" (33.3%), and none advised them to remain silent.[40] Parents may unwittingly sabotage their child's ability to exercise rights by siding with authority.[41] Anecdotal evidence reports that parents push their children to talk with police and to tell the truth.[42] Moreover, parents may be no more able to weigh the impact of waiver or to resist police pressures than their children are.[43]

Jennifer Woolard and her colleagues examined whether parents understand *Miranda* and police tactics sufficiently to compensate for their children's lack of knowledge.[44] They interviewed 170 pairs of parents and adolescents of varying ages about *Miranda* rights and interrogation practices. They confirmed that juveniles' understanding of *Miranda* increases with age and that parents have a somewhat greater understanding of *Miranda* than do adolescents. However, both parents and adolescents share fundamental misconceptions about police interrogation practices:

> Virtually all parents and adolescents expect that police will notify them if the adolescent is considered a witness or suspect. About half believe that the police must tell the truth during interrogation and up to two-thirds believe that police must wait for parents before questioning an adolescent. . . . [A] majority of parents and adolescents anticipate parental and individual protections during the interrogation process that simply are not constitutionally required and do not (necessarily) exist.[45]

Despite parents' greater understanding of *Miranda*, several factors contribute to their limited role and effectiveness at interrogations. They may be emotionally upset or angry at their child's arrest. They may believe that their child's confessing will produce a better outcome. They may think that children should respect authority or assume responsibility.[46] They may misunderstand how police interrogate suspects. "[P]arents do not play an active role in interrogation because they believe that the police 'play fair' and would not take advantage of youthful immaturity. If parents knew that the police can lie or that special protections are not necessarily afforded to youth, would they be more likely to be present, to participate actively, or to offer advice to their youth?"[47]

Parents advise their children to cooperate with police for three reasons: morality, strategy, and belief in assuming responsibility.[48] Most parents endorse cooperation with police because "honesty is the best policy." Some make a strategic calculus that cooperation will result in more lenient disposition. Others believe that children should assume responsibility and learn the consequences of their actions. The conflicting interests may prevent parents from playing the protective role the law envisions:

> [I]f a parent approaches police interrogation with a set of goals and preferred outcomes that is different from her child's, the advice she gives (if any) may not align with the best interests of her child (as the child or defense attorney defines them), regardless of her understanding of *Miranda* rights and their implications. Moreover, parents may be disadvantaged if children do not fully disclose to them the nature of their involvement in the acts in question. Incongruent parent and youth goals, incomplete or inaccurate knowledge of the youth's behavior, lack of knowledge about interrogation practices, and an incorrect understanding of *Miranda* rights may all result in an interrogation environment in which the parent may not be positioned to compensate for youth's developmental deficits as the law presumes.[49]

Several juvenile justice personnel described the dilemma of parental presence at interrogations. One urban public defender noted,

> Usually a parent is not a good thing because they might not appreciate the seriousness of the situation, and they might encourage their kid to talk without realizing that, "Hey, this kid is going to be facing some long-term consequences from talking." So if you're an informed parent and if you know about your *Miranda* rights and you know about the criminal justice system, it helps. But if you're not informed and just kind of an overbearing parent that's trying to hold

your kid accountable and is mad at your kid for getting into trouble, sometimes that can backfire for the kid to have a parent present.

This section examines whether the juveniles in this study spontaneously asked to have a parent present at questioning. It assesses whether police notified parents that their child was in custody or sought permission to question the child. Urban and suburban police departments had different policies to notify parents of impending interrogations, and parental presence varied with geography. If parents attended juveniles' interrogations, then police developed strategies—to enlist parents as allies or to neutralize their presence—to facilitate questioning youths. Finally, the section considers what assistance parents provided when they attended their child's interrogation.

1. JUVENILES' SPONTANEOUS REQUEST FOR A PARENT

The Minnesota Supreme Court has held that if police disregard youths' repeated requests for a parent, then their refusal might render a waiver or confession involuntary.[50] In *State v. Burrell*, a sixteen-year-old juvenile asked for his mother three times before police administered the *Miranda* warning and ten times after the warning.[51] Police denied his request, secured a *Miranda* waiver, and obtained an incriminating statement. *Burrell* reviewed previous cases in which the Minnesota court had rejected a per se rule of parental presence. It held, "Although we reiterate that there is no per se rule requiring a parent's presence before a juvenile waives his *Miranda* rights, the circumstances of this case suggest that Burrell's repeated requests for a parent were enough to render his *Miranda* waiver ineffective."[52] *Burrell* is an exceptional case in which a juvenile repeatedly asked for a parent. More commonly, Minnesota judges treat parental absence as just one factor in the totality of the circumstances. Some suburban police departments give the *Burrell* decision greater credence.

The police I interviewed did not regard a juvenile's request for a parent as an invocation of the right to remain silent or to have counsel present. Some officers referred to in-service training in which county attorneys told them that if a younger juvenile—twelve, thirteen, or fourteen years old—requests a parent, then that is "pretty much the same as asking for a lawyer, because they're so young and naïve about the system, especially if it's their first time. It's really not unreasonable for them to get advice from their parent about what to do."

Unlike states that allow or require a parent or interested adult to attend a youth's interrogation, juveniles in Minnesota do not have a right to have a parent present. The standard *Miranda* warning does not include an advisory about parental presence. As one urban officer explained, "It's not my responsibility or my obligation to tell them that they can have their parent present. That's something they have to bring up on their own. We don't offer that 'if you want your mom here or your dad here, we can call them and have them come down.'" As a result, a public defender observed, "I don't think it's clear to them [juveniles] that they can ask for a parent." Suburban officers occasionally broached the subject of parents during the *Miranda* formalities: "I do want to make you aware at this time, because you are a juvenile, you do also have the right to have your parents in here with you." The juvenile in that case declined: "No, that's fine. We can just get it done right now." Another juvenile flatly refused—"No"—when an officer asked him, "Do you want me to contact your parent and let them know that you're here? Are you interested in having them present when we talk with you?"

In a few cases (2.9%), and even without an advisory, a juvenile spontaneously requested a parent to be present. Research in Canada reported that in a sample of fifty cases, only 2% of interrogated juveniles requested a parent, even though the law gave them a legal right to be present.[53] Woolard et al.'s research attributed the rarity with which juveniles sought parental assistance to several factors: "lack of knowledge concerning the right and police practices or instructions discouraging it . . . [and concern] that notifying their parents would have negative effects (e.g., anger, worry) or that there was no benefit."[54]

Police officers whom I interviewed described juveniles' unprompted requests for parents as rare occurrences. When asked how often juveniles spontaneously ask for a parent, one veteran officer stated, "I would say in my career, maybe once every two years." In the few instances in which juveniles ask for a parent, police said they do not feel obliged to terminate questioning. One urban officer said, "If the child requests a parent present, that's going to be a discretionary call up to us as the investigator. It's my discretionary call if I want to honor that." Most officers said they would not honor the request, and one officer explained,

As far as the older kids, like sixteen or seventeen years old, and particularly if they've been around the block a few times, and they say,

"Well, I want to talk to my mom," I have not typically honored that as a valid request. If they say they want a lawyer, then the interview stops. If they say they want their mom, then I'll continue on to probe to find out why—to tell them [parent] that they're at the jail—you know to find out more why.

Another officer said, "Even if parents were outside in the lobby screaming, 'I want to see my kid,' they wouldn't allow it. They didn't. You would tell him, 'He's under arrest now. He's going through the process. We will let you know when you can talk to him.'" A judge confirmed that police prevent parents who arrive at the station house from seeing their child until the police complete an interview: "Parents would show up to see their kids, and the police wouldn't let them in while they were interrogating the kids." In the few cases in this study in which a juvenile asked for a parent, officers put off the request and continued the interview. When a juvenile asked, "Is there any way that I can see my dad tonight?" the officer replied, "When we finish up here, you probably can."

Police attributed youths' spontaneous requests for a parent to anxiety and fear, rather than a need for assistance. Police observed that requests for parents occur "very rarely": "Usually when that happens, what you've got is a kid that's starting to panic, because he knows he's in big trouble, and now his last chance is 'I want my mommy.' It's not so much they want them in the room, but they want their mommies, like we all did at one time." Another officer confirmed, "It seems like the spontaneous request for a parent after you Mirandize and start questioning them kind of comes at the point where they've just spilled their guts, and they feel like—they kind of realize, 'Uh-oh, I'm in some trouble now.' I think that's the time at which it comes most often."

Police and juvenile justice personnel suggested several reasons why so few youths request parents unbidden. If police do not tell suspects they may have a parent present, then youths may lack the awareness or fortitude to request one repeatedly, as did Burrell. A public defender noted, "The power dynamic is such that it takes a lot of courage for that kid to just ask for a parent once, let alone several times. So they feel like they don't have any control over the situation. So if the cop says no or kind of dismisses the question or ignores the question, they don't persist." Many delinquents feel estranged from their parents. Others may not feel that their parents can provide any meaningful assistance. A judge observed of delinquents,

[They] have complex relationships with their parent or parents. I think it's a mistake to project a normal home environment on that kid. So often the parent might have their own chemical or abuse issue. So they're not that close to their parent. They don't need them there. They don't feel like it's one of your parents or my parents. They don't think they're going to get much help from them. Their parents may whale on them.

Police described youths' domestic relationships as an impediment to a parental request: "They don't have a parent at home, or if they do have a parent at home, there's not much contact. It is very rare that you see a kid that has a close relationship with Mom or Dad. And so I think because of that, there's just not the relationship, or they just don't think about it."

Youths may be especially embarrassed to have parents present during investigations of certain types of crimes, for example, criminal sexual conduct or intrafamilial sexual abuse. One officer said, "Sometimes it's the nature of what the topic is that makes kids uncomfortable to have their parents there." Prosecutors agreed, "It's harder to say what you did in front of your parents." Justice personnel described interrogations about sex crimes as especially difficult for juveniles if parents attend: "They don't want their parents there. They might be embarrassed, like, for example, in a crim sex case, or the parent may be harsher than the police officer." Prior to one interrogation, an investigator described a prior discussion about how a mother's presence would discomfit her child and chill his candor: "All right, now we had a conversation before the recorder went on about whether or not you wanted your parents here. I think we came down to an issue that there's an embarrassment issue as far as being totally honest and up-front about what has happened in the past. You said you wanted to be up-front and honest, but because your parents are here, more of an embarrassment, and you didn't know if you wanted to say everything."

In addition to embarrassment, officers said that some juveniles were ashamed to tell their parents what they had done but wanted them to know. Juveniles sometimes used police to communicate with their parents—to tell them what happened without having to face them directly. An officer said, "They're embarrassed that they got in trouble, and they know that if they tell us the truth, the truth is going to come out. They may never have to tell their parents, because we'll tell them for them. So it's their way of being able to tell the story, get it out in the open, get it off their chest, out into the open without telling their parents."

Many juveniles do not want their parents to know that they are in trouble. One defender aptly described their quandary: "They perceive themselves as in trouble, so the last person they want to call is their parent, because that would just bring on more trouble." Some youths naïvely believe that their parents will not learn that police had arrested them for a felony and hope to resolve the case quickly in the interrogation room without their awareness:

> They usually don't want their parent to know. One, they're thinking, like, at the end of the day—this is my assumption—maybe mom and dad won't know. They're sitting in the backseat of the squad car going to Lino [detention center]—your parents are going to know. But maybe in their brain, they're thinking they won't know. Like, you get a speeding ticket, and mom and dad won't know, until they get their insurance statement.

One officer noted, "More times than not, they don't want their parents to find out. At their first contact with me, they probably have not even talked with their parents, a lot of times. They want to try to keep it under the covers." However, juveniles' hopes or expectations that their parents will remain unawares are disappointed. One officer said, "I think a lot are thinking, 'I don't want mom or dad to find out,' and they don't realize that we have to notify parents in the end." A public defender observed, "They don't want their parents to know. There's a shame element asking for a parent. And I do see that with older kids who are relatively new to the system. They react by 'Don't tell my mom. Please don't tell my mom.' So they're just hoping they can put off the conversation with the parent as long as possible." Another defender echoed, "A lot of kids don't want their parents to know how much they've screwed up, so the last thing they want is for the parent to know all the details."

Police speculated that some young men might view a request for a parent as a sign of weakness: "In their eyes, I'm envisioning a lot of these young males, maybe it shows weakness." Others speculated that juveniles fear that their parents will be able to tell if they are lying more readily than an interrogator might: "It could be, 'OK, I'm going to tell a lie now, and my mom will know that part of what I'm going to say isn't true.'"

Justice system personnel most commonly proffered that youths fear the domestic consequences if parents find out about their offense. The foregoing excerpts from the interviews adverted to juveniles' fear of parental discipline—for example, "Their parents may whale on them," or "the parent may be harsher than the police officer." One judge observed, "They're afraid of their parents. They're more afraid of their parents than they are of the judge or the cops or anybody else. They're terrified." Sometimes, juveniles fear the physical discipline. One officer observed, "A lot of them have said, 'My dad is going to kick my butt. I'm in trouble. My mom is going to be so mad.' So they're really not that excited to have their parent show up." A prosecutor noted, "A lot of times, kids are scared of their parents. It's not uncommon that while the cops are investigating a crime, the kid will say, 'My parents are going to beat me when they hear this.' So then we have to get the whole child-protection thing going."

Juveniles do not request parental assistance for several reasons. Minnesota law does not require parental presence, police do not notify juveniles of the possibility, and few youths spontaneously request a parent. Some delinquents are estranged from their parents or do not view them as capable of assisting them. Many youths fear domestic consequences more than the sanctions of the justice system. In some instances, youths are embarrassed about the type of crime. More often, youths know that they have disappointed their parents, do not want them to know the details of how they got into trouble, or hope that their parents will not learn of their arrest. Many fear domestic consequences—physical discipline or other parental sanctions. Because most juveniles are reluctant to ask for a parent, any policy that requires them to make an affirmative request will leave the vast majority unprotected.

2. URBAN AND SUBURBAN VARIATION IN PARENTAL PRESENCE

Police questioned juveniles alone in the vast majority of cases (90.2%) (see table 3.4). In some cases, a parent (8.1%) or a school official or probation officer (1.7%) attended interrogations. Significantly, three times as many suburban parents as urban parents (13.3% versus 3.7%) attended their child's interrogation (see table 6.5). In part, this reflected differences in the parental notification policies of urban and suburban police departments.

Urban police notified parents in less than one-quarter (22.7%) of cases in which they had taken a juvenile into custody and planned to question the child. Urban police reports did not include notations about officers' efforts to notify or secure parents' permission prior to questioning. Urban police explained that they regard parental notification as a self-defeating policy: "A lot of the kids that we deal with unfortunately they're a product of their environment. Their parents are just as anti–law enforcement

Table 6.5

People Present at Interrogation: Urban and Suburban

	Urban		Suburban	
	N	%	N	%
Police interrogators				
One	143	87.2	121	84.6
Two	21	12.8	22	15.4
Others[a]				
Parent	6	3.7	19	13.3
Other[b]	2	1.2	3	2.1
None	156	95.1	121	84.6

[a] Statistically significant at χ²(2, N = 307) = 9.993, $p < .01$
[b] Probation officer or school official

and establishment as the children are, and you say, 'Can I talk with your kid?' and they say, 'Hell no, I'm coming to get them.' It's basically not really conducive." Urban public defenders reported, "Parents are shocked that the cops can talk to their kids without them present, let alone letting them know."

By contrast, suburban police attempted to contact a youth's parents in more than three-quarters of cases (77.3%) and sought permission to question the child. Policy manuals in some suburban departments instruct officers to contact parents: "The arresting officer will, as soon as practical, notify the juvenile's parents or guardians of the fact that their child has been taken into custody. The following information shall be given to the parent or guardian in addition to the notification: a. Reason for detention. b. Place of detention, appropriate contact person and phone number."[55] Departmental instructions for processing and interrogating juveniles in custody require a "full *Miranda* advisory" and note that courts gauge the validity of a waiver by the "totality of circumstances." In addition to age, maturity, education, and experience, the manual refers to "[p]resence and competence of juvenile's parents (their presence is *not* constitutionally required, *State vs. Jones*, 1997)."[56] Some suburban officers regard parental notification as a legal requirement—for example, *State v. Burrell*—or at least a departmental policy:

If it's not a law here in the state, it is definitely a policy within our department that we will make every effort to reach out to a parent before we proceed with any type of interview. I wouldn't say it's a hard and fast rule, but it's definitely something we make every attempt to do. There are kids who maybe have been through the system an unbelievable amount of times. Maybe that would be an exception, where you would say, "This kid knows how the system works." If I can't get ahold of a parent at that time, I might not wait.

Because courts consider a parent's presence as a factor under the totality of circumstances, suburban officers view notification as a way to eliminate one basis on which defense lawyers could challenge a youth's waiver and statement:

> As a rule, we'll try and make contact with a parent and kind of get permission to talk. If you do get the permission, that really solidifies your position during the interview. You Mirandize them, and you got permission from the parents, you're okay, you're on solid ground there. If you don't get permission from the parent or ask permission from the parent, then you kind of have to lay the groundwork that this kid is okay to make the [waiver] decision for himself.

A suburban prosecutor agreed that parental notification deprives defense lawyers of one ground on which to challenge a waiver or statement: "It's one of the factors that courts look at about voluntariness of a statement, if a parent is there. It helps make the statement stronger on that basis, if the officer has attempted to contact the parent." A suburban defender agreed that police contact parents to foreclose that avenue of defense challenge:

> I think it just makes things cleaner and smoother down the road. If we are going to challenge a statement, that is one of the factors we can look at: was the parent contacted, or were they present? If they do it on the front end, if the cops are following all of the rules they're supposed to be following, I don't think it makes a difference for them if the parents are there or not. It is something for us to challenge down the road if we spot problems with the statement. That's one area we can challenge, if the parent wasn't contact—although that's just one factor of many they can look at when we're challenging a statement.

Suburban police documented efforts to contact parents in their reports and at the start of an interrogation. As one officer explained, "With cell phones nowadays, you always get ahold of them. My general rule, usually each parent has a home phone, work phone, and a cell phone. I'll call three numbers or four numbers and give it a half hour before I get to the point of talking to them. Usually, all parents are spoken with before." Police summarized attempts to contact and speak with parents in their reports. For example, one report included the notation, "Richard Chandler, Katie Chandler's father, gave permission for me to speak to Katie about the incident." At the start of Katie's questioning, the officer documented on the *Scales* tape that he had received parental permission: "We're here investigating the attempted auto theft that you were involved in or that we think you were involved in. I talked to your father. He's already given permission to get a statement from you." In another case, the report stated, "Prior to reading [juvenile] his rights, I contacted his mother over the phone and informed her of the situation regarding her son. I asked her if I had permission to speak with her son. She said I had her permission to speak with him." At the conclusion of a juvenile's *Miranda* warning, an officer confirmed with the juvenile that his mother gave him permission to question the youth: "Keeping those rights in mind, do you wish to speak with me? Did I also contact your mother? And she agreed to let me talk to you?"

When police contacted parents, none of them denied permission to question their child. One officer said, "Parents usually are pretty cooperative. I think parents want to know the truth as well or at least find out what I know." Another suburban officer attributed parents' consent to frustration with troubled children: "Most parents are fed up with their kids. 'Yeah, go ahead. I can't believe he's in trouble again.'" When police contacted parents, most of them declined the opportunity to attend the interrogation. As one officer told a suspect, "I spoke with your mom on the phone, and I talked with her that I'd be interviewing you about this and what I was interviewing you about. And she said that she didn't have an interest in coming down here and sitting with you." Even when parents were present at the police station, most chose not to attend. Again, officers documented in reports and on tape that these parents declined to join the interview. After an officer called a youth's parents to the station house, he stated in the report, "I asked [mother] if I could have permission to speak to her son and interview him in regard to this case. She told me that I did. The statement was taped with her permission; however, she elected not to be in the room at the time it was made." A suburban public defender confirmed, "I've seen cases where the parents took them down there and just kind of handed them over to the police, instead of insisting that they be in there with them."

If parents appeared at their child's interrogation, then at the start of the *Scales* tape and prior to the *Miranda* warning, the officer stated, "And also present here at the police station is [suspect's mother], and she was advised of this interview and provided me with permission to speak to her son." After police secured a juvenile's *Miranda* waiver, they also elicited a waiver from the parents: "While we are on that, because you're a minor, Penny and John [parents], is it okay if we proceed?"

Justice system personnel attributed differences in parental notification and request policies to differences in urban and suburban police cultures or community politics. An urban officer disparagingly attributed suburban parental notification policy to local police chiefs' "sensitivity" to their constituencies and desire to foster transparency:

> There's a lot of departments that are—I'll just say a little more touchy-feely. They want to make sure they're doing the right thing, and the right thing is to let the parents know. If you get a new chief of police, you see those kinds of [parental notification] policy changes: "I want to be more transparent. When it comes to juveniles, do nothing unless the parents are there." It's bad policy, but there are places that do that. And I think you do see it in the suburbs more than—you're never going to see it in Minneapolis or St. Paul. A lot of suburbs, it's their own policy that says you won't interview a kid without a parent there.

An urban prosecutor speculated that suburban parents' education, affluence, and influence heighten pressures for departments to notify them and to permit their presence:

> My sense is you may be dealing with a more—parents that live in suburban areas tend to be more educated. They maybe feel like they have the right to be there. Sometimes, suburban jurisdictions, their citizens would be more upset if their kids are being interviewed without their parents present. The chief of police may hear more from disgruntled parents than they would in an urban setting.

An urban judge theorized that more suburban juveniles reside in "two-parent families, and they're going to raise more hell." A suburban defender confirmed, "When parents aren't contacted and their kids are talked to, they are not happy about that."

Despite some suburban departments' policies to notify parents, officers prefer to question juveniles alone. Suburban officers described parental presence as a two-edged sword—helpful in some instances and counterproductive in others:

> Sometimes when they actually go in, parents can be very helpful. Certain juveniles can't lie to their parents or don't lie to their parents, but they have no problem lying to me. On the flip side, they lie to their parents all the time or they hate their parents, and they're not going to talk to me because their mom's sitting there, or they're going to get beat when they go home or get grounded or get their cell phone taken away or whatever it may be.

Suburban officers said they feel that parents' presence can inhibit juveniles' honesty: "I definitely avoid at all costs having a parent in the room, because children, regardless of their relationship with their parent, children are not as forthcoming with their parent in the room as they are with a parent out of the room." In addition to parents' hindering youths' openness, suburban officers feared that parents could impede their ability to question juveniles effectively:

> I think sometimes with parents present, kids will hang up on what they're going to tell. As soon as you remove the parents from a room, they're more willing to tell you what actually happened, because maybe they've already created a lie with their parent, maybe there's already conflict there. The other reason we don't like to have parents there is because they start getting in the way of your questioning or the interviewing process.

In the absence of a departmental policy, most police would not call parents prior to interrogation because they feel that nothing good can come of it: "I don't want to muddy things up, give them the opportunity to invoke the kid's rights."

3. NEUTRALIZING PARENTAL PRESENCE

If parents attend a juvenile's interrogation, then police try either to enlist them as allies or to neutralize their presence. Inbau and Reid advise officers to assure parents that no one blames them for their child's misconduct.[57] Officers emphasize to parents that the role of the police is to learn the truth and try to enlist parents as collaborators. Prior to an interview, officers advise parents that they will be better able to help their child if they know what happened. One officer explained that he asked parents, "'Do you want the truth here?' And they'll all say yes. Most normal people do. 'Good, this is my goal. I cannot give you a crystal ball of what's going to happen at the end of the day, but we all need the truth.'"

Officers understand that juveniles might have denied wrongdoing to their parents and that parents may arrive at the station house feeling defensive. Police explained to parents that they share a common goal—to learn the truth—but cautioned them that their presence could inhibit their child's ability to be honest:

> More times than not, they already are aware of the allegations. And their child usually has denied the allegations to the parents, so they come in somewhat biased. I will talk to the parents prior to the interview and give them a kind of a spiel that, "We understand you feel your child is being falsely accused or did not do this. If they did do this, would you want to know, as a good parent?" They all say yes, they would. At this point, I say, "Do you think there would be a better chance that he would admit to his error with just me and him or her, or with me, him or her, and two parents also sitting there? I never say they can't, but more times than not they will say, "We would just as soon not be in the interview." I never talk them out of it. I just let them know that we have a better chance of getting to the truth here, and that's what we all want.

When an officer frames the question that way, what good parent does not want to know the truth about whether their child committed a crime?

Police question most suspects alone and have a strong preference to do so. Isolation increases the compulsive pressures of interrogation. To interview juveniles without a parent present, officers develop strategies to separate them at the station house. One office explained, "We would orchestrate it so that I could say, 'I'm going to take your child back here and interview him.' If they pushed it, of course, they were invited to come back. But otherwise I would try to get the kid alone first."

The same reasons that juveniles do not spontaneously request parents —for example, shame, fear, or estrangement—can also inhibit their truthfulness if parents attend interviews. Parental presence also can prevent juveniles from telling their story. For example, if a juvenile already had lied to his parents, then the parents could react defensively and make it more difficult for the child to change his story. Police discourage parents' participation by cautioning that their presence could impede their mutual quest for the truth:

> We normally would suggest to the parents that they don't sit in on the interview, for two reasons. One is it's easier for a kid to tell the truth to somebody they don't know—the cops—than to have Mom and Dad sit there, that he's already told them "the lie." It's a bad idea to have parents in there because—part of the problem, the kids won't tell the truth, and parents may interject things to get the kid to say certain things, and then you're just wasting your time.

Police said they reassure parents of their honorable intentions: "We always offer to them, 'If you want to watch the tape when we're done, go right ahead. We're not going to hide anything from you.'"

If a parent attends an interrogation, then Inbau and Reid advise the officer to seat the parent behind the child and not to engage him or her in questioning—to render the parent passive and unobtrusive: "A parent who is present during the interrogation should be advised to refrain from talking, confining his or her function to that of an observer. The parent should be asked to sit in the chair set aside for an observer. . . . The investigator should then proceed with the interrogation as though he were alone with the suspect."[58]

Officers described procedures they use to neutralize parents' presence and to render them as passive observers rather than active participants. Passivity reduces parents' psychological role as an ally and increases police's ability to get a statement. Officers described how they physically orchestrate the interrogation room:

> The parents can sit in the back corner. They've been instructed, "This is an interview that is between the child and myself. So if you want to sit in the back"—basically, the parent sees their own child's back of them. There's no eye-to-eye contact or anything like that that can influence or make an interview difficult. I don't want the child to direct the questions back to their parents or look to their parents for answers.

In addition to physically separating parent and child, officers instruct parents, "This is an interview that is between the child and myself. There will be no coaching or telling the child what to say." Officers admonish parents that if they intervene, then the officers will terminate the interview: "I don't want the parents to answer. If I get a parent in there that sits there and answers for the child, I say, 'Look, I need to talk to this person individually. If you're going to continue to interrupt this interview, we're not going to continue with it.' If they're going to answer the questions, it's not an interview anymore. And if they're going to interrupt, there's no point to continue."

Police strategies to obviate parents' assistance to their children—either to enlist them as allies to learn the truth or to neutralize their participation—probably explain why so few parents adequately protect their children's rights. Apart from the effectiveness of those strategies, a judge noted that parents often are in state of shock at their child's arrest and interrogation: "I see parents not having much of a role. I see them as acquiescing and generally being quiet and not being all that helpful. I wouldn't expect them to just sit there and be obsequious, but at times, it seems to me they are. Certain parents are overcome by the whole situation, so they're kind of numb, I think, when the kid is being interviewed."

4. PARENTS' ROLE AT INTERROGATION: "TELL THE TRUTH"

If parents attend an interview, then police try to enlist them as allies in their joint quest to learn the truth. Several justice system personnel said that parents' collaboration adversely affects their child's interests. One prosecutor said that when a parent attends, "it's more likely they will confess. The parents usually tell their kids, 'Tell the truth, and tell them what you did.'" One officer observed that he will "very often see a parent joining with the police officer, depending on the family circumstances. The police are seen as the helpers. The police probably get quicker confessions if the parents are in there, simply because the parents are saying, 'Officer Smith isn't going to lie. You lied to us last week when you told us you were in school.'" Another officer reported that when he interviews juveniles at home with parents present, "I would say 90% of mine—it went a little better. Mom or Dad got on them about telling the truth and to talk versus to not talk." A public defender commented that parents often persuade their child to talk and then express perplexity when cooperation leads to adverse consequences:

> I have many, many cases where there is no doubt in my mind that the kid would not have given a statement but for the fact that Mom

or Dad said, "You will talk to the police." And in talking to the parents at the first court appearance, when they're looking at the kid charged with a felony, saying, "The cop never told me that my kid would be charged with anything. I thought we were just doing the right thing by cooperating with law enforcement." So the parents are tricked as well.

Parents socialize children to tell the truth, and this predisposition compromises their children's interests. One prosecutor said, "Sometimes parents will march their kids into the police department and tell them, 'I want you to tell them what you just told me.'" At one interrogation attended by a parent, the officer asked the juvenile, "Would it be more comfortable talking without your mom here." The juvenile assured him, "She already knows. She knows all about it." His mother replied, "It's all right. I know all about it. We've had that talk. I'd rather have him tell you the truth." Police used the mother's urging to their own advantage: "It wouldn't be the end of the world if you just told me that you did this. We could straighten this out. Your mom wants you to tell the truth. I want you to tell the truth." A suburban defender noted that it is difficult for adult suspects to invoke *Miranda* rights and even more so for juveniles whose parents encourage them to waive and confess:

> I think it's pretty intimidating for any adult and especially kids, even if you're sixteen or seventeen, to exercise your rights with a police officer. I think they hear the words, but to actually get up and walk away, especially if you do have a parent in the room telling you, "You should talk," it's hard to make your own decision when you're sixteen or seventeen. You're answering to the cops. You're answering to your parents.

During some of the interrogations in this study, parents switched sides, became active allies of the police, and urged the child to tell the truth. A mother and grandfather attended an interview at which police questioned a youth about a burglary. At the beginning, the grandfather observed, "I've interrogated him several times, and he just doesn't look guilty or act guilty or anything to me. I realize how some people can look pretty sensible, even if they're lying. He didn't look like it to me, and I've known him ever since he was in diapers." After the officer questioned the juvenile for a few minutes and revealed some evidence of his involvement, his mother said, "Brady, just tell the truth, because it's gonna get a lot worse if —I don't know—one way, one way or the other, I just want what's best for you." Thereafter, the grandfather, who previously defended the youth, instructed him, "Tell him the truth now, Brady. Do you know anything about it? Were you in that trailer at all? Were you in that trailer that got robbed?"

In most of the interviews in which parents were present, parents did not participate after police advised them of the child's *Miranda* rights. Police see parents' role as to furnish emotional support, rather than to provide advice: "Almost like a calming presence for the kid. I've never had any parents intervene on behalf of their kids or try to shut it down. It's almost like emotional support." When parents did participate, they frequently helped police to obtain information. At one interrogation, a juvenile's mother advised him, "We want to be as helpful as possible to the police, right, Nick? You will tell the detective how to find this guy or help them out in any way possible." One officer observed that parents often do his job for him:

> Sometimes I'm sitting there, and Mom or Dad will kind of take over the interrogation for you. This is useful for me, because they're getting somewhere that I wasn't getting. They're calling them, they're doing certain things—maybe they're saying, "I can tell you're lying. You've done this before"—certain things that are useful for breaking down barriers, even things I wouldn't have known.

Parents attended twenty-five interrogations in this study and played a protective role in only two (8%). In one instance, a father confronted an officer for confusing his son and putting words in his mouth:

> I'm not minimizing anything here. We've already told Ron he's gonna suffer the consequences that are due him. And you're kind of suggesting—you're interjecting in a sentence your opinion and that this is a little game you're trying to get him to agree or get him to stumble up. He's doing his best right now to answer truthfully what happened. . . . You really are [trying to get him to stumble] because you're kind of confusing me, and I'm forty-five years old. So you're kind of—in one sense, I don't really appreciate what you're doing. I know you want to get to the truth, and I'm not trying to stop you. But he's seventeen years old, and I just wish that you would treat him that way right now.

Despite the father's challenge to the officer's questions, the youth confessed. In another interview, a youth's mother protected him so aggressively that the officer ended the interview. He tried to question the youth in the squad car about a beer burglary. His report of the encounter stated, "Johnson's mother asked to be present during the suspect interview and was allowed to. However, the statement was cut short after repeated interruptions from the suspect's mother." Parents played a protective role in only these two cases, and police still obtained an admission in one of them.

C. Waiving Miranda Rights

The vast majority (92.8%) of all the juveniles in this study waived their *Miranda* rights. However, a significantly larger proportion of suburban youths (96.5%) waived than did their urban counterparts (89.6%). Youths with one or more prior felony arrests were more likely to invoke their rights in both settings, but more urban than suburban youths had prior felony arrests (35.4% versus 19.4%). Proportionally twice as many urban juveniles as suburban youths (15.8% versus 7.4%) with one or more prior felony arrests invoked their rights.

D. Urban and Suburban Interrogation Tactics

Most police receive instruction in the Reid Method, and they tend to use similar tactics. In this study, both urban and suburban officers used

Table 6.6

Juveniles Who Waived or Invoked Their *Miranda* Rights by Offense and Prior Arrests: Urban and Suburban

| | Urban | | | | Suburban | | | |
| | Waived | | Invoked | | Waived | | Invoked | |
	N	%	N	%	N	%	N	%
Offense*								
Person	58	95.1	3	4.9	34	94.4	2	5.6
Property	68	87.2	10	12.8	89	97.8	2	2.2
Drugs	8	72.7	3	27.3	8	100.0	0	0.0
Firearm	10	90.9	1	9.1	5	83.3	1	16.7
Other	3	100.0	0	0.0	2	100.0	0	0.0
Total	147	89.6	17	10.4	138	96.5	5	3.5
Prior arrests								
Nonfelony	96	92.3	8	7.7	109	97.3	3	2.7
One or more felony	48	84.2	9	15.8	25	92.6	2	7.4
Total	144	89.4	17	10.6	134	96.4	5	3.6

* Statistically significant at $\chi^2(1, N = 307) = 5.419, p < .05$

Table 6.7

Maximization Questions: Types and Frequency

	Urban		Suburban	
	N	%	N	%
Interrogation strategy				
Confront with evidence*	73	49.7	82	59.4
Accuse of lying	51	34.7	42	30.4
Urge to tell the truth	39	26.5	45	32.6
Ask BAI questions	44	29.9	38	27.5
Use confrontational tactics	30	20.4	27	19.6
Warn about causing trouble for others	24	16.3	17	12.3
Accuse of other crimes**	18	12.2	6	4.3
Number of tactics per interrogation				
None	44	29.9	36	26.1
One	37	25.2	32	23.2
Two	17	11.6	27	19.6
Three	20	13.6	16	11.6
Four	7	4.8	15	10.9
Five	14	9.5	9	6.5
Six	6	4.1	3	2.2
Seven	2	1.4	0	0.0

Note: Based on juveniles (N = 285) who waived *Miranda* rights and whom police questioned

* Statistically significant at $\chi^2(1, N = 285) = 2.733, p < .1$; ** statistically significant at $\chi^2(1, N = 285) = 5.756, p < .05$

comparable maximization tactics—exhorting youth to tell the truth, accusing them of lying, confronting them with inconsistencies, and warning them of causing trouble for others. However, two significant differences in strategies emerged. Suburban officers were significantly more likely to confront youths with evidence than were urban officers (59.4% versus 49.7%). Recall that suburban police questioned a larger proportion of juveniles immediately after the offense and had stronger evidence available, which provided some advantage in the interrogation room. Also, urban police accused youths of other crimes or referred to their prior crimes significantly more often than did suburban officers (12.2% versus 4.3%). This likely reflects urban delinquents' more serious offenses and more extensive prior records. One urban defender confirmed that youths' backgrounds likely affect interrogation practices: "The felonies they [white youths] get charged with are different, so already you've got a different setup in terms of what's going to be asked and what kind of proof that you need."

Officers used fewer minimization tactics than maximization tactics during all interrogations. However, urban police used significantly more minimization tactics than their suburban colleagues did. Proportionally, urban police were four times as likely to minimize the seriousness of the offense (8.2% versus 2.2%), three times more likely to express empathy (15.0% versus 5.8%), and twice as likely to make appeals to honor (11.6% versus 5.8%) as were suburban officers. Urban police used more tactics and offered more rationales than did suburban officers.

E. Juveniles' Responses

The suburban juveniles in this study gave significantly more fulsome statements and provided police with more corroborating evidence than the urban delinquents did. Although both groups gave similar short positive responses, suburban youths gave significantly more long explanations, rationalizations, and justifications for their offenses than urban juveniles gave. By contrast, urban juveniles gave significantly more negative responses and denials and more often sought information about their case from police than suburban youths did. These differences in patterns of responses—suburban rationalizations and extended narratives and urban denials and seeking of information—are consistent with my interpretation that suburban police questioned less sophisticated delinquents and did not have to interview them vigorously to elicit admissions.

Table 6.8

Minimization Questions: Types and Frequency

	Urban		Suburban	
	N	%	N	%
Interrogation strategy				
Neutralize guilt	26	17.7	18	13.0
Appeal to self-interest	15	10.8	19	13.8
Express empathy*	22	15.0	8	5.8
Appeal to honor**	17	11.6	8	5.8
Minimize seriousness***	12	8.2	3	2.2
Blame third parties	7	4.8	3	2.2
Number of tactics per interrogation				
None	114	77.6	119	86.2
One	17	11.6	16	11.6
Two	10	6.8	3	2.2
Three	5	3.4	0	0.0
Four	1	0.7	0	0.0

Note: Based on juveniles (N = 285) who waived Miranda rights and whom police questioned
* Statistically significant at $\chi^2(1, N = 285) = 6.353, p < .05$; ** statistically significant at $\chi^2(1, N = 285) = 2.959, p < .1$; *** statistically significant at $\chi^2(1, N = 285) = 5.121, p < .05$

Table 6.9

Form of Juveniles' Responses: Urban and Suburban

	Urban		Suburban	
Response	N	%	N	%
Short positive	142	96.6	135	97.8
Rationalization*	89	60.5	98	71.0
Extended positive**	86	58.5	98	71.0
Negative—denial***	66	44.9	40	29.0
Seeking information****	42	28.6	23	16.7

Note: Based on juveniles (N = 285) who waived *Miranda* rights and whom police questioned

* Statistically significant at $\chi^2(1, N = 285) = 3.459, p < .1$; ** statistically significant at $\chi^2(1, N = 285) = 4.870, p < .05$; *** statistically significant at $\chi^2(1, N = 285) = 7.715, p < .01$; **** statistically significant at $\chi^2(1, N = 285) = 5.730, p < .05$

Table 6.10

Outcome of Interrogation and Corroborating Evidence: Urban and Suburban

	Urban		Suburban	
	N	%	N	%
Outcome*				
Confession	70	47.6	97	70.3
Admission	52	35.4	33	23.9
Denial	25	17.0	8	5.8
Corroborating evidence provided[a]	22	15.0	30	21.7

Note: Based on juveniles (N = 285) who waived *Miranda* rights and whom police questioned

[a] Includes providing leads to physical evidence, identifying a witness, creating a diagram, and identifying a codefendant

* Statistically significant at $\chi^2(1, N = 285) = 17.1, p < .001$

The outcomes of urban and suburban interrogations differed. A somewhat larger proportion of suburban than urban delinquents (82.6% vs. 76.9%) exhibited a cooperative attitude during questioning. A significantly larger proportion of suburban youths (70.3%) gave full confessions than did urban juveniles (47.6%). A larger proportion of suburban youths provided police with leads to other evidence than did urban delinquents (21.7% versus 15%). Urban delinquents denied criminal involvement about three times as frequently as did suburban youths (17.0% versus 5.8%). By all of these measures—rates of confession, corroboration, and denial—suburban youths were more cooperative, forthcoming, and self-incriminating than were urban youths.

II. Interrogation and Race

The overlap of geography and race—suburban and white, urban and minority—requires separate analysis of whether police questioned minority juveniles differently than they did white youths. Disproportionate minority confinement characterizes juvenile justice administration, and differences in interrogation practices could contribute to that phenomenon.[59] Juvenile justice involves sequential decisions by different personnel: arrest, intake, petition, detention, adjudication or waiver, and disposition. Even small racial disparities during successive stages can produce larger cumulative differences. For example, juveniles' prior records reflect earlier decisions by justice system personnel, and previous dispositions influence later sentences. Minority youths are disproportionately overrepresented at every stage of the juvenile justice process.[60] The National Academy of Sciences reported that black youths constituted about 15% of the population aged ten to seventeen, 26% of juvenile arrests, 30% of delinquency referrals, one-third of petitioned delinquency cases, and 40% of inmates in institutions.[61] At each succeeding step in the juvenile justice system, the proportion of minority youths increases, and the largest disparities occur in the initial stages.[62] "[A]t almost every stage in the juvenile justice process the racial disparity is clear, but not extreme. However, because the system operates cumulatively the risk is compounded and the end result is that black juveniles are three times as likely as white juveniles to end up in residential placement."[63]

In 1988, Congress amended the Juvenile Justice and Delinquency Prevention (JJDP) Act and required states that receive federal funds to examine disproportionate minority confinement (DMC) in detention facilities and institutions.[64] Most states responded to the JJDP Act requirement and found racial disparities. Forty-one of forty-two states found minority youth overrepresented in detention facilities, and all thirteen states that examined postadjudication institutional placements found disproportionate minority confinement.[65] Minority youths receive more out-of-home placements and serve longer periods in custody than do white youths convicted of similar crimes.[66]

Analysts attribute disproportionate minority representation to several factors: differential offending by race, differential justice system responses to race, and the structural context of juvenile courts.[67] Differences in rates and seriousness of offending by race, especially for violent crimes, contribute somewhat to the processing of more minority youths than white juveniles. In addition, juvenile court personnel respond to real or perceived dissimilarities among youths of different races, and their decisions play a role in minority overrepresentation.[68] For example, justice system personnel may view black youths as more threatening than white youths or may ascribe their delinquency to personal choices rather than to external forces.[69] Either attribution—being threatening or having personal responsibility—could produce harsher sanctions for minority youths. A larger proportion of black youths than white youths reside in single-parent households, which may indicate a greater need for services. If justice system personnel refer more youths for formal processing on the basis of family structure or service needs, then juvenile courts' treatment decisions indirectly mirror racial disparities.[70] Finally, the structural context of juvenile courts contributes to disproportionate minority contact. Urban courts tend to be more formal and to sentence all juveniles more severely.[71] Urban courts have greater access to detention facilities, and youths held in pretrial detention typically receive more severe sentences than do those who remain at liberty.[72] Proportionally more minority youths live in urban environs, police disproportionately arrest them for violent and drug crimes, and juvenile courts detain them at higher rates.[73] Thus, a juvenile's race interacts with locale, crime patterns, underclass threat, and justice system responses to produce disproportionate minority confinement.[74]

Donna Bishop analyzed police encounters with juveniles and ways in which geography and race interact to affect arrest decisions.[75] Serious crime is concentrated in disadvantaged neighborhoods; police therefore allocate more resources to these neighborhoods, which exposes minority youths to heightened surveillance, creates more opportunities for their contact with police, and increases their risk of arrest. Police view people in dangerous neighborhoods with suspicion and engage in more aggressive, proactive intervention.[76] Aggressive patrol or proactive intervention—experienced by juveniles as hassling—reinforces minority youths' hostility and distrust of police. For less serious crimes, youths' demeanor influences police discretion. Police may perceive minority youth to be more threatening, more gang involved, and less cooperative than white youth are. "At all stages of police processing, differential treatment of white and minority youths seems to be affected most by behavioral and attitudinal indicators of risk (danger and hostility) that are perceived to be linked to class and race. The overrepresentation of minorities in police arrest data, especially for violent offenses, reinforces racist expectancies."[77]

Although county attorneys charged all of the youths in this study with felony offenses, I examine whether youths of different races—white, black, and other—varied on other dimensions. Did they present different delinquency profiles? Did police question them in different venues? Did they waive *Miranda* at different rates? Did police question them differently? What attitudes did they exhibit in the interrogation room? How did they respond to questioning? Do interrogation practices contribute to minority overrepresentation in juvenile courts and disproportionate confinement?

A. Offender Characteristics

Chapters 3, 4, and 5 reported aggregate data, and the analyses here focus on significant differences among youths of different races. The present offenses, prior records, and juvenile court histories of youths of different races varied significantly. Recall that the racial composition in the urban and suburban counties differed, with larger proportions of minority youth living in urban counties (see tables A.1, 6.1, and 6.2). Table 6.11 reports that one-third (33.8%) of white youths whom police questioned were in the urban counties and two-thirds (66.3%) in the suburban counties. By contrast, nearly three-quarters (72.9%) of black youths whom police questioned lived in urban counties and only about one-quarter (27.1%) in suburban counties. Interrogations of minorities of other races also were concentrated in the urban counties (78.4%). The geographic variable—urban and suburban—and county racial composition overlap, and these analyses enable us to identify the separate effects of geography and race.

There were statistically significant differences in the crimes with which prosecutors charged youths of different races. Police questioned nearly two-thirds (64.4%) of white youths for property crimes, as compared with less than half (49.5%) of black youths and about one-third (35.1%) of youths of other races. Conversely, they questioned less than one-quarter (22.5%) of white youths for violent crimes, as contrasted with more than one-third (37.4%) of black youths and nearly half (48.6%) of youths of other races. Proportionally, police questioned about twice as many white youths for drug crimes (white, 8.8%; black, 3.7%; other, 2.7%) and twice as many racial minority youths for firearms offenses (white, 3.1%; black, 6.5%; other, 13.5%). Prosecutors charged proportionally more minority youths than white youths with person and firearms crimes (white, 25.6%; black, 43.9%; other, 62.1%) which we saw earlier produced some differences in interrogation tactics (see, e.g., tables 3.6 and 5.3).

Youths' prior arrests and court involvement varied significantly by race. Proportionally, twice as many white youths as black youths or youths of other races had no prior arrests (white, 43.9%; black, 20%; other, 20.0%). Conversely, less than one-fifth (19.1%) of white youths had one or more prior felony arrests, compared with about one-third of black youths (38.1%)

Table 6.11

Characteristics of Juveniles Interrogated: Race Comparison

	White		Black		Other	
	N	%	N	%	N	%
Gender						
Male	144	90.0	95	88.8	32	86.5
Female	16	10.0	12	11.2	5	13.5
Age						
16	82	51.2	65	60.7	23	62.2
17	74	46.3	42	39.3	14	37.8
18	4	2.5	0	0.0	0	0.0
County type*						
Urban	54	33.8	78	72.9	29	78.4
Suburban	106	66.3	29	27.1	8	21.6
Offense[a]**						
Property	103	64.4	53	49.5	13	35.1
Person	36	22.5	40	37.4	18	48.6
Drugs	14	8.8	4	3.7	1	2.7
Firearms	5	3.1	7	6.5	5	13.5
Other	2	1.3	3	2.8	0	0.0
Prior arrests***						
None	69	43.9	21	20.0	7	20.0
Status	29	18.5	12	11.4	6	17.1
Misdemeanor	29	18.5	32	30.5	11	31.4
One felony	19	12.1	21	20.0	5	14.3
Two or more felonies	11	7.0	19	18.1	6	17.1
Prior juvenile court referrals****						
None	82	53.9	31	30.1	13	37.1
One or more	70	46.1	72	69.9	22	62.9
Court status at time of interrogation*****						
None	89	57.8	36	35.0	17	48.6
Prior supervision	27	17.5	28	27.2	6	17.1
Current probation/parole	32	20.8	32	31.1	11	31.4
Current placement	6	3.9	7	6.8	1	2.9
Total	160	52.1	107	34.9	37	12.1

[a] For offense details, see table 4.1.

* Statistically significant at $\chi^2(2, N = 304) = 50.369, p < .001$; ** statistically significant at $\chi^2(8, N = 304) = 25.712, p < .001$ (5 cells have expected cell count less than 5); *** statistically significant at $\chi^2(4, 8 = 297) = 29.416, p < .001$ (1 cells has expected cell count less than 5); **** statistically significant at $\chi^2(2, N = 290) = 14.858, p < .001$; ***** statistically significant at $\chi^2(6, N = 292) = 14.109, p < .05$

and of juveniles of other races (31.4%). More than half (53.9%) of white youths had no prior court referrals, as compared with about one-third of blacks (30.1%) and of youths of other races (37.1%). Less than one-quarter (24.7%) of white youths were under court supervision, as compared with more than one-third of black youths (37.9%) and of youths of other races (34.3%). By every measure—present offense, prior arrests, and court status —white youths were significantly less delinquent than were black youths and youths of other races.

B. Race and Custody, Location, and Detention

The arrest status, detention status, and location of interrogations differed significantly for juveniles of different races. Although police had arrested 86.6% of all juveniles whom they interrogated, table 6.12 reports that they arrested a significantly larger proportion of black youths (91.6%) and youths of other races (94.6%) than of white youths (81.3%). Police detained about two in five white youths (41.9%), as contrasted with more than three-quarters of black youths (76.6%) and of youths of other races (86.5%). Youths' present offense and prior records likely account for some racial differences in arrest and detention status.

The locations in which police questioned youth varied with their race. Police questioned most juveniles (55.7%) at police stations (see table 3.2),

Table 6.12

Custody Status, Detention Status, and Location of Interrogation, by Race

	White		Black		Other	
	N	%	N	%	N	%
Custody status*						
Arrested	130	81.3	98	91.6	35	94.6
Not arrested	30	18.8	9	8.4	2	5.4
Detention status**						
Detained	67	41.9	82	76.6	32	86.5
Not detained	87	54.4	23	21.5	4	10.8
Location of interrogation***						
Police/sheriff's department	87	54.4	65	60.7	19	51.4
Detention-correction	21	13.1	31	29.0	16	43.2
Place of arrest	21	13.1	3	2.8	1	2.7
School	16	10.0	3	2.8	0	0.0
Home	13	8.1	5	4.7	1	2.7
Hospital	2	1.3	0	0.0	0	0.0

* Statistically significant at $\chi^2(2, N = 304) = 8.232$, $p < .05$; ** statistically significant at $\chi^2(2, N = 304) = 45.413$, $p < .001$ (3 cells have expected count less than 5); *** statistically significant at $\chi^2(10, N = 304) = 37.732$, $p < .001$ (6 cells have expected count less than 5)

Table 6.13

People Present at Interrogation, by Race

	White		Black		Other	
	N	%	N	%	N	%
Police interrogators						
One	136	85.0	92	86.0	33	89.2
Two	24	15.0	15	14.0	4	10.8
Others[a]						
Parent	18	11.3	6	5.6	1	2.7
Other[b]	5	3.1	0	0.0	0	0.0
None	137	85.6	101	94.4	36	97.3

[a] Statistically significant at χ^2(2, N = 304) = 9.331, p < .1 (4 cells have expected count less than 5)
[b] Probation officer or school official

and they interrogated similar proportions of white youths, black youths, and youths of other races at the station house (54.4%, 60.7%, and 51.4%, respectively). Because police detained fewer white youths than those of other races, they interrogated a significantly larger proportion of minority youths at detention facilities (white, 13.1%; black, 29.0%; other, 43.2%). By contrast, police questioned proportionally two or three times as many white juveniles as minority youths at the place of arrest, at school, or at home. While suburban police were more likely to questions youths at the place of arrest, school, or home than were urban officers, the proportion of white youths questioned in these locations exceeds those attributable to geography. Although police made *Scales* recordings of all these interrogations, they questioned white delinquents under somewhat softer conditions than they did minority youths: fewer were arrested, fewer were detained, and more were in non-police-dominated locations.

C. People Present at the Interrogation

A parent attended only 8.1% of all juveniles' interrogations. Suburban parents were proportionally three times as likely to be present as were urban parents: 13.3% versus 3.7% (see table 6.5). Three-quarters (74.1%) of suburban delinquents were white. Table 6.13 reports that proportionally twice as many parents of white youths (11.3%) attended their child's interrogation than did parents of black youths (5.6%) or those of other races (2.7%). Thus, both geographic locale—specifically, differences in urban and suburban parental notification policies—and a youth's race affected whether parents attended a juvenile's interrogation.

D. Race and Whether Suspects Waived or Invoked Their Miranda Rights

There was *no* statistically significant relationship between youths' race and their decision to waive or invoke their *Miranda* rights. Police obtained waivers from 93.1% of white youths, 91.6% of black youths, and 94.6% of youths of other races—nonsignificant differences. Juveniles of each race with one or more prior felony arrests were more likely to invoke *Miranda* rights than were less criminally sophisticated delinquents. Within racial groups, the relationship between prior felony arrests and *Miranda* invocations prevailed and was strongest for white youths. White juveniles with prior felony arrests were significantly more likely to invoke *Miranda* than were repeat offenders of other races. Prosecutors charged more black juveniles with crimes against the person, and a larger proportion had prior involvement with police and juvenile courts (see table 6.11). However, no relationship appeared between type of offense and *Miranda* waivers, and that pattern held true within racial groups as well.

Justice system personnel expressed mixed views about whether juveniles of different races invoke *Miranda* at different rates. Most said they had not observed differences in waiver rates by race: "I don't see any difference in that. I think it comes down to their prior contacts with law enforcement—no matter white, black, Asian—is the driving force behind whether they're going to waive their rights." Some people thought that

Table 6.14

Juveniles Who Waived or Invoked Their *Miranda* Rights by Offense and Prior Arrests, by Race

	White				Black*				Other			
	Waived		Invoked		Waived		Invoked		Waived		Invoked	
	N	%	N	%	N	%	N	%	N	%	N	%
Offense**												
Person	34	94.4	2	5.6	38	95.0	2	5.0	17	94.4	1	5.6
Property	96	93.2	7	6.8	49	92.5	4	7.5	12	92.3	1	7.7
Drugs	13	92.9	1	7.1	2	50.0	2	50.0	1	100.0	0	0.0
Firearm	4	80.0	1	20.0	6	85.7	1	14.3	5	100.0	0	0.0
Other	2	100.0	0	0.0	3	100.0	0	0.0	0	0.0	0	0.0
Total	149	93.1	11	6.9	98	91.6	9	8.4	35	94.6	2	5.4
Prior arrests												
Nonfelony	122	96.1	5	3.9	61	93.8	4	6.2	22	91.7	2	8.3
One or more felony	24	80.0	6	20.0	35	87.5	5	12.5	11	100.0	0	0.0
Total	146	93.0	11	7.0	96	91.4	9	8.6	33	94.3	2	5.7

* Statistically significant at $\chi^2(4, N = 107) = 10.225$, $p < .05$ (7 cells have expected count less than 5); ** statistically significant at $\chi^2(1, N = 157) = 9.610$, $p < .01$

minority juveniles invoke *Miranda* more frequently because of prior experience with the justice system: "What I think I'm going by here is exposure to the criminal justice system. I think some of our minority kids have been more exposed to the system, especially in the sixteen- to seventeen-year-old range. They're a little more savvy, and they don't waive as frequently as nonminority kids." Others attributed minority youths' greater likelihood to invoke to cultural distrust and parental socialization. One judge said, "I think black children—socioeconomic studies I'm sure explain it—those kids tend to distrust the system much more. Inner-city kids have grown up with parents who distrust the system. Therefore, that impacts their distrust of the system." Another judge observed that minority youth likely have had more extensive contacts with other governmental agencies—county welfare, child protection, and law enforcement—which could foster distrust.

On the other hand, some justice system personnel view black youths as more likely to waive *Miranda* than their white counterparts are. An urban public defender said, "Black kids waive a lot more. Here in Hennepin County, I think at least 95% of my caseload are kids of color. It's very rare for us to get a kid—a Caucasian kid. Almost all of them are African Americans, and they do waive their rights a lot more. They just do." Some police said they prefer to question minority youths more than whites: "Minority kids I've dealt with are a little more willing to play the game, willing to engage in conversation. I have found the white kids to be more about 'Call my attorney.'"

Other justice system personnel thought that white youths invoke more frequently than minorities because they are children of privilege. One public defender said, "Kids from the 'burbs that we get, they're a lot less likely to talk to the police. They're a lot less likely to have a *Scales* tape on them." Similarly, some police view white youths as more likely than minority juveniles to invoke counsel: "Give me black kids from the inner city any day over these obnoxious suburban little white pricks, because every one of them dropped the attorney word. There is a difference by race. White kids are more confrontational, more in your face." By contrast, other justice system personnel thought that white juveniles waive *Miranda* more frequently than minority juveniles do. They attributed the difference to parental socialization and a greater tendency to trust the system.

While justice personnel speculated whether and why white or minority youths invoke *Miranda* more often, I found *no* significant differences in rates of waiver by race. The vast majority of juveniles of all races waived

Miranda: white, 93.1%; black, 91.6%; and other races, 94.6%. White delinquents with prior felony arrests invoked *Miranda* significantly more often
than did minority delinquents with similar arrest histories. This finding
reappears in the logistic regression and interaction effects of geography
and race.

E. Interrogation Tactics

I examined whether police used similar tactics—maximization or minimization—to question youths of different races. There were *no* significant
differences in police's use of maximization techniques with white youths,
black youths, or youths of other races. Police used the same techniques
(see table 4.2) and in about the same proportion with all youths, regardless of race. Recall, police used minimization tactics much less frequently
than they did maximization techniques when they questioned youths—
69.1% versus 17.3% (see tables 4.2 and 4.3). Table 6.15 reports that police
used minimization tactics significantly more frequently with nonwhite
youths than with white youths. They were significantly more likely to offer
themes or scenarios, to express empathy, and to minimize the seriousness
of the offense with minority youths than with whites.

Table 6.15

Minimization Questions: Types and Frequency, by Race

	White		Black		Other	
	N	%	N	%	N	%
Interrogation strategy						
Neutralize guilt*	18	12.1	16	16.3	10	28.6
Appeal to self-interest	16	10.9	12	12.6	6	18.8
Express empathy**	10	6.7	11	11.2	8	22.9
Appeal to honor	10	6.7	10	10.2	5	14.3
Minimize seriousness***	3	2.0	8	8.2	4	11.4
Blame third parties****	2	1.3	5	5.1	3	8.6
Number of tactics per interrogation*****						
None	130	87.2	77	78.6	24	68.6
One	15	10.1	14	14.3	3	8.6
Two	2	1.3	5	5.1	6	17.1
Three	1	.7	2	2.0	2	5.7
Four	1	.7	0	0.0	0	0.0

Note: Based on juveniles (N = 285) who waived *Miranda* rights and whom police questioned

* Statistically significant at $\chi^2(2, N = 282) = 5.913, p < .1$; ** statistically significant at $\chi^2(1, N = 282) = 8.152, p < .05$; *** statistically significant at $\chi^2(2, N = 282) = 7.401, p < .05$; **** statistically significant at $\chi^2(2, N = 282) = 5.394, p < .1$; ***** statistically
significant at $\chi^2(8, N = 282) = 23.058, p < .05$

Table 6.16

Form of Juveniles' Responses, by Race

	White		Black		Other	
Response	N	%	N	%	N	%
Short positive	145	97.3	96	98.0	33	94.3
Rationalization	102	68.5	63	64.3	19	54.3
Extended positive**	105	70.5	56	57.1	21	60.0
Negative-denial**	38	25.5	51	52.0	17	48.6
Seeking information***	20	13.4	29	29.6	14	40.0

Note: Based on juveniles (N = 285) who waived *Miranda* rights and whom police questioned

* Statistically significant at $\chi^2(2, N = 282) = 4.948, p < .1$; ** statistically significant at $\chi^2(2, N = 282) = 19.801, p < .001$; *** statistically significant at $\chi^2(2, N = 282) = 16.091, p < .001$

F. Juveniles' Responses

Juveniles of different races waived *Miranda* at comparable rates, and police used similar tactics to question them. However, youths of different races responded significantly differently to their interrogators. Table 6.16 reports that white juveniles were significantly more likely to provide police with one or more extended answers—three sentences or longer—than were black youths or those of other races (white, 70.5%; black, 57.1%; other, 60.0%). By contrast, white juveniles were half as likely as youths of other races to respond negatively or to deny criminal involvement (white, 25.5%; black, 52.0%; other, 48.6%). White juveniles were half as likely as youths of color to seek information from police, for example, the status of the case, their likely disposition (white, 13.4%; black, 29.6%; other, 40.0%). Thus, white juveniles appeared to speak more freely and to be more forthcoming in their responses than were youths of other races. Juvenile justice personnel corroborated these differences between white and black youths' responses. One public defender observed, "Kids of color are more inclined to shorter answer, which sometimes protects them a little bit. Kids of color tend to give those monosyllabic answers, and kids who tend to be more chatty, once they hit sixteen or seventeen, are the suburban white kids."

Table 6.17 confirms that youths of different races responded differently and that their interviews produced somewhat dissimilar outcomes. Recall, more than half (58.6%) of youths confessed, nearly one-third (29.8%) made incriminating admissions, and only about one-tenth (11.6%) denied involvement (see table 5.2). In addition, outcomes varied with youths' attitudes—cooperative or resistant. Cooperative youths confessed significantly more often (71.4%), and the small group of resistant youths denied their involvement (43.8%).

There were significant differences in interrogation outcomes by race. First, significantly more white juveniles exhibited cooperative attitudes than did black youths (85.2% versus 70.4%). Conversely, black juveniles were twice as likely as white youths to display a resistant attitude (29.6% versus 14.8%). Youths of other races were neither as cooperative as white youths nor as resistant as black youths. A meta-analysis of the effect of race on police arrest decisions reported that "officers making a decision to arrest may not be reacting to a suspect's race but to his or her disrespectful behavior, with Black suspects showing a greater tendency to exhibit disrespectful behaviors during encounters."[78] However, earlier research reports that youths' attitude primarily affected arrest decisions for less serious offenses, rather than for felonies.

Other factors may account for racial differences in juveniles' attitudes. In data not shown in tables here, police questioned three-quarters (74.4%) of white youths within less than one day of the offense, as compared with less than two-thirds of black youths (66.4%) and those of other races (64.9%). Reflecting the relationship between strength of evidence and time to interrogation (see table 3.3), police had strong evidence in a larger proportion of interviews with white youths (67.9%) than they did with black youths (55.7%) or youths of other races (64.9%). Police questioned larger proportions of minority than white youths who were under arrest, placed

Table 6.17

Outcome of Interrogation, Corroborating Evidence, and Youths' Attitude, by Race

	White		Black		Other	
	N	%	N	%	N	%
Outcome*						
Confession	108	72.5	43	43.9	14	40.0
Admission	33	22.1	39	39.8	12	34.3
Denial	8	5.4	16	16.3	9	25.7
Corroborating evidence provided[a]	27	18.1	18	18.4	6	17.1
Attitude**						
Cooperative	127	85.2	69	70.4	28	80.0
Resistant	22	14.8	29	29.6	7	20.0

Note: Based on juveniles (N = 285) who waived *Miranda* rights and whom police questioned

[a] Includes providing leads to physical evidence, identifying a witness, creating a diagram, and identifying a codefendant

* Statistically significant at χ^2(4, N = 282) = 29.831, $p < .001$; ** statistically significant at χ^2(4, N = 282) = 7.963, $p < .05$

in detention, and in custodial settings—a police station or detention center. By contrast, police questioned larger proportions of white youths in softer settings—home or school—and accompanied by parents. The combination of factors—celerity to interrogation, strength of evidence, and setting—could contribute to minority youths' more resistant attitude.

A prosecutor attributed more black juveniles' having a resistant attitude to criminal sophistication—experience and background: "With black kids, I think to the extent that they are criminally sophisticated or have a family history of being in and out of the system, my bet would be that they would be the group that is resistant. More African American kids would be more defiant: 'Fuck you, I'm not going to talk to you.'" However, a public defender attributed attitudinal differences to minority youths' experiences with the dominant culture: "Recognizing that I'm dealing with an inner-city population, and with that [population there's] just general distrust of police officers and people of authority in the African American community."

Reflecting the relationship between attitude and interrogation outcomes, nearly three-quarters (72.5%) of white youths gave police full confessions, as compared with about two-fifths of youths of color (black, 43.9%; other, 40%). Conversely, black youths (16.3%) and youths of other races (25.7%) were far more likely than white youths (5.4%) to give denials (see table 6.17). The relationship between attitudes and outcomes corresponds with the types of responses juveniles made—white youths gave significantly more extended positive answers, and minority youths made twice as many negative responses and denials (see table 6.16).

Justice personnel's experiences confirm these findings. An urban public defender thought that white juveniles would be more cooperative and forthcoming than black youths because of black youths' experiences with police:

Kids of color who've had some experience with the criminal justice system and also come from families that have had a lot of police contacts, they've kind of been raised in an environment where they distrust the police. They've had lots of negative experiences with the police, and so they tend to be more hostile and suspicious of the motives of police. Whereas the kids that tend to be more cooperative with information are kids who are white and come from more privileged backgrounds.

Many justice personnel echoed the reference to white youths' "more privi-leged backgrounds" and attributed differences in attitudes and outcomes to socioeconomic factors rather than to race. A judge expressed the dif-ference, noting, "I'm probably more comfortable drawing a distinction between lower socioeconomic kids, and that being a more telling feature of their background than their race." An urban officer also attributed per-ceived differences in responses by race to socioeconomic background and culture rather than to youths' ethnicity:

> I think it has to do with their attitudes they've been raised with, the culture in which they've grown up in, how they've been told to view the police and what the police are there for and the whole system. Kids I deal with that are white are pretty middle-class kids that have gotten in trouble, and my assumption is they grew up learning about Officer Friendly, [being] there to help you. [They're] more trusting. Whereas a lot of the black kids are lower income, come from pov-erty. They've seen a lot of stuff. And the family, they've heard stories about police corruption, or the police did this or that, whether it's true or not. They've had an image impressed on them that the police are out to get black people and don't trust them.

Police in this study concluded all the interrogations very quickly, and they questioned youths of all races for similar lengths of time. The rela-tionship between the length of interrogations and the involvement of guns appeared for youths of all races and was strongest for white youths. When I examined case-processing outcomes of youths of different races who waived or invoked *Miranda*, some significant within-group differ-ences emerged, but none between groups. For example, white youths who waived *Miranda* were significantly more likely to receive probation sen-tences than were those who invoked. By contrast, black youths who in-voked *Miranda* were more likely to have their cases dismissed than black youths who waived. However, the small numbers of youths who invoked *Miranda* do not allow me to control for other variables.

These analyses document similarities more than differences among youths of different races during questioning. Police questioned larger proportions of minority youths in more custodial settings, but youths of different races waived *Miranda* at similar rates. Those with prior felony arrests invoked more frequently, regardless of race. Although police used minimization tactics somewhat more often with minority youths, overall those techniques appeared in only a small proportion of all interrogations. In general, police used similar tactics and questioned youths for similar lengths of time regardless of race. Minority youths were more criminally sophisticated delinquents (present offense, prior record, and court involvement) than were white youths, and their attitudes (cooperative or resistant) and outcomes (confession or denial) reflected those background differences. However, none of the differences in attitudes or responses affected sentencing outcomes.

G. Multivariate Analysis: Geography, Race, and Invoking Miranda

Logistic regression enables us to estimate the factors that influence the outcome of the categorical dependent variable—whether youths waive or invoke their *Miranda* rights. Table 6.18 includes factors that bivariate analyses indicated would be associated with juveniles' greater probability to invoke *Miranda*. Previous bivariate analyses associated a greater likelihood to invoke *Miranda* with youths who have had prior felony arrests (table 3.6) and who reside in urban counties (table 6.6). Model I examines

Table 6.18

Logistic Regression Predicting *Miranda* Invocation

Predictor	Model I			Model II		
	B	SE B	e^B	B	SE B	e^B
Demographics						
Black	-.53	.52	.59	1.08	1.04	2.95
Male	.74	1.08	2.11	.83	1.08	2.28
Urban	1.50**	.61	4.50	2.21***	.81	9.16
Prior arrests						
Felony	1.21*	.64	3.35	1.19*	.65	3.30
Status offense	.07	.70	1.07	.08	.71	1.09
Interaction						
Black*Urban				-2.00*	1.17	.14
Constant	-4.43			-5.01		
Wald chi-square				2.899		

* $p < .1$; ** $p < .05$; *** $p < .01$

Predicting Invocation by Race and Geography

	Black urban male	Black suburban male	White urban male	White suburban male
log odds	-1.70	-1.92	-0.78	-3.00
odds	0.18	0.15	0.46	0.05
probability	0.15	0.13	0.31	0.05

factors predicting *Miranda* invocation, holding other variables constant. Model II examines factors predicting *Miranda* invocation, holding other variables constant and with the addition of interaction terms for race and geography. Logistic regression confirms the salience of prior felony arrests and geographic locale and reveals that white youths in urban counties are more likely to invoke *Miranda* than are youths of other races or those in suburban venues.

In Model I, the race variable—black as compared with white—is not significant. Similarly, the gender variable—male as compared with female —is not significant. The geography variable—urban as compared with suburban—is statistically significant. As compared with suburban youths, and holding race, gender, and prior record constant, we expect a 1.5 increase in the odds of urban youths invoking rights. In other words, the odds of invoking are four and a half times greater for urban youths than for suburban youths, holding race, gender, and prior record constant.

In bivariate analyses, juveniles with prior felony arrests invoked *Miranda* at significantly higher rates than did those with less serious or no prior arrests. Similarly, in the logistic regression, we expect a 1.2 increase in the log odds (or an increase in the odds by a factor of 3.35) of juveniles with felony arrests to invoke their rights, as compared with juveniles with no prior record and holding other independent variables constant. By contrast, the log odds coefficient for juveniles with prior arrests for misdemeanors or status offenses only is not significant. In Model I, without the interaction term, it appears that geography—residing in an urban county —and prior felony arrests are the strongest predictors for invoking rights.

Model II of the logistic regression introduces an interaction term of two predictor variables to describe how the effect of one of these predictors (i.e., race) depends on the value of another predictor variable (i.e., geography). If the interaction term is significant, then there is a difference between how white juveniles and black juveniles in urban or suburban locations invoke their rights. In Model II, the interaction term is significant at the .1 threshold ($p = .089$) but not the .05 standard. In Model II, being black and urban decreases the odds of invoking rights by a factor of two, holding other variables constant. With the inclusion of the interaction term into the model, no significant difference appears between urban and suburban black youths. However, a difference does emerge when we compare urban and suburban white youths. White youths with prior felony arrests were significantly more likely to invoke *Miranda* than were youths of other races. In Model II, urban white juveniles are more likely to invoke *Miranda* than are suburban white youths. The probability that a white juvenile will invoke *Miranda* increased from 5% for youths in suburban counties to 31% for those in urban counties. Overall, accounting for geography washes out the race effect when predicting the log odds that a juvenile will invoke *Miranda*. Thus, the significant factors in bivariate analyses—urban county and prior felony arrests—emerge as the most significant variables associated with invocations.

Summary and Conclusion

Urban and suburban police officers in this study questioned somewhat different offender populations. The youths whom urban police questioned were charged by prosecutors with more serious crimes, had accumulated more extensive prior records, and had more justice system experience than suburban youths had. Suburban police arrested and detained youths at somewhat lower rates and questioned proportionally more youths in less custodial venues—school and home—than urban officers did. These differences in arrest and detention status and location of interrogation likely reflect the underlying differences in youths' offense and prior record.

Urban youths invoked *Miranda* rights at higher rates than did their suburban counterparts. Urban and suburban police used somewhat different tactics when they questioned youths. Suburban police arrested a larger proportion of youths immediately after they committed an offense and had somewhat stronger evidence with which to confront youths when they questioned them. By contrast, urban delinquents had more extensive prior records, and officers referred to these records or accused youths of other crimes. Urban police used some minimization tactics more extensively than did suburban officers to induce youths to confess. Suburban youths exhibited a more cooperative attitude, gave fuller explanations, confessed more completely, and provided police with more collateral evidence than did urban youths.

Parental notification and presence marked the most significant difference between urban and suburban interrogation practices. Suburban police were three times more likely to contact youths' parents and to request their permission to question the youths. Justice professionals attributed these differences in notification and presence to suburban departments' policies to increase accountability and transparency. Quite likely, these policies reflect the greater affluence and influence of suburban parents compared with their urban peers. Although a larger proportion of parents attended interrogations in the suburbs, they did *not* provide their children with substantial assistance. Police described strategies to enlist parents as allies or to neutralize their presence. In the vast majority of cases, parents remained silent and did not intervene, and police questioned youths as if the parent was not there. In other instances, parents actually increased the pressure on their child to talk—"tell the truth." Parents acted protectively on behalf of their child in only two cases (8%) of those at which a parent was present.

Although parents only attended twenty-five interrogations (8.1%), we can draw some conclusions about how effectively they protected children's legal interests. First, the vast majority of youths did not spontaneously ask for a parent. Any policy that requires youths affirmatively to request a parent will fail, because so few do so. Second, a requirement that police obtain parental consent prior to an interrogation is likely to fail because every parent whom police contacted allowed officers to question their child. Finally, only a small fraction of parents present at an interrogation acted protectively on their child's behalf. The vast majority either sat by passively during the interrogation or actively interceded on behalf of police. Most parents, like other adults, do not fully understand *Miranda* or feel empowered to exercise rights.[79] Police adopted strategies to reduce parents' ability to help their child. They spoke with parents prior to the interrogation to enlist their assistance and conducted interviews in a manner orchestrated to minimize their participation. Accordingly, states' policies to require the presence of parents at interrogations are unlikely to achieve protective goals.

Racial differences in the criminal sophistication of delinquents, in interrogation practices, and in youths' responses overlap urban and suburban differences. Prosecutors charged a larger proportion of black youths with crimes of violence. Minority youths had more extensive records and court involvement. Police arrested and subsequently detained larger proportions of minority youths than they did white youths. They interrogated a larger proportion of minority youths in more custodial settings—for example, detention facilities—and more white youths in less coercive environments such as school and home. These differences are consistent with differences in youths' offense and prior record and do not suggest discriminatory law enforcement. A larger proportion of parents of white delinquents attended interrogations than did parents of youths of other races.

Despite significant differences in racial groups' present offense, prior record, juvenile court history, arrest and detention status, and location of interrogation, youths of all races waived *Miranda* at virtually identical rates, and police used similar tactics in their interrogations. Although police used more minimization techniques with minority youths than they did with white youths, they employed these tactics in only a small subset of all interrogations.

Youths of different races responded significantly differently to their interrogators. White youths exhibited a more cooperative attitude, gave longer explanations, and confessed at significantly higher rates. By contrast, proportionally twice as many blacks displayed a resistant attitude, gave negative responses, and denied criminal involvement. These differences are consistent with racial differences in experience with the juvenile justice system. Whether justice system personnel attributed these differences to youths' race or social class, they confirmed these findings. Despite differences in the ways these youths responded to questioning, the justice system did not sentence youths of different races differently based on whether they waived or invoked *Miranda* or subsequently confessed or denied involvement. Racial disparities have long plagued juvenile justice administration and contributed to disproportional minority confinement.[80] Against the historical backdrop of racial inequalities in juvenile justice administration, police in this study questioned youths of different racial groups similarly.

True and False Confessions

Different Outcomes, Different Processes

[B]y any standards of human discourse, a criminal confession can never truly be called voluntary. With rare exception, a confession is compelled, provoked and manipulated from a suspect by a detective who has been trained in a genuinely deceitful art. That is the essence of interrogation, and those who believe that a straightforward conversation between a cop and a criminal—devoid of any treachery—is going to solve a crime are somewhere beyond naïve. If the interrogation process is, from a moral standpoint, contemptible, it is nonetheless essential. Deprived of the ability to question and confront suspects and witnesses, a detective is left with physical evidence and in many cases, precious little of that. Without a chance for a detective to manipulate a suspect's mind, a lot of bad people would simply go free.[1]

No system of justice is foolproof, but when errors occur, the state may convict an innocent person. Juvenile and criminal justice personnel inevitably make mistakes as byproducts of human fallibility or, more rarely, deliberate misconduct. Constitutional safeguards—for example, proof beyond a reasonable doubt, the right to confront and cross-examine witnesses, and the privilege against self-incrimination—function to reduce risks of error and to prevent the state from convicting the innocent.

The Due Process model stresses the risk of mistakes and emphasizes reliability—a high level of quality control—in the justice process. It sacrifices some efficiency to maintain greater confidence in the justice system's decisions. Concerns about reliability "lead to a rejection of *informal fact-finding processes* as definitive of factual guilt and to an insistence on formal, adjudicative, adversary fact-finding processes in which the factual case against the accused is publicly heard by an impartial tribunal and is evaluated only after the accused has had a full opportunity to discredit the case against him."[2] The Due Process and Crime Control models diverge sharply regarding the need for and the risk of error in police interrogation of suspects—"informal fact-finding." The Crime Control model posits that a suspect is often the best source of information and affords police an opportunity to question a person shortly after arrest and before the person has had a chance to decide not to cooperate.[3] Whether police use tactics that elicit involuntary or unreliable confessions are post hoc judicial questions.

The Due Process model assumes that if police have conducted an independent investigation and have established probable cause prior to arrest, then the need to gather additional evidence from the suspect should be minimal.[4] It emphasizes individual autonomy and limits state power. Police arrest people to hold them to answer to charges and not to use them as a source of evidence. Accordingly, once they arrest someone, they should promptly conclude booking formalities and bring the person before a magistrate without unreasonable delay. "[T]here is all the difference in the world between an interrogation conducted during the relatively brief span of time necessary to get the suspect before a magistrate and an interrogation whose length is measured by the time necessary to get him to confess."[5] The two models clash regarding the appropriate role and scope of pretrial questioning—informal fact-finding and whether police examine suspects fairly and reliably. They differ whether guilt should be determined in an informal administrative proceeding (the interrogation room) without a record or in a formal proceeding (trial) in public view. They differ about the reliability of the process and the risks of error.

Innocent people confess falsely, some plead guilty, and juries convict others with disturbing regularity.[6] Studies of cases of DNA exonerations and postconviction exculpations report that false confessions occurred in about 15–25% of cases.[7] Along with mistaken eyewitness identification, false confessions are one of the leading causes of wrongful convictions.[8] Scholars debate the frequency with which false confessions occur, the interrogation techniques most likely to elicit them, the appropriate safeguards to reduce their incidence, and the impact of restricting coercive tactics on innocent suspects and public safety.[9]

We have no way to measure how frequently false confessions occur or lead to wrongful convictions.[10] They represent the proverbial needle in the haystack of true confessions. Analysts attribute our inability to estimate the incidence of police-induced false confessions to three factors:

> First, American police typically do not record interrogations in their entirety. Therefore, it is not possible to ascertain the ground truth of the interrogation. . . . Second, because no criminal justice agency keeps records or collects statistics on the number or frequency of interrogations in America, no one knows how often suspects are

interrogated or how often they confess, whether truthfully or falsely. Third, many, if not most, cases of false confessions are likely to go entirely unreported by the media and therefore unacknowledged and unnoticed by researchers.[11]

Despite our ignorance about prevalence rates, DNA exonerations of defendants who confessed falsely highlight the risk of imprisoning and executing innocent people.[12]

While we cannot estimate the rate or prevalence of false confessions, they appear frequently in post hoc analyses of wrongful convictions. Brandon Garrett found false confessions in 16% of wrongful convictions.[13] Others estimate that false confessions occur in between 14% and 25% of cases of wrongful convictions.[14] Surveys of police officers estimate that innocent people falsely confess in 5% of cases.[15]

Consistently with the expectations of developmental psychologists, youth appear especially susceptible to give false confessions. Steven Drizin and Richard Leo examined 125 cases of false confessions in which DNA evidence conclusively established the suspect's innocence.[16] Nearly one-third (32%) of those who confessed falsely to murder and rape were juveniles, even though only 8% of the people arrested for homicide and only 16% of the people arrested for rape are juveniles.[17] Another study of 340 cases of criminal exonerations between 1989 and 2003 reported that 42% of juveniles gave false confessions, compared with 13% of adults, and among juveniles fifteen years of age and younger, 69% gave false confessions.[18] An analysis of the trials and postconviction relief of two hundred DNA exonerees reported that false confessions occurred in 16% of cases and that juveniles accounted for 39% of false confessors.[19] Nearly all juvenile false confessions occurred in investigations of murders and rapes, where pressures to solve crimes are greatest.[20]

Disproportionate overrepresentation of young false confessors stems from their inadequate understanding of *Miranda*, immature judgment, impaired decision-making, susceptibility to stress, and heightened suggestibility.[21] Wrongful convictions represent a fundamental breakdown in the justice system, and youthfulness is a significant risk factor for false confessions that contribute to those miscarriages.

This chapter examines how and when false confessions occur and how the processes that produce them differ from routine interrogations. Part I reviews the sequences of events and interrogation tactics that lead innocent people to inculpate themselves. False confessions occur when police erroneously misclassify an innocent person as guilty and then use confrontational tactics—maximization and minimization—to elicit an admission. They may confront a suspect with false evidence to create a sense of despair. Interrogation conducted over a lengthy period heightens an innocent person's feelings of isolation and weakens his or her resistance. Individual vulnerabilities—youthfulness, mental retardation, and the like—increase the risks of false confessions. Part II contrasts the conditions that produce false confessions with the routine interrogations reported in this study. This study provides a baseline of ordinary questioning against which to identify false confessions as extraordinary outliers of a different process. This will enable decision-makers to scrutinize more closely confessions in which those exceptional factors appear, in order to assure their voluntariness and reliability.

I. False Confessions

A false confession occurs when an innocent person admits responsibility for a crime someone else committed and DNA or other evidence conclusively establishes the person's innocence.[22] We have no way to determine how often false confessions occur because no government agencies collect the data, and it is difficult to determine the ground truth—that is, a confessor's innocence.[23]

False confessions and wrongful convictions occur almost exclusively in high-visibility, serious crimes such as murder and rape.[24] "In high profile cases, the police are under significant pressure to solve a crime and, because of the magnitude of the investigation, are able to devote an unusually large amount of time to interrogating suspects."[25] A study of youthful exonerees reported that 96.1% of the juveniles and 98.6% of the young adults were charged by the state with murder, sexual assault, or both.[26] Police feel the greatest imperatives to solve these violent crimes and to use all means available. Without a victim or witness, police may have less evidence with which to find the true perpetrator and must rely more heavily on suspects' confessions to solve cases. Analysts attribute the disproportionate concentration of wrongful convictions in murder cases to "the extraordinary pressure to secure convictions for heinous crimes; the difficulty of investigating many homicides because, by definition, the victims are unavailable; [and] extreme incentives for the real killers to frame innocent fall guys when they are facing the possibility of execution."[27]

Although false confessions and wrongful convictions likely occur in less serious cases, it takes a long time and a lot of work to prove that justice miscarried, and states often will release defendants sentenced for shorter terms before they can establish innocence.[28] Also, delinquents receive shorter sentences, which reduces their incentive or ability to challenge wrongful convictions based on false confessions.[29]

A. Misclassification of the Innocent as Guilty

Personal and situational factors combine to produce false confessions.[30] These risk factors play out through a succession of investigative missteps: classification error, coercion error, and contamination error.[31] Police first must erroneously decide that an innocent person is guilty. Once they conclude an innocent person is guilty, they subject the person to coercive psychological tactics.[32] Officers' tunnel vision and confirmation bias, lengthy interrogation, and coercive tactics can elicit false confessions from normal adults without unique susceptibilities.[33]

> Investigators first misclassify an innocent person as guilty; they next subject him to a guilt-presumptive, accusatory interrogation that invariably involves lies about evidence and often the repeated use of implicit and explicit promises and threats as well. Once they have elicited a false admission, they pressure the suspect to provide a post-admission narrative that they jointly shape, often supplying the innocent suspect with the (public and nonpublic) facts of the crime.[34]

Misclassification occurs because poor investigation leads detectives mistakenly to conclude that an innocent person is guilty.[35] Police believe that they can accurately distinguish between truthful and deceptive suspects, and this mistaken belief leads to both classification errors and misplaced confidence in those judgments.[36] Police are no better able than laypeople to discriminate between true and false denials of guilt, and neither amateurs nor professionals accurately distinguish liars at rates better than chance. Psychological research has not independently evaluated the Reid Method, the scientific soundness of BAI questions, or claims of their diagnostic validity.[37]

Interrogation manuals discount the likelihood of false confessions, minimize the role of interrogation tactics to elicit them, and make scientifically unsubstantiated claims about police's ability to assess suspects' guilt or innocence.[38] Police express greater confidence in their ability to distinguish between truthful and lying suspects than do laypeople, even though they do not perform more accurately.[39] "Research has consistently demonstrated that interviewers cannot detect deception through non-verbal cues. Indeed, those cues which interviewers 'read' as indicators of lying often are a result of their own behavior (e.g., being too close to the interviewee) and are instead signs of anxiety with the situation."[40] Officers' length of service and training correlates negatively with accuracy in discerning deception.[41] Many criminal defendants *do* lie and the vast majority of those who confess *are* guilty, and this reinforces interrogators' confidence in their ability to discriminate liars. This guilt-presumptive baseline expectancy predisposes police to disbelieve true claims of innocence and to attend to information that confirms their belief.

> Interrogation is a guilt-presumptive process, a theory-driven social interaction led by an authority figure who holds a strong a priori belief about the target and who measures success by the ability to extract an admission from that target. . . . [O]nce people form a belief, they selectively seek and interpret new data in ways that verify the belief, . . . [which] makes beliefs resistant to change, even in the face of contradictory evidence.[42]

Analysts have developed taxonomies to classify different types of false confessions: voluntary, coerced-compliant, and persuaded or coerced-internalized.[43] A voluntary false confession occurs when an innocent person claims responsibility for a crime without any pressure from police. A person may voluntarily confess falsely for a variety of reasons: a pathological desire for notoriety in sensational crimes, a psychological need for self-punishment, or a desire to protect the real offender or others.[44] Most people who confess falsely do so to protect other people rather than because of police pressure.[45] A coerced-compliant false confession occurs when a suspect succumbs to psychological pressures and confesses to avoid prolonging an aversive interrogation experience.[46] An internalized or persuaded false confession occurs when an innocent but malleable suspect confesses to a crime of which the person is innocent and comes to believe his or her own guilt.[47] For a suspect to assume responsibility for a crime of which he or she has no memory, the interrogator must provide an explanation—for example, a blackout or repressed memory—to account for the absence of recollection.[48]

B. Confrontational Interrogation

Coercive interrogation compounds the risks for innocent suspects. After police misclassify an innocent person as guilty, they may employ coercive tactics. Accusatorial questioning—maximization and minimization tactics—prolonged interrogation, and false-evidence ploys may induce an innocent person to confess falsely to escape a stressful situation. Police may hear what they want to hear—confirmation bias—and disregard inconsistent evidence of innocence. A false confession may contain a veneer of verisimilitude if police deliberately or inadvertently contaminate a postadmission narrative by providing undisclosed facts and details.[49] Without a complete recording of the entire interrogation, neither police nor suspect can demonstrate whether and how contamination occurred.

If police presume guilt, then they may confront and question more aggressively innocent suspects. No diagnostic behaviors or responses reliably distinguish between truthful and deceptive suspects, and many factors on which police rely—nervousness, fidgeting, and the like—are equally indicative of stress as of falsehood.[50] Many behaviors that police use to indicate deception in juveniles—for example, slouching in a chair, failing to make eye contact, and delayed responses to questions—are normal adolescent conduct.[51]

The psychological processes used in the Reid Method—isolation, confrontation, and minimization—increase the risks of false confessions.[52] Research in England describes similar psychological tactics to overcome suspects' resistance as "Intimidation (e.g., increasing the suspect's anxiety over denial), Robust Challenge (e.g., aggressively challenging lies and inconsistencies), and Manipulation (e.g., justifying or excusing the offense)."[53] Isolation heightens stress and anxiety. Confrontation, fatigue, and sleep deprivation increase susceptibility to social influences, impair complex decision-making, and heighten suggestibility.[54] Minimization provides a moral justification on which some suspects seize to escape from isolation. Confronting suspects with strong assertions of guilt and presenting them with false evidence increase their sense of hopelessness.[55] Offering moral justifications to neutralize guilt may induce innocent people to adopt the proffered excuses as a mean to end questioning.[56]

Saul Kassin contends that innocence actually increases the risks that suspects will confess falsely. He concludes that innocent people may confess falsely because they believe the legal process ultimately will vindicate them:

> Those who stand falsely accused . . . believe that truth and justice will prevail. . . . Reflecting a fundamental belief in a just world and in the transparency of their own blameless status, however, those who stand falsely accused also have faith that their innocence will become self-evident to others. As a result, they cooperate with police, often not realizing that they are suspects, not witnesses; they waive their rights to silence, counsel, and a lineup; they agree to take lie-detector tests; they vehemently protest their innocence, unwittingly triggering aggressive interrogation behavior; and they succumb to pressures to confess when isolated, trapped by false evidence, and offered hope via minimization and the leniency it implies.[57]

Even after detectives elicit a false confession, police, justice system personnel, and juries do not readily recognize a confessor's innocence. Both police and laypeople intuitively trust confessions as they do other behavior that runs contrary to self-interest. "[M]ost people reasonably believe that they would never confess to a crime they did not commit and have only rudimentary understanding of the predispositional and situational factors that would lead someone to do so."[58] Neither professionals nor laypeople can readily distinguish between true and false confessions.[59]

The credibility of false confessions derives from the crime details they contain. "[I]nnocent people not only falsely confess[], but they also offer[] surprisingly rich, detailed, and accurate information."[60] Although police are trained to assess whether a "suspect can freely volunteer specific details that only the true culprit could know,"[61] they may contaminate a confession by supplying crucial details during interrogation, which a suspect incorporates unknowingly into a final, scripted narrative that enhances its credibility.[62] Police sometimes bring suspects to a crime scene to test their knowledge of how the crime occurred.[63] If suspects visit a crime scene prior to questioning, viewing it may reveal facts and contaminate any ensuing confession. One study reports that police brought 38% of exonerated false confessors to the crime scene.[64] Final confessions often are carefully constructed, police-guided narratives that do not reveal the backdrop of how the police and suspect produced them.[65] Police typically record "only part of the interrogation, often a final confession statement," and there often is "no recording of what came before."[66]

Two additional features compound the dangers of misclassification and confrontational interrogation. Police use of false-evidence ploys may cause even innocent people to despair and to confess to end the torment. Also, lengthy interrogation may amplify a suspect's sense of helplessness and futility. Confrontational tactics, false evidence, and prolonged questioning exact a greater toll from younger suspects than from adults.

1. FALSE EVIDENCE

The Supreme Court does not prohibit police from using trickery, deception, and false evidence during interrogation.[67] Trial courts routinely admit confessions that police elicited by confronting a suspect with false evidence.[68] Some people justify police trickery and deception on crime-control grounds—deceit is necessary.[69] "The greatest objection to a ban on deceptive interrogations of juveniles is likely utilitarian: without some trickery, police will be less able to extract confessions from suspects, and thus less likely to convict the guilty and clear the innocent."[70]

If many suspects lie, then should the law afford police similar latitude? Lying is a form of manipulation that uses a person for ulterior purposes. "[T]he rules and expectations governing discourse between citizens does not necessarily apply to police questioning of criminal suspects. Given society's interest in catching criminals, lying during interrogation can be justified as an appropriate means toward achieving this important social end."[71] Although lies and deception violate social norms, they may be necessary to elicit confessions from guilty suspects.[72] Some people condone duplicity as a last resort after other strategies have failed.[73]

However, government-sanctioned dishonesty carries risks. People are social creatures and highly susceptible to manipulations created by false appearances and by authority figures.

> Misinformation renders people vulnerable to manipulation.... Presentations of false information—via confederates, witnesses, counterfeit test results, bogus norms, false physiological feedback, and the like—can substantially alter subjects' visual judgments, beliefs, perceptions of other people, behaviors toward other people, emotional states, self-assessments, memories for observed and experienced events, and even certain medical outcomes, as seen in studies of the placebo effect. Scientific evidence for human malleability in the face of misinformation is broad and pervasive.[74]

Lying is a common and effective form of manipulation. Because of its effectiveness, use of false evidence during interrogation is fraught with peril.

Some analysts oppose police deception on ethical and prudential grounds.[75] Police can solve most crimes without resort to fraud during interrogation.[76] Constitutional safeguards function to preserve individual autonomy, and government deception deliberately manipulates a person and undermines those values. Sometimes, false evidence may seep into the fact-finding process and undermine the integrity of the justice system. Finally, state-sanctioned deception is corrosive and "has a tendency to expand into other areas of police work (i.e., it inevitably leads to police lying in other contexts, such as at trial); and . . . produces false and unreliable confessions."[77]

While scholars debate the utility of false-evidence ploys, initially we encounter definitional difficulties. What is false evidence? Should courts prohibit police from feigning sympathy or creating an illusion of a therapeutic relationship with suspects?[78] Is the use of themes to neutralize guilt or to provide justifications impermissibly deceptive? May police falsely tell a suspect that the homicide victim survived, in order to minimize seriousness and to induce a confession? Have police lied by omission if they fail to inform a suspect that the victim died and thereby obtain a confession to assault rather than to murder?[79] May police confront a suspect with false evidence—for example, nonexistent accomplice confessions, made-up witness identification, or fabricated physical or scientific evidence?[80] Should courts distinguish between verbal lies and falsified physical evidence or laboratory reports that may subsequently contaminate the criminal process?[81]

Without empirical studies of interrogation, we do not know how often or effectively police use false-evidence ploys when they question suspects. And we do not know how many *additional* guilty suspects respond to false-evidence ruses who did not respond previously when confronted with true evidence. Because we do not know the prevalence of false-evidence tactics or of false confessions, or the relationship between the two, we do not know how false-evidence ploys affect the ratio of true confessions by guilty people to false confessions by innocent ones—that is, true and false positives.

Even without empirical basis, some analysts argue that "police-induced false confessions occur frequently enough to create a serious societal problem and that current interrogation practices tend to produce these false confessions."[82] Some fear that to condone lying during interrogation may encourage police perjury.[83] We do not know whether legitimating lying during interrogation would generalize to increase perjury at suppression hearings or trials.[84]

Scholars debate the desirability of categorically prohibiting police from confronting suspects with false evidence.[85] Some recommend that judges focus on the reliability of statements and decide whether a particular strategy elicited a false confession, while others advocate sweeping prohibitions.[86] Analysts recognize the difficulty of distinguishing between false evidence (e.g., a claim to possess nonexistent fingerprints), exaggerated evidence (e.g., the certainty of a witness's identification), and anticipated evidence (e.g., evidence police predict they *will* uncover during an investigation). Police write offense reports and interrogation notes contemporaneously, but a judge at a suppression hearing may be unable to ascertain whether they had evidence to which they referred during questioning. Even if courts or legislators categorically prohibit use of false evidence, then prosecutors, defense attorneys, and judges must establish a causal relationship between police references to false evidence and a defendant's subsequent decision to confess. Interrogation is a cumulative process of social influence, and it would be difficult to attribute a suspect's decision to confess to a single, misleading element.[87]

Deceit, trickery, and false evidence play a significant role in eliciting some false confessions.[88] Confronting suspects with false evidence puts the innocent especially at risk.[89] Innocent people who waive *Miranda* in a guilt-presumptive process encounter officers whose preconceptions and professional expectancies lead them to misinterpret and more aggressively question those who deny guilt. Confronting innocent people with false evidence—laboratory reports, fingerprints or footprints, eyewitness identification—may cause them to disbelieve their own innocence. People whom police have misled with false evidence succumb to despair and confess to escape interrogation in the naïve belief that investigators will establish their innocence rather than seek to confirm their guilt.[90]

Good investigations should precede every interrogation. Police should possess enough real evidence with which to confront a suspect so that they should not need to resort to false evidence. If they do not have substantial evidence of guilt, then the likelihood increases that they have misclassified an innocent person and that false evidence may elicit a false confession. Analysts distinguish between the impact of true and false evidence on those who are questioned: "[T]he practice of confronting suspects with real evidence, or even just their own inconsistent statements, is a necessary tool that should increase the diagnosticity of the statements ultimately elicited. To the extent that police misrepresent the evidence, however, both guilty and innocent suspects become similarly trapped, reducing diagnosticity."[91] The United Kingdom prohibits police from using false evidence, and it has not adversely affected the success of interviews.[92]

2. LENGTHY INTERROGATION

It takes police a long time to elicit a false confession. Inbau and Reed estimate that a competent interviewer can obtain a confession in four hours or less, if a suspect is willing to talk.[93] By contrast, interrogations in which police elicit a false confession are lengthy affairs in which interviewers wear down an innocent person's resistance.[94] One study reported that in fifteen of sixteen cases of false confessions for which the length of interrogation was documented, police questioned suspects for six hours or more, usually continuously.[95] Another study reported, "in proven false-confession cases in which records were available, the interrogations lasted for an average of 16.3 hours."[96] The largest study of proven false confessions reported that police questioned suspects for less than six hours in 16% of cases, interrogated another one-third (34%) for between six and twelve hours, interviewed another one-third of suspects (39%) for twelve to twenty-four hours, and persisted from one to three days in the remaining 11% of cases.[97] A study of exonerations reported that false confessions "are usually the product of long, intensive interrogations that eventually frighten or deceive or break the will of a suspect to the point where he will admit to a terrible crime that he did not commit. Some of these interrogations stretch over days and involve relays of police interrogators."[98] Clearly, the risk of false confession increases with the length of interrogation, and there may be a tipping point after police question a suspect for more than a few hours.

D. Vulnerable Populations

Young people and suspects with mental retardation are especially vulnerable to coercive questioning and are more likely to give false confessions.[99] Juveniles are greatly overrepresented among those who give false confessions, and younger adolescents are at greater risk than older ones.[100] A study of 125 cases of proven false confessions found that juveniles constituted one-third (35%) of all offenders who confessed falsely, and those fifteen years of age or younger (19%) constituted the majority, even though police arrest far fewer younger offenders for the most serious crimes.[101] A study of DNA exonerations reported that juveniles constituted one-third (32.5%) of all suspects who confessed falsely despite making up less than 10% of those convicted.[102]

A study of 340 exonerations reported that false confessions occurred in 15% of cases, that juveniles accounted for 42% of all false confessors, and that among the youngest juveniles—those aged twelve to fifteen—more than two-thirds (69%) confessed to crimes they did not commit.[103] Significantly, exonerated juveniles who confess falsely involve only the small population of youths whom states prosecuted as adults.[104] This reflects the greater seriousness of their crimes, the greater pressure on police to solve them, and the longer period available to youths and their attorneys subsequently to correct the errors.

Another study focused on factors associated with wrongful convictions of 103 youths—defined as those under the age of twenty at the time of their offense.[105] One-third (31.1%) of juvenile exonerees gave false confessions, a rate of false confessions almost double that of young-adult DNA exonerees (17.8%).[106] Moreover, youths who confessed falsely tended to be younger than those who did not. These two findings—a higher rate of false confessions by juveniles and an age skew toward younger offenders —highlight the special vulnerability of young suspects.

Developmental psychologists and legal analysts attribute juveniles' overrepresentation among false confessors to developmental immaturity, diminished competence relative to adults, and increased susceptibility to interrogation techniques.[107] Juveniles have fewer life experiences or psychological resources on which to draw and with which to resist the pressures of interrogation.[108] Their impulsive decision-making, limited ability to consider long-term consequences, and greater desire to obey and please authority figures heightens their risk.[109] Their nascent judgment makes them less likely to appreciate the gravity of talking.[110]

Juveniles' immaturity, inexperience, and propensity to comply with authority increases the likelihood that they will waive *Miranda* without understanding the warning or appreciating the consequences. Juveniles' lower social status relative to adult interrogators and societal expectations of youthful obedience to authority create additional pressures to waive.[111] The isolation, stress, and anxiety associated with interrogation intensify their desire to extricate themselves by the short-term expedient of confessing.[112] Because the judgmental controls that regulate risk-taking lag behind emotional responses, "youth may be particularly willing to risk the potential long-term negative consequences of waiving rights for the positive consequence of ending an unpleasant interrogation and potentially being released."[113]

Juveniles have limited language skill, understanding, and attention compared with adults, and these differences affect their performance during interrogation.[114] Their reduced appreciation of legal rights or consequences increases their vulnerability to manipulative tactics.[115] They think less strategically and more readily assume responsibility for or confess falsely to protect a peer than do adults.[116] Limited ability to appreciate consequences renders them more susceptible than adults to police tactics and even alters their perceptions of events.[117] Suspects with low IQs erroneously believe that false confessions have minimal consequences and therefore comply more readily with police suggestion.[118] Juveniles are more likely than are adults to comply with authority figures, to tell police what they think they want to hear, and to respond more submissively to negative feedback.[119]

Developmental immaturity and diminished competence heighten juveniles' suggestibility. Police can more easily pressure, persuade, or manipulate them to make statements—including false ones—than they can adults.[120] "They tend to be immature, naïvely trusting of authority, acquiescent, and eager to please adult figures. They are thus predisposed to be submissive when questioned by police. Juveniles also tend to be highly suggestible. . . . [T]hey are easily pressured, manipulated, or persuaded to make false statements, including incriminating ones."[121]

The generic vulnerabilities of youth multiply when coupled with mental illness, mental retardation, or compliant personalities. These cumulative risk factors heighten susceptibility to give false confessions.[122] People with mental impairments and/or low IQs exhibit greater vulnerability during interrogation than do those of normal intelligence. People with mental illness understand *Miranda* less well and exhibit greater suggestibility.[123] Many youths in the juvenile justice system have mental health and substance abuse problems.[124] "[B]etween 70% and 100% of justice-involved youths have a diagnosable disorder, with a majority having multiple disorders. These rates stand in stark contrast to the rate for youths in the general population, which is around 20%."[125] Thus, delinquent youths are at greater risk during interrogation.

Despite the heightened vulnerability of youth, police do not recognize or respond to developmental differences between juveniles and adults.[126]

They use the same interrogation techniques on adults without mental health issues as they do with juveniles with mental health problems.[127] Tactics designed to manipulate adults may be much more effective and problematic when used on vulnerable children.[128] "Interrogation procedures designed for adults but used with children increase the likelihood of false confessions and may even undermine the integrity of the fact-finding process."[129]

Tactics such as aggressive questioning, presenting false evidence, and using leading questions may create unique dangers when employed with youths. Analysts note the disjunction between how investigators question child victims or witnesses using developmentally appropriate strategies tailored to immaturity and how they interrogate juvenile suspects using the same tactics employed with adult defendants.[130] Because many juveniles will find arrest, detention, and interrogation frightening, they are especially vulnerable to "readily admit to offences in order to obtain as quick a release as a possible from an uncomfortable situation."[131] Stressful conditions may cause children to change their stories and to actually believe their distorted version of the event.[132]

II. Routine Interrogation and True Confessions: Comparison and Contrast

False confessions result from a dynamic, interactive social process that involves both personal and situational elements. Contextual factors include the seriousness of the crime, the amount and strength of evidence available to police, and pressure on them to solve the crime.[133] Personal vulnerability factors include youthfulness, mental illness or retardation, or a suggestive or compliant personality. Personal and contextual factors interact with length and aggressiveness of questioning and protective features such as the presence of a lawyer for a vulnerable suspect.[134]

This study consists of sixteen- and seventeen-year-old delinquents changed with felony offenses. They constitute a youthful population theoretically at heightened risk to confess falsely. Despite their vulnerability, I have no reason to question the veracity of the statements they gave to police or their pleas in court. Many interrogations corroborated evidence that police already possessed. About one-fifth of suspects gave police additional evidence they did not already have.

False confessions occur primarily in cases of murder and stranger rape, for which police experience the most pressure to obtain a confession to secure a conviction.[135] Although this sample included a few youths charged with murder or attempted murder (1.3%) and criminal sexual conduct (5.5%), county attorneys filed waiver motions and juvenile courts transferred the most serious young offenders to adult criminal court.[136] It excludes the types of cases in which problematic questioning most often occur.

Police misclassification of an innocent person as a guilty suspect must precede every interrogation that elicits a false confession. In this sample, I judged that police had strong enough evidence to convict independently of youths' statements in more than two-thirds of cases and had more than enough probable cause to arrest them in all cases. Prompt arrests and independent investigations reduce the likelihood that police will misclassify and question the wrong suspects.

Although I looked for use of Reid Method tactics, police did not employ confrontational maximization techniques extensively. They most commonly confronted juveniles with real or hypothetical evidence. Although there may have been a few false-evidence ploys, as best I can discern from the files, they occurred infrequently. Police more often used hypothetical or implied evidence—"What if I told you somebody saw you?" or "Will we find your DNA on the gun?"—rather than fabricating nonexistent evidence. Although implied evidence may increase a suspect's uncertainty and anxiety, it is probably not as potent or likely to undermine a person's ability to resist as a false assertion that evidence conclusively establishes his or her guilt.

Every study of wrongful convictions and false confessions reports that they emerge as the product of lengthy interrogation—a minimum of six hours and more often twelve to eighteen hours of continuous questioning. Police completed the interrogations in this study very quickly—three-quarters in fifteen minutes or less and 90% in half an hour or less. Other research corroborates that routine interrogation is short.[137] A survey of police investigators reported that four hours was about the longest interrogations they conducted.[138] By contrast, another study reported that police required an average of more than sixteen hours of interrogation to elicit false confessions.[139] Thus, false confessions emerge almost exclusively during very lengthy interrogations, which constitute extreme outliers from routine questioning.

Summary and Conclusion
If we assume the criminal and juvenile justice systems are 99% reliable —an unrealistically high level of accuracy—then the sheer volume of

cases they process annually still would produce about ten to twenty thousand erroneous felony convictions and pleas. The wrongful convictions of which we occasionally become aware are only the tip of the iceberg of a much more deeply flawed justice system. False confessions feature prominently in about 20% of those wrongful convictions.

Proven false confessions occur almost exclusively during interrogations for murder and rape, for which police experience the greatest pressures to solve crimes. Police interrogators, in turn, use their full battery of tactics on suspects in these investigations. If they misclassify innocent people as guilty, subject them to aggressive and confrontational tactics, and question them for extended periods, then they create substantial dangers of false confessions.

The apparent relationship between serious crimes and false confessions should not allay concerns about interrogation practices in other investigations. Rather, cases in which the stakes are the highest—life and death—and innocent convicts have the strongest incentive and longest time to prove their blamelessness raise the visibility of these injustices. The lengthy sentences imposed on people wrongly convicted give them and lawyers more time in which to establish their innocence.[140] By contrast, people wrongfully convicted of less serious crimes garner less media or legal scrutiny, and prisons may release them before they can mobilize resources to prove their innocence.

Good investigation must precede every interrogation. To conduct a custodial interview, police already must possess probable cause. As the Supreme Court has said repeatedly, "probable cause is a fluid concept—turning on the assessment of probabilities in particular factual contexts—not readily or even usefully, reduced to a neat set of legal rules."[141] The Court characterizes probable cause as a "fluid," "common-sense," and "practical" standard,[142] and it requires at least a "fair probability" or a "substantial chance" that the person was involved in criminal activity.[143] Assuring that police possess probable cause prior to questioning may reduce somewhat the likelihood of initial errors that classify innocent people as guilty.

False confessions occur when police use some of the aggressive and confrontational tactics that the Reid Method endorses. Police employ these tactics to intimidate and to prevent a person from making a free-will choice to remain silent—the antithesis of voluntariness. The use of false evidence heightens feelings of despair, overwhelms innocent people's confidence in their own guiltlessness, and creates powerful incentives for them to escape from the situation, even by confessing falsely. The pressure mounts with the length of interrogation. All of these dangers compound when police question vulnerable suspects—youths and persons with mental illness or disabilities. Each of these elements—classification errors, confrontational interrogation, false evidence, length of questioning, and vulnerable populations—may require separate policy safeguards to reduce the cumulative likelihood of eliciting a false confession.

False confessions and wrongful convictions represent a fundamental breakdown in the justice system's quality control. The Crime Control and Due Process models diverge sharply in their concerns about the reliability of the justice process and mechanisms to prevent or control errors. The Crime Control model

> places heavy reliance on the ability of investigative and prosecutorial officers, acting in an informal setting in which their distinctive skills are given full sway, to elicit and reconstruct a tolerably accurate account of what actually took place in an alleged criminal event. The Due Process Model rejects this premise and substitutes for it a view of informal, nonadjudicative fact-finding that stresses the possibility of error. People are notoriously poor observers of disturbing events. . . . [C]onfessions and admissions by persons in police custody may be induced by physical or psychological coercion so that the police end up hearing what the suspect thinks they want to hear rather than the truth.[144]

The Crime Control model discounts the likelihood of error and tolerates a higher error rate than does the Due Process model. In the Crime Control model, mistakes become a problem if they undermine the deterrent function and legitimacy of the system.

The Due Process model rejects efficiency as a primary goal in favor of enhancing reliability.

> The aim of the process is at least as much to protect the factually innocent as it is to convict the factually guilty. It is a little like quality control in industrial technology: tolerable deviation from standard varies with the importance of conformity to standard in the destined uses of the product. The Due Process Model resembles a factory that has to devote a substantial part of its input to quality control.[145]

The interrogation room lies at the heart of the Crime Control model. It is where investigators conduct "informal, non-adjudicative fact-finding" during the narrow window of opportunity before formal commencement of the adversary process. "Facts can be established more quickly through interrogation in a police station than through the formal process of examination and cross-examination in a court; it follows that extrajudicial processes should be preferred to judicial processes, informal to formal operations."[146] The goal of the process is to elicit a confession that leads to a guilty plea and obviates the need for formal adjudication. If investigators underestimate the risk of classification error and use dangerous tactics—confrontation, false evidence, and lengthy interrogation—on vulnerable suspects, then they heighten the risk of false confessions. Incommunicado questioning amplifies these hazards because we do not know what happens when police interrogate suspects in secret. Without an independent record, we have no way to assure the reliability of the process, to assess how aggressively police questioned a suspect, to ascertain whether they possessed evidence with which they confronted a person, to determine whether police contaminated a suspect's statement, or even to measure how long they questioned a suspect.

Policy Reforms

The Supreme Court decided *Miranda* in an empirical vacuum because researchers and nonpolice observers lacked access to interrogation rooms. Four decades later, police still control admission, and we have few studies of a low-visibility but outcome-determinative stage of criminal and juvenile justice. Audio and video recordings can expose the inner workings of interrogation rooms to external scrutiny. Four Minnesota county attorneys provided me with access to *Scales* tapes and their associated files, and that entrée enabled me to describe and analyze routine felony interrogation of older delinquents. These findings have implications for interrogation policy and the special case of adolescents.

After three constitutional theories and decades of cases, the Court settled on *Miranda* to supervise interrogation. The Court's regulatory efforts have foundered on the same obstacle—the lack of a record of what actually happens in the interrogation room. Without an objective record, trial judges have to conduct suppression hearings, reconcile conflicting stories, resolve credibility disputes, and apply an imprecise legal standard—voluntariness—to contested facts. *Miranda* was supposed to remedy those deficiencies by providing a per se rule—the warning—and an objective basis for courts to decide admissibility of statements. The Court assumed that empowered suspects aware of their rights would assert them and maintain the adversarial balance.

Miranda did not empower suspects. Despite the warning, people succumb to the compulsive pressures the warning is supposed to dispel, and they waive constitutional protections at very high rates. Moreover, subsequent decisions shrunk the ambit of custodial interrogations that require warnings and limit the exclusionary impact when violations occur.[1] Police interrogation practices did not change after *Miranda*. Analysts note that rather than handcuff the police, the warnings have liberated them. *Miranda* "permit[s] the officer to continue questioning his isolated suspect. . . . *Miranda*'s warnings unquestionably serve—and from the outset were designed to serve—the function of permitting custodial interrogation to continue."[2] Finally, police question juveniles just like adults.

Miranda alone is inadequate to empower suspects, to maintain a properly functioning adversary process, or to ensure voluntary and reliable statements. A warning is especially problematic for younger juveniles, who may not understand the words or concepts it conveys. Courts and legislatures should adopt protections for youths and policies to increase reliability and to reduce risks of false confessions. Only mandatory recording can enable judges to know what happened when police elicited a statement and to assure its voluntariness and reliability.

Part I of this chapter argues that Court decisions have minimized *Miranda*'s impact in theory, undermined it in practice, and rendered it a nullity. If only 10%–20% of suspects—primarily the more sophisticated ones—avail themselves of this basic procedural safeguard, then how effectively does it protect the adversary system? After suspects waive *Miranda*, interrogation tactics remain essentially unchanged from those used prior to *Miranda*. Most damaging, *Miranda* displaced judicial scrutiny of the voluntariness and reliability of statements. Adherence to *Miranda* provides safe passage to admissibility. Despite *Miranda*'s shortcomings, it remains a necessary but not sufficient condition for admissibility of statements. The Court in *Dickerson v. United States* acknowledged that *Miranda* does not significantly restrict law enforcement and that "warnings have become part of our national culture."[3]

Part II argues for invigorated judicial scrutiny of voluntariness—the voluntariness of youths' *Miranda* waivers and the reliability of statements. The Court long has recognized the heightened vulnerability of youths in the interrogation room and has distinguished between the competence of younger and older youths. Developmental psychological research and the age skew of suspects who confess falsely corroborate the different abilities of younger and older adolescents. Younger juveniles' incomplete understanding, impaired judgment, and heightened vulnerability warrant greater assistance—a nonwaivable right to counsel—to assure voluntariness of *Miranda* waivers and statements. Strategies to enhance reliability and factual accuracy and to reduce risk of involuntary and false confessions include a shift from confrontational interrogation to investigative interviewing, as well as time limits on the length of interrogations.

Part III concludes that no procedural safeguard is stronger than the means available to enforce it. Mandatory recording of *all* questioning by police of suspects is necessary to assure factual accuracy, to minimize coercion, and to increase police professionalism. In the Crime Control model of American justice, the inquisitorial stage—the interrogation room—effectively determines the outcome. Even guilty defendants deserve an opportunity to appeal on the record and to obtain judicial review. Every state should require recording of custodial interrogation.

I. *Miranda*'s Waning Protections

The Court intended *Miranda* to bolster the privilege against self-incrimination—"the main-stay of our adversary system"—and to protect "the dignity and integrity of its citizens."[4] The warning failed to achieve that goal. Post-*Miranda* decisions limited its scope and adverse consequences when police fail to comply.[5] *Dickerson v. United States* affirmed, "our subsequent cases have reduced the impact of the *Miranda* rule on legitimate law enforcement."[6]

Miranda's failure in practice mirrors its narrow doctrinal scope. *Miranda* requires only shallow understanding of the warning's words to enable informed individuals to choose whether to invoke its safeguards. *Miranda* provides a limited protection (awareness of rights and ability to terminate questioning) that only comes into play under restrictive conditions (custodial interrogation). Awareness of rights does not extend to collateral facts—for example, the seriousness of the crime or the availability of an attorney who is seeking access—or an appreciation of the consequences of waiver.[7] Suspect must assert their constitutional right to remain silent by speaking—an unambiguous invocation of the right.[8] Suspects enmeshed in the most inquisitorial stage of the adversary process make waiver decisions without advice of counsel, unless they explicitly request it. Despite *Miranda*'s insistence that the state bears a "heavy burden" to show a valid waiver, *Berghuis v. Thompkins* effectively shifted the burden to the defendant to invoke clearly.

Charles Weisselberg analyzed strategies police use to evade even *Miranda*'s limited protection and found that police manipulate conditions of custody to avoid giving a warning, soften up suspects prior to warning them, and question outside of *Miranda* those who invoke their rights:

> [W]e have a *Miranda* rule that is somewhat limited in reach, which sometimes locates warnings and waivers within the heart of a highly structured interrogation process, provides admonitions that many suspects do not understand, and appears not to afford many suspects a meaningful way to assert their Fifth Amendment rights. As a prophylactic device to protect suspects' privilege against self-incrimination . . . *Miranda* is largely dead.[9]

Miranda's limited protection—the right to cut off questioning—only comes into play after police isolate a suspect and subject him or her to the compulsive pressure of custodial interrogation, and 80% of adult and

90% of juvenile suspects succumb to those pressures and waive. Sophisticated suspects—those with prior felony arrests—invoke *Miranda* more frequently, but they would be more likely to resist interrogators even without a warning. If nearly everyone waives, then warnings fail to safeguard the adversarial process. Rather, the compulsive pressures that *Miranda* recognized as a threat provide police with a window of opportunity for an inquisitorial process.

Perversely, *Miranda* allows judges to focus on ritualistic compliance with a procedural formality rather than to examine closely the voluntariness of a waiver or reliability of statements. Critics note that "following *Miranda*'s hollow ritual often forecloses a searching inquiry into the voluntariness of a statement."[10] Judges focus primarily on *Miranda* and attend less closely to the voluntariness of a confession, as required by pre-*Miranda* jurisprudence.[11] In *Missouri v. Seibert*, Justice Souter recognized that "giving the warning and getting a waiver has generally produced a virtual ticket of admissibility; maintaining that a statement is involuntary even though given after warnings and a voluntary waiver of rights requires unusual stamina, and litigation over voluntariness tends to end with the finding of a valid waiver."[12] Similarly, the *Dickerson* Court noted, "Cases in which a defendant can make a colorable argument that a self-incriminating statement was 'compelled' despite the fact that the law enforcement authorities adhered to the dictates of *Miranda* are rare."[13] Thus, judicial review of a *Miranda* waiver is the beginning *and* the end of regulating interrogation.

As a matter of constitutional law and legal policy, *Miranda* remains a necessary but not sufficient predicate for any admissible statement. The decision in *Dickerson* concluded, "*Miranda* announced a constitutional rule."[14] After limiting *Miranda*'s scope and effectiveness, the Court declined to overrule it, and it remains the law. Despite its ineffectiveness, *Miranda* symbolized limits to police power, professionalized interrogation, and civilized police behavior.[15] It assures suspects that police will respect their legal rights, enables suspects to terminate an interrogation, and provides a device to preserve the adversary process. Despite *Miranda*'s primarily symbolic function, "the symbolic effects of criminal procedural guarantees are important; they underscore our societal commitment to restraint in an area in which emotions easily run uncontrolled."[16]

II. Reinvigorating Voluntariness

Miranda recognized that the compulsive pressure of custodial interrogation threatens the balance of equals in the adversarial process. However, a warning alone may be inadequate to enable people to make voluntary decisions, and it may provide even less effective protection for younger offenders. *Miranda* provides the information a person needs to make an informed waiver decision—that is, one that is knowing and intelligent. However, the voluntariness of a waiver depends on whether the person makes a "free and deliberate choice," rather than succumbs to "intimidation, coercion, or deception."[17] Any subsequent statement must be voluntary,[18] and the *Dickerson* Court reaffirmed, "We have never abandoned this due process jurisprudence, and thus continue to exclude confessions that were obtained involuntarily."[19]

Although the Court pays lip service to voluntariness, critics note that *Miranda* has diverted judicial attention from the substance of confessions and the tactics used to elicit them:

> *Miranda* may act as a cover . . . by leading to judicial myopia about voluntariness, supposedly the ultimate issue in interrogation regulation. Many have noted that once the warnings are given and a "valid" waiver obtained, courts are extremely likely to find confessions "voluntary." . . . By shifting the constitutional foundation of interrogation analysis from due process and "fundamental fairness" to the Fifth Amendment and compulsion, *Miranda* seems to have made it easier for courts to ignore police tactics that rely on trickery rather than coercion.[20]

Miranda provides an objective first step to assure a valid statement, but the voluntariness test provides the "only check on police conduct in the high percentage of interrogations where *Miranda* warnings have been provided and waived."[21]

A. Voluntariness, Youthfulness, and Vulnerability

The voluntariness of waivers and statements by youth are even more problematic. It is important to distinguish between youths' cognitive ability (capacity to understand) and maturity of judgment (capability to make grown-up decisions). *Miranda* requires only cognitive competence—the ability to understand the words. Developmental psychologists report that most sixteen- and seventeen-year-old youths can understand the meaning of *Miranda*. However, laboratory studies may overstate their competence, and youths' limited cognitive ability may be further compromised if they have a low IQ. In this study, older delinquents charged with serious crimes purported to understand the warnings and exercised their rights similarly to adults. The objective indicators—*Scales* tapes, waiver forms, and express waivers—provide the evidentiary basis on which trial courts find valid waivers. I attribute the differences between youths' and adults' waiver rates to youths' inexperience with the process, rather than to their inability to understand the warning.

The vast majority of older delinquents in this study waived their *Miranda* rights, and police questioned them about the same way as they do adults. These juveniles cooperated with or resisted the tactics police used about as well or badly as do adults.[22] Police concluded most interviews quickly and did not resort to coercive tactics beyond those inherent in a police-dominated environment. This study confirms developmental psychologists' findings that older adolescents function about on a par with adults and that police treat them that way. If psychologists are correct about the relative competence of older adolescents, then they are also likely correct about the inability of younger juveniles to exercise legal rights. Police elicit a disproportionate number of false confessions from the small group of the youngest offenders, and states should provide additional protections for these vulnerable suspects.

1. THE COURT'S FUNCTIONAL LINE: YOUNGER JUVENILES AND ENHANCED PROTECTIONS

Over the past quarter century, developmental psychologists consistently report that many, if not most, children fifteen years of age or younger are neither able to understand *Miranda* nor competent to participate in legal proceedings.[23] Research on false confessions underscores the heightened vulnerability of younger juveniles. In one study, police obtained one-third (35%) of proven false confessions from suspects under the age of eighteen and obtained most of them from youths fifteen years of age or younger.[24] Research on adolescent brain development, judgment, maturity, and self-control demonstrates why younger juveniles are especially at risk. The neuroscience bolsters developmental psychologists' findings and influences Court decisions.[25]

The Court's rulings in juvenile interrogation cases—*Haley v. Ohio, Gallegos v. Colorado, In re Gault, Fare v. Michael C., Yarborough v. Alvarado*, and *J.D.B. v. North Carolina*—excluded statements taken from youths fifteen years of age or younger and admitted those obtained from sixteen- and seventeen-year-olds. The due process decisions—*Haley* and *Gallegos*—recognized children's developmental limitations and required protective safeguards to assure that their statements were voluntary.[26] *J.D.B.* reaffirmed the relevance of age to assessments of custody and to a heightened vulnerability to coercion. The Court in *J.D.B.* asserted, "[A] child's age 'would have affected how a reasonable person' in the suspect's position 'would perceive his or her freedom to leave.' That is, a reasonable child subjected to police questioning will sometimes feel pressured to submit when a reasonable adult would feel free to go."[27] The Court concluded, "[O]fficers and judges need no imaginative powers, knowledge of developmental psychology, training in cognitive science, or expertise in social and cultural anthropology to account for a child's age. They simply need the common sense to know that a 7-year-old is not a 13-year-old and neither is an adult."[28] For more than half a century, the Court has recognized that youthfulness heightens vulnerability, and immaturity and inexperience increase the likelihood that youths' waivers and confessions may be involuntary.[29]

The Court's de facto functional line—fifteen years of age and younger versus sixteen and older—closely tracks developmental research findings that younger juveniles lack the ability to understand the words of the *Miranda* warning, much less to exercise their rights. Developmental psychologists report that older juveniles exhibit relatively adultlike understanding and perform more or less on par with adults in the interrogation room. This study corroborates that sixteen- and seventeen-year-old juveniles appear to understand and exercise *Miranda* rights about the same way as do adults. This consistency inferentially bolsters the research findings that juveniles fifteen years of age and younger lack competence to exercise *Miranda* rights.

Courts and legislatures should formally adopt the functional line that the Court drew and that psychologists discern between youths sixteen years of age and older and those fifteen years of age and younger. Some states attempt to protect vulnerable juveniles by requiring parents to be present and to consult with them. States that rely on parental presence make several unjustified assumptions about parents' competence and motivation. Parents may have little more understanding of *Miranda* than their children do.[30] Even with adequate understanding, they may be unable to resist the compulsive pressures of the interrogation room. Parents may have financial disincentives to pay for an attorney, or they may have a conflict of interest with their child.[31] Parental presence does not increase juveniles' ability to assert their rights, most parents provide little advice, and they often encourage children to cooperate with police.[32] This study provides strong evidence of parents' limited ability to assist their child during interrogation.

Analysts advocate that juveniles fifteen years of age or younger "should be accompanied and advised by a professional advocate, preferably an attorney, trained to serve in this role."[33] Juveniles should consult with an attorney, rather than rely on parents, before they exercise or waive constitutional rights.[34] "[Y]outhfulness supports a per se rule prohibiting juveniles from waiving either the Fifth Amendment privilege against self-incrimination in the interrogation room or the Sixth Amendment right to counsel in delinquency proceedings. In both contexts, the assistance of counsel should be mandatory."[35]

The Court emphasized repeatedly in *Fare* that lawyers play a unique role in the *Miranda* framework that other people—for example, probation officers, parents, or coaches—cannot duplicate. The *Fare* Court reaffirmed *Miranda*'s core understanding that "the lawyer occupies a critical position in our legal system because of his unique ability to protect the Fifth Amendment rights of a client undergoing custodial interrogation."[36] *Miranda*'s per se element was "based on the unique role the lawyer plays in the adversary system."[37] No other actor—parent or guardian —has the training, testimonial privilege, independence, and judgment to perform this critical role. "The Court in *Miranda* recognized that 'the attorney plays a vital role in the administration of criminal justice under our Constitution. It is this pivotal role of legal counsel that justifies the *per se* rule established in *Miranda*, and that distinguishes the request for counsel from the request for a probation officer, a clergyman, or a close friend."[38] To require a child to consult with an attorney prior to a waiver assures an informed and voluntary waiver decision and relieves parents of the burden that may follow from their misguided advice.[39] "The best practice to ensure accuracy in confessions and knowing and intelligent waivers of counsel is to require a per se rule that children cannot waive their *Miranda* rights without first consulting an attorney."[40]

I am not naïve about the implications of this proposal. To require youths fifteen years of age or younger to consult with counsel prior to a *Miranda* waiver will limit somewhat police's ability to secure confessions. However, *Gault* recognized youths' constitutional right to a fundamentally fair proceeding. If the majority of younger juveniles do not understand

and cannot exercise rights without legal assistance, then to treat them as if they do denies fundamental fairness. Formal equality produces practical inequality and enables the state to take advantage of them. The Court in *Escobedo v. Illinois* observed, "No system worth preserving should have to *fear* that if an accused is permitted to consult with a lawyer, he will become aware of, and exercise, these rights. If the exercise of constitutional rights will thwart the effectiveness of a system of law enforcement, then there is something very wrong with that system."[41] Procedural safeguards assure factual accuracy, promote equality between the citizen and the state, and protect individuals from governmental overreaching. Respecting the rule of law inevitably diminishes somewhat the state's ability to fight crime—that is what constitutional protections do.

I long have complained of juvenile courts' failure to provide counsel for delinquent youths at trial.[42] I am equally dubious about states' ability to provide lawyers for youths at pretrial interrogations. More than three decades ago, the American Bar Association proposed that "the right to counsel should attach *as soon as the juvenile is taken into custody* by an agent of the state, when a petition is filed against the juvenile, or when the juvenile appears personally at an intake conference, whichever occurs first."[43] The ABA endorsed mandatory, nonwaivable counsel because it recognized that "[f]ew juveniles have the experience and understanding to decide meaningfully that the assistance of counsel would not be helpful."[44] For more than a quarter of a century, I have criticized juvenile courts for failing to appoint counsel for juveniles, for failing to conduct meaningful waiver colloquies, for allowing incompetent youths to waive counsel, and for removing unrepresented juveniles from their homes.[45] Over the past decade, federal and state-by-state assessments in nineteen jurisdictions conducted by the American Bar Association and the National Juvenile Defender Center confirm the continuing validity of those criticisms.[46] In some states, nearly as many youths waive the right to counsel at trial as waive *Miranda*.[47] Despite long-persisting failures, *Fare* emphasized lawyers' unique role, and *Haley*, *Gallegos*, and *Gault* recognized juveniles' exceptional need for assistance.

B. Enhancing Reliability

Constitutional concerns about involuntary confessions focus, in part, on factual reliability. However, *Colorado v. Connelly* relegated the reliability of confessions to states' evidence law rather than to constitutional regulation, if police did not act to elicit the statement.[48] Although the schizophrenic defendant in *Connelly* confessed while suffering from auditory command hallucinations—the "voice of God"—the Court concluded that while the statement "might be proved to be quite unreliable, . . . this is a matter to be governed by the evidentiary laws of the forum" and not constitutional requirements of due process.[49] Courts should focus on factual reliability and examine the fit between suspects' admissions and facts known to police.[50]

Several analysts have advocated for safeguards to enhance reliability, to avoid police contamination, and to evaluate suspects' suggestibility.[51] Indicia of reliability would include whether the statement led police to evidence of which they previously were unaware, whether it contained highly unusual facts not disclosed to the public, and whether it contained accurate details of mundane aspects of the crime.[52] To evaluate questionable statements, Richard Leo and colleagues describe a procedure akin to a suppression hearing to ascertain "whether the suspect's post-admission narrative 'fits' (or fails to fit) with the crime facts and existing objective evidence."[53] Brandon Garrett proposes that courts conduct evidentiary reliability hearings to assess whether police contaminated a contested confession.[54] Expert evaluations of juveniles and people suffering from mental disabilities would assess their vulnerability and suggestibility.

Other analysts have focused on objective police practices that pose a risk of producing unreliable confessions.[55] For example, Welsh White has identified interrogation practices likely to elicit untrustworthy statements —threats of punishment, promises of leniency, threats of adverse consequences to others, presentation of false evidence, and the like.[56] Mark Godsey has identified tactics that create a penalty—compulsion—when police question a suspect.[57]

The contrasts between the routine interrogations analyzed here and those in which police elicit false confessions identify several fruitful areas for reform. First, police should conduct interviews to elicit information and to determine the truth, rather than to interrogate suspects to elicit a confession and to obtain a guilty plea. The police practices described in this study appear less confrontational or aggressive than the strategies prescribed by the Reid Method. They more closely resemble those employed in the United Kingdom. Second, false confessions emerge almost exclusively at the end of lengthy interrogations. Courts or legislatures should create a sliding-scale presumption that police coerced a confession as the length of questioning increases. Third, a prompt judicial determination of probable cause would improve screening, reduce the risk of misclassifying innocent people as guilty, and limit prolonged incommunicado questioning.

1. CONFRONTATIONAL INTERROGATION VERSUS INVESTIGATIVE INTERVIEWING

Police questioning should elicit accurate information from guilty perpetrators without simultaneously extracting incorrect facts from innocent people—to distinguish between true and false positive admissions. Youthful immaturity and vulnerability to confessing falsely require developmentally appropriate forms of questioning.[58] Police should reorient interrogation practices from a confrontational to a more investigative form of questioning.[59] It is anomalous to use developmentally appropriate techniques to interview child victims and witness but to use more confrontational tactics when police question young suspects.[60]

Recording of interrogations in the United Kingdom under PACE and the PEACE model of information gathering indicates that police can employ less confrontational methods to question suspects without adversely affecting their ability to elicit incriminating information.[61] Rebecca Milne and Ray Bull describe the PEACE approach, the training programs employed to implement it, and evaluations of its effectiveness.[62] PACE prohibited UK interrogators from using false-evidence ploys, required them to record the entire interrogation, and changed the culture of police interrogation. "After PACE, British interrogation moved to a model of investigative interviewing that is more conversational and designed to obtain information, not confessions."[63] *Scales* interviews in Minnesota probably resemble more closely UK practices than traditional Reid Method interrogations. The many successful interviews police conducted in this study demonstrate the effectiveness of less confrontational methods.

Investigative interviewing also reduces the need to employ minimization techniques that "can communicate promises of leniency indirectly through pragmatic implication."[64] Although explicit promises of leniency render a statement involuntary, psychologists contend that themes and scenarios convey implicit promises of leniency that may induce innocent suspects to confess.

> Minimization techniques come in essentially three forms: those that minimize the *moral* consequences of confessing, those that minimize

the *psychological* consequences of confessing, and those that minimize the *legal* consequences of confessing. One possible compromise . . . would be to permit moral and psychological forms of minimization, but ban legal minimization that communicates promises of leniency via pragmatic implication.[65]

Analysts suggest other reforms to enhance the reliability of statements obtained from young suspects, such as avoiding the use of suggestive or leading questions.[66] Leading questions did not figure prominently in any of the interviews analyzed in this study.

Leo describes other reforms to improve training of police investigators. Police cannot accurately distinguish between innocent and guilty suspects on the basis of nonverbal behavioral cues. They should not subject people to high-pressure tactics without strong independent evidence of guilt. Police training should raise awareness that psychological interrogation can induce even normal, innocent people to confess falsely and that youth are especially vulnerable.[67]

2. LIMITING THE LENGTH OF INTERROGATIONS

The Court has long recognized that lengthy interrogations produce involuntary confessions.[68] Questioning a juvenile for even five or six hours can produce an involuntary statement.[69] However, the Court avoided stating time limits after it approved "stop and frisk" encounters in *Terry v. Ohio*[70] and did not find forty-eight hours of pretrial detention to be unreasonable before the state must show probable cause.[71] While judicial restraint and considerations of federalism may explain the Court's reluctance to specify time limits for police practices, state courts and legislatures have the authority to restrict the length of time that police may interrogate suspects.

The vast majority of interrogations in this study were surprisingly brief, and police concluded 90% in less than thirty minutes. Every empirical study reports that police complete the vast majority of interrogations in less than an hour, and fewer than 10% require as long as two hours.[72] By contrast, prolonged interrogation—especially combined with youthfulness, mental retardation, or other vulnerabilities—is strongly associated with eliciting false confessions.[73] "[A]n interrogation's length seems directly related to its likelihood of producing a false confession. In nearly all of the documented cases involving false confessions by suspects of normal intelligence, the interrogation proceeded for several hours, generally more than six."[74] Samuel Gross and colleagues' study of exonerations emphasized that false confessions "are usually the product of long, intensive interrogations that eventually frighten or deceive or break the will of a suspect to the point where he will admit to a terrible crime that he did not commit. Some of these interrogations stretch over days and involve relays of police interrogators."[75] Garrett's analysis of false confessions in DNA exonerations reported that police interrogated only 10% of exonerees for less than three hours and interrogated the others "for far longer, typically in multiple interrogations over a period of days, or interrogations lasting for more than a day with interruptions only for meals and sleep."[76] A review of the psychological conditions under which police elicit false confessions concluded that they

> tend to occur after long periods of time—which indicates a dogged persistence in the face of denial. The human needs for belonging, affiliation, and social support, especially in times of stress, are a fundamental human motive. People under stress seek desperately to affiliate with others for psychological, physiological, and health benefits that social support provides. Hence prolonged isolation from significant others in this situation constitutes a form of deprivation that can heighten a suspect's distress and incentive to remove himself or herself from the situation.[77]

I cannot prescribe specific time limits for interrogations because I did not encounter either lengthy or factually problematic interviews in this study. However, courts should create a sliding-scale presumption that police coerced an involuntary confession as the interrogation length increases. Police complete nearly all felony interrogations of juveniles and adults in less than one hour and extract the vast majority of false confessions after prolonged questioning of six hours or longer. Inbau and Reid recognize the diminishing utility of prolonged questioning and conclude, "Rarely will a competent interrogator require more than approximately four hours to obtain a confession from an offender, even in cases of a very serious nature. . . . Most cases require considerably fewer than four hours."[78] These times provide guidance to frame the length of interrogation and the strength of the presumption of coercion. Based on the short duration of routine questioning and the fact that lengthy interrogations are associated with most police-induced false confessions, some analysts contend that "[r]egardless of the interrogation practices employed, an interrogation should not be allowed to extend beyond some prescribed limit, say six hours."[79] An American Psychological Association study group proposes that

> policy discussions should begin with a proposal for the imposition of time limits, or at least flexible guidelines, when it comes to detention and interrogation, as well as periodic breaks from questioning for rest and meals. At a minimum, police departments should consider placing internal time limits on the process that can be exceeded—initially and at regular intervals thereafter, if needed—only with authorization from a supervisor of detectives.[80]

Some suspects confess falsely to terminate a seemingly endless interrogation. A limit of four or six hours gives police ample opportunity to obtain true confessions from guilty suspects without increasing the risk of eliciting false confessions from innocent people.[81] It also comports with proposals to promptly present suspects before a magistrate to determine probable cause and to provide an independent *Miranda* advisory.

3. CLOSING THE WINDOW OF OPPORTUNITY:
PROMPT PRESENTMENT AND PROBABLE CAUSE

To elicit a false confession, police must initially misclassify an innocent person as guilty. If police lack evidence of guilt and rely on hunch or ambiguous circumstances, then they increase the likelihood of a classification error. Police must have probable cause to arrest a suspect and to conduct a custodial interrogation. The Supreme Court excludes statements obtained from a suspect arrested without probable cause, regardless of whether police complied with *Miranda*.[82] Although probable cause sets a low factual threshold,[83] it defines Fourth Amendment limits to the state's authority to hold a person for investigation. To reduce dangers of misclassification, police should justify to a neutral fact-finder why they want to question someone.

Federal Rule of Criminal Procedure 5(a) provides that "[a] person making an arrest within the United States must take the defendant *without unnecessary delay* before a magistrate judge, or before a state or local judicial officer."[84] Prompt presentment avoids isolation and secrecy and brings a suspect in custody quickly into the open. It allows judges to inform suspects of the charges against them and to advise them of their *Miranda* rights, and it enables suspects to process that information in a non-police-dominated setting. "[C]ustodial police interrogation, by its very nature, isolates and pressures the individual and there is mounting empirical evidence that these pressures can induce a frighteningly high percentage of people to confess to crimes they never committed."[85]

The Court in *McNabb v. United States* and *Mallory v. United States* exercised supervisory authority over federal criminal justice administration, interpreted Rule 5(a) to prohibit "unreasonable delay," and required police to present an arrestee before a magistrate within six hours.[86] Prompt judicial presentment reinforces the Fourth Amendment's probable cause requirements, restricts the time within which police may question a suspect unencumbered, and reinforces the constitutional values of the adversary system. The Court in *Mallory* noted,

> The police may not arrest upon mere suspicion but only on "probable cause." The next step in the proceeding is to arraign the arrested person before a judicial officer as quickly as possible so that he may be advised of his rights and so that the issue of probable cause may be promptly determined. The arrested person may, of course, be "booked" by the police. But he is not to be taken to police headquarters in order to carry out a process of inquiry that lends itself, even if not so designed, to eliciting damaging statements to support the arrest and ultimately his guilt. . . . Circumstances may justify a brief delay between arrest and arraignment, as for instance, where the story volunteered by the accused is susceptible of quick verification through third parties. But the delay must not be of a nature to give opportunity for the extraction of a confession.[87]

The *McNabb-Mallory* rule "aimed not only at checking the likelihood of resort to the third degree but meant generally to 'avoid all the evil implications of secret interrogations of persons accused of crime.'"[88] *Corley v. United States* reaffirmed that unreasonable delay of more than six hours renders a statement inadmissible, regardless of whether a court might otherwise find it voluntary.[89]

A few jurisdictions have adopted state versions of the *McNabb-Mallory* rule to reduce police incentives to arrest suspects on suspicion and to limit their ability to interrogate without probable cause.[90] Some use advanced communication technology to conduct a preliminary arraignment and to enable judges to advise suspects without requiring police physically to transport suspects to the courthouse. Texas requires a magistrate to give a juvenile a *Miranda* warning without a police officer present unless one is necessary for courtroom safety.[91] It requires a judge to oversee a youth's signing a *Miranda* advisory and to assure he or she understands the content of the warning.

A rule to require prompt presentment serves several important functions. First, it assures that police have probable cause to question a suspect and reduces somewhat the inherent coercion of custodial interrogation. A suspect who receives a *Miranda* warning from a judge in a noncustodial setting may be better able to make an informed choice than one who receives the warning from law enforcement in a police-dominated environment. "Police could be required to present the evidence establishing probable cause to a judge or magistrate before being allowed to interrogate. Although many suspects are now interrogated after they have been arrested, this does not necessarily mean that probable cause of their guilt was established prior to their arrest."[92] Prompt presentment enables police to complete the booking process without creating a prolonged opportunity for incommunicado interrogation.[93]

III. On the Record

Justice Harlan's *Miranda* dissent correctly observed that a verbal warning provides no evidence of what actually occurs during interrogation. "Those who use third-degree tactics and deny them in court are equally able and destined to lie as skillfully about warnings and waivers."[94] Requiring a recording of all police-suspect conversation provides an obvious solution. Within the past decade, criminologists, psychologists, legal scholars, police, and justice system personnel have reached consensus that recording interrogations reduces coercion, diminishes dangers of false confessions, and increases reliability of the process.[95] In the decades since Alaska[96] and Minnesota[97] mandated recordings, about a dozen states have required police to record some custodial interrogations, although some do so only for capital crimes, homicide, or very young suspects.[98] Some states require trial judges to give juries cautionary instructions about any nonrecorded statements that the state offers, and police record statements to avoid the negative instruction.[99] Several hundred police departments around the country have adopted policies to record custodial interrogations for some crimes—for example, homicides, violent crimes, young suspects, and the like.[100] In the United Kingdom, PACE has required police to record interviews for two decades.[101] Courts should adopt rules of procedure or decide cases and legislatures should enact laws to require police to record all custodial interrogations.

Audio or video recording creates an objective record of testimonial evidence. "[A]n exact accounting of interrogation events—from the way the warnings are given to the precise nature of any threats, promises, and deceptions that occur—is needed to determine whether statements are voluntary in the totality of the circumstances. . . . [T]his kind of record is very difficult to generate solely from testimony by the police and the suspect, even if we assume that they try to be honest."[102] It provides an independent basis by which to resolve disputes between police and defendants about *Miranda* warnings, waivers, or statements. A cynic might suspect that some police oppose recording because an objective basis to resolve credibility disputes shifts "the balance of advantage between police and suspects in the 'swearing contest.'"[103] Without an independent record, police almost invariably prevail in a swearing contest because an arrest and subsequent charges diminish a person's credibility at a suppression hearing or trial.

A complete record reduces risks of false confessions. It enables the fact-finder to decide whether a statement contains facts known to a guilty perpetrator or whether police supplied them to an innocent suspect during questioning.[104] "When custodial interrogations are not recorded in their entirety, one cannot easily discern whether facts were volunteered by the suspect or disclosed by law enforcement."[105]

Recording does not adversely affect any legitimate state interests and provides prosecutors with convincing evidence to avoid suppression hearings, negotiate better pleas, and obtain convictions more quickly. Recording protects police from false claims of abuse and protects innocent suspects from false confessions and wrongful convictions.[106] It enhances police professionalism by enabling an investigator to review details of an interview not captured in written notes and to test them against newly discovered facts.[107] It enables police to focus on suspects' responses and to review previously overlooked information. It reduces the need for police to take notes or for a second officer to witness suspects' statements, which may chill their willingness to talk. Recordings avoid distortions that occur when interviewers rely on memory or notes to interpret or summarize a statement.[108] Recording may deter police from using some coercive tactics; one officer told me, "Everything you do on tape lives forever."

Police administrators enthusiastically endorse the practice and express no desire to revert to nonrecorded interrogations.[109] They note that recordings

> protect officers from claims of misconduct, and practically eliminate motions to suppress based on alleged police use of overbearing, unlawful tactics; remove the need for testimony about what was said and done during the interviews; allow officers to concentrate on the suspects' responses without the distraction of note taking; permit fellow officers to view interviews by remote hookup and make suggestions to those conducting the interview; disclose previously overlooked clues and leads during later viewings; protect suspects who are innocent; make strong, often invincible cases against guilty suspects who confess or make guilty admissions by act or conduct; increase guilty pleas; serve as a training tool for the officers conducting interviews, as well as for officers aspiring to become detectives; and provide protection against civil damage awards based on police misconduct.[110]

A recorded confession greatly strengthens prosecutors' plea bargain advantage. Prosecutors affirm the value of recorded interrogations to bolster the strength of their cases because "proof of confessions or admissions, or evasions and signs of guilty conscience, is immeasurably stronger when established by electronic recordings, rather than by police testimony based on notes, typewritten reports, and testimonial descriptions."[111]

Defense lawyers can review recordings rather than rely on their clients' imperfect recollection of a highly stressful event. An objective record drastically reduces the number of pretrial suppression motions filed because it enables lawyers to evaluate what happened. This generates substantial savings to the justice system because police, prosecutors, and defense counsel do not spend time preparing for suppression hearings and judges do not conduct pretrial hearings to resolve disputes about *Miranda* warnings, coercive tactics, or statements' accuracy.

Thomas Sullivan addresses and rebuts police objections to recording.[112] Some complain that recording may interfere with officers' efforts to establish rapport with suspects. Because suspects have no reasonable expectation of privacy in the interrogation room, they cannot object to a recording. Several officers told me that their departments use hidden cameras and recorders that automatically activate when they enter the interrogation room. Others described a subterfuge in which they turn off a visible recorder while a hidden one tapes the interrogation.

Some police fear that judges or jurors may find some valid interrogation techniques distasteful or improper. If community representatives find certain tactics offensive even to protect public safety, then police policymakers should reevaluate them and prepare to justify their use in exceptional cases. Although psychological techniques have supplanted physical coercion, confrontational maximization tactics may be as obsolete and unnecessary as earlier police use of the "third degree" to obtain confessions.[113] Others worry that equipment failures may lead to suppression of some unrecorded confessions. State court decisions create exceptions for unintentional or inadvertent equipment failures. Some critics object to the costs associated with recording in times of fiscal constraints. Cost savings in justice administration more than offset the expense of recording.

For recordings effectively to safeguard the integrity of the justice system, police must document *all* communications with a suspect. Police must record all conversations—preliminary interviews and interrogations—rather than just a final statement.[114] Otherwise, police may conduct preinterrogation interviews, elicit incriminating information, and then conduct a recorded confession only after the cat is out of the bag —the type of practice that the Court condemned in *Missouri v. Seibert*.[115] Garrett found that police contamination occurred in false confessions because "[o]nly part of the interrogation, often a final confession statement, was recorded. There was no recording of what came before. . . . [I]t is 'not uncommon' for police to conduct an initial interview in which they 'use a gamut of techniques' to secure admissions, but do not tape that interview. Rather, police tape a second interview only once the admissions have been secured."[116] Only a complete record of every interaction can protect against a final statement that ratifies an earlier coerced one or against a false confession in which a suspect repeats back facts previously furnished by police.[117] Only a complete record of every communication between a suspect and police will enable a judge to determine whether police supplied facts not available to the public. Moreover, recordings themselves— for example, the camera angle—can bias perceptions. A video recording that depicts a suspect alone versus one that shows both the suspect and the interrogator affects how people evaluate the voluntariness and accuracy of a statement.[118]

Recorded interrogations are not self-executing, although voice-recognition software may ease transcription burdens in the future. Mandatory recording imposes an administrative burden on the justice system. Police must record each conversation during an investigation without knowing whether they will obtain useful statements. Thereafter, both prosecution and defense must review it or incur transcription costs to evaluate whether statements have evidentiary value. Police reports may alert prosecutors that a suspect made useful admissions, but their reports may not disclose *Miranda* errors, coercive questions, or exculpatory evidence that prosecutors must disclose to the defense.[119] Similarly, a defense lawyer, paralegal, or law clerk must review each tape to determine whether police gave proper warnings or used improper techniques.

The quality of some recordings is poor. Research that compares police reports about interrogations with taped interviews often reveals substantial discrepancies. "In some cases the police record of the interview stated that the suspect had made a confession and in others there was no clear statement about whether or not the suspect had confessed when in the researchers' judgment the suspect had clearly denied the offence."[120] Minnesota's Rules of Criminal Procedure require a party who offers a tape in evidence to furnish the court with a transcript.[121] Because of tedium and transcription errors, someone must verify the accuracy of the transcript. As one study found, "The simple expedient of checking the typed transcript with the audiotape recording cannot be overlooked, for, without exception, discrepancies were unearthed. In a number of these cases these were major errors, which if left unchallenged would present a serious example of misrepresentation."[122]

Savings to juvenile and criminal justice administration far outweigh these costs.[123] Recording interrogations "can actually *save* money (e.g., saving costs of lengthy contested pretrial and trial hearings on what occurred during custodial interrogations, because recordings make extensive testimony unnecessary)."[124] Police do not need to testify at suppression hearings; prosecutors and defense lawyers can focus on truly contestable cases; and judges minimize the need to conduct suppression hearings. This study amply corroborates those expectations. *Scales* recordings virtually have eliminated defense motions to suppress confessions and contested hearings. Prosecutors, defense lawyers, and judges consistently reported few motions to suppress evidence because tapes provide clear evidence of police compliance. Even without a pre- and post-*Scales* study of interrogation practices before and after the advent of recording, one could reasonably infer that recordings contribute to the high level of police professionalism observed. One judge who has presided over delinquency and criminal proceedings before and after *Scales* reflected, "*Scales* cleaned up the process both in adult and juvenile court. It made law enforcement dot the *i*'s and cross the *t*'s."

Recording is easy and essential to increase visibility and reliability of police interrogations. There are *no* valid objections to require police to record and prosecutors to provide a tape and transcript when the state offers a defendant's statements as evidence. Courts control the evidence they allow parties to introduce in, and judges should insist on the best evidence. The Wisconsin Supreme Court in *In re Jerrell C.J.* exercised its supervisory power and required police to record custodial interrogations of juveniles: "Plainly, this court has authority to adopt rules governing the admissibility of evidence . . . [and] can regulate the flow of evidence in state courts, including the nature of the evidence developed and presented by law enforcement."[125]

Police create the conditions—isolation, incommunicado questioning, and stress—that make after-the-fact determinations of what occurred during interrogation problematic. No legitimate reasons exist to rely on fallible, biased, and contradictory human memories about a secret and stressful event that occurred months earlier when it is so easy to create an objective record. Courts should exclude unrecorded statements unless the prosecution proves that the failure to record is not attributable to police conduct. Those might include nonnegligent equipment failure, a spontaneous confession outside the interrogation room without police questioning, or police documentation that a suspect refused to speak "on the record."[126]

This study demonstrates that recordings provide a unique opportunity for systematic evaluation and research of what happens in the interrogation room. As more states institute recording requirements and more researchers obtain access, we can finally address *Miranda*'s concerns about what transpires in secret and develop policies based on knowledge rather than surmise.

Conclusion

The Court repeatedly maintains that American criminal and juvenile justice is an adversary system. *Miranda* required the warning "to make the individual more acutely aware that he is faced with a phase of the adversary system—that he is not in the presence of persons acting solely in his interest."[127] Despite the Court's repeated assertions, in reality states decide most defendants' guilt through an inquisitorial system rather than in an adversarial one. Most defendants seal their fate in the interrogation room and render trial procedures a nullity—interrogation elicits confessions and confessions produce guilty pleas. Packer's Due Process model is highly distrustful of the "reliability of informal administrative fact-finding activities that take place in the early stages of the criminal process."[128] Concern about reliability requires procedures to prevent and eliminate mistakes to the greatest extent possible. Cases of false confessions and wrongful convictions attest to the validity of those concerns. Because states do not and need not provide full adversarial testing of every case, we need stronger mechanisms to assure the factual reliability of inquisitorial justice—to elicit true confessions from guilty people.

For more than half a century, the Court has used three constitutional strategies to regulate police interrogation. The Court's limited and ineffectual forays have relieved public officials of their responsibility to assure the fairness and accuracy of the justice system. Although *Miranda* invited states to experiment with alternatives to protect citizens during custodial interrogation, none has done so. The judicial and legislative abdication of responsibility reflects the "recognition that virtually any alternative that meets *Miranda*'s concerns about custodial pressures will impose infinitely greater burdens on law enforcement than do the *Miranda* rules themselves."[129] Recording imposes no great burdens on police, illuminates the inner workings of the interrogation room, and provides an objective record on which a defendant may appeal from inquisitorial fact-finding to a judge. Because the vast majority of defendants will not receive a trial, judicial review of the record of a confession provides an alternative basis to assure its reliability.

We know more than the *Miranda* Court did about the features of routine interrogation, the risks of false confessions and wrongful convictions, and the special vulnerability of young suspects. Courts, legislatures, police, and prosecutors should institute reforms to assure factual accuracy, to limit state power to take advantage of the weak and vulnerable, to safeguard individual autonomy, and to enhance the integrity of the justice system. Our adversary system of justice reflects a constitutional commitment to individual autonomy and equality with the state. Police interrogation, as practiced in many states, undermines those values and transforms investigations into an inquisitorial system in which police use individuals to build a case against themselves. Police can conduct legitimate investigations, interview suspects, and elicit truthful information without undercutting constitutional values.

From the Court's earliest to most recent decisions—*Haley, Gallegos, Gault,* and *J.D.B.*—it has recognized youths' heightened vulnerability and drawn a functional line to protect youths fifteen years of age and younger. Developmental psychological research corroborates that line of significantly diminishing competence for younger juveniles. The disproportionate concentration of false confessions elicited from the youngest suspects confirms their greater vulnerability. Since *Haley* ("counsel to advise him") and *Gallegos* ("a lawyer . . . to give petitioner the protection [from] his own immaturity") the Court has recognized that younger offenders need protection of counsel at interrogation.[130] For too long, juvenile courts have failed to provide the fundamental fairness that *Gault* mandated and that justice requires.

Appendix 1

Data and Methodology

More than four decades ago, the *Miranda* Court decried, "Interrogation still takes place in privacy. Privacy results in secrecy and this in turn results in a gap in our knowledge as to what in fact goes on in the interrogation rooms."[1] Then and now, police control access to interrogation rooms and grant few civilians access to the inner sanctum. The increasingly widespread adoption of electronic recordings provides researchers with an alternative to get inside the interrogation room and to lift some of the shroud of secrecy.

Alaska and Minnesota have long required police to record interrogation of criminal suspects. In 1985, the Alaska Supreme Court in *Stephan v. State* held that an unexcused failure to record a custodial interrogation violated a defendant's state constitutional rights.[2] In 1994, the Minnesota Supreme Court in *State v. Scales* used its supervisory power to regulate the admissibility of evidence and required police to record custodial interrogations.[3] *Scales* held that "all custodial interrogation including any information about rights, any waiver of those rights, and all questioning shall be electronically recorded where feasible and must be recorded when questioning occurs at a place of detention."[4] The Minnesota Supreme Court adopted the reasoning in *Stephan* and found that

> [a] recording requirement . . . provides a more accurate record of a defendant's interrogation and thus will reduce the number of disputes over the validity of *Miranda* warnings and the voluntariness of purported waivers. In addition, an accurate record makes it possible for a defendant to challenge misleading or false testimony and, at the same time, protects the state against meritless claims. Recognizing that the trial and appellant [*sic*] courts consistently credit the recollections of police officers regarding the events that take place in an unrecorded interview, the [*Stephan*] court held that recording "is now a reasonable and necessary safeguard, essential to the adequate protection of the accused's right to counsel, his right against self incrimination and, ultimately, his right to a fair trial." A recording requirement also discourages unfair and psychologically coercive police tactics and thus results in more professional law enforcement.[5]

Since *Stephan* and *Scales*, more states require police to record some custodial interrogations,[6] and many police agencies do so as a matter of departmental policy.[7] The increased availability of recordings will greatly expand opportunities for criminologists, psychologists, lawyers, and criminal justice professionals to analyze interrogation practices and policies.

This study analyzes *Scales* tapes and transcripts, police reports, juvenile court petitions, sentence reports, and dispositions associated with the offense for which police interrogated youth. County attorneys in four Minnesota counties—Anoka, Dakota, Hennepin, and Ramsey—provided unrestricted access to their files. This appendix summarizes county characteristics to frame the context within which police conducted the interviews. It describes how I collected, coded, analyzed, and interpreted the data. Chapter 6 presents additional data about structural characteristics of these counties and analyzes how differences between urban and suburban counties affected interrogation practices.

I. County Context

Police conducted the interrogations in this study between about 2003 and 2006. Table A.1 presents 2005 census data to compare and summarize county demographics, youth population, and juvenile court filings. Anoka, Dakota, Hennepin, and Ramsey Counties are the four most populous of Minnesota's eighty-seven counties. They account for almost half (47.6%) the state's population, nearly half (45%) the youth aged ten to seventeen eligible for juvenile court, and nearly half (45.6%) the delinquency petitions filed.

A. Anoka County

Anoka County is a suburban and rural county with nearly one-third of a million residents and about 6.2% of the state's total population. About 12.8% of the county population falls within the age jurisdiction of the juvenile court. Nine out of ten (90.9%) juveniles in Anoka County are white, with smaller proportions of black (4.7%), Native American (0.9%), and Asian youths (3.5%). The Anoka County Sheriff, Anoka Police Department, and eight municipal police departments provide law enforcement service.[8] In 2003, the Anoka County Attorney filed 1,459 delinquency petitions, about 4.3% of the total delinquency petitions filed in the state.

B. Dakota County

Dakota County is a suburban and rural county with more than one-third of a million people and 7.7% of the state population. About 12.8% of the county's population falls within the age jurisdiction of the juvenile court. The vast majority of juveniles in Dakota County are white (89.5%). Black youths (5.7%), Native American youths (0.8%), and Asian youths (4.1%) compose the rest of the juvenile population. The Dakota County Sheriff and ten municipal police departments provide law enforcement service.[9] In 2003, the Dakota County Attorney filed 3,231 delinquency petitions, or 9.4% of the state total.

C. Hennepin County

Hennepin County is an urban and suburban county that includes Minneapolis, the largest city in Minnesota. It includes several suburban cities and a population of 1.1 million people. Nearly one-quarter (23.5%) of Minnesota residents live in Hennepin County, and about 10.4% of the population falls within the age jurisdiction of the juvenile court. The juvenile population is ethnically diverse—about three-quarters (74%) of the youths are white, about 16.5% are black, about 1.7% are Native American, and about 7.8% are Asian. The Hennepin County Sheriff's Department, twenty-five municipal police departments (e.g., Minneapolis, Bloomington, Brooklyn Center) and five specialty agencies (e.g., Metropolitan Transit Police, MSP Airport Police, and the like) provide law enforcement service.[10] In 2003, the Hennepin County Attorney filed 7,728 delinquency petitions, nearly one-quarter (22.5%) of the state total.

D. Ramsey County

Ramsey County is an urban and suburban county that includes St. Paul —Minnesota's state capital—and several smaller suburban cities. It is the second most populous county in the state, with nearly half a million residents and 10.2% of the state population. About 11.3% of the county residents fall within the age jurisdiction of the juvenile court. About 65.9% of the juveniles are white, 17.8% Asian, 15% African American, and 1.3% Native American. The St. Paul Police, Ramsey County Sheriff, and seven suburban police departments provide law enforcement service.[11] In 2003, the Ramsey County Attorney filed 3,227 delinquency petitions, nearly one-tenth (9.4%) of the state total.

County Youth Population and Juvenile Court Filings

	Anoka		Dakota		Hennepin		Ramsey	
	N	%	N	%	N	%	N	%
County population	320,213	6.2[a]	381,027	7.7[a]	1,121,369	23.5[a]	497,047	10.2[a]
Juvenile population 2005								
Age 10–17	40,848	12.8	48,919	12.8	116,754	10.4	56,147	11.3
Gender								
Male	20,856	51.1	25,087	51.3	59,883	51.3	28,984	51.6
Female	19,992	48.9	23,832	48.7	56,871	48.7	27,163	48.4
Race								
White	37,121	90.9	43,775	89.5	86,421	74.0	36,980	65.9
Black	1,918	4.7	2,785	5.7	19,256	16.5	8,422	15.0
Native American	378	0.9	371	0.8	1,989	1.7	746	1.3
Asian	1,431	3.5	1,988	4.1	9,088	7.8	9,999	17.8
Delinquency petitions 2003	1,459	4.3[b]	3,231	9.4[b]	7,728	22.5[b]	3,227	9.4[b]
Status offense petitions 2003	567	3.3[b]	1,447	8.5[b]	7057	41.2[b]	703	4.1[b]

Source: Office of Juvenile Justice and Delinquency Protection 2011; Stahl, Livsey, and Kang 2006

[a] Percentage of total state population (5,104,890)

[b] Percentage of total state delinquency petitions filed (34,273) in 2003

II. Quantitative Data

Delinquency trials of sixteen- and seventeen-year-old youths charged with felony-level offenses are public proceedings in Minnesota.[12] Delinquency hearings for younger juveniles and those charged with less serious crimes remain closed and confidential. This study focused on older felony delinquents to obviate some confidentiality concerns. However, many files included information about younger juveniles—for example, co-offenders—whose identity remained private. In addition to securing the county attorneys' endorsement, I obtained orders from county juvenile courts to authorize access to the files. The court orders included confidentiality stipulations to protect the identity of all juveniles.[13] The University of Minnesota Institutional Review Board (IRB) approved the study. I have changed the names of all youths interrogated and all juvenile justice personnel interviewed to preserve confidentiality.

Each county generated a list of closed cases of sixteen- and seventeen-year-old youths whom prosecutors charged with a felony. In two counties a paralegal staff person and in two counties a law-student research assistant culled all closed cases that prosecutors had not stored in archives. Armed with a list of names, they individually searched every closed felony file to find cases that contained an interrogation transcript, a tape or digital record, a *Miranda* form and no confession, or a police report that indicated a juvenile had invoked his or her rights. The latter enabled me to compare juveniles who waived or invoked their *Miranda* rights.

A. Interrogation Files

About fourteen hundred cases met the search criteria—sixteen- or seventeen-year-old youths charged with a felony in a closed case that prosecutors had not placed in archives; 307 files included either an interrogation tape or transcript, or a police report that indicated a juvenile had invoked *Miranda* rights. Under Minnesota court rules, the party that offers an audio- or videotape as evidence provides the court with a transcript. "If either party offers into evidence a videotape or audiotape exhibit, that party may also provide to the court a transcript of the proposed exhibit which will be made a part of the record."[14]

Data collection proceeded from one county to the next between 2005 and 2007. Police conducted most of the interrogations between 2003 and 2006. The 307 files involved felony delinquency, waiver, or Extended Jurisdiction Juvenile (EJJ) prosecutions that remained in juvenile court.[15]

Every time a paralegal or research assistant found a tape, transcript, or police report of a *Miranda* invocation, he or she copied the entire file associated with that offense—police reports, *Miranda* form, transcript or tape of interrogation, juvenile court petition, certification study, probation report, and sentencing record. County attorneys provided me with complete, unrestricted access to all available files and allowed me to copy all cases that contained tapes, transcripts, or invocations. They did not cherry-pick or select only self-serving good cases. Two hundred and sixty (84.7%) files contained only a transcript and the remainder only interrogation tapes. Pursuant to confidentiality restrictions, I personally transcribed the latter. No one had transcribed or listened to those tapes since the police recorded them. This bolsters my confidence that prosecutors did not censor files to withhold problematic interrogations. Listening to and transcribing tapes immersed me in the tenor of the interrogation room.

Even unrestricted access to tapes and transcripts provides limited entrée to the reality of interrogation. "They can never reveal everything that has happened while a suspect is in custody, since only the 'formal' interview is recorded, and an observer can do no more than make an intuitive assessment of what might have happened 'off-stage.' The tapes may indeed on occasion provide a misleading picture of the whole encounter and may represent no more than the final act in what might have been a lengthy drama."[16] Interviews with police, prosecutors, and defense attorneys reported that very few "off-stage" substantive interviews occurred prior to creating a *Scales* record because the information would be inadmissible. Police training manuals sometimes distinguish between preliminary interviews to separate innocent from guilty suspects and more accusatory interrogations to elicit confessions from the latter.[17] Despite the supposed distinction between interviews and interrogations, I use the terms interchangeably in this study to describe post-*Miranda* custodial questioning of suspects. I closely examined the files and transcripts for any indication of interviews or questioning prior to *Scales* interrogation. Police reports or interrogations referred to *any* prior conversation in only 16.9% of cases, and none involved the substance of the offense. For example, when an officer asked a youth if he knew why police arrested him, the juvenile replied, "Your partner told me for burglary." Minnesota police had worked under *Scales*'s recording requirement for about a decade when they conducted these interrogations and had adapted to life "on the record."

Police, prosecutors, defense attorneys, and judges described how a recorded interrogation becomes a transcript or tape in the county attorneys' files. Transcription is expensive and time-consuming. The decision to transcribe an interrogation varies from county to county and among police departments. One officer explained, "They don't do it for everyone, because it's very costly. So it would be going to trial, where it is contested." Typically, police reports summarize the interview, and county attorneys request a tape or transcript when the reports indicate that statements have evidential value *and* the juvenile might contest the case. One officer explained,

> You only need transcripts when it's going to trial, and it's down to the last 5% of cases. Transcripts are only there if it's only going to trial. My guess is because it's because it's an easy disclosure issue, when a case gets charged, the county does get a copy of that interview, so they can share with the defense. The idea of transcribing it doesn't get started until the defense attorney says, "We're taking this case to trial. We're not going to settle." Very few of them [county attorneys] have them transcribed until it's pretty obvious they're going to trial.

Prosecutors identified several factors that affect whether they transcribe a tape—the seriousness of a case, the evidentiary value of the interview, whether a youth is in custody, and whether the case appears likely to go to trial. The files from which I obtained transcripts or tapes likely reflect more serious or contested cases.

Interviews with justice system personnel suggested other ways in which files with tapes or transcripts might differ from the larger universe of cases in which police questioned youths. Suspects are more likely to confess when police have stronger evidence, and prosecutors prefer to charge cases with strong evidence *and* confessions. One officer said, "What percentage of cases are there confessions without strong evidence? You have a solid witness or you have solid physical evidence, it probably lends itself more to a confession than others if you don't have solid witness. Most cases that get charged have a confession, because they're a slam dunk." A prosecutor concurred, "There may be some correlation between how good the evidence is and whether there's a confession or not." Another prosecutor thought she observed higher rates of *Miranda* invocations in cases in which they did not file charges: "If you were to look at all Mirandized statements of sixteen- to seventeen-year-olds being investigated for a felony, it [invocations] would be a lot higher if you put the uncharged ones in there."

Since I completed the data collection, digital technology has superseded cassette recordings and enhanced file sharing. With digital technology, after officers complete an interview, they download the digital file onto a departmental server. Thereafter, police stenographers or county attorney secretaries can access the server, select the audio or video file, transcribe it, and save the transcript as a digital file. Under rules of discovery, prosecutors must provide defense attorneys with tapes, CDs, or digital files of an interrogation and transcript. Public defenders follow a similar protocol to interview a client about an interrogation, review a tape or digital files, arrange for transcription, and provide copies to the prosecutors.

B. Coding Files
I reviewed police reports, witness statements, evidence inventories, and other documents to learn about the crime, the interrogation, and the evidence police possessed when they questioned a suspect. I obtained codebooks used in other studies[18] and constructed a 180-variable codebook. I coded for where, when, and who was present at an interrogation, how and when police administered *Miranda* warnings, whether juveniles invoked or waived, how officers interrogated them, how they responded, and how invoking *Miranda* affected case processing. I coded whether interrogators

used Reid Method tactics—for example, Behavioral Analysis Interview questions and maximization and minimization techniques. I extracted excerpts from interrogations to illustrate tactics officers used and juveniles' responses. I coded court records and sentences to assess how the decision to invoke or waive *Miranda* affected case processing and sentences. The codebook and interview protocol are available upon request: feldx001@umn.edu.

C. Data Limitations

The 307 files reflect sample-selection bias. I could not randomly select files from a larger universe of interrogation files because such an array did not exist. The sample includes only juveniles whom prosecutors charged with a felony and whose files reported an interrogation or *Miranda* invocation. Other evidence being equal, prosecutors are more likely to charge suspects who waive than those who invoke *Miranda* because they have plea-bargain advantage. Police made these *Scales* recordings during custodial interrogation, and the files do not include unrecorded, noncustodial interviews.[19] I do not know how the felony cases that prosecutors charged and that contained transcripts differ from those in which juveniles invoked *Miranda* and police did not forward the cases, cases that prosecutors did not charge, or cases that they charged but that did not contain transcripts. The study includes only sixteen- and seventeen-year-old youths charged with a felony and sheds only indirect light on problems posed when police question younger or less sophisticated juveniles.[20] Finally, Minnesota prosecutors filed motions to transfer to criminal court some older youths charged with serious offenses such as murder, rape, and armed offenses.[21] If a judge waived a youth for trial as an adult, then the county attorney transferred the file to the criminal division. Minnesota law excludes sixteen- or seventeen-year-old youths charged with Murder 1 from juvenile court jurisdiction, so the sample lacks some of the most serious cases.

More than 150 officers from more than fifty different police agencies conducted these interrogations. Interrogation is more of an art than a science, and these files reflect the personalities of the individuals who conducted them.[22] The variability of strategies used reflects officers' training and experience, learning on the job, personalities, and styles, rather than scientifically evaluated techniques,[23] and these officers' practices may not represent those of other departments in Minnesota. We do not know how community contexts, police department cultures, or interrogation practices vary or how those variations affect suspects' waivers or invocations.[24] *Scales* had required police to record interrogations for more than a decade when I collected these data, and police likely adjusted their tactics to accommodate recordings.[25] Their interrogation practices may differ from those used in other states. For example, other research has reported that police continue to question suspects after they have invoked *Miranda*,[26] whereas only one officer in this study "questioned outside of *Miranda*" after a juvenile invoked his or her rights.

I transcribed interrogation tapes and coded all the files to address county attorneys' and juvenile court judges' concerns about data confidentiality. Court-ordered confidentiality restrictions precluded use of multiple coders, so I did not obtain interrater reliability scores.

Despite these caveats, this study analyzes the largest number of routine felony interrogations in the United States. Notorious cases of juvenile false confessions—for example, Ryan Harris, the youths in the Central Park jogger case, and Michael Crowe—properly garner policymaker and media attention. However, analysts cannot estimate how often false confessions occur or how those cases differ from routine interrogations.[27] We need a baseline of routine interrogations with which to compare those exceptional ones. "In an era of electronic recording, the ideal way for scholars to measure and study actual police practices and their outcomes—and thus the best way to find out what is common practice and what is extraordinary—is to observe large numbers of videotaped interrogations, randomly selected from across the country, involving a full range of crimes."[28] This study gathers a large number of interrogations involving a range of serious crimes in several Minnesota counties and thereby controls for the applicable legal framework. It allows for analyses of structural, contextual, and demographic variations in interrogation practices to shed light on routine interrogation of older juveniles.

Minnesota tried these sixteen- and seventeen-year-old youths charged with felonies as juveniles. Two states try youths sixteen years of age or older as adults, and ten states try seventeen-year-olds as adults.[29] Transfer policies and juvenile court age limits place about 250,000 older youths in criminal court annually.[30] Minnesota's older, serious delinquents represent these young adults tried in criminal courts in other states.

III. Qualitative Data

Preliminary quantitative data analyses helped to generate questions about interrogation.[31] I conducted purposive interviews with police, prosecutors, defense lawyers, and juvenile court judges to elicit their views about interrogation, to learn from their experience, and to validate my findings. The interviews provide thick descriptions of the process. Literature review and preliminary analyses provided the theoretical and conceptual framework for interview questions that paralleled the structure of the codebook. I sought qualitative data to triangulate with the quantitative data and to strengthen my interpretation.

I conducted structured, open-ended interviews with additional probes with nineteen police officers, six juvenile prosecutors, nine juvenile defense lawyers, and five juvenile court judges in the urban and suburban counties. I purposely recruited juvenile justice system professionals to interview in several ways. I called juvenile court judges—elected public officials—directly, some of whom were professional colleagues. I recruited prosecutors and defense attorneys through their juvenile administrators. I contacted prosecutor and defender juvenile division heads and explained the project and my reasons to interview their staff. They, in turn, sent e-mails to their staff attorneys that described the project and sought volunteers for me to interview. The administrators provided me with a list of attorney volunteers whom I contacted. I recruited police officers in several ways. Police departments differ in organizational characteristics and internal structure—for example, divisions within departments based on legal categories such as juvenile, homicide, property, and the like.[32] In some instances, I contacted police juvenile division administrators who, in turn, recruited juvenile officer volunteers for me to interview. In several departments, I used a snowball sampling technique: initial police interviewees recruited other officers with relevant background and experience from their own and other departments. In those instances, officers acted as referrals and intermediaries to put me in contact with other officers. I conducted saturation interviews with justice system personnel until I reached a point of diminishing returns—no new data, themes, or conceptual relationships emerged.

In each interview, I explained the nature of the project and the information I sought. I assured them that I would not attribute comments to specific individuals but only to justice system roles. After answering their questions, I obtained their informed consent to record our interviews. I conducted five interviews face-to-face and thirty-four by telephone. The recorded interviews lasted between thirty and eighty minutes and averaged about forty-five minutes. After I elicited their responses, I corroborated my findings with their experiences and sought their interpretations of the data. The justice system personnel were remarkably forthcoming, candid, and generous with their time, insights, and experience. They strongly confirmed that my quantitative data corresponded with their experiences and provided valuable insights to aid my interpretation.

The interviewees had extensive experience in the justice system. The police officers averaged 18.4 years of professional experience, the prosecutors averaged 14.5 years, the public defenders averaged 13.3 years, and the juvenile court judges averaged 16 years. Four of the five judges presided in urban juvenile courts. Half of the prosecutors worked in urban counties and the other half in suburban counties. Two-thirds of the defense lawyers worked in urban counties and one-third in suburban counties. Seven police officers worked in suburban counties and twelve in urban counties. I interviewed sergeants, detectives or investigators, and school resource officers (SROs)—the ranks and specialties that conduct most custodial interrogations of juveniles.

In the included excerpts from interviews with justice system professionals and interrogations of juveniles, I edited to eliminate verbal fillers —"um," "er," "you know," and so on—repetitions, and digressions. I inserted punctuation for clarity. Apart from this editing, I want the juveniles and professionals to speak for themselves.

Appendix 2

Where the Girls Are

Historically, juvenile courts processed boys primarily for criminal misconduct and girls for noncriminal status offenses—for example, incorrigibility, being a runaway, and immorality.[1] The status jurisdiction reflected Progressives' cultural construction of childhood overlaid with paternalistic sexual attitudes.[2] Judges detained and incarcerated females primarily for minor and status offenses and at higher rates than they did boys.[3]

By the early 1970s, juvenile courts' status jurisdiction came under criticism because judges confined noncriminal offenders in institutions with delinquents, stigmatized them with delinquency labels, discriminated against females, and provided few services.[4] The 1974 federal Juvenile Justice and Delinquency Prevention Act (JJDPA) prohibited states from confining status offenders in secure facilities with delinquents.[5] Increased formality after *In re Gault* and JJDP-sponsored efforts to deinstitutionalize status offenders prompted states to divert them. Deinstitutionalization produced a dramatic decline in the number of females and status offenders in secure facilities by the early 1980s.[6] However, analysts warned that states could charge status offenders with crimes, relabel them as delinquents, and evade deinstitutionalization.[7] Punitive get-tough policies adopted in the mid-1980s to mid-1990s adversely affected girls—who were not the intended target—because states could charge incorrigible girls with assault in lieu of status offenses.[8] The crackdown on youth violence and the rise in girls' arrests for assault coincided with the removal of status offenders from institutions.

Police arrest and juvenile courts handle fewer females than their makeup of the juvenile population, especially for felony-level crimes.[9] However, changes in attitudes toward domestic assaults and mandatory arrest policies for family violence increased girls' vulnerability to arrest.[10] Sensitivity to domestic violence and restrictions on incarcerating status offenders encourage police to arrest girls for assault rather than incorrigibility.[11] Many cases of girls being charged with assault involve nonserious altercations with parents.[12] However, mandatory arrest for domestic violence—initially adopted to restrain abusive men—provides a tool with which to control unruly daughters.

Police arrest fewer girls than boys for serious crimes—the boy-girl ratio of felony arrests is about nine to one.[13] With fewer serious female offenders, juvenile courts respond to girls' misconduct differently than they do boys' criminality.[14] Research on *Miranda* comprehension reports few differences between how boys and girls respond: "Nearly all of the studies that have examined gender differences in *Miranda* comprehension have found no differences between males' and females' understanding and/or appreciation of rights."[15] However, one study attributed female delinquents' poorer understanding of *Miranda* to inexperience with the justice system and with lawyers.[16]

Offender Characteristics and Gender

Table A2.1 describes the boys and girls whom police interrogated in this study. Only one-tenth (10.7%) of the youths whom prosecutors charged with felony offenses were girls, about the same ratio at which police arrest girls and boys for serious crimes.[17] Although the girls constitute a small portion of the felons whom police questioned, they were in other respects strikingly similar to the boys. A significantly larger proportion of girls than boys were seventeen years old (66.7% versus 40.1%). However, no other significant differences between genders appeared in offense or offense histories. Of the girls whom police questioned, nearly two-thirds (63.6%) lived in urban counties and one-third (36.4%) in suburban counties. Prosecutors charged more girls with property and drug crimes and fewer with violent crimes than they did boys, and girls had fewer prior arrests and for less serious offenses. None of the differences was statistically significant. The similar offenses and histories of the boys and girls enable me to attribute any differences in interrogation tactics and responses to gender rather than to other variables.

Interrogation and Gender

Few differences appeared in the way police interrogated boys and girls, and they do not require tabular displays to describe. Police arrested, detained, and questioned equal proportions of girls and boys in similar locations. They questioned a larger proportion of girls than they did boys within twenty-four hours of the offense (78.8% versus 68.6%), and they were more likely to have strong evidence when they interrogated them (78.8% versus 61.8%). Girls were significantly more likely to be interviewed by a single police officer than were boys (97.0% versus 84.7%). Boys and girls waived *Miranda* rights at statistically similar rates (boys, 92.3%; girls, 97%). The marginal difference in waiver rates by gender is consistent with differences in prior experience with police. When I asked officers about

Table A2.1

Characteristics of Juveniles Interrogated, by Gender

	Male		Female	
	N	%	N	%
Age*				
16	161	58.8	10	30.3
17	110	40.1	22	66.7
18	3	1.1	1	3.0
Race				
White	144	53.1	16	48.5
Black	95	35.1	12	36.4
Other	32	11.8	5	15.2
County type				
Urban	143	52.2	21	63.6
Suburban	131	47.8	12	36.4
Offense[a]				
Property	148	54.0	21	63.6
Person	91	33.2	6	18.2
Drugs	15	5.5	4	12.1
Firearms	16	5.8	1	3.0
Other	4	1.5	1	3.0
Prior arrests				
None	84	31.3	13	40.6
Status	40	14.9	7	21.9
Misdemeanor	63	23.5	9	28.1
One felony	42	15.7	3	9.4
Two or more felonies	39	14.6	0	0.0
Prior juvenile court referrals				
None	111	42.2	15	50.0
One or more	152	57.8	15	50.0
Court status at time of interrogation				
None	125	47.3	17	54.8
Prior supervision	56	21.2	5	16.1
Current probation/parole	67	25.4	8	25.8
Current placement	16	6.1	1	3.2
Total	274	89.3	33	10.7

[a] For offense details, see table 4.1.

* Statistically significant at $\chi^2(2, N = 307) = 9.946, p < .05$

differences between males and females, one observed, "They [females] may be a little less likely to refuse to talk to you. I don't think I've ever had a female refuse to talk to me. They always want to say something, even if it's a denial." Males and females with prior felony arrests invoked *Miranda* significantly more often than did those with less experience.

Once juveniles waived *Miranda*, police used significantly more maximization techniques to question boys than they did girls. They confronted a larger proportion of boys than girls with evidence. Police were twice as likely to accuse boys of lying as they were girls (34.4% versus 18.8%) and more than twice as likely to urge boys to tell the truth (31.6% versus 12.5%). There were no statistically significant differences between boys and girls in police use of minimization tactics. Boys and girls responded to police questioning very similarly. Girls gave more extended responses and fewer denials than boys did, but the differences were not significant. One public defender reported, "Girls talk more. The girls will volunteer information," which makes the task for a defense lawyer "a giant nightmare."

Girls were more likely to fully confess than were boys (68.8% versus 57.3%) and less likely to completely deny their involvement (3.1% versus 12.6%), but these differences were not significant. Boys were significantly more likely to provide police with leads to other corroborating evidence than girls were (19.8% versus 6.3%). Both boys and girls manifested similarly cooperative attitudes when police questioned them (boys, 79.1%; girls, 84.4%). Police questioned boys and girls for similar, brief periods and questioned both longer when the case involved a firearm. No significant differences appeared between boys' and girls' decisions to waive *Miranda* and the level of offense for which the state convicted them, whether the state reduced charges, or the type of disposition they received.

In short, the girls and boys whom police interrogated presented comparable offenses, prior records, and previous juvenile court involvement, and police questioned them similarly. Apart from use of more maximization

Table A2.2

Maximization Questions: Types and Frequency, by Gender

Interrogation strategy	Male		Female	
	N	%	N	%
Confront with evidence*	142	56.1	13	40.6
Accuse of lying**	87	34.4	6	18.8
Urge to tell the truth***	80	31.6	4	12.5
Ask BAI questions	75	29.6	7	21.9
Use confrontational tactics	52	20.6	5	15.6
Warn about causing trouble for others	36	14.2	5	15.6
Accuse of other crimes	23	9.1	1	3.1

Note: Based on juveniles (N = 285) who waived *Miranda* rights and whom police questioned

* Statistically significant at $\chi^2(1, N = 285) = 2.752, p < .1$; ** statistically significant at $\chi^2(1, N = 285) = 3.160, p < .1$; *** statistically significant at $\chi^2(1, N = 285) = 4.996, p < .05$

techniques with boys, police questioned juveniles of both genders similarly, the youths responded the same ways, and they confessed at the same rates.

I asked police and justice system personnel to reflect on differences between boys and girls in the interrogation room. Many noted why it was difficult to answer: "we have very few girls." One public defender commented, "We don't see many girls come through. I could probably count on my hand the number of serious felonies I've had where the respondent was female, one hand."

With that caveat, interviewees generally described girls as "more likely to talk, less likely to invoke their rights"—an observation consistent with the data. One prosecutor attributed girls' greater likelihood to waive and to talk to the fact that they are talking to "an authority figure. Girls tend to be more cooperative and talk more." Several suggested that girls talk more freely because they usually have played a secondary role in the offense, even when charged with a felony offense: "Usually the girls are kind of just along for the ride and usually tell it as best they can, minimizing their activities." Girls who play a minor role have less to lose and more incentive to implicate others:

> Usually in felony-level offenses, they play more of a peripheral role. In the ag[gravated] robbery cases, they're the getaway driver. But they're usually not the one going in brandishing the gun, jumping over the counter, grabbing the money out of the till. That's usually the boys. So my sense is they talk more because they're, "I'm not going down. He's the one that did all that." My sense is they would talk more.

A study of probation officers' perceptions of delinquent girls characterized females as "Criers, Liars, and Manipulators."[18] When I asked justice system personnel to describe girls' attitudes in the interrogation room, they proffered two contradictory views that include criers, liars, and manipulators. On the one hand, they described the girls as emotional or manipulative. On the other hand, they described girls as hostile and confrontational.

Emotional

Some police described girls as more emotional about their crimes than boys are: "Girls are usually more emotional. They cry more often." A suburban officer said, "You get a lot more crying, a lot more emotion from juvenile females than you do from juvenile males—emotions and attitude." Larger proportions of girls than boys exhibited a positive attitude (84.4% versus 79.1%) and confessed (68.8% versus 57.3%). Girls' emotional distress can contribute to statements that are more fulsome. A public defender observed, "Girls in general tend to be much more emotional at the scene and disclose information right then and there. So those cases tend to resolve because the girls are pretty straightforward. They don't tend to be manipulative or play games. They kind of like just tell it like it is. And usually they're quite emotional about it."

Other justice system personnel described girls as more apt to justify their behavior rather to deny or minimize their role. A public defender contrasted the responses of female and male delinquents: "Girls are more likely to spin a story of self-justification. Boys are more likely to deny or to admit their involvement and try to minimize that way. Girls are more likely to tell why what they did wasn't wrong." A prosecutor thought that girls try to persuade interrogators to view the crime from their perspective: "They feel like they had some justification in doing what they did because the person who they directed their violence toward had mistreated them somehow. So their explanation always had the tone of 'if you just hear what I have to say, you'll understand that I was the one that was in the right.'"

If girls respond more emotionally during interrogation, then justice system personnel attributed it to the personal difficulties they confront: "Girls in court are probably struggling more with sex abuse perpetrated on them, mental illness. Girls are more likely to be seriously into drugs. They're such a different delinquent than boys." A police officer contrasted his experiences of questioning adolescent females and adult women: "When you deal with adult women—whether they're in the system, whether they have a history with the system or not—adult women are different from adolescent girls. It's really striking: they're [girls are] so quick to start screaming at you—much more emotional."

Hostile and Confrontational

Most police described girls as more confrontational than boys during their interrogations. Some speculated that serious female offenders tend to be further into a delinquent career before they encounter police: "Encountering a female offender happened less. They probably get away with a lot more. They probably get further into a life of crime before they get caught. I think they probably hold dope, they mule. They're the last person you look at. You just don't think like that as a cop."

A majority of the officers who had interrogated girls expressed negative opinions about their experiences: "I don't have good memories." One officer complained, "The toughest to interview, by the way, is a sixteen-year-old female. They don't care. They'll lie like their talking to you." Several officers felt that teenage females have a greater sense of being untouchable than boys: "They have an attitude of arrogance, a naïve belief that they're untouchable. They tend to be more noncompliant." Officers described girls as more resistant, more difficult to question, and more prone to lie than boys are: "Especially the hard-core girls, they come off real harsh with a real attitude. It's kind of interesting sometimes, when you see—they're not meek or timid. The girls I talk to have always been very abrasive. A lot of them do not like to admit they did anything wrong. I get boys saying, 'Hey, I screwed up. I did it,' and the girls deny until they turn blue in the face." Police regularly described girls in the interrogation room in unfavorable terms: "Attitude is pretty negative. They're almost like false bravado. They're going to be tough." Another office complained, "When we're dealing with a lot of girls, they have a tendency to be more loud, bitchy—for lack of a better word. Girls that want to be the tough guys, they're kind of a pain in the ass to deal with. They're not afraid to yap at you. They're less apt to be afraid of you than guys are." Several officers repeated the theme that girls do not seem to be as cowed in police presence as boys are: "Girls are a lot more hostile in their interviewing. They are more apt to raise the level of the interview in the interrogation into a more aggressive type of environment. They're a lot more hostile, a lot more quick to get into your face. They just don't seem to appear to feel—they're not afraid of you. I don't know why. They're sometimes not afraid of you." Officers felt that some girls use confrontational responses to intimidate them: "having that nasty bear attitude gets you to back off."

Police descriptions of girls in the interrogation room mirror those proffered by probation officers in other studies.[19] Despite officers' negative portrayals, the data report that girls exhibit a more cooperative attitude and give confessions more often than boys do. I observed few differences between boys and girls in the interrogation process. Gender disparities have long plagued juvenile justice administration. Against the historical backdrop of gender inequalities, these findings are reassuring. Police interrogation of boys and girls was evenhanded.

NOTES

Notes to the Introduction

1 Baldwin 1993:334.
2 Feld 1999.
3 Feld 2003b, 2008; Feld and Bishop 2011, 2012.
4 Feld 1999.
5 Feld 2003a; Feld and Bishop 2011.
6 *Allen v. Illinois* 1986:373; *In re Gault* 1967.
7 *Breed v. Jones* 1975:529.
8 Leo 2008.
9 Milne and Bull 1999.
10 Leo 1996c; Feld 2006a, 2006b.
11 Damaska 1975.
12 E.g., *Brown v. Mississippi* 1936.
13 E.g., *Massiah v. United States* 1964; *Escobedo v. Illinois* 1964.
14 *Miranda v. Arizona* 1966.
15 Packer 1968.
16 Graham 1970.
17 Baldwin 1993:331.
18 Inbau et al. 2004; Leo 2008.
19 *Fare v. Michael C.* 1979
20 Feld 1991; Feld and Schaefer 2010a, 2010b.
21 Feld 1999.
22 Bishop 2005; Bishop and Leiber 2012.
23 E.g., Drizin and Leo 2004; Leo 2008; Garrett 2010, 2011.
24 *State v. Scales* 1994.
25 Feld 2009; Kempf-Leonard 2012.

Notes to Chapter 1

1 *Watts v. Indiana* 1949:54.
2 Damaska 1975.
3 Stone 1977.
4 Stone 1977.
5 Graham 1970.
6 Weisselberg 1998.
7 Leo 2008.
8 Leo 2008:32.
9 "Developments in the Law" 1966; White 2003; Godsey 2005.
10 Leo 2004, 2008.
11 *Rogers v. Richmond* 1961:544.
12 *Culombe v. Connecticut* 1961:602.
13 E.g., *Brown v. Mississippi* 1936.
14 White 2003:44.

15 *Schneckloth v. Bustamonte* 1973:225–26.

16 Godsey 2005:468–69.

17 *Miller v. Fenton* 1985:116.

18 *Culombe* 1961:603.

19 Grano 1979; White 2003.

20 White 2003:42.

21 Leo 2008.

22 Grano 1979; Godsey 2005; Leo 1992, 2004, 2008.

23 *Massiah v. United States* 1964; *Escobedo v. Illinois* 1964.

24 *Escobedo* 1964:486–89.

25 *Miranda v. Arizona* 1966.

26 *Murphy v. Waterfront Comm'n* 1964:84.

27 Stone 1977.

28 Packer 1968.

29 Leo 2008:11.

30 E.g., *Massiah* 1964.

31 Packer 1968:187–88.

32 Packer 1968:190.

33 Schulhofer 1987:436.

34 Packer 1968; Graham 1970.

35 Feld 1999, 2003b.

36 Graham 1970:157.

37 Packer 1968:194.

38 Weisselberg 1998, 2008.

39 *Harris v. New York* 1971; Weisselberg 1998.

40 *Moran v. Burbine* 1986.

41 *Moran* 1986:422.

42 *Davis v. United States* 1994:450.

43 *Colorado v. Spring* 1987.

44 *Fare v. Michael C.* 1979; *Davis* 1994.

45 *Berghuis v. Thompkins* 2010:2264: "A suspect who has received and understood the *Miranda* warnings, and has not invoked his *Miranda* rights, waives the right to remain silent by making an uncoerced statement to the police."

46 *Berghuis* 2010:2264.

47 *Dickerson v. United States* 2000:443–44.

48 White 2003:119.

49 Malone 1986:368.

50 Godsey 2005; Weisselberg 2008.

51 White 1998, 2001, 2003.

52 Slobogin 2003:310.

53 *Miranda* 1966:448.

54 Graham 1970:180.

55 *Miranda* 1966:448.

56 Leo and White 1999; Kassin and Gudjonsson 2004.

57 Weisselberg 1998, 2008.

58 *Miranda* 1966:449.

59 Inbau et al. 2004.

60 *Miranda* 1966:449–55.

61 Gudjonsson 2003; Kassin 1997.

62 Kassin 1997:222.

63 Kassin et al. 2009:15.

64 Milne and Bull 1999.

65 Milne and Bull 1999:55–56.

66 Milne and Bull 1999.

67 Leo 2008.

68 Leo 2008:23.

69 *Miranda* 1966:449–55.

70 Kassin 1997; Kassin and Gudjonsson 2004.

71 Kassin et al. 2009:12.

72 Kassin et al. 2009:12.

73 E.g., Kassin et al. 2009; Kassin and Gudjonsson 2004.

74 Grano 1986; Leo 2008.

75 See http://www.reid.com; King and Snook 2009.

76 E.g., Leo 1996b; Gudjonsson 2003; Feld 2006a, 2006b; King and Snook 2009.

77 Inbau et al. 2004.

78 Gudjonsson 2003:12

79 Russano et al. 2005:485.

80 Leo 2008; Gudjonsson 2003.

81 Schulhofer 1987:452.

82 Inbau et al. 2004; Gudjonsson 2003.

83 Leo 2008:119.

84 Kassin and Gudjonsson 2004:43.

85 Leo 2008.

86 Owen-Kostelnik, Reppucci, and Meyer 2006; Reppucci, Meyer, and Kostelnik 2010.

87 Inbau et al. 2004:298.

88 Meyer and Reppucci 2007; Kostelnik and Reppucci 2009.

89 Meyer and Reppucci 2007; Kostelnik and Reppucci 2009.

90 Kostelnik and Reppucci 2009:362.

91 Kassin et al. 2009; Milne and Bull 1999; Bull and Milne 2004; Bull and Soukara 2010.

92 Milne and Bull 1999; Bull and Soukara 2010; Gudjonsson 2003.

93 Gudjonsson 2003; Milne and Bull 1999.

94 Milne and Bull 1999.

95 Milne and Bull 1999

96 Kassin et al. 2009; Milne and Bull 1999; Bull 2010.

97 Milne and Bull 1999; Bull 2010.

98 Bull and Milne 2004:182.

99 Milne and Bull 1999; Bull and Soukara 2010.

100 Milne and Bull 1999:77.

101 *State v. Scales* 1994.

102 Nelson 2006.

103 Nelson 2006:17.

104 Nelson 2006:11–12.

105 Nelson 2006:4.

106 Nelson 2006:10.

107 Nelson 2006:18.

108 Nelson 2006:18–19.

109 Leo 2008.

110 Leo 1996a, 1996b, 1996c.

111 Feld 2006a, 2006b.

112 Leo 1996c:267–68.

113 E.g., Cassel and Hayman 1996; Leo 1996a, 1996c.

114 Milne and Bull 1999; Gudjonsson 2003; Bull and Soukara 2010.

115 E.g., Leiken 1970; Medalie 1968; Seeburger and Wettick 1967; Wald et al. 1967; Witt 1973.

116 Leiken 1970.

117 Seeburger and Wettick 1967.

118 Medalie 1968.

119 Wald et al. 1967.

120 Witt 1973.

121 Schulhofer 1996; Thomas 1996.

122 Leo 1996a:645.

123 Schulhofer 1996:503.

124 E.g., Cassel 1996, 1998.

125 E.g., Thomas 1996; Feeney 2000.

126 Wald et al. 1967.

127 Leo 1996a, 1996b, 1996c.

128 Feld 2006a, 2006b.

129 King and Snook 2009.

130 Cassel and Hayman 1996.

131 Weisselberg 1998, 2008.

132 Weisselberg 1998.

133 Gudjonsson 2003; Kassin et al. 2009. PACE provides that "[i]t shall be the duty of the Secretary of State—(a) to issue a code of practice in connection with the tape-recording of interviews of persons suspected of the commission of criminal offences which are held by police officers at police stations; and (b) to make an order requiring the tape-recording of interviews of persons suspected of the commission of criminal offences" (1984: Code E 60(1)).

134 Kassin et al. 2009.

135 Milne and Bull 1999.

136 Soukara et al. 2009; Bull and Soukara 2010.

137 Gudjonsson 2003; and associates, e.g., Pearse et al. 1998.

138 Evans 1993, 1994.

139 Soukara et al. 2009; Bull and Milne 2004; Bull 2010.

140 Kassin 1997, 2005; Kassin and Gudjonsson 2004; Kassin et al. 2009.

141 Kassin and Gudjonsson 2004.

142 Kassin 2005; Kassin et al. 2009.

143 Drizin and Leo 2004; Garrett 2008, 2011; Scheck, Neufeld, and Dwyer 2000.

144 Drizin and Leo 2004; Leo and Ofshe 1998.

145 Gross et al. 2005.

146 Garrett 2008, 2011.

147 Drizin and Leo 2004; Leo and Ofshe 1998; Ofshe and Leo 1997a.

148 Leo 2008.

149 Leo 2004, 2008.

150 Leo 1996b; Feld 2006a, 2006b.

151 Milne and Bull 1999.

152 Redlich and Meissner 2009.

Notes to Chapter 2

1 *Fare v. Michael C.* 1979.

2 Feld 1999; Owen-Kostelnik, Reppucci, and Meyer 2006.

3 Feld 1999.

4 Minow 1990.

5 *Haley v. Ohio* 1948.

6 *Haley* 1948:600–601.

7 *Haley* 1948:599–601.

8 *Gallegos v. Colorado* 1962.

9 *Gallegos* 1962:55.

10 *Gallegos* 1962:54.

11 *In re Gault* 1967.

12 *Gault* 1967:52.

13 *Gault* 1967:45, 55.

14 *Gault* 1967:44.

15 *Gault* 1967:49–50.

16 *Gault* 1967:47.

17 E.g., Rothman 1980; Feld 1999; Tanenhaus 2004.

18 Ryerson 1978; Feld 1984; Tanenhaus 2004.

19 Feld 1999.

20 Feld 1984.

21 *In re Winship* 1970.

22 *Breed v. Jones* 1975.

23 *McKeiver v. Pennsylvania* 1971; Feld 2003a.

24 Feld 1984, 1988a, 1999.

25 Feld 1999, 2003b.

26 Blumstein 1996; Zimring 1998; Feld 1999.

27 Feld 1999, 2003b; Zimring 1998; Tonry 2011 (punishing race).

28 Feld 1999; Zimring 1998; Garland 2001.

29 Feld 1988a, 1999; Feld and Bishop 2011.

30 Feld 1998, 1999; Feld and Bishop 2012.

31 Feld 2003a.

32 Feld 1984, 1988a, 1999.

33 E.g., Scott and Grisso 2005; Slobogin and Fondacaro 2011.

34 Slobogin and Fondacaro 2011:116–17.

35 *Fare* 1979.

36 King 2006.

37 *Haley* 1948:599.

38 Rosenberg 1980; McCarthy 1981; Feld 1984.

39 Larson 2003.

40 *J.D.B. v. North Carolina* 2011.

41 *Miranda* 1966:444.

42 *J.D.B.* 2011:2401.

43 *J.D.B.* 2011:2403–4.

44 *J.D.B.* 2011:2403.

45 *J.D.B.* 2011:2407.

46 *Haley* 1948; *Gallegos* 1962.

47 *Colorado v. Spring* 1987.

48 *Moran v. Burbine* 1986.

49 *Moran* 1986:421.

50 Larson 2003; King 2006.

51 *West v. United States* 1968:469; see also *Fare* 1979.

52 Feld 1984, 2000, 2006a.

53 Kassin et al. 2009.

54 Bishop and Farber 2007.

55 Garrett 2008.

56 King 2006; Feld 2000, 2006a.

57 Farber 2004; Feld 2006a; King 2006.

58 *In re E.T.C.* 1982:929.

59 *In re B.M.B.* 1998; *Commonwealth v. A Juvenile* 1983.

60 *State v. Presha* 2000.

61 Krzewinski 2002; King 2006.

62 Krzewinksi 2002; Chao 2000; Drizin and Colgan 2004; Reba, Waldman, and Woodhouse 2011.

63 Feld 2000; Farber 2004.

64 *In re Dino* 1978.

65 Huang 2001.

66 *Presha* 2000.

67 Farber 2004.

68 Reba, Waldman, and Woodhouse 2011.

69 Grisso 1981; Farber 2004; Reba, Waldman, and Woodhouse 2011.

70 E.g., *Anglin v. State* 1972; *In re Omar L.* 2002; *Postell v. State* 1980.

71 Larson 2003; Grisso 1981; Kaban and Tobey 1999; Woolard et al. 2008; Reba, Waldman, and Woodhouse 2011.

72 Grisso 1981.

73 Grisso and Ring 1979.

74 *State v. Loyd* 1973; *State v. Nunn* 1980.

75 *State v. Hogan* 1973:671.

76 *State v. Burrell* 2005.

77 *Roper v. Simmons* 2005; Feld 2008.

78 *Roper* 2005:569–70.

79 *Graham v. Florida* 2010.

80 *Graham* 2010:2026

81 Steinberg and Cauffman 1999; Scott and Steinberg 2008; Steinberg et al. 2009.

82 Morse 1997.

83 Steinberg et al. 2009:584.

84 Steinberg and Cauffman 1996; Spear 2000.

85 Steinberg et al. 2009:586.

86 See http://www.adjj.org; Feld 2008; Scott and Steinberg 2008.

87 Bishop and Farber 2007.

88 Scott and Steinberg 2003; Steinberg and Scott 2003.

89 Scott and Steinberg 2008; Feld 2008.

90 Scott and Steinberg 2003; Morse 1997.

91 Steinberg 2005.

92 Scott, Reppucci, and Woolard 1995; Scott and Grisso 1997; Scott and Steinberg 2003; Morse 1997.

93 Aaronson 2007; Dahl 2001; Steinberg et al. 2009.

94 Scott 1992; Steinberg and Cauffman 1996.

95 Gardner 1993; Scott and Steinberg 2003, 2008; Spear 2000.

96 Furby and Beyth-Marom 1992; Gardner 1993; Grisso 2000.

97 Scott 2000.

98 See http://www.adjj.org; Steinberg and Scott 2003.

99 See http://www.adjj.org; Steinberg and Scott 2003, 2008.

100 Scott 1992; Scott and Steinberg 2003, 2008.

101 Scott and Grisso 1997; Spear 2000.

102 See http://www.adjj.org.

103 Furby and Beyth-Marom 1992.

104 Spear 2000; Dahl 2001; Sowell et al. 2001.

105 Gruber and Yurgelun-Todd 2006; Paus et al. 1999; Giedd 2002; Sowell et al. 1999.

106 Paus et al. 1999; Sowell et al. 2001.

107 Paus et al. 1999; Gruber and Yurgelun-Todd 2006.

108 Baird et al. 1999; Arredondo 2003.

109 Dahl 2001.

110 Bishop and Farber 2007:159.

111 Scott and Steinberg 2003:816.

112 Dahl 2001; Gruber and Yurgelun-Todd 2006; Morse 2004, 2006.

113 Redlich, Silverman, and Steiner 2003.

114 *Graham* 2010:2032.

115 *Haley* 1948; *Gallegos* 1962; *J.D.B.* 2011.

116 *Duckworth v. Eagan* 1988.

117 Rogers et al. 2007.

118 Rogers et al., "An Analysis of *Miranda* Warnings," 2008; Rogers et al., "Comprehensibility and Content," 2008.

119 Rogers et al., "Comprehensibility and Content," 2008.

120 Goldstein and Goldstein 2010.

121 Rogers et al., "Comprehensibility and Content," 2008.

122 Rogers et al., "An Analysis of *Miranda* Warnings," 2008.

123 Grisso 1980, 1981, 1983, 1997a, 1997b, 1998; Grisso et al. 2003.

124 Grisso 1980, 1981.

125 Grisso 1998.

126 Grisso 1998; Bishop and Farber 2007.

127 Grisso 1980.

128 Grisso 1980:1160.

129 Grisso 1997a.

130 Viljoen and Roesch 2005:736.

131 Kassin et al. 2009.

132 Viljoen, Zapf, and Roesch 2007.

133 Viljoen, Zapf, and Roesch 2007.

134 Viljoen and Roesch 2005.

135 Goldstein et al. 2003:366.

136 Viljoen and Roesch 2005.

137 Grisso 2004.

138 Rogers et al., "Comprehensibility and Content," 2008; Rogers 2008.

139 Rogers et al., "Comprehensibility and Content," 2008:80.

140 Beyer 2000; Abramovitch, Higgins-Biss, and Biss 1993; Abramovitch, Peterson-Badali, and Rohan 1995; Redlich, Silverman, and Steiner 2003; Viljoen and Roesch 2005; Goldstein and Goldstein 2010.

141 Viljoen, Klaver, and Roesch 2005.

142 Grisso and Pomiciter 1977; Beyer 2000.

143 Grisso 1981, 1997a; Larson 2003.

144 Grisso 1997b, 2002.

145 Grisso 1997b:11.

146 Grisso 1981, 2000.

147 Viljoen and Roesch 2005:738.

148 Viljoen, Klaver, and Roesch 2005.

149 Grisso 1983; Redlich and Goodman 2003.

150 Owen-Kostelnik, Reppucci, and Meyer 2006:287.

151 Meissner, Russano, and Narchet 2010.

152 Bishop and Farber 2007.

153 Viljoen, Klaver, and Roesch 2005.

154 Grisso 1997a:13.

155 Grisso 1997a:14.

156 *Dusky v. United States* 1960:402.

157 *Drope v. Missouri* 1975:171.

158 Bonnie and Grisso 2000; Grisso et al. 2003.

159 Grisso et al. 2003:335.

160 Redding and Frost 2001; Scott and Grisso 2005; Grisso 1997a.

161 Grisso et al. 2003.

162 Bonnie and Grisso 2000; Redding and Frost 2001; Cowden and McKee 1995.

163 Grisso et al. 2003.

164 Grisso et al. 2003.

165 Grisso et al. 2003:356.

166 Scott and Grisso 1997; Steinberg and Cauffman 1999.

167 Gudjonsson 2003:345.

168 Milne and Bull 1999.

169 Milne and Bull 1999

170 Singh and Gudjonsson 1992; Gudjonsson 2003; Goldstein et al. 2003.

171 Owen-Kostelnik, Reppucci, and Meyer 2006.

172 Drake, Bull, and Boon 2008.

173 Koocher 1992; Larson 2003; Owen-Kostelnik, Reppucci, Meyer 2006.

174 Kassin et al. 2009.

175 Meyer and Reppucci 2007; Richardson, Gudjonsson, and Kelly 1995; Billings et al. 2007.

176 Ainsworth 1993; Kaban and Tobey 1999.

177 Billings et al. 1997.

178 Meyer and Reppucci 2007:764.

179 Goldstein et al. 2003.

180 Steinberg and Cauffman 1996; Grisso 1981; Grisso et al. 2003.

181 Owen-Kostelnik, Reppucci, and Meyer 2006:292.

182 *Berghuis v. Thompkins* 2010; *Davis v. United States* 1994.

183 Ainsworth 1993; Beyer 2000.

184 *Davis* 1994:460.

185 Drizin and Leo 2004:1005.

Notes to Chapter 3

1 E.g., Wald et al. 1967; Leo 1996b, 1996c, 2008.

2 E.g., Grisso 1981; Viljoen, Klaver, and Roesch 2005.

3 E.g., Baldwin 1993; Evans 1993; Milne and Bull 1999; Gudjonsson 2003.

4 Feld and Schaefer 2010a, 2010b.

5 *Miranda* 1966:444.

6 *J.D.B. v. North Carolina* 2011.

7 Weisselberg 2008.

8 Grisso 1981.

9 Inbau et al. 2004:57.

10 Minn. Stat. §206B.176 (West 2006).

11 Milne and Bull 1999.

12 Owen-Kostelnik, Reppucci, and Meyer 2006; Redlich 2007.

13 Inbau et al. 2004:51.

14 Milne and Bull 1999.

15 Evans 1993:26.

16 *State v. Burrell* 2005.

17 Leo 1996a, 2008.

18 *Duckworth v. Eagan* 1988.

19 Rogers et al. 2007.

20 Rogers et al., "Language of *Miranda* Warnings," 2008.

21 Rogers 2008.

22 Rogers et al., "Comprehensibility and Content," 2008.

23 Rogers et al., "Comprehensibility and Content," 2008:72.

24 Rogers 2008.

25 Viljoen, Zapf, and Roesch 2007.

26 Oberlander and Goldstein 2001:459.

27 Cassel and Hayman 1996:888.

28 Weisselberg 2008.

29 Malone 1986:377.

30 Leo 1996b:259.

31 Leo 1996b:265.

32 Leo 1996b.

33 Inbau et al. 2004.

34 Leo 2008:26.

35 *Missouri v. Seibert* 2004; Weisselberg 2008.

36 Weisselberg 2008; Mosteller 2007; Leo 2008.

37 *Rhode Island v. Innis* 1980; *Pennsylvania v. Muniz* 1990.

38 Leo 1996a:661.

39 Weisselberg 2008:1548.

40 Leo and White 1999:432; White 2003.

41 Redlich and Drizin 2007.

42 Weisselberg 2008.

43 Leo 1996a:660.

44 White 2003:80.

45 Baldwin 1993:337.

46 White 2003:82.

47 Leo and White 1999:433.

48 *Dickerson v. United States* 2000:430.

49 Leo and White 1999:434–35.

50 Goldstein et al. 2003:366.

51 *Colorado v. Spring* 1987; *Moran v. Burbine* 1986.

52 White 2003:81.

53 Grisso et al. 2003.

54 *Fare v. Michael C.* 1979; *Davis v. United States* 1994; *Berghuis v. Thompkins* 2010.

55 Grisso 1980, 1981; Grisso et al. 2003.

56 E.g., Saywitz, Jaenicke, and Camparo 1990; Smith 1985; Huerter and Saltzman 1992; Rogers 2008.

57 Bull 2010:8.

58 Rogers 2008.

59 Drizin and Colgan 2004.

60 *Miranda* 1966:536.

61 White 1997; Godsey 2005; Weisselberg 2008.

62 Leo 1996c:260.

63 Wald et al. 1967:1563.

64 Leo 1996c.

65 Cassell and Hayman 1996.

66 Kassin et al. 2007.

67 Pearse et al. 1998.

68 Grisso and Pomiciter 1977; Grisso 1981.

69 Viljoen, Klaver, and Roesch 2005.

70 Goldstein and Goldstein 2010:50.

71 Viljoen and Roesch 2005.

72 Grisso 1981; Grisso and Pomiciter 1977; Viljoen, Klaver, and Roesch 2005.

73 Leo 1996c; Cassell and Hayman 1996; Wald et al. 1967.

74 Malone 1986:370

75 Grisso 1981:64.

76 Leo 1996b:286.

77 Kassin 2005:218.

78 Leiken 1970.

79 Grisso and Pomiciter 1977; Grisso 1981.

80 Viljoen and Roesch 2005.

81 *Harris v. New York* 1971.

82 *Michigan v. Tucker* 1974.

83 *United States v. Patane* 2004.

84 Weisselberg 1998, 2008; Alschuler 1987; Clymer 2002.

85 Weisselberg 1998.

86 Leo 1996c.

Notes to Chapter 4

1 Cicourel 1995:115 (emphasis added).

 2 Cicourel 1995:115–16 (emphasis added).

 3 Packer 1968.

 4 E.g., Wald et al. 1967; Leo 1996b, 1996c, 2008.

 5 Grisso 1981; Viljoen and Roesch 2005.

 6 E.g., Inbau et al. 2004; Milne and Bull 1999.

 7 Nelson 2006.

 8 Leo 2008.

 9 Inbau et al. 2004.

10 Inbau et al. 2004; Garrett 2010.

11 Leo 1996a; Evans 1993.

12 Milne and Bull 1999.

13 Milne and Bull 1999.

14 Milne and Bull 1999.

15 Drizin and Leo 2004; Garrett 2011.

16 Inbau et al. 2004.

17 Milne and Bull 1999.

18 Kassin 1997.

19 Kassin 1997.

20 Leo 2008:133.

21 Kassin 1997; Kassin and Gudjonsson 2004; Kassin et al. 2009.

22 Leo 1996c.

23 Inbau et al. 2004.

24 Leo 2008:139.

25 Evans 1993; Soukara et al. 2009; Leo 1996c.

26 Zimring 1981; Snyder and Sickmund 2006.

27 White 1997, 2003.

28 Leo 1996c:279.

29 E.g., Young 1998; Kassin et al. 2009.

30 Inbau et al. 2004:173.

31 Inbau et al. 2004:173–206 recommends interrogators use response-provoking BAI questions such as "Do you know why I have asked to talk to you here today?"; "Did you commit [the crime]?"; "Who do you think committed [the crime]?"; "Is there any reason you can think of that someone would name you as a suspect?"; "Who would eliminate you from suspicion?"; "How do you feel about being interviewed about [the crime]?"; "Why do you think the victim is saying you are the one who did this?"; "Who do you think would have had the best chance to do [the crime]?"; "Why do you think someone would have done [the crime]?"; "Did you ever think about doing [the crime] even though you didn't go through with it?"; "Tell me why you wouldn't do something like this?"; "What do you think should happen to the person who did this?"; "How do you think the results of the investigation will come out on you?"; "If it becomes necessary, would you be willing to take a polygraph test to verify that what you have told me about this issue is the truth?"; "Do you think the person who did this would deserve a second chance under any circumstances?"; "Is there any reason why you would have done [the crime]?"

32 Vrij, Mann, and Fisher 2006.

33 Leo 1996c.

34 Leo 1996c, 2008.

35 Kassin 1997; Kassin et al. 2009; Inbau et al. 2004.

36 Leo 2008:153.

37 Ofshe and Leo 1997a.

38 Soukara et al. 2009:502.

39 Inbau et al, 2004:232. Inbau and Reid describe various themes to provide suspects with a justification or excuse for their crime: assuring suspect that anyone in a similar situation would have behaved as they did; minimizing moral seriousness; suggesting a more acceptable reason for suspects' actions; and blaming the victim or accomplices. Additional themes recommended for use with juveniles include attributing the offense to youthful boredom, craving excitement, youths' propensity to make mistakes, the presence of too many temptations, and inadequate parental supervision (232–303).

40 Inbau et al. 2004:232.

41 Sykes and Matza 1957.

42 Matza 1964.

43 Matza 1964:74.

44 Matza 1964:84.

45 Snyder and Sickmund 2006.

46 Nelson 2006.

47 Inbau et al. 2004:353.

48 Kassin 2005; Kassin et al. 2009.

49 Minn. Stat. § 609.035 (West 2005).

50 Milne and Bull 1999.

51 Leo 2008:175.

52 Leo 1996b, 2008.

Notes to Chapter 5

1 Pearse and Gudjonsson 2003; Leo 1996c; Wald et al. 1967.

2 *Oregon v. Bradshaw* 1983.

3 Cassell and Hayman 1996; Wald et al. 1967.

4 Soukara et al. 2009:495.

5 Milne and Bull 1999:81.

6 Evans 1993:36.

7 Leo 1996c.

8 Wald et al. 1967.

9 Kassin et al. 2007.

10 Bull and Milne 2004.

11 Milne and Bull 1999.

12 Evans 1993:29.

13 Viljoen, Klaver, and Roesch 2005.

14 Soukara et al. 2009; Baldwin 1993; Pearse and Gudjonsson 1996.

15 Baldwin 1993:333.

16 Baldwin 1993.

17 Clarke and Sykes 1974.

18 Clarke and Sykes 1974; Bittner 1976.

19 LaFave 1965; Skolnick 1967; Piliavin and Briar 1964; Cicourel 1995.

20 Bittner 1976:82.

21 Piliavin and Briar 1964.

22 Cicourel 1995; Emerson 1974.

23 Bittner 1976; Bridges and Steen 1998; Black and Reiss 1970.

24 Cicourel 1995:xv.

25 Baldwin 1993.

26 Baldwin 1993:332.

27 Baldwin 1993.

28 Kamisar 1995:1000.

29 Cassell and Hayman 1996:881.

30 Leo 2008:166.

31 Leo 2008:168.

32 Drizin and Leo 2004.

33 White 2001:1225.

34 Drizin and Leo 2004.

35 Inbau et al. 2004.

36 Wald et al. 1967.

37 Leo 1996c.

38 Cassell and Hayman 1996.

39 Kassin et al. 2007:384.

40 Evans 1993:26.

41 Gudjonsson 2003.

42 Baldwin 1993:331.

43 Bull and Soukara 2010.

44 Kassin and Gudjonsson 2004:46.

45 Milne and Bull 1999.

46 Leo 1996c.

47 Feld 2006b.

48 E.g., Podkopacz and Feld 1996.

49 *Rhode Island v. Innis* 1980:295–96.

50 "Developments in the Law" 1966; Godsey 2005; White 1998.

51 "Developments in the Law" 1966; White 2001; Young 1998; Skolnick and Leo 1992.

52 *Brown v. Mississippi* 1938.

53 *Arizona v. Fulminante* 1991.

54 *Ashcraft v. Tennessee* 1944.

55 *Brooks v. Florida* 1961.

56 White 1998, 2001.

57 *Arizona v. Fulminante* 1991; White 2001.

58 *Chavez v. Martinez* 2003:770.

59 Feld 1995; Podkopacz and Feld 2001.

60 Leo 2008:31.

61 Leo 2009.

62 Neubauer 1974.

63 Cassell 1996; Ofshe and Leo 1997a; Cassell and Hayman 1996; Pearse et al. 1998; Kassin et al. 2009.

64 Cassell and Hayman 1996:909.

65 Nardulli, Eisenstein, and Fleming 1988; Wald et al. 1967.

66 Puritz et al. 1995; Goldstein and Goldstein 2010.

67 Cassell 1996; Goldstein and Goldstein 2010.

68 Goldstein and Goldstein 2010:54.

69 Sullivan 2010:131–32.

70 Ruback and Vardaman 1997:66.

71 Podkopacz and Feld 1996.

72 Cassell and Hayman 1996; Schulhofer 1996.

73 Ruback and Vardaman 1997:65.

74 Viljoen, Klaver, and Roesch 2005:274.

75 Emerson 1974; Ruback and Vardaman 1997.

Notes to Chapter 6

1 Feld 1991; Feld and Schaefer 2010a, 2010b; U.S. General Accounting Office 1995; Burruss and Kempf-Leonard 2002; Bray, Sample, and Kempf-Leonard 2005.
2 Feld 1991, 1993; Feld and Schaefer 2010a.
3 Feld 1991; Feld and Schaefer 2010a, 2010b; Burruss and Kempf-Leonard 2002.
4 Feld 1991; Burruss and Kempf-Leonard 2002; GAO 1995; Feld and Schaefer 2010b.
5 Sampson and Laub 1993; Ruback and Vardaman 1997.
6 Feld 1999; Bishop 2005; Bishop and Leiber 2012.
7 Ruback and Vardaman 1997; Feld and Schaefer 2010a, 2010b.
8 Sampson and Laub 1993.
9 Feld 1999; McCord, Widom, and Crowell 2001; Bishop 2005.
10 Manning 1997.
11 See tables A1.1 and 6.1; "Minnesota Police Departments" 2010.
12 Paoline 2003; Paoline and Terrill 2005.
13 Skolnick 1967; Manning 1997.
14 Rubenstein 1973; Skolnick 1967; Westley 1970; Paoline 2003.
15 Bittner 1976.
16 Wilson 1968b.
17 Wilson 1968b:233.
18 Manning 1997; Paoline and Terrill 2005.
19 Paoline 2003.
20 Hassell, Zhao, and Maguire 2003; Zhao, Ren, and Lovrich 2010.
21 Paoline and Terrill 2005; Terrill, Paoline, and Manning 2003.
22 Wilson 1968a.
23 Meehan 1993.
24 Meehan 2000.
25 Evans 1993:21.
26 Feld 1999; Snyder and Sickmund 2006.
27 Feld 1999.
28 Bishop 2005; Bishop and Leiber 2012.
29 Feld 1999, 2008; McCord, Widom, and Crowell 2001.
30 Wilson 1968b; Meehan 1993.
31 Feld 1991; Sampson and Laub 1993.
32 Feld and Schaefer 2010a, 2010b.
33 Feld and Schaefer 2010a, 2010b.
34 Farber 2004:1305.
35 Grisso 1981; Farber 2004.
36 *Anglin v. State* 1972; *In re Omar L.* 2002; *Postell v. State* 1980.
37 *Anglin v. State* 1972:752.
38 Grisso and Ring 1979.
39 Grisso 1981.
40 Viljoen, Klaver, and Roesch 2005.
41 Rogers et al., "Comprehensibility and Content," 2008.
42 Kaban and Tobey 1999.
43 Kassin et al. 2009.

44 Woolard et al. 2008.

45 Woolard et al. 2008:694.

46 Grisso and Pomiciter 1977; Goldstein and Goldstein 2010.

47 Woolard et al. 2008:695.

48 Grisso 1981.

49 Woolard 2008: 696.

50 *State v. Burrell* 2005.

51 *State v. Burrell* 2005.

52 *State v. Burrell* 2005:597.

53 Peterson-Badali et al. 1999.

54 Woolard et al. 2008:688.

55 Eagan Police Department 2006:4.

56 Eagan Police Department 2006:3

57 Inbau et al. 2004.

58 Inbau et al. 2004:301.

59 Feld 1999; Snyder and Sickmund 2006; Bishop and Leiber 2012.

60 Feld 1999; Bishop 2005; Bishop and Leiber 2012; McCord, Widom, and Crowell 2001

61 McCord, Widom, and Crowell 2001.

62 Snyder and Sickmund 2006; Sampson and Lauritsen 1997.

63 McCord, Widom, and Crowell 2001:257.

64 42 U.S.C. 5633(a)(16) (1994).

65 Pope 1994; Feld 1999.

66 Poe-Yamagata and Jones 1999; Bishop 2005; Bishop and Leiber 2012.

67 Sampson and Lauritsen 1997; Feld 1999; Leiber 2003; Bishop 2005.

68 Bridges and Steen 1998; McCord, Widom, and Crowell 2001.

69 Sampson and Laub 1993; Bridges and Steen 1998.

70 Bishop and Frazier 1988; Bishop 2005.

71 Feld 1991, 1993.

72 Feld 1999.

73 Snyder and Sickmund 2006.

74 Sampson and Laub 1993; Feld 1999; Leiber 2003.

75 Bishop 2005; Bishop and Leiber 2012.

76 Bittner 1976.

77 Bishop 2005:45.

78 Kochel, Wilson, and Mastrofski 2011:496.

79 Leo 1996c; Woolard et al. 2008.

80 Feld 1999; Bishop and Leiber 2012.

Notes to Chapter 7

1 Simon 1991:211–12.

2 Packer 1968:163–64 (emphasis added).

3 Packer 1968:187–88.

4 Packer 1968:190.

5 Packer 1968:191.

6   Garrett 2008, 2010, 2011; Scheck, Neufeld, and Dwyer 2000.
7   Drizin and Leo 2004; Garrett 2010, 2011; Gross et al. 2005.
8   Alschuler 1997; Ofshe and Leo 1997b; Leo and Ofshe 1998; White 1997; Gross et al. 2005; Garrett 2011.
9   Leo and Ofshe 1998; Magid 2001; White 1998, 2001; Cassell 1998.
10 Kassin and Gudjonsson 2004; Gudjonsson 2010.
11 Leo and Ofshe 1998:560.
12 Kassin and Gudjonsson 2004; Leo and Ofshe 1998; Ofshe and Leo 1997a; Gross et al. 2005; Leo 2009.
13 Garrett 2008, 2010, 2011.
14 Drizin and Leo 2004; Scheck, Neufeld, and Dwyer 2000.
15 Kassin et al. 2007.
16 Drizin and Leo 2004.
17 Drizin and Leo 2004; Snyder and Sickmund 2006.
18 Gross et al. 2005.
19 Garrett 2008, 2011.
20 Drizin and Leo 2004; Gross et al. 2005; Leo 2008; Garrett 2008.
21 Kostelnik and Reppucci 2009.
22 Kassin et al. 2009; Garrett 2011.
23 Kassin et al. 2009; Leo 2009.
24 Drizin and Leo 2004; Gross et al. 2005; Leo 2008; Tepfer, Nirider, and Tricarico 2010.
25 White 2001:1225.
26 Tepfer, Nirider, and Tricarico 2010.
27 Gross et al. 2005:532.
28 Gross et al. 2005.
29 Drizin and Luloff 2007; Tepfer, Nirider, and Tricarico 2010.
30 Kassin and Gudjonsson 2004; Gudjonsson 2010.
31 Leo 2008, 2009; Leo and Drizin 2010.
32 Leo 2008, 2009; Leo and Drizin 2010.
33 Drizin and Leo 2004; Redlich and Meissner 2009.
34 Leo 2009:333–34.
35 Leo 2008; Leo and Drizin 2010.
36 Meissner and Kassin 2002, 2004; Vrij, Mann, and Fisher 2006; Leo 2008, 2009.
37 Leo 2008; Vrij, Mann, and Fisher 2006.
38 Kassin and Fong 1999; Kassin and Gudjonsson 2004; Kassin, Meissner, and Norwick 2005; Redlich and Meissner 2009.
39 Kassin and Fong 1999; Kassin, Meissner, and Norwick 2005; Leo and Drizin 2010; Vrij, Mann, and Fisher 2006.
40 Milne and Bull 1999:64.
41 Meissner and Kassin 2002; Redlich and Drizin 2007.
42 Kassin and Gudjonsson 2004:41.
43 Kassin and Wrightsman 1985; Kassin 1997; Ofshe and Leo 1997a, 1997b; Leo 2008.
44 Kassin et al. 2009.
45 Gudjonsson 2010.

46 Gudjonsson 2003.
47 Kassin et al. 2009; Ofshe and Leo 1997a, 1997b; Leo 2008.
48 Leo 2008.
49 Leo 2008, 2009; Garrett 2011.
50 Redlich and Meissner 2009; Milne and Bull 1999.
51 Meyer and Reppucci 2007; Vrij, Mann, and Fisher 2006.
52 Kassin 2005.
53 Kassin and Gudjonsson 2004:47.
54 Kassin 2005.
55 Kassin and Keichel 1996.
56 Kassin and Fong 1999; Kassin, Meissner, and Norwick 2005.
57 Kassin 2005:224.
58 Kassin et al. 2009.
59 Meissner and Kassin 2002, 2004.
60 Garrett 2010:1054.
61 Garrett 2011:20.
62 Kassin et al. 2009; Leo 2008.
63 Garrett 2010.
64 Garrett 2010.
65 Leo 2008; Garrett 2010.
66 Garrett 2011:32.
67 *Frazier v. Cupp* 1969; *Miller v. Fenton* 1985.
68 Gohara 2006; Thomas 2007.
69 Slobogin 2007; Magid 2001.
70 McMullen 2005:999.
71 Magid 2001:1185.
72 Grano 1993; Magid 2001.
73 Slobogin 2007.
74 Kassin et al. 2009.
75 Skolnick and Leo 1992.
76 Cassell and Hayman 1996; Wald et al. 1967; Seeburger and Wettick 1967.
77 Leo 2008:191.
78 Magid 2001.
79 Klein 2007; *Colorado v. Spring* 1987.
80 Gohara 2006; McMullen 2005; Skolnick and Leo 1992.
81 E.g., *State v. Cayward* 1989; *State v. Patton* 2003.
82 White 2001:1222.
83 Young 1998; Gohara 2006.
84 Leo 2008; Dripps 1996.
85 White 2001; Magid 2001.
86 Magid 2001; Gohara 2006.
87 Ofshe and Leo 1997a; White 2001.
88 Drizin and Leo 2004; McMullen 2005.
89 Kassin 2005, 2008.
90 White 1997, 2001; Young 1998; Kassin 2005.

91 Kassin 2005:225.

92 Gudjonsson 2003; Kassin et al. 2009.

93 Inbau et al. 2004:xiv.

94 Drizin and Leo 2004.

95 Leo and Ofshe 1998.

96 Kassin and Gudjonsson 2004:60.

97 Drizin and Leo 2004.

98 Gross et al. 2005:544.

99 Drizin and Leo 2004; Redlich and Drizin 2007; Garrett 2011.

100 Drizin and Leo 2004; Gross et al. 2005; Tepfer, Nirider, and Tricarico 2010.

101 Drizin and Leo 2004.

102 Garrett 2011.

103 Gross et al. 2005.

104 Gross et al. 2005; Tepfer, Nirider, and Tricarico 2010.

105 Tepfer, Nirider, and Tricarico 2010.

106 Tepfer, Nirider, and Tricarico 2010.

107 Bonnie and Grisso 2000; Redlich et al. 2004; Tobey, Grisso, and Schwartz 2000; Drizin and Luloff 2007.

108 Drizin and Leo 2004; Drizin and Luloff 2007.

109 Redlich 2010.

110 Leo 2009.

111 Milne and Bull 1999; Redlich et al. 2004.

112 Owen-Kostelnik, Reppucci, and Meyer 2006.

113 Goldstein and Goldstein 2010:63.

114 Tobey, Grisso, and Schwartz 2000.

115 Tobey, Grisso, and Schwartz 2000; Cooper 1997.

116 Gudjonsson 2010.

117 Drizin and Luloff 2007.

118 Gudjonsson 1991.

119 Gudjonsson 2003; Lyon 1999; Bull 2010.

120 Leo 2009.

121 Leo 2008:233.

122 Leo 2008.

123 Redlich 2004, 2007.

124 Grisso 2004; Redlich 2007.

125 Redlich 2007:610.

126 Owens-Kostelnik, Reppucci, and Meyer 2006.

127 Redlich 2007.

128 Tanenhaus and Drizin 2002.

129 Kaban and Tobey 1999:158.

130 Redlich and Drizin 2007.

131 Evans 1993:4.

132 Johnson and Hunt 2000.

133 Gudjonsson 2010.

134 Gudjonsson 2010.

135 Leo 2008; Gross et al. 2005; Garrett 2010.

136 Podkopacz and Feld 1996.

137 Wald et al. 1967; Baldwin 1993; Leo 1996c; Gudjonsson 2003.

138 Kassin et al. 2007.

139 Drizin and Leo 2004.

140 Gross et al. 2005.

141 *Illinois v. Gates* 1983:232.

142 *Gates* 1983:232, 238.

143 *Safford v. Redding* 2009:2639.

144 Packer 1968:163.

145 Packer 1968:165.

146 Packer 1964:13.

Notes to Chapter 8

1 E.g., *Harris v. New York* 1971; *United States v. Patane* 2004.

2 Schulhofer 1987:454.

3 *Dickerson v. United States* 2000:430.

4 *Miranda v. Arizona* 1966:460

5 Weisselberg 2008; Slobogin 2007.

6 *Dickerson* 2000:443.

7 *Colorado v. Spring* 1987; *Moran v. Burbine* 1986.

8 *Berghuis v. Thompkins* 2010.

9 Weisselberg 2008:1592.

10 Weisselberg 2008:1523.

11 Godsey 2005; Leo 2008.

12 *Missouri v. Seibert* 2004:608–609.

13 *Dickerson* 2000:444

14 *Dickerson* 2000:444

15 Leo 1996a; Kamisar 2007.

16 Schulhofer 1987:460.

17 *Moran v. Burbine* 1986:421.

18 Godsey 2005.

19 *Dickerson* 2000:434.

20 Slobogin 2003:310.

21 Godsey 2005:508.

22 Leo 1996c, 2008.

23 Grisso 1980; Grisso et al. 2003.

24 Drizin and Leo 2004; see also Garrett 2011.

25 Birckhead 2008; Maroney 2009.

26 King 2006.

27 *J.D.B.* 2011:2403.

28 *J.D.B.* 2011:2407

29 *Haley v. Ohio* 1948; *Gallegos v. Colorado* 1962.

30 Woolard et al. 2008.

31 Drizin and Luloff 2007.

32 Grisso and Ring 1979; Oberlander and Goldstein 2001.

33 Kassin et al. 2009:30.

34 Farber 2004; King 2006; Drizin and Luloff 2007.

35 Bishop and Farber 2007:149.

36 *Fare v. Michael C.* 1979:719

37 *Fare* 1979:719.

38 *Fare* 1979:722.

39 Farber 2004.

40 Drizin and Luloff 2007:313.

41 *Escobedo v. Illinois* 1964:490

42 Feld 1988b, 1989, 1993; Feld and Schaefer 2010a, 2010b.

43 American Bar Association 1980:89 (emphasis added); ABA 1995.

44 American Bar Association 1980:92.

45 Feld 1984, 1988b, 1989, 1993; Feld and Schaefer 2010a, 2010b.

46 ABA 1995; Jones 2004; National Juvenile Defender Center 2011.

47 Bishop and Farber 2007.

48 *Colorado v. Connelly* 1986.

49 *Connelly* 1986:167.

50 Schulhofer 1981; Godsey 2005; Garret 2010; Leo et al. 2006; Leo 2008.

51 Kassin et al. 2009; Leo 2008.

52 Leo et al. 2006; Leo 2008.

53 Leo et al. 2006:531.

54 Garrett 2010, 2011.

55 Godsey 2005; White 2001, 2003.

56 White 2001, 2003.

57 Godsey 2005.

58 Tepfer, Nirider, and Tricarico 2010

59 Milne and Bull 1999; Bull 2010; Kassin et al. 2009; Garrett 2010.

60 Milne and Bull 1999; Tepfer, Nirider, and Tricarico 2010.

61 Bull and Soukara 2010.

62 Milne and Bull 1999.

63 Leo 2008:326.

64 Kassin et al. 2009:29.

65 Kassin et al. 2009:30.

66 Tepfer, Nirider, and Tricarico 2010.

67 Leo 2008.

68 *Ashcraft v. Tennessee* 1944.

69 *Haley* 1948; *Gallegos* 1962.

70 E.g., *Sharpe v. United States* 1985.

71 *County of Riverside v. McLaughlin* 1991.

72 E.g., Feld 2006b; Leo 1996c; Wald et al. 1967; Gudjonsson 2003.

73 Drizin and Leo 2004.

74 White 1997:143.

75 Gross et al. 2005:544.

76 Garrett 2011:38.

77 Kassin et al. 2009:16.

78 Inbau et al. 2004:597.

79 White 2001:1233.

80 Kassin et al. 2009:28.

81 White 2003; Leo 2008.

82 *Brown v. Illinois* 1975.

83 *Illinois v. Gates* 1983.

84 Federal Rule of Criminal Procedure 5(a) (emphasis added).

85 *Corley v. United States* 2009:321.

86 *McNabb v. United States* 1943; *Mallory v. United States* 1957.

87 *Mallory* 1957:455.

88 *Corley* 2009:307

89 Reid 2010.

90 LaFave et al. 2009.

91 Tex. Fam. Code 51.095(a)(1) (2005).

92 Leo 2008:308.

93 E.g., *Moran* 1986.

94 *Miranda* 1966:505.

95 E.g., Gudjonsson 2003; Cassell 1998; Drizin and Reich 2004; Leo 2008; Kassin et al. 2009; Sullivan 2006, 2010; Garrett 2008, 2010, 2011; Milne and Bull 1999; Schlam 1995.

96 *Stephan v. State* 1985.

97 *State v. Scales* 1994.

98 Leo 2008; Sullivan 2004, 2006, 2010; Garrett 2011.

99 Sullivan 2006, 2010.

100 Sullivan 2006, 2010.

101 Milne and Bull 1999; Gudjonsson 2003.

102 Slobogin 2003:316.

103 Leo 1996a:687.

104 White 1997.

105 Garrett 2010:1058.

106 Cassell 1998; White 1997.

107 Drizin and Reich 2004; Leo 1996a.

108 Milne and Bull 1999.

109 Sullivan 2006, 2010.

110 Sullivan 2006:178–79.

111 Sullivan 2006:179.

112 Sullivan 2010.

113 Leo 1992, 2008.

114 Gudjonsson 2003; White 1998.

115 Slobogin 2003.

116 Garrett 2011:32.

117 Kassin 1997; White 1997, 1998; Garrett 2010, 2011.

118 Kassin et al. 2009; Lassiter and Geers 2004; Lassiter et al. 2007.

119 *Brady v. Maryland* 1963.

120 Evans 1993:47.

121 Minn. R. Crim. P. 11.02 (2005).

122 Gudjonsson 2003:85.

123 Sullivan 2010.

124 Owen-Kostelnik, Reppucci, and Meyer 2006:301.

125 *In re Jerrell C.J.* 2005:121.

126 E.g., *Connelly* 1986; Leo et al. 2006.

127 *Miranda* 1966:469.

128 Packer 1968:161.

129 Schulhofer 1996:556.

130 *Haley* 1948:600; *Gallegos* 1962:54.

Notes to Appendix 1

1 *Miranda v. Arizona* 1966:448.

2 *Stephan v. State* 1985.

3 *State v. Scales* 1994.

4 *Scales* 1994:592.

5 *Scales* 1994:591.

6 Sullivan 2006; Redlich and Drizin 2007; Garrett 2011:341n. 23.

7 Sullivan 2004, 2006, 2010; Leo 2008.

8 "Minnesota Police Departments" 2010.

9 "Minnesota Police Departments" 2010.

10 "Minnesota Police Departments" 2010.

11 "Minnesota Police Departments" 2010.

12 Minn. Stat. § 260B.163 (1)(c)(2) (West 2005).

13 The county attorneys and juvenile court judges imposed several conditions under which I obtained access to confidential juvenile court data. One of the conditions included in each court order was that "Prof. Barry C. Feld shall retain personal custody of all edited files and no one else shall have access to those files. He shall personally transcribe all tapes not already transcribed and report his research findings only in ways that preserve the confidentiality of the information contained therein." Order *In re* Request of Professor Barry C. Feld to Access Ramsey County Attorney's Juvenile Delinquency Felony Files (June 1, 2004).

14 Minn. R. Crim. P. 11.02 (2005).

15 Minn. Stat. § 260B.130 (West 2005) authorizes judges to impose juvenile "blended sentences" in lieu of transferring a youth to criminal court. With "blended sentences," the state tries youths in juvenile court with all adult criminal procedural safeguards, including the right to a jury trial, and following conviction, judges impose both a longer juvenile EJJ sentence and a stayed criminal sentence pending successful completion of the juvenile disposition. Feld 1995; Podkopacz and Feld 2001.

16 Baldwin 1993:328.

17 Inbau et al. 2004.

18 E.g., Wald et al. 1967; Leo 1996b; Pearse and Gudjonsson 2003.

19 Cassel and Hayman 1996.

20 Drizin and Leo 2004; Kassin and Gudjonsson 2004.

21 Podkopacz and Feld 1996.

22 Leo 2004; Redlich and Meissner 2009.

23 Redlich and Meissner 2009.

24 Evans 1993.

25 Nelson 2006.

26 Leo 1996c; Weisselberg 1998.

27 Drizin and Leo 2004; Kassin and Gudjonsson 2004.

28 Kassin et al. 2007:397.

29 Snyder and Sickmund 2006.

30 Feld and Bishop 2012.

31 Corbin and Strauss 2008.

32 Manning 1997.

Notes to Appendix 2

1 Schlossman 1977; Sutton 1988.

2 Schlossman and Wallach 1978; Bishop and Frazier 1992; Kemp-Leonard and Johansson 2007; Kempf-Leonard 2012.

3 Schlossman 1977; Tanenhaus 2004; Chesney-Lind 1988.

4 Schwartz, Steketee, and Schneider 1990; Feld 1999.

5 42 U.S.C. § 223 (a)(12); Schwartz 1989.

6 Handler and Zatz 1982; Maxson and Klein 1997.

7 Handler and Zatz 1982; Kempf-Leonard and Sample 2000.

8 Chesney-Lind and Belknap 2004; Feld 2009.

9 Steffensmeier et al. 2005; Feld 2009; Kempf-Leonard 2012.

10 Chesney-Lind and Belknap 2004; Miller 2005.

11 Feld 2009.

12 Feld 2009.

13 Feld 2009; Kempf-Leonard 2012.

14 Chesney-Lind and Pasko 2004; Zahn 2009.

15 Goldstein and Goldstein 2010:68.

16 Viljoen and Roesch 2005.

17 Feld 2009; Kempf-Leonard 2012.

18 Gaarder, Rodriguez, and Zatz 2004.

19 Gaarder, Rodriguez, and Zatz 2004.

REFERENCES

Aaronson, Jay D. 2007. "Brain Imaging Culpability and the Juvenile Death Penalty." *Psychology, Public Policy and Law* 13:115–42.

Abramovitch, Rona, Karen L. Higgins-Biss, and Stephen R. Biss. 1993. "Young Persons' Comprehension of Waivers in Criminal Proceedings." *Canadian Journal of Criminology* 35:309–22.

Abramovitch, Rona, Michele Peterson-Badali, and Meg Rohan. 1995. "Young People's Understanding and Assertion of Their Rights to Silence and Legal Counsel." *Canadian Journal of Criminology* 37:1–18.

Ainsworth, Janet E. 1993. "In a Different Register: The Pragmatics of Powerlessness in Police Interrogation." *Yale Law Journal* 103:259–322.

Allen v. Illinois, 478 U.S. 364 (1986).

Alschuler, Albert W. 1987. "Failed Pragmatism: Reflections on the Burger Court." *Harvard Law Review* 100:1436–56.

Alschuler, Albert W. 1997. "Constraint and Confessions. " *Denver University Law Review* 74:957–78.

American Bar Association. 1980. *Juvenile Justice Standards Relating to Pretrial Court Proceedings.* Institute of Judicial Administration. Cambridge, MA: Ballinger.

American Bar Association. 1995. *A Call for Justice: An Assessment of Access to Counsel and Quality of Representation in Delinquency Proceedings.* Washington, DC: American Bar Association.

Anglin v. State, 259 So. 2d 752 (Fla. Dist. Ct. App. 1972).

Arizona v. Fulminante, 499 U.S. 279 (1991).

Arredondo, David E. 2003. "Child Development, Children's Mental Health and the Juvenile Justice System: Principles of Effective Decision-Making." *Stanford Law & Policy Review* 14:13–28.

Ashcraft v. Tennessee, 322 U.S. 143 (1944).

Baird, Abigail A., Staci A. Gruber, Deborah A. Fein, Luis C. Maas, Ronald J. Steingard, Perry F. Renshaw, Bruce M. Cohen, and Deborah A. Yurgelun-Todd. 1999. "Functional Magnetic Resonance Imaging of Facial Affect Recognition in Children and Adolescents." *Journal of the American Academy of Child & Adolescent Psychiatry* 38:195–99.

Baldwin, John. 1993. "Police Interview Techniques: Establishing Truth or Proof?" *British Journal of Criminology* 33:325–52.

Berghuis v. Thompkins, 130 S. Ct. 2250 (2010).

Beyer, Marty. 2000. "Immaturity, Culpability and Competency in Juveniles: A Study of 17 Cases." *Criminal Justice* 15 (2): 26–37.

Billings, F. James, Tanya Taylor, James Burns, Deb L. Corey, Sena Garven, and James M. Wood. 2007. "Can Reinforcement Induce Children to Falsely Incriminate Themselves?" *Law and Human Behavior* 31:125–39.

Birckhead, Tamar R. 2008. "The Age of the Child: Interrogating Juveniles after *Roper v. Simmons.*" *Washington and Lee Law Review* 65:385–450.

Bishop, Donna M. 2005. "The Role of Race and Ethnicity in Juvenile Justice Processing."

In *Our Children, Their Children: Confronting Racial and Ethnic Differences in American Juvenile Justice*, edited by Darnell F. Hawkins and Kimberly Kempf-Leonard, 23–82. Chicago: University of Chicago Press.

Bishop, Donna M., and Hillary B. Farber. 2007. "Joining the Legal Significance of Adolescent Developmental Capacities with the Legal Rights Provided by *In re Gault*." *Rutgers Law Review* 60:125–73.

Bishop, Donna M., and Charles Frazier. 1988. "The Influence of Race in Juvenile Justice Processing." *Journal of Research in Crime & Delinquency* 25:242–63.

Bishop, Donna M., and Charles Frazier. 1992. "Gender Bias in Juvenile Justice Processing: Implications of the JJDP Act." *Journal of Criminal Law and Criminology* 82:1162–86.

Bishop, Donna M., and Michael J. Leiber. 2012. "Racial and Ethnic Differences in Delinquency and Justice System Responses." *The Oxford Handbook of Juvenile Crime and Juvenile Justice*, edited by Barry C. Feld and Donna M. Bishop, 445–84. New York: Oxford University Press.

Bittner, Egon. 1976. "Policing Juveniles: The Social Context of Common Practice." In *Pursuing Justice for the Child*, edited by Margaret K. Rosenheim, 69–93. Chicago: University of Chicago Press.

Black, Donald J., and Albert J. Reiss, Jr. 1970. "Police Control of Juveniles." *American Sociological Review* 35:63–77.

Blumstein, Alfred. 1996. "Youth Violence, Guns, and the Illicit-Drug Industry." *Journal of Criminal Law and Criminology* 86:10–36.

Bonnie, Richard J., and Thomas Grisso. 2000. "Adjudicative Competence and Youthful Offenders." In *Youth on Trial: A Developmental Perspective on Juvenile Justice*, edited by Thomas Grisso and Robert G. Schwartz, 73–104. Chicago: University of Chicago Press.

Brady v. Maryland, 373 U.S. 83 (1963).

Bray, Timothy M., Lisa L. Sample, and Kimberly Kempf-Leonard. 2005. "Justice by Geography: Racial Disparity and Juvenile Courts." In *Our Children, Their Children: Confronting Racial and Ethnic Differences in American Juvenile Justice*, edited by Darnell F. Hawkins and Kimberly Kempf-Leonard, 270–99. Chicago: University of Chicago Press.

Breed v. Jones, 421 U.S. 519 (1975).

Bridges, George, and Sarah Steen. 1998. "Racial Disparities in Official Assessments of Juvenile Offenders: Attributional Stereotypes as Mediating Mechanisms." *American Sociological Review* 63:554–70.

Brooks v. Florida, 389 U.S. 413 (1961).

Brown v. Illinois, 422 U.S. 590 (1975).

Brown v. Mississippi, 297 U.S. 278 (1938).

Bull, Ray. 2010. "The Investigative Interviewing of Children and Other Vulnerable Witnesses: Psychological Research and Working/Professional Practice." *Legal and Criminological Psychology* 15:5–23.

Bull, Ray, and Becky Milne. 2004. "Attempts to Improve the Police Interviewing of Suspects." In *Interrogations, Confessions, and Entrapment*, edited by G. Daniel Lassiter, 181–96. New York: Kluwer Academic.

Bull, Ray, and Stavroula Soukara. 2010. "Four Studies of What Really Happens in Police Interviews." In *Police Interrogations and False Confessions: Current Research, Practice, and Policy Recommendations*, edited by G. Daniel Lassiter and Christian A. Meissner, 81–96. Washington, DC: American Psychological Association.

Burruss, George W., Jr., and Kimberly Kempf-Leonard. 2002. "The Questionable Advantage of Defense Counsel in Juvenile Court." *Justice Quarterly* 19:37–68.

Cassell, Paul G. 1996. "*Miranda*'s Social Costs: An Empirical Reassessment." *Northwestern University Law Review* 90:387–499.

Cassell, Paul G. 1998. "Protecting the Innocent from False Confessions and Lost Confessions—And from *Miranda*." *Journal of Criminal Law and Criminology* 88:497–556.

Cassell, Paul G., and Bret S. Hayman. 1996. "Police Interrogation in the 1990s: An Empirical Study of the Effects of *Miranda*." *UCLA Law Review* 43:839–932.

Chao, Raymond. 2000. "Mirandizing Kids: Not as Simple as A-B-C." *Whittier Law Review* 21:521–56.

Chavez v. Martinez, 538 U.S. 760 (2003).

Chesney-Lind, Meda. 1988. "Girls and Status Offenses: Is Juvenile Justice Still Sexist?" *Criminal Justice Abstracts* 20:144–65.

Chesney-Lind, Meda, and Joanne Belknap. 2004. "Trends in Delinquent Girls' Aggression and Violent Behavior: A Review of the Evidence." In *Aggression, Antisocial Behavior, and Violence among Girls: A Developmental Perspective*, edited by Martha Putallaz and Karen L. Bierman, 203–22. New York: Guilford.

Chesney-Lind, Meda, and Lisa Pasko. 2004. *The Female Offender: Girls, Women, and Crime*. 2nd ed. Thousand Oaks, CA: Sage.

Cicourel, Aaron V. 1995. *The Social Organization of Juvenile Justice*. New Brunswick, NJ: Transaction. First published 1968.

Clarke, John P., and Richard E. Sykes. 1974. "Some Determinants of Police Organization and Practice in a Modern Industrial Democracy." In *Handbook of Criminology*, edited by Daniel Glaser, 455–94. Chicago: Rand-McNally.

Clymer, Stephen D. 2002. "Are Police Free to Disregard *Miranda*?" *Yale Law Journal* 112:447–552.

Colorado v. Connelly, 479 U.S. 157 (1986).

Colorado v. Spring, 479 U.S. 564 (1987).

Commonwealth v. A Juvenile, 449 N.E.2d 654 (Mass. 1983).

Cooper, Deborah K. 1997. "Juveniles' Understanding of Trial-Related Information: Are They Competent Defendants?" *Behavioral Sciences & the Law* 15:167–80.

Corbin, Juliet, and Anselm Strauss. 2008. *Basics of Qualitative Research: Techniques and Procedures for Developing Grounded Theory*. 3rd ed. Thousand Oaks, CA: Sage.

Corley v. United States, 129 S. Ct. 1558 (2009).

County of Riverside v. McLaughlin, 500 U.S. 44 (1991).

Cowden, Vance L., and Geoffrey R. McKee. 1995. "Competency to Stand Trial in Juvenile Delinquency Proceedings: Cognitive Maturity and the Attorney-Client Relationship." *University of Louisville Journal of Family Law* 33:629–60.

Culombe v. Connecticut, 367 U.S. 568 (1961).

Dahl, Ronald E. 2001. "Affect Regulation, Brain Development, and Behavioral/Emotional Health in Adolescence." *CNS Spectrums* 6:60–72.

Damaska, Mirjan. 1975. "Structures of Authority and Comparative Criminal Procedure." *Yale Law Journal* 84:480–544.

Davis v. United States, 512 U.S. 452 (1994).

"Developments in the Law: Confessions." 1966. *Harvard Law Review* 79:935–1119.

Dickerson v. United States, 530 U.S. 428 (2000).

Drake, Kim E., Ray Bull, and Julian C. W. Boon. 2008. "Interrogative Suggestibility, Self-Esteem, and the Influence of Negative Life-Events." *Legal and Criminological Psychology* 13:299–307.

Dripps, Donald A. 1996. "Police, Plus Perjury, Equals Polygraphy." *Journal of Criminal Law and Criminology* 86:693–716.

Drizin, Steven A., and Beth A. Colgan. 2004. "Tales from the Juvenile Confession Front: A Guide to How Standard Police Interrogation Tactics Can Produce Coerced and False Confessions from Juvenile Suspects." In *Interrogations, Confessions, and Entrapment*, edited by G. Daniel Lassiter, 127–62. New York: Kluwer Academic.

Drizin, Steven A., and Richard A. Leo. 2004. "The Problem of False Confessions in the Post-DNA World." *North Carolina Law Review* 82:891–1008.

Drizin, Steven A., and Greg Luloff. 2007. "Are Juvenile Courts a Breeding Ground for Wrongful Convictions?" *Northern Kentucky Law Review* 34:257–322.

Drizin, Steven A., and Marissa J. Reich. 2004. "Heeding the Lessons of History: The Need for Mandatory Recording of Police Interrogations to Accurately Assess the Reliability and Voluntariness of Confessions." *Drake Law Review* 52:619–46.

Drope v. Missouri, 420 U.S. 162 (1975).

Duckworth v. Eagan, 492 U.S. 195 (1988).

Dusky v. United States, 362 U.S. 402 (1960).

Eagan Police Department. 2006. Police Department Manual. In author's possession.

Emerson, Robert M. 1974. "Role Determinants in Juvenile Court." In *Handbook of Criminology*, edited by Daniel Glaser, 621–50. Chicago: Rand-McNally.

Escobedo v. Illinois, 378 U.S. 478 (1964).

Evans, Roger. 1993. *The Conduct of Police Interviews with Juveniles*. Royal Commission on Criminal Justice Report. London: HMSO.

Evans, Roger. 1994. "Police Interrogations and the Royal Commission on Criminal Justice." *Policing and Society: An International Journal of Research and Policy* 4:73–81.

Farber, Hillary B. 2004. "The Role of the Parent/Guardian in Juvenile Custodial Interrogations: Friend or Foe?" *American Criminal Law Review* 41:1277–1312.

Fare v. Michael C., 442 U.S. 707 (1979).

Feeney, Floyd. 2000. "Police Clearances: A Poor Way to Measure the Impact of *Miranda* on the Police." *Rutgers Law Journal* 32:1–114.

Feld, Barry C. 1984. "Criminalizing Juvenile Justice: Rules of Procedure for the Juvenile Court." *Minnesota Law Review* 69:141–276.

Feld, Barry C. 1988a. "The Juvenile Court Meets the Principle of Offense: Punishment, Treatment, and the Difference It Makes." *Boston University Law Review* 68:821–915.

Feld, Barry C. 1988b. "*In re Gault* Revisited: A Cross-State Comparison of the Right to Counsel in Juvenile Court." *Crime & Delinquency* 34:393–424.

Feld, Barry C. 1989. "The Right to Counsel in Juvenile Court: An Empirical Study of

When Lawyers Appear and the Difference They Make." *Journal of Criminal Law and Criminology* 79:1185–1346.

Feld, Barry C. 1991. "Justice by Geography: Urban, Suburban, and Rural Variations in Juvenile Justice Administration." *Journal of Criminal Law and Criminology* 82:156–210.

Feld, Barry C. 1993. *Justice for Children: The Right to Counsel and the Juvenile Courts.* Boston: Northeastern University Press.

Feld, Barry C. 1995. "Violent Youth and Public Police: A Case Study of Juvenile Justice Law Reform." *Minnesota Law Review* 79:965–1128.

Feld, Barry C. 1998. "The Juvenile Court." In *The Handbook of Crime and Punishment,* edited by Michael Tonry, 509–41. New York: Oxford University Press.

Feld, Barry C. 1999. *Bad Kids: Race and the Transformation of the Juvenile Court.* New York: Oxford University Press.

Feld, Barry C. 2000. "Juveniles' Waiver of Legal Rights: Confessions, *Miranda,* and the Right to Counsel." In *Youth on Trial: A Developmental Perspective on Juvenile Justice,* edited by Thomas Grisso and Robert G. Schwartz, 105–38. Chicago: University of Chicago Press.

Feld, Barry C. 2003a. "The Constitutional Tension between *Apprendi* and *McKeiver:* Sentence Enhancements Based on Delinquency Convictions and the Quality of Justice in Juvenile Courts." *Wake Forest Law Review* 38:1111–1224.

Feld, Barry C. 2003b. "Race, Politics, and Juvenile Justice: The Warren Court and the Conservative 'Backlash.'" *Minnesota Law Review* 87:1447–1577.

Feld, Barry C. 2006a. "Juveniles' Competence to Exercise *Miranda* Rights: An Empirical Study of Policy and Practice." *Minnesota Law Review* 91:26–100.

Feld, Barry C. 2006b. "Police Interrogation of Juveniles: An Empirical Study of Policy and Practice." *Journal of Criminal Law and Criminology* 97:219–316.

Feld, Barry C. 2008. "A Slower Form of Death: Implications of *Roper v. Simmons* for Juveniles Sentences to Life without Parole." *Notre Dame Journal of Law, Ethics, and Public Policy* 22:9–65.

Feld, Barry C. 2009. "Violent Girls or Relabeled Status Offenders? An Alternative Interpretation of the Data." *Crime & Delinquency* 55:241–65.

Feld, Barry C., and Donna M. Bishop. 2011. "Juvenile Justice." In *The Oxford Handbook of Crime and Criminal Justice,* edited by Michael Tonry, 627–59. New York: Oxford University Press.

Feld, Barry C., and Donna M. Bishop. 2012. "Transfer of Juveniles to Criminal Court." In *The Oxford Handbook of Juvenile Crime and Juvenile Justice,* edited by Barry C. Feld and Donna M. Bishop, 801–41. New York: Oxford University Press.

Feld, Barry C., and Shelly Schaefer. 2010a. "The Right to Counsel in Juvenile Court: The Conundrum of Attorneys as an Aggravating Factor at Disposition." *Justice Quarterly* 27:713–41.

Feld, Barry C., and Shelly Schaefer. 2010b. "The Right to Counsel in Juvenile Court: Law Reform to Deliver Legal Services and Reduce Justice by Geography." *Criminology & Public Policy* 9:327–56.

Frazier v. Cupp, 394 U.S. 731 (1969).

Furby, Lita, and Ruth Beyth-Marom. 1992. "Risk Taking in Adolescence: A Decision-Making Perspective." *Developmental Review* 12:1–44.

Gaarder, Emily, Nancy Rodriguez, and Marjorie S. Zatz. 2004. "Criers, Liars, and Manipulators: Probation Officers' Views of Girls." *Justice Quarterly* 21:547–78.

Gallegos v. Colorado, 370 U.S. 49 (1962).

Gardner, William. 1993. "A Life-Span Rational Choice Theory of Risk Taking." In *Adolescent Risk Taking*, edited by Nancy J. Bell and Robert W. Bell, 66–83. Thousand Oaks, CA: Sage.

Garland, David. 2001. *The Culture of Control: Crime and Social Order in Contemporary Society*. Chicago: University of Chicago Press.

Garrett, Brandon L. 2008. "Judging Innocence." *Columbia Law Review* 108:55–142.

Garrett, Brandon L. 2010. "The Substance of False Confessions." *Stanford Law Review* 62:1051–1118.

Garrett, Brandon L. 2011. *Convicting the Innocent: Where Criminal Prosecutions Go Wrong*. Cambridge: Harvard University Press.

Giedd, Jay. 2002. "Inside the Teenage Brain: Interview with Jay Giedd." *Frontline*, PBS, March 31. http://www.pbs.org/wgbh/pages/frontline/shows/teenbrain/interviews/giedd.html.

Godsey, Mark A. 2005. "Rethinking the Involuntary Confession Rule: Toward a Workable Test for Identifying Compelled Self-Incrimination." *California Law Review* 93:465–540.

Gohara, Miriam S. 2006. "A Lie for a Lie: False Confessions and the Case for Reconsidering the Legality of Deceptive Interrogation Techniques." *Fordham Urban Law Journal* 33:791–842.

Goldstein, Alan, and Naomi E. Sevin Goldstein. 2010. *Evaluating Capacity to Waive Miranda Rights*. New York: Oxford University Press.

Goldstein, Naomi E. Sevin, Lois Oberlander Condie, Rachel Kalbeitzer, Douglas Osman, and Jessica L. Geier. 2003. "Juvenile Offenders' *Miranda* Rights Comprehension and Self-Reported Likelihood of Offering False Confessions." *Assessment* 10:359–69.

Graham v. Florida, 130 S. Ct. 2011 (2010).

Graham, Fred P. 1970. *The Due Process Revolution and the Warren Court's Impact on Criminal Law*. New York: Hayden.

Grano, Joseph D. 1979. "Voluntariness, Free Will, and the Law of Confessions." *Virginia Law Review* 65:859–946.

Grano, Joseph D. 1986. "Selling the Idea to Tell the Truth: The Professional Interrogator and Modern Confessions Law." *Journal of Criminal Law and Criminology* 89:1465–98.

Grano, Joseph D. 1993. *Confessions, Truth, and the Law*. Ann Arbor: University of Michigan Press.

Grisso, Thomas. 1980. "Juveniles' Capacities to Waive *Miranda* Rights: An Empirical Analysis." *California Law Review* 68:1134–66.

Grisso, Thomas. 1981. *Juveniles' Waivers of Rights: Legal and Psychological Competence*. Vol. 3, *Perspectives in Law & Psychology*. New York: Plenum.

Grisso, Thomas. 1983. "Juveniles' Consent in Delinquency Proceedings." In *Children's Competence to Consent*, edited by Gary B. Melton, Gerald P. Koocher, and Michael J. Saks, 131–48. New York: Plenum.

Grisso. Thomas. 1997a. "The Competence of Adolescents as Trial Defendants." *Psychology, Public Policy & Law* 3:3–32.

Grisso, Thomas. 1997b. "Juvenile Competency to Stand Trial: Questions in an Era of Punitive Reform." *Criminal Justice* 12 (3): 4–11.

Grisso, Tomas. 1998. *Instruments for Assessing Understanding and Appreciation of* Miranda *Rights*. Sarasota, FL: Professional Resource Press.

Grisso, Thomas. 2000. "What We Know about Youths' Capacities as Trial Defendants." In *Youth on Trial: A Developmental Perspective on Juvenile Justice*, edited by Thomas Grisso and Robert G. Schwartz, 139–72. Chicago: University of Chicago Press.

Grisso, Thomas. 2002. "Juveniles' Competence to Stand Trial: New Questions for an Era of Punitive Juvenile Justice Reform." In *More Than Meets the Eye: Rethinking, Assessment, Competency and Sentencing for a Harsher Era of Juvenile Justice*, edited by Patricia Puritz, Alycia Capozello, and Wendy Shang, 23–38. Washington, DC: American Bar Association Juvenile Justice Center.

Grisso, Thomas. 2004. *Double Jeopardy: Adolescent Offenders with Mental Disorders*. Chicago: University of Chicago Press.

Grisso, Thomas, and Carolyn Pomiciter. 1977. "Interrogation of Juveniles: An Empirical Study of Procedures, Safeguards and Rights Waiver." *Law and Human Behavior* 1:321–42.

Grisso, Thomas, and Melissa Ring. 1979. "Parents' Attitudes toward Juveniles' Right in Interrogation." *Criminal Justice and Behavior* 6:211–26.

Grisso, Thomas, Laurence Steinberg, Jennifer Woolard, Elizabeth Cauffman, Elizabeth Scott, Sandra Graham, Fran Lexcen, N. Dickon Reppucci, and Robert Schwartz. 2003. "Juveniles' Competence to Stand Trial: A Comparison of Adolescents' and Adults' Capacities as Trial Defendants." *Law and Human Behavior* 27:333–63.

Gross, Samuel R., Kristen Jacoby, Daniel J. Matheson, Nicholas Montgomery, and Sujata Patil. 2005. "Exonerations in the United States: 1989 through 2003." *Journal of Criminal Law and Criminology* 95:523–60.

Gruber, Staci A., and Deborah A. Yurgelun-Todd. 2006. "Neurobiology and the Law: A Role in Juvenile Justice." *Ohio State. Journal of Criminal Law* 3:321–40.

Gudjonsson, Gisli H. 1991. "Suggestibility and Compliance among Alleged False Confessors and Resisters in Criminal Trials." *Medicine, Science and the Law* 31:147–51.

Gudjonsson, Gisli H. 2003. *The Psychology of Interrogations and Confessions: A Handbook*. Chichester, UK: Wiley.

Gudjonsson, Gisli H. 2010. "The Psychology of False Confessions: A Review of the Current Evidence." In *Police Interrogations and False Confessions: Current Research, Practice, and Policy Recommendations*, edited by G. Daniel Lassiter and Christian A. Meissner, 32–47. Washington, DC: American Psychological Association.

Haley v. Ohio, 332 U.S. 596 (1948).

Handler, Joel F., and Julie Zatz, eds. 1982. *Neither Angels nor Thieves: Studies in Deinstitutionalization of Status Offenders*. Washington, DC: National Academy Press.

Harris v. New York, 401 U.S. 222 (1971).

Hassell, Kimberly D., Jihong "Solomon" Zhao, and Edward R. Maguire. 2003. "Structural Arrangements in Large Municipal Police Organizations: Revisiting Wilson's Theory of Local Political Culture." *Policing: An International Journal of Police Strategies & Management* 26:231–50.

Huang, David T. 2001. "Less Unequal Footing: State Courts' Per Se Rules for Juvenile Waivers during Interrogations and the Case for Their Implementation." *Cornell Law Review* 86:437–82.

Huerter, Regina M., and Bonnie E. Saltzman. 1992. "What Do 'They' Think? The Delinquency Court Process in Colorado as Viewed by the Youth." *Denver University Law Review* 69:345–58.

Illinois v. Gates 462 U.S. 213 (1983).

Inbau, Fred E., John E. Reid, Joseph P. Buckley, and Brian C. Jayne. 2004. *Criminal Interrogation and Confessions.* 4th ed. Sudbury, MA: Jones & Bartlett Learning. First edition published 1962.

In re B.M.B., 955 P.2d 1302 (Kan. 1998).

In re Dino, 359 So. 2d 586 (La. 1978).

In re E.T.C., 449 A.2d 937 (Vt. 1982).

In re Gault, 387 U.S. 1 (1967).

In re Jerrell C.J., 699 N.W.2d 110 (Wis. 2005).

In re Omar L., 748 N.Y.S.2d 209 (Fam. Ct. 2002).

In re Winship, 397 U.S. 358 (1970).

J.D.B. v. N. Carolina, 131 S. Ct. 2394 (2011).

Johnson, Matthew B., and Ronald C. Hunt. 2000. "The Psycholegal Interface in Juvenile Assessment of *Miranda.*" *American Journal of Forensic Psychology* 18 (3): 17–35.

Jones, J. B. 2004. *Access to Counsel.* Washington, DC: Office of Juvenile Justice and Delinquency Prevention.

Kaban, Barbara, and Ann E. Tobey. 1999. "When Police Question Children, Are Protections Adequate?" *Journal of the Center for Children and the Courts* 1:151–60.

Kamisar, Yale. 1995. "On the 'Fruits' of *Miranda* Violations, Coerced Confessions, and Compelled Testimony." *Michigan Law Review* 93:929–1010.

Kamisar, Yale. 2007. "On the Fortieth Anniversary of the *Miranda* Case: Why We Needed It, How We Got It—and What Happened to It." *Ohio State Journal of Criminal Law* 5 (1): 163–203.

Kassin, Saul M. 1997. "The Psychology of Confession Evidence." *American Psychologist* 52:221–33.

Kassin, Saul M. 2005. "On the Psychology of Confessions: Does *Innocence* Put *Innocents* at Risk?" *American Psychologist* 60:215–28.

Kassin, Saul M. 2008. "False Confessions: Causes, Consequences, and Implications for Reform." *Current Directions in Psychological Science* 17:249–53.

Kassin, Saul M., Steven A. Drizin, Thomas Grisso, Gisli H. Gudjonsson, Richard A. Leo, and Allison Redlich. 2009. "Police-Induced Confessions: Risk Factors and Recommendations." *Law and Human Behavior* 34:49–52.

Kassin, Saul M., and Christina T. Fong. 1999. "'I'm Innocent!': Effects of Training on Judgments of Truth and Deception in the Interrogation Room." *Law and Human Behavior* 23:499–516.

Kassin, Saul M., and Gisli H. Gudjonsson. 2004. "The Psychology of Confession

Evidence: A Review of the Literature and Issues." *Psychological Science in the Public Interest* 5:33–67.

Kassin, Saul M., and Katherine L. Keichel. 1996. "The Social Psychology of False Confessions: Compliance, Internalization, and Confabulation." *Psychological Science* 7:125–28.

Kassin, Saul M., Richard A. Leo, Christian A. Meissner, Kimberly D. Richman, Lori H. Colwell, Amy-May Leach, and Dana La Fon. 2007. "Police Interviewing and Interrogation: A Self-Report Survey of Police Practices and Beliefs." *Law and Human Behavior* 31:381–400.

Kassin, Saul M., Christian A. Meissner, and Rebecca J. Norwick. 2005. "'I'd Know a False Confession If I Saw One': A Comparative Study of College Students and Police Investigators." *Law and Human Behavior* 29:211–27.

Kassin, Saul M., and Lawrence S. Wrightsman. 1985. "Confession Evidence." In *The Psychology of Evidence and Trial Procedure*, edited by Saul M. Kassin and Lawrence S. Wrightsman, 67–94. Beverly Hills, CA: Sage.

Kempf-Leonard, Kimberly. 2012. "The Conundrum of Girls and Juvenile Justice Processing." In *The Oxford Handbook of Juvenile Crime and Juvenile Justice*, edited by Barry C. Feld and Donna M. Bishop, 485–525. New York: Oxford University Press.

Kempf-Leonard, Kimberly, and Pernilla Johansson. 2007. "Gender and Runaways: Risk Factors, Delinquency, and Juvenile Justice Experiences." *Youth Violence and Juvenile Justice* 5:308–27.

Kempf-Leonard, Kimberly, and Lisa L. Sample. 2000. "Disparity Based on Sex: Is Gender-Specific Treatment Warranted?" *Justice Quarterly* 17:89–128.

King, Kenneth J. 2006. "Waiving Childhood Goodbye: How Juvenile Courts Fail to Protect Children from Unknowing, Unintelligent, and Involuntary Waivers of *Miranda* Rights." *Wisconsin Law Review* 2006:431–78.

King, Lesley, and Brent Snook. 2009. "Peering inside the Canadian Interrogation Room: An Examination of the Reid Model of Interrogation, Influence Tactics, and Coercive Strategies." *Criminal Justice and Behavior* 36:674–94.

Klein, Susan R. 2007. "Lies, Omissions, and Concealment: The Golden Rule in Law Enforcement and the Federal Criminal Code." *Texas Tech Law Review* 39:1321–53.

Kochel, Tammy R., David B. Wilson, and Stephen D. Mastrofski. 2011. "Effect of Suspect Race on Officers' Arrest Decisions." *Criminology* 49 (2): 473–512.

Koocher, Gerald P. 1992. "Different Lenses: Psycho-Legal Perspectives on Children's Rights." *Nova Law Review* 16:711–32.

Kostelnik, Jessica O., and N. Dickon Reppucci. 2009. "Reid Training and Sensitivity to Developmental Maturity in Interrogation: Results from a National Survey of Police." *Behavioral Sciences & the Law* 27:361–79.

Krzewinski, Lisa M. 2002. "But I Didn't Do It: Protecting the Rights of Juveniles during Interrogation." *Boston College Third World Law Journal* 22:355–88.

LaFave, Wayne R. 1965. *Arrest*. Boston: Little, Brown.

LaFave, Wayne R., Jerold H. Israel, Nancy J. King, and Orin S. Kerr. 2009. *Criminal Procedure*. 5th ed. St. Paul, MN: Thomson Reuters.

Larson, Kimberly. 2003. "Improving the 'Kangaroo Courts': A Proposal for Reform in Evaluating Juveniles' Waiver of *Miranda.*" *Villanova Law Review* 48:629–68.

Lassiter, G. Daniel, Shari Seidman Diamond, Heather C. Schmidt, and Jennifer K. Elek. 2007. "Evaluating Videotaped Confessions: Expertise Provides No Defense against the Camera-Perspective Effect." *Psychological Science* 18:224–26.

Lassiter, G. Daniel, and Andrew L. Geers. 2004. "Bias and Accuracy in the Evaluation of Confession Evidence." In *Interrogations, Confessions, and Entrapment*, edited by G. Daniel Lassiter, 197–214. New York: Kluwer Academic.

Leiber, Michael J. 2003. *The Contexts of Juvenile Justice Decision Making: When Race Matters.* Albany: SUNY Press.

Leiken, Lawrence S. 1970. "Police Interrogation in Colorado: The Implementation of *Miranda.*" *Denver Law Journal* 47:1–53.

Leo, Richard A. 1992. "From Coercion to Deception: The Changing Nature of Police Interrogation in America." *Crime, Law, and Social Change* 18:35–59.

Leo, Richard A. 1996a. "The Impact of *Miranda* Revisited." *Journal of Criminal Law and Criminology* 86:621–92.

Leo, Richard A. 1996b. "Inside the Interrogation Room." *Journal of Criminal Law and Criminology* 86:266–303.

Leo, Richard A. 1996c. "*Miranda*'s Revenge: Police Interrogation as a Confidence Game." *Law & Society Review* 30:259–88.

Leo, Richard A. 2004. "The Third Degree and the Origins of Psychological Interrogation in the United States." In *Interrogations, Confessions, and Entrapment*, edited by G. Daniel Lassiter, 37–84. New York: Kluwer Academic.

Leo, Richard A. 2008. *Police Interrogation and American Justice.* Cambridge: Harvard University Press.

Leo, Richard A. 2009. "False Confessions: Causes, Consequences and Implications." *Journal of American Academy of Psychiatry and the Law* 37:332–43.

Leo, Richard A., and Steven A. Drizin. 2010. "The Three Errors: Pathways to False Confession and Wrongful Conviction." In *Police Interrogations and False Confessions: Current Research, Practice, and Policy Recommendations*, edited by G. Daniel Lassiter and Christian A. Meissner, 9–30. Washington, DC: American Psychological Association.

Leo, Richard, Steven A. Drizin, Peter J. Neufeld, Bradley R. Hall, and Amy Vatner. 2006. "Bringing Reliability Back In: False Confessions and Legal Safeguards in the Twenty-First Century." *Wisconsin Law Review* 2006:479–539.

Leo, Richard A., and Richard J. Ofshe. 1998. "The Consequences of False Confessions: Deprivations of Liberty and Miscarriages of Justice in the Age of Psychological Interrogation." *Journal of Criminal Law and Criminology* 88:429–96.

Leo, Richard A., and Welsh S. White. 1999. "Adapting to *Miranda*: Modern Interrogators' Strategies for Dealing with the Obstacles Posed by *Miranda.*" *Minnesota Law Review* 84:397–472.

Lyon, Thomas D. 1999. "The New Wave in Children's Suggestibility Research: A Critique." *Cornell Law Review* 84:1004–87.

Magid, Laurie. 2001. "Deceptive Police Interrogation Practices: How Far Is Too Far?" *Michigan Law Review* 99:1168–1210.

Mallory v. United States, 354 U.S. 449 (1957).

Malone, Patrick. 1986. "You Have the Right to Remain Silent: *Miranda* after Twenty Years." *American Scholar* 55:367–89.

Manning, Peter K. 1997. *Police Work: The Social Organization of Policing.* 2nd ed. Long Grove, IL: Waveland.

Maroney, Terry A. 2009. "The False Promise of Adolescent Brain Science in Juvenile Justice." *Notre Dame Law Review* 85:89–176.

Massiah v. United States 377 U.S. 201 (1964).

Matza, David. 1964. *Delinquency and Drift.* New York: Wiley.

Maxson, Cheryl L., and Malcolm W. Klein. 1997. *Responding to Troubled Youth.* New York: Oxford University Press.

McCarthy, Francis Barry. 1981. "Pre-adjudicatory Rights in Juvenile Court: An Historical and Constitutional Analysis." *University of Pittsburgh Law Review* 42:457–514.

McCord, Joan, Cathy Spatz Widom, and Nancy A. Crowell. 2001. *Juvenile Crime, Juvenile Justice.* Washington DC: National Academy Press.

McKeiver v. Pennsylvania 403 U.S. 528 (1971).

McMullen, Patrick M. 2005. "Questioning the Questions: The Impermissibility of Police Deception in Interrogations of Juveniles." *Northwestern University Law Review* 99:971–1006.

McNabb v. United States, 318 U.S. 332 (1943).

Medalie, Richard J. 1968. "Custodial Police Interrogation in Our Nation's Capital: The Attempt to Implement *Miranda.*" *Michigan Law Review* 66:1347–1422.

Meehan, Albert J. 1993. "Internal Police Records and the Control of Juveniles." *British Journal of Criminology* 33:504–24.

Meehan, Albert J. 2000. "The Organizational Career of Gang Statistics: The Politics of Policing Gangs." *Sociological Quarterly* 41:337–70.

Meissner, Christian A., and Saul M. Kassin. 2002. "'He's Guilty!': Investigator Bias in Judgments of Truth and Deception." *Law and Human Behavior* 26:469–80.

Meissner, Christian A., and Saul M. Kassin. 2004. "'You're Guilty, So Just Confess!': Cognitive and Behavioral Confirmation Biases in the Interrogation Room." In *Interrogations, Confessions, and Entrapment,* edited by G. Daniel Lassiter, 85–106. New York: Kluwer Academic.

Meissner, Christian A., Melissa B. Russano, and Fadia M. Narchet. 2010. "The Importance of Laboratory Science for Improving the Diagnostic Value of Confession Evidence." In *Police Interrogations and False Confessions: Current Research, Practice, and Policy Recommendations,* edited by G. Daniel Lassiter and Christian A. Meissner, 49–66. Washington, DC: American Psychological Association.

Meyer, Jessica R., and Dickon N. Reppucci. 2007. "Police Practices and Perceptions Regarding Juvenile Interrogation and Interrogative Suggestibility." *Behavioral Sciences & the Law* 25:757–80.

Michigan v. Tucker, 417 U.S. 433 (1974).

Miller v. Fenton, 474 U.S. 104 (1985).

Miller, Susan L. 2005. *Victims as Offenders: The Paradox of Women's Violence in Relationships.* New Brunswick: Rutgers University Press.

Milne, Rebecca, and Ray Bull. 1999. *Investigative Interviewing: Psychology and Practice*. Chichester, UK: Wiley.

"Minnesota Police Departments." 2010. USA Cops: The Nation's Law Enforcement Website. http://www.usacops.com/mn/ (accessed July 1, 2010).

Minow, Martha L. 1990. *Making All the Difference: Inclusion, Exclusion, and American Law*. Ithaca: Cornell University Press.

Miranda v. Arizona, 384 U.S. 436 (1966).

Missouri v. Seibert, 542 U.S. 600 (2004).

Moran v. Burbine, 475 U.S. 412 (1986).

Morse, Stephen J. 1997. "Immaturity and Irresponsibility." *Journal of Criminal Law and Criminology* 88:15–67.

Morse, Stephen J. 2004. "New Neuroscience, Old Problems." In *Neuroscience and the Law: Brain, Mind and the Scales of Justice*, edited by Brent Garland, 157–98. New York: Dana.

Morse, Stephen J. 2006. "Brain Overclaim Syndrome and Criminal Responsibility: A Diagnostic Note." *Ohio State Journal of Criminal Law* 3:397–412.

Mosteller, Robert P. 2007. "Police Deception before *Miranda* Warnings: The Case for Per Se Prohibition of an Entirely Unjustified Practice at the Most Critical Moment." *Texas Tech Law Review* 39:1239–74.

Murphy v. Waterfront Comm'n, 378 U.S. 52 (1964).

Nardulli, Peter F., James Eisenstein, and Roy B. Fleming. 1988. *The Tenor of Justice: Criminal Courts and the Guilty Plea Process*. Urbana: University of Illinois Press.

National Juvenile Defender Center. 2011. "National Juvenile Defender Centers Assessments." http://www.njdc.info/assessments.php (accessed February 11, 2011).

Nelson, Neil. 2006. *Strategies for the Recorded Interview*. St. Paul, MN: St. Paul Police Department.

Neubauer, David W. 1974. "Confessions in Prairie City: Some Causes and Effects." *Journal of Criminal Law and Criminology* 65:103–12.

Oberlander, Lois B., and Naomi E. Goldstein. 2001. "A Review and Update of the Practice of Evaluating *Miranda* Comprehension." *Behavioral Sciences & the Law* 19:453–71.

Office of Juvenile Justice and Delinquency Protection. 2011. "Easy Access to Juvenile Populations: 1990–2008." http://www.ojjdp.ncjrs.org/ojstatbb/ezapop/.

Ofshe, Richard J., and Richard A. Leo. 1997a. "The Decision to Confess Falsely: Rational Choice and Irrational Action." *Denver University Law Review* 74:979–1122.

Ofshe, Richard J. and Richard A. Leo. 1997b. "The Social Psychology of Police Interrogation: The Theory and Classification of True and False Confessions." *Studies in Law, Politics and Society* 16:189–251.

Oregon v. Bradshaw, 462 U.S. 1039 (1983).

Owen-Kostelnik, Jessica, N. Dickon Reppucci, and Jessica R. Meyer. 2006. "Testimony and Interrogation of Minors: Assumptions about Maturity and Morality." *American Psychologist* 61:286–304.

Packer, Herbert L. 1964. "Two Models of the Criminal Process." *University of Pennsylvania Law Review* 113:1–68.

Packer, Herbert L. 1968. *The Limits of the Criminal Sanction*. Stanford: Stanford University Press.

Paoline, Eugene A., III. 2003. "Taking Stock: Toward a Richer Understanding of Police Culture." *Journal of Criminal Justice* 31:199–214.

Paoline, Eugene A., III, and William Terrill. 2005. "The Impact of Police Culture on Traffic Stop Searches: An Analysis of Attitudes and Behavior." *Policing: An International Journal of Police Strategies & Management* 28:455–72.

Paus, Tomáš, Alex Zijdenbos, Keith Worsley, D. Louis Collins, Jonathan Blumenthal, Jay N. Giedd, Judith L. Rapoport, and Alan C. Evans. 1999. "Structural Maturation of Neural Pathways in Children and Adolescents: In Vivo Study." *Science* 283:1908–11.

Pearse, John, and Gisli H. Gudjonsson. 1996. "Police Interview Techniques at Two South London Police Stations." *Psychology, Crime & Law* 3:63–74.

Pearse, John, and Gisli H. Gudjonsson. 2003. "The Identification and Measurement of 'Oppressive' Police Interviewing Tactics in Britain." In *The Psychology of Interrogations and Confessions: A Handbook*, by Gisli H. Gudjonsson, 75–114. Chichester, UK: Wiley.

Pearse, John, Gisli H. Gudjonsson, I. C. H. Clare, and S. Rutter. 1998. "Police Interviewing and Psychological Vulnerabilities: Predicting the Likelihood of a Confession." *Journal of Community & Applied Social Psychology* 8:1–21.

Pennsylvania v. Muniz, 496 U.S. 582 (1990).

Peterson-Badali, Michele, Rona Abramovitch, Christopher J. Koegl, and Martin D. Ruck. 1999. "Young People's Experience of the Canadian Youth Justice System: Interacting with Police and Legal Counsel." *Behavioral Sciences and the Law* 17:455–65

Piliavin, Irving, and Scott Briar. 1964. "Police Encounters with Juveniles." *American Journal of Sociology* 7:206–14.

Podkopacz, Marcy Rasmussen, and Barry C. Feld. 1996. "The End of the Line: An Empirical Study of Judicial Waiver." *Journal of Criminal Law and Criminology* 86:449–92.

Podkopacz, Marcy Rasmussen, and Barry C. Feld. 2001. "The Back-Door to Prison, Waiver Reform, 'Blended Sentencing,' and the Law of Unintended Consequences." *Journal of Criminal Law and Criminology* 91:997–1072.

Poe-Yamagata, Eileen, and Michael A Jones. 1999. *And Justice for Some*. Washington, DC: Building Blocks of Youth.

Police and Criminal Evidence Act (PACE). 1984. c. 60, pt. V (Eng.) (revised 1991).

Pope, Carl E. 1994. "Racial Disparities in the Juvenile Justice System." *Overcrowded Times* 5:1–4.

Postell v. State, 383 So. 2d 1159 (Fl. Ct. App. 1980).

Puritz, Patricia, Sue Burrell, Robert Schwartz, Mark Soler, and Loren Warboys. 1995. *A Call for Justice: An Assessment of Access to Counsel and Quality of Representation in Delinquency Proceedings*. Washington, DC: American Bar Association, Juvenile Justice Center.

Reba, Stephen M., Randee J. Waldman, and Barbara Bennett Woodhouse. 2011. "'I Want to Talk to My Mom': The Role of Parents in Police Interrogation of Juveniles."

In *Justice for Kids: Keeping Kids Out of the Juvenile Justice System*, edited by Nancy E. Dowd, 219–38. New York: NYU Press.

Redding, Richard E., and Lynda E. Frost. 2001. "Adjudicative Competence in the Modern Juvenile Court." *Virginia Journal of Social Policy & the Law* 9:353–409.

Redlich, Allison D. 2004. "Mental Illness, Police Interrogations, and the Potential for False Confessions." *Psychiatric Services* 55:19–21.

Redlich, Allison D. 2007. "Double Jeopardy in the Interrogation Room: Young Age and Mental Illness." *American Psychologist* 62:609–11.

Redlich, Allison D. 2010. "False Confessions, False Guilty Pleas: Similarities and Differences." In *Police Interrogations and False Confessions: Current Research, Practice, and Policy Recommendations*, edited by G. Daniel Lassiter and Christian A. Meissner, 49–66. Washington, DC: American Psychological Association.

Redlich, Allison D., and Steven Drizin. 2007. "Police Interrogation of Youth." In *The Mental Health Needs of Young Offenders: Forging Paths toward Reintegration and Rehabilitation*, edited by Carol L. Kessler and Louis J. Kraus, 61–78. Cambridge: Cambridge University Press.

Redlich, Allison D., and Gail S. Goodman. 2003. "Taking Responsibility for an Act Not Committed: The Influence of Age and Suggestibility." *Law and Human Behavior* 27:141–56.

Redlich, Allison D., and Christian A. Meissner. 2009. "Techniques and Controversies in the Interrogation of Suspects." In *Psychological Science in the Courtroom: Consensus and Controversy*, edited by Jennifer L. Skeem, Kevin S. Douglas, and Scott O. Lilienfeld, 124–48. New York: Guilford.

Redlich, Allison D., Melissa Silverman, Julie Chen, and Hans Steiner. 2004. "The Police Interrogation of Children and Adolescents." In *Interrogations, Confessions, and Entrapment*, edited by G. Daniel Lassiter, 107–26. New York: Kluwer Academic.

Redlich, Allison, Melissa Silverman, and Hans Steiner. 2003. "Pre-adjudicative and Adjudicative Competence in Juveniles and Young Adults." *Behavioral Sciences & the Law* 21:393–410.

Reid, Christopher M. 2010. "Voluntary Confessions: An Examination of the Need to Restore a Pure Voluntary Confession Rule in *Corley v. United States*, 129 S. Ct. 1558 (2009)." *Nebraska Law Review* 89:184–217.

Reppucci, N. Dickon, Jessica Meyer, and Jessica Kostelnik. 2010. "Custodial Interrogation of Juveniles: Results of a National Survey of Police." In *Police Interrogations and False Confessions: Current Research, Practice, and Policy Recommendations*, edited by G. Daniel Lassiter and Christian A. Meissner, 67–80. Washington, DC: American Psychological Association.

Rhode Island v. Innis, 446 U.S. 291 (1980).

Richardson, Graeme, Gisli H. Gudjonsson, and Thomas P. Kelly. 1995. "Interrogative Suggestibility in an Adolescent Forensic Population." *Journal of Adolescence* 18:211–16.

Rogers, Richard. 2008. "A Little Knowledge Is a Dangerous Thing . . . Emerging *Miranda* Research and Professional Roles for Psychologists." *American Psychologist* 63:776–87.

Rogers, Richard, Kimberly S. Harrison, Daniel W. Schuman, Kenneth W. Sewell, and

Lisa L. Hazelwood. 2007. "An Analysis of *Miranda* Warnings and Waivers: Comprehension and Coverage." *Law and Human Behavior* 31:177–92.

Rogers, Richard, Lisa L. Hazelwood, Kenneth W. Sewell, Kimberly S. Harrison, and Daniel W. Schuman. 2008. "The Language of *Miranda* Warnings in American Jurisdictions: A Replication and Vocabulary Analysis." *Law and Human Behavior* 32:124–36.

Rogers, Richard, Lisa L. Hazelwood, Kenneth W. Sewell, Daniel W. Schuman, and Hayley L. Blackwood. 2008. "The Comprehensibility and Content of Juvenile *Miranda* Warnings." *Psychology, Public Policy and Law* 14:63–87.

Rogers v. Richmond 365 U.S. 534 (1961).

Roper v. Simmons, 543 U.S. 551 (2005).

Rosenberg, Irene Merker. 1980. "The Constitutional Rights of Children Charged with Crime: Proposal for a Return to the Not So Distant Past." *UCLA Law Review* 27:656–721.

Rothman, David. 1980. *Conscience and Convenience: The Asylum and Its Alternative in Progressive America*. Boston: Little, Brown.

Ruback, R. Barry, and Paula J. Vardaman. 1997. "Decision Making in Delinquency Cases: The Role of Race and Juveniles' Admission/Denial of the Crime." *Law and Human Behavior* 21:47–69.

Rubenstein, Jonathan. 1973. *City Police*. New York: Farrar, Straus, and Giroux.

Russano, Melissa B., Christian A. Meissner, Fadia M. Narchet, and Saul M. Kassin. 2005. "Investigating True and False Confessions within a Novel Experimental Paradigm." *Psychological Science* 16:481–86.

Ryerson, Ellen. 1978. *The Best-Laid Plans: America's Juvenile Court Experiment*. New York: Hill and Wang.

Safford v. Redding, 557 U.S. 364 (2009).

Sampson, Robert J., and John Laub. 1993. "Structural Variations in Juvenile Court Processing: Inequality, the Underclass, and Social Control." *Law & Society Review* 27:285–311.

Sampson, Robert J., and Janet L. Lauritsen. 1997. "Racial and Ethnic Disparities in Crime and Criminal Justice Research in the United States." *Crime and Justice: A Review of Research* 23:311–74.

Saywitz, Karen, Carol Jaenicke, and Lorinda Camparo. 1990. "Children's Knowledge of Legal Terminology." *Law and Human Behavior* 14:523–35.

Scheck, Barry, Peter Neufeld, and J. Dwyer. 2000. *Actual Innocence*. Garden City, NY: Doubleday.

Schlam, Lawrence. 1995. "Police Interrogation of Children and State Constitutions: Why Not Videotape the MTV Generation?" *University of Toledo Law Review* 26:901–36.

Schlossman, Steven L. 1977. *Love and the American Delinquent: The Theory and Practice of "Progressive" Juvenile Justice, 1825–1920*. Chicago: University of Chicago Press.

Schlossman, Steven L., and Stephanie Wallach. 1978. "The Crime of Precocious Sexuality: Female Juvenile Delinquency in the Progressive Era." *Harvard Educational Review* 48:655–94.

Schneckloth v. Bustamonte, 412 U.S. 218 (1973).

Schulhofer, Stephen J. 1981. "Confessions and the Court." *Michigan Law Review* 79:865–928.

Schulhofer, Stephen J. 1987. "Reconsidering *Miranda*." *University of Chicago Law Review* 54:435–61.

Schulhofer, Stephen J. 1996. "*Miranda*'s Practical Effect: Substantial Benefits and Vanishingly Small Social Costs." *Northwestern University Law Review* 90:500–563.

Schwartz, Ira M. 1989. *(In)Justice for Juveniles: Rethinking the Best Interests of the Child*. Lexington, MA: Lexington Books.

Schwartz, Ira M., Martha W. Steketee, and Victoria W. Schneider. 1990. "Federal Juvenile Justice Policy and the Incarceration of Girls." *Crime & Delinquency* 36:511–20.

Scott, Elizabeth S. 1992. "Judgment and Reasoning in Adolescent Decisionmaking." *Villanova Law Review* 37:1607–69.

Scott, Elizabeth S. 2000. "The Legal Construction of Childhood." *Hofstra Law Review* 29:541–88.

Scott, Elizabeth S., and Thomas Grisso. 1997. "The Evolution of Adolescence: A Developmental Perspective on Juvenile Justice Reform." *Journal of Criminal Law and Criminology* 88:137–89.

Scott, Elizabeth S., and Thomas Grisso. 2005. "Developmental Incompetence, Due Process, and Juvenile Justice Policy." *North Carolina Law Review* 83:793–846.

Scott, Elizabeth S., Dickon Reppucci, and Jennifer L. Woolard. 1995. "Evaluating Adolescent Decision Making in Legal Contexts." *Law and Human Behavior* 19:221–44.

Scott, Elizabeth S., and Laurence Steinberg. 2003. "Blaming Youth." *Texas Law Review* 81:799–840.

Scott, Elizabeth S., and Laurence Steinberg. 2008. *Rethinking Juvenile Justice*. Cambridge: Harvard University Press.

Seeburger, Richard H., and R. Stanton Wettick, Jr. 1967. "*Miranda* in Pittsburgh—A Statistical Study." *University of Pittsburgh Law Review* 29:1–26.

Sharpe v. United States, 470 U.S. 675 (1985).

Simon, David. 1991. *Homicide: A Year on the Killing Streets*. New York: Holt.

Singh, Krishna, and Gisli H. Gudjonsson. 1992. "Interrogative Suggestibility among Adolescent Boys and its Relationship with Intelligence, Memory, and Cognitive Set." *Journal of Adolescence* 15:155–61.

Skolnick, Jerome H. 1967. *Justice without Trial: Law Enforcement in Democratic Society*. New York: Wiley.

Skolnick, Jerome H., and Richard A. Leo. 1992. "The Ethics of Deceptive Interrogation." *Criminal Justice Ethics* 11:3–12.

Slobogin, Christopher. 2003. "Toward Taping." *Ohio State Journal of Criminal Law* 1:309–22.

Slobogin, Christopher. 2007. "Lying and Confessing." *Texas Tech Law Review* 39:1275–92.

Slobogin, Christopher, and Mark R. Fondacaro. 2011. *Juveniles at Risk: A Plea for Preventive Justice*. New York: Oxford University Press.

Smith, Trudie. 1985. "Law Talk: Juveniles' Understanding of Legal Language." *Journal of Criminal Justice* 13:339–53.

Snyder, Howard, and Melissa Sickmund. 2006. *Juvenile Offenders and Victims: 2006 National Report*. Washington, DC: Office of Juvenile Justice and Delinquency Prevention.

Soukara, Stavroula, Ray Bull, Aldert Vrij, Michael Turner, and Julie Cherryman. 2009. "What Really Happens in Police Interviews of Suspects? Tactics and Confessions." *Psychology, Crime & Law* 15:493–506.

Sowell, Elizabeth R., Paul M. Thompson, Colin J. Holmes, Terry L. Jernigan, and Arthur W. Toga. 1999. "In Vivo Evidence for Post-Adolescent Brain Maturation in Frontal and Striatal Regions." *Nature Neuroscience* 2:859–61.

Sowell, Elizabeth R., Paul M. Thompson, Kevin D. Tessner, and Arthur W. Toga. 2001. "Mapping Continued Brain Growth and Gray Matter Density Reduction in Dorsal Frontal Cortex: Inverse Relationships during Postadolescent Brain Maturation." *Journal of Neuroscience* 21:8819–29.

Spear, L. P. 2000. "The Adolescent Brain and Age-Related Behavioral Manifestations." *Neuroscience & Biobehavioral Reviews* 24:417–63.

Stahl, A., S. Livsey, and W. Kang. 2006. "Easy Access to State and County Juvenile Court Case Counts, 2003." http://www.ojjdp.ncjrs.gov/ojstatbb/ezaco/.

State v. Burrell, 697 N.W.2d 579 (Minn. 2005).

State v. Cayward, 552 So. 2d 971 (Fla. Dist. Ct. App. 1989).

State v. Hogan, 212 N.W. 2d 664 (Minn. 1973).

State v. Loyd, 212 N.W.2d 671 (Minn. 1973).

State v. Nunn, 297 N.W.2d 752 (Minn. 1980).

State v. Patton, 826 A.2d 783 (N.J. Super. Ct. App. Div. 2003).

State v. Presha, 748 A.2d 1108 (N.J. 2000).

State v. Scales, 518 N.W.2d 587 (Minn. 1994).

Steffensmeier, Darrell, Jennifer Schwartz, Sara Hua Zhong, and Jeffery Ackerman. 2005. "An Assessment of Recent Trends in Girls' Violence Using Diverse Longitudinal Sources: Is the Gender Gap Closing?" *Criminology* 43:355–405.

Steinberg, Laurence. 2005. "Cognitive and Affective Development in Adolescence." *Trends in Cognitive Science* 9:69–74.

Steinberg, Laurence, and Elizabeth Cauffman. 1996. "Maturity of Judgment in Adolescence: Psychosocial Factors in Adolescent Decision-Making." *Law and Human Behavior* 20:249–72.

Steinberg, Laurence, and Elizabeth Cauffman. 1999. "The Elephant in the Courtroom: A Developmental Perspective on the Adjudication of Youthful Offenders." *Virginia Journal of Social Policy & the Law* 6:389–418.

Steinberg, Laurence, Sandra Graham, Lia O'Brien, Jennifer Woolard, Elizabeth Cauffman, and Marie Banich. 2009. "Age Differences in Future Orientation and Delay Discounting. *Child Development* 80:28–44.

Steinberg, Laurence, and Elizabeth Scott. 2003. "Less Guilty by Reason of Adolescence: Developmental Immaturity, Diminished Responsibility, and the Juvenile Death Penalty." *American Psychologist* 58:1009–18.

Stephan v. State, 711 P.2d 1156 (Alaska 1985).

Stone, Geoffrey R. 1977. "The *Miranda* Doctrine in the Burger Court." *Supreme Court Review* 1977:99.

Sullivan, Thomas P. 2004. *Police Experiences with Recording Custodial Interrogations.* Chicago: Northwestern University School of Law.

Sullivan, Thomas P. 2006. "The Time Has Come for Law Enforcement Recordings of Custodial Interviews, Start to Finish." *Golden Gate University Law Review* 37:175–90.

Sullivan, Thomas P. 2010. "The Wisdom of Custodial Recording." In *Police Interrogations and False Confessions: Current Research, Practice, and Policy Recommendations,* edited by G. Daniel Lassiter and Christian A. Meissner, 127–42. Washington, DC: American Psychological Association.

Sutton, John. 1988. *Stubborn Children: Controlling Delinquency in the United Sates, 1640–1981.* Berkeley: University of California Press.

Sykes, Gresham M., and David Matza. 1957. "Techniques of Neutralization: A Theory of Delinquency." *American Sociology Review* 22:664–70.

Tanenhaus, David S. 2004. *Juvenile Justice in the Making.* New York: Oxford University Press.

Tanenhaus, David S., and Steven A. Drizin. 2002. "'Owing to the Extreme Youth of the Accused': The Changing Legal Response to Juvenile Homicide." *Journal of Criminal Law and Criminology* 92:641–706.

Tepfer, Joshua A., Laura H. Nirider, and Lynda M. Tricarico. 2010. "Arresting Development: Convictions of Innocent Youth." *Rutgers Law Review* 62:887–941.

Terrill, William, Eugene A. Paoline III, and Peter K. Manning. 2003. "Police Culture and Coercion." *Criminology* 41:1003–34.

Terry v. Ohio, 392 U.S. 1 (1968).

Tex. Fam. Code Ann. § 51.095(a)(1) (Vernon Supp. 2005).

Thomas, George C. 1996. "Is *Miranda* a Real-World Failure? A Plea for More (and Better) Empirical Evidence." *UCLA Law Review* 43:821–38.

Thomas, George C. 2007. "Regulating Police Deception during Interrogation." *Texas Tech Law Review* 39:1293–1319.

Tobey, Ann, Thomas Grisso, and Robert G. Schwartz. 2000. "Youths' Trial Participation as Seen by Youths and Their Attorneys: An Exploration of Competence-Based Issues." In *Youth on Trial: A Developmental Perspective on Juvenile Justice,* edited by Thomas Grisso and Robert G. Schwartz, 225–42. Chicago: University of Chicago Press.

Tonry, Michael. 2011. *Punishing Race: A Continuing American Dilemma.* New York: Oxford University Press.

United States v. Patane, 542 U.S. 630 (2004).

U.S. General Accounting Office. 1995. *Juvenile Justice: Representation Rates Varied as Did Counsel's Impact on Court Outcomes.* Washington, DC: Government Printing Office.

Viljoen, Jodi, Jessica Klaver, and Ronald Roesch. 2005. "Legal Decisions of Preadolescent and Adolescent Defendants: Predictors of Confessions, Pleas, Communication with Attorneys, and Appeals." *Law and Human Behavior* 29:253–78.

Viljoen, Jodi, and Ronald Roesch. 2005. "Competence to Waive Interrogation Rights and Adjudicative Competence in Adolescent Defendants: Cognitive Development, Attorney Contact, and Psychological Symptoms." *Law and Human Behavior* 29:723–42.

Viljoen, Jodi, Patricia Zapf, and Ronald Roesch. 2007. "Adjudicative Competence and Comprehension of *Miranda* Rights in Adolescent Defendants: A Comparison of Legal Standards." *Behavioral Sciences & the Law* 25:1–19.

Vrij, Aldert, Samantha Mann, and Ronald P. Fisher. 2006. "An Empirical Test of the Behavior Analysis Interview." *Law and Human Behavior* 30:329–45.

Wald, Michael, Richard Ayres, David W. Hess, Mark Schantz, and Charles H. Whitebread II. 1967. "Interrogations in New Haven: The Impact of *Miranda*." *Yale Law Journal* 76:1519–1648.

Watts v. Indiana, 338 U.S. 49, 54 (1949).

Weisselberg, Charles D. 1998. "Saving *Miranda*." *Cornell Law Review* 84:109–92.

Weisselberg, Charles D. 2008. "Mourning *Miranda*." *California Law Review* 96:1519–1601.

West v. United States, 399 F.2d 467 (5th Cir. 1968).

Westley, William A. 1970. *Violence and the Police: A Sociological Study of Law, Custom, and Morality*. Cambridge: MIT Press.

White, Welsh S. 1997. "False Confessions and the Constitution: Safeguards against Unworthy Confessions." *Harvard Civil Rights–Civil Liberties Law Review* 17:105–58.

White, Welsh S. 1998. "What Is an Involuntary Confession Now?" *Rutgers Law Review* 50:2001–58.

White, Welsh S. 2001. "*Miranda*'s Failure to Restrain Pernicious Interrogation Practices." *Michigan Law Review* 99:1211–47.

White, Welsh S. 2003. *Miranda's Waning Protections: Police Interrogation Practices after Dickerson*. Ann Arbor: University of Michigan Press.

Wilson, James Q. 1968a. "The Police and the Delinquent in Two Cities." In *Controlling Delinquents*, edited by Stanton Wheeler, 9–30. New York: Wiley.

Wilson, James Q. 1968b. *Varieties of Police Behavior: The Management of Law and Order in Eight Communities*. Cambridge: Harvard University Press.

Witt, James W. 1973. "Non-coercive Interrogation and the Administration of Criminal Justice: The Impact of *Miranda* on Police Effectuality." *Journal of Criminal Law and Criminology* 64:320–33.

Woolard, Jennifer L., Hayley M. D. Cleary, Samantha A. S. Harvell, and Rusan Chen. 2008. "Examining Adolescents' and their Parents' Conceptual and Practical Knowledge of Police Interrogation: A Family Dyad Approach." *Journal Youth Adolescence* 37:685–98.

Yarborough v. Alvarado, 541 U.S. 652 (2004).

Young, Deborah. 1998. "Unnecessary Evil: Police Lying in Interrogations." *Connecticut Law Review* 28:425–78.

Zahn, Margaret A., ed. 2009. *The Delinquent Girl*. Philadelphia: Temple University Press.

Zhao, Jihong, Ling Ren, and Nicholas Lovrich. 2010. "Wilson's Theory of Local Political Culture Revisited in Today's Police Organizations: Findings from Longitudinal Panel Study." *Policing: An International Journal of Police Strategies & Management* 33:287–304.

Zimring, Franklin E. 1981. "Kids, Groups, and Crime: Some Implications of a Well-Known Secret." *Journal of Criminal Law and Criminology* 72:867–85.

Zimring, Franklin E. 1998. *American Youth Violence*. New York: Oxford University Press.

INDEX

Crime Control Model, 5–6, 10, 11, 18, 19–20, 33, 104, 141, 161, 166, 170, 177, 228, 245–46, 248; and inquisitorial system, 5, 18, 33, 104, 141, 161, 229, 245–46; presumption of guilt, 20; and risk of error, 19, 228–29, 245. *See also* Due Process Model; Inquisitorial system

Criminal Interrogation and Confessions, 23

Criminal justice administration, 1, 13, 17, 254; constitutional dimensions of criminal procedure, 12–18, 255

Cruel trilemma, 4

Custodial interrogation, 13, 18, 22, 56, 63, 93, 249, 261, 267. *See also* Isolation of suspects

Data. *See* Methodology and data

Davis v. United States, 57, 58, 89, 98

Defense attorneys: and electronic recording of interrogations, 173–76, 264; for juveniles, 2, 38–39, 40, 173–76, 254–55; role in adversary system, 12, 16–17, 254

Delinquency and Drift, 128

Demeanor. *See* Juveniles interrogated

Denials, 9, 146, 147, 153

Detectives. *See* Police investigators

Developmental psychology, 2, 7–8, 9, 35, 45–50, 51–56, 82, 85, 87, 88–89, 101, 253; cognitive ability, 8, 35, 82, 87, 88–89, 101, 251–52; competence, 35, 45, 50, 240–41; judgment, 8, 35, 82, 87, 90, 165; and juveniles' false confessions, 240–42; and juveniles' understanding of *Miranda,* 9, 35, 51–56, 72–73, 82–86, 87–89, 101, 247, 248, 251, 252, 253; and neuroscience, 46, 49–50. *See also* Juveniles, generally

Dickerson v. United States, 22, 81, 249, 250

Disproportionate minority confinement, 10, 178, 180–81, 210, 227–228. *See also* Race

DNA evidence, 115; exonerations, 43, 229, 230, 231, 240, 259. *See also* Wrongful convictions

Double jeopardy, 2

Drizin, Steven, 230

Drope v. Missouri, 55

Duckworth v. Eagan, 72

Due Process Clause, 13, 14, 161. *See also* Fourteenth Amendment; Voluntary confessions

Due Process Model, 5–6, 7, 19–20, 21, 33, 170, 177, 178, 228, 245–46, 268; adversarial system, 5, 18, 166, 178, 268; and risk of error, 19, 20, 228–29, 245, 268. *See also* Adversary system; Crime Control Model

Dusky v. United States, 54–55

Electronic recording of interrogations, 6, 22, 28, 73–74, 139, 166–70, 246, 248, 262–67; and appeal on the record, 170, 248, 262–67, 268; calls for, 10, 248, 262–63, 267; cautionary instructions to juries, 262; costs associated with, 265–67; and false confessions, 229, 235, 263; felony cases, 6; impact on justice administration, 166–70, 263–65, 266–67; judicial review of, 6, 265; jurisdictions mandating full or partial, 11, 28, 32, 257, 263–64; of juveniles, 73, 267; law enforcement, use of, 71, 73–74, 139, 262, 263, 272; need for, 32, 262–65; and police professionalism, 168, 262, 271; reduces suppression hearings, 167–68, 263–66, 267–68; research using, 31–32, 247, 267, 271, 272; selective recording, 235, 248, 257, 262, 265; state legislatures, 262, 263; value of, 262–65

Empower suspects, 5, 13, 18, 21, 22, 42, 57, 93, 102, 226, 247, 267–68

Escobedo v. Illinois, 17, 18, 255

Evans, Roger, 180

Evidence, admissibility of, 100–101

Evidence ploys, 112, 115–18

Factual accuracy, 1, 4, 14, 19, 20, 38, 228, 237, 245, 248, 255, 256, 268

False confessions, 3, 6, 8, 14, 32, 155, 156, 229, 234–35, 237, 238, 244–45, 246, 248, 256, 268, 279; classification error, 10, 232–34, 243; coercion error, 232; coercive interrogation, 232, 234–36; contamination error, 106, 107–8, 232, 235, 236, 246, 256, 263, 265; contrasted with routine interrogation, 10, 155, 230; disbelief in, 232–33, 235; electronic recording of interrogations, 10, 229, 263; false-evidence ploy, 10, 116–18, 231, 232, 235, 237, 238; frequency, 32–33, 229, 231, 237–38, 240, 243, 279; high-profile cases, 31, 156, 230, 231, 240, 242, 243, 244; investigative work prior to interrogation, 238–39, 244; juveniles, 32–33, 230; leading questions and, 109; length of time and, 8, 10, 155, 156, 231, 239, 243, 256, 258–59; lying about evidence, 232; police-induced, 229, 233–34; police interrogation manuals, 31–32, 232–33; and probable cause to interrogate, 10, 229; reliability of confessions, 10; types of, 233–34; research studying, 32–33, 229–32, 237–38; vulnerable suspects, 231, 234–35, 236–37, 239–42, 252, 258; wrongful convictions, 3, 229, 231, 240–42, 245, 246, 268. *See also* Classification error; Wrongful convictions

False evidence, 117–18, 231, 232, 234, 236–38, 242, 243, 244, 256; impact on innocent, 236–38

Leo, Richard, 30, 31, 76, 78, 79, 82, 101, 117, 120, 147, 154, 156, 159, 230, 256, 258
Lie detection: ability of police to distinguish truth-telling from deception, 232–33, 243; behavioral symptom analysis, 26, 232–33; nonverbal behaviors, 26, 233; police investigators as lie detectors, 232–33
Lying about evidence, 107, 232. *See also* False evidence

MacArthur Foundation Network on Adolescent Development, 47–48
Mallory v. United States, 261
Matza, David, 128
Maximization techniques, 9, 24, 25–27, 104, 106, 109, 110–26, 140, 160, 176, 206–7, 218, 231, 234, 243, 265, 278; accuse of other crimes, 126, 207; accuse of lying, 110, 113, 118–19; BAI questions, 110, 120–21, 140; challenge, 121–24; confront with evidence, 110, 111, 112–18, 140, 207, 285; false evidence, 110, 117–18; frequency used, 112; hypothetical evidence, 115–16, 243; increase uncertainty, 122; overstate seriousness, 110, 122–23; tell the truth, 119–20, 285; trouble for others, 124–26. *See also* Evidence ploys; Minimization techniques; Psychological interrogation
McKeiver v. Pennsylvania, 39
McNabb v. United States, 261
Media, 3, 6, 81, 84, 157, 230
Meehan, Albert, 181
Mentally ill suspects, 29, 42, 55, 128, 241, 242
Mentally retarded suspects, 29, 55, 239, 241, 242
Methodology and data, 271–81; counties, 272–73; data limitations, 278–79, qualitative data, 279–81; quantitative data, 274–78
Milne, Rebecca, 28, 257
Minimization techniques, 8, 9, 23, 24, 26–27, 104, 106, 110, 126–37, 140, 160, 176, 207–8, 218, 222, 227, 234, 257–58, 278; appeal to honor, 135–36, 140; appeal to self-interest, 127, 133–35, 140; blame the victim, 131–32; empathy and understanding, 122, 127, 135, 137; frequencies, 127–128; and investigative interview, 127–28, 257–58; minimize seriousness, 132, 136–37; mistake, 108, 128, 130–31, 134, 135, 136, 164; neutralization, 128–32, 140. *See also* Themes/scenarios
Minority juveniles. *See* Race
Miranda v. Arizona, 2, 5, 18–23, 104; Court decision's limiting impact, 22, 247, 248, 249, 250; custodial interrogation, 13, 18, 22,

41–42, 56, 63, 93, 249, 261, 267; empirical research, 30–31, 247; empower suspects, 5, 13, 18, 21, 22, 42, 57, 93, 102, 226, 247, 267–68; impact of, 2, 23, 30–31, 73; impeachment exception to, 22, 100; inherent coercion, 13, 18, 21, 22, 25, 93, 150; internal contradiction, 76, 93; police interrogation manuals, 8, 24–25; psychological interrogation, 23–25, 94; questioning outside of, 32, 100–101, 249, 279; secrecy in police interrogation, 23, 60, 70, 247, 267, 271; as symbolism, 7, 250
Miranda advisory form, 75, 89
Miranda rights: assert, 5, 12, 20, 22, 57, 74, 88–89, 97–100, 190, 249; deception during interrogation, 22, 76; failure to give, 32 ; Fifth Amendment, 7, 13, 18–19; Fourteenth Amendment, 13; invoke, 97–100; proper administration of, effect of, 7, 30–31, 32, 60, 73, 75–76, 89, 93–96
Miranda violations, 22, 100–101
Miranda waivers, 7, 93–96, 101, 104; appreciate legal consequences, 42, 53, 82–86, 248; electronic recording of, 7, 22, 71, 75; express waivers, 93–96, 97, 101; impact on charges, 174–75; implied waivers, 22, 93, 97; juveniles, 9, 35–42, 51–54, 93–96; low IQ, 52–53; in Minnesota, 45, 190; persuading suspects to waive *Miranda* rights, 7, 31, 76; and prior records, 98–100, 223–25; during police interrogation, 7, 56, 75; questioning following, 31, 32; rates of, 30–31, 93–96, 247, 249–50; reasons suspects waive, 95–96; requirement for knowing, intelligent, and voluntary, 7, 9, 22, 32, 35, 42–43, 50–51, 57, 60, 82–86, 98–99, 138, 249; voluntariness of, 9, 42, 46, 50, 90, 190; voluntariness of confessions, 32
Miranda warnings, 21, 104, 191; about parental presence, 190, 191; administering of, 9, 60, 63, 72–73, 75–82, 92–93; custody, 41–42; deemphasizing significance of, 76, 77–82; dumbed-down, 73, 90; during police interrogation, 7, 72–73, 76–82, 89; electronic recording of, 7; to empower suspects, 13, 21, 22, 42, 57, 93, 247, 267–68; impact on confessions, 30–31, 97–100; juveniles' understanding of, 9, 51, 72, 82–86, 87–89; offset inherent coercion, 13, 21, 22, 262; repeat back, 90–93; speed of administering, 9, 76–78; typical, 75; verbal complexity, 51, 72–73; versions of 51, 72–73
Misclassification. *See* Classification error
Missouri v. Seibert, 77, 250, 265
Moran v. Burbine, 22

Neuroscience, 46, 49–50, 58, 86, 143, 252
Nonverbal behaviors: anxiety, 26, 122, 234; belief in their validity as indicia of lying, 26, 232, 233, 258

Open-ended question, 30, 106–108
Oregon v. Bradshaw, 144

Packer, Herbert, 5–6, 19–20, 141, 268
Parental presence, 10, 29, 43–45, 58, 71–72, 181, 182, 187–206, 215, 253–54; legal requirement of, 43–44, 187; notification of, 10, 72, 190, 191, 195–98, 215, 225–26; police strategies to neutralize, 191–92, 200–203; policies underlying, 187–88, reasons for limited effectiveness, 188–89; reasons why youths do not request, 192–95; role of, 44–45, 181, 187–90, 203–6, 226, 254; and urging to tell the truth, 44, 187–89, 203–5, 226, 257
PEACE interviewing, 28–39, 32
Pennsylvania v. Muniz, 77
Phases of interrogation, 104; closure, 138, 154–55; constructing culpability, 154–55; free will, voluntary, 138–39, 154; interrogation, 106–37; *Miranda* phase, 78–82, 89–96; postadmission narratives, 235, 256, 265; softening up phase, 76–78, 249. *See also* Police interrogation; Psychological interrogation
Plea bargaining, 13–14, 86, 141, 166, 169, 173–76, 177, 264, 278; impact of electronic recording on, 166–70, 264–65
Police administration, 178–81; and community characteristics, 179–80, 181–82, 199–200, 211, 225; and parental notification, 195–200; and police culture, 179–80, 199–200
Police and Criminal Evidence Act (PACE), 28, 30, 32, 257, 262; and appropriate adult, 29; and electronic recording, 32, 257, 262, 263
Police interrogation, 24, 103–4; adversarial nature of, 20, 25, 29, 76; biased interpretations of, 104 ; as carrier of facts, 30, 105–6, 108, 119–20, 124, 139; closure, 138, 146; constructing culpability, 154–55; criminal investigation, 24; emphasis on convictions, 20, 28, 30, 104, 158–59, 246, 256; emphasis on incrimination, 24, 25, 28, 30, 32, 158–59, 246, 256; establishing rapport, 76–78, 105, 149, 264; form of question, 106–9; free-will and voluntary, 138–39, 154–55; guilt presumptive, 158–59, 232, 233, 234, 238; justification of, 9; juveniles and adults, 101, 241–42, 247, 252; maximization techniques, 110–126, 265; minimization techniques, 126–37; in Minnesota, 6, 29, 45, 72, 105–6, 141, 257, 266;

Miranda v. *Arizona*, impact of, 13, 30–31, 93–96; outcomes, 147–50; parental presence at, 10, 29; people present during, 9, 70–72; preparing for, 105–6, 108, 244; psychological tactics, 24, 26–27; questioning outside of *Miranda*, 100–101; Sixth Amendment right to counsel, 13, 17–18; training about juveniles, 70, 76, 110, 241–42, 247. *See also* Electronic recording of interrogations; Interrogation training manuals; Investigative interviewing; Maximization techniques; Minimization techniques; Phases of interrogation; Police interrogation manuals; Psychological interrogation
Police interrogation manuals, 8, 13, 24–25, 31–32, 100–101, 105; discount false confessions, 232–33. *See also* Interrogation training manuals
Police investigators, 103–4, 105; ability to distinguish truth-telling from deception, 25, 119, 120, 122, 232–33, 234, 235, 258; classification error, 232–34, 236, 238, 243, 244, 246, 257, 260; counselors compared to, 135, 149, 237; disbelief in false confessions, 25, 232–33, 235; establishing rapport, 76–78, 105, 149, 264; evidence possessed by, 103–4; goals of interrogation process, 20, 25, 28, 76, 96, 154–55, 158–59, 256; as lie detectors, 25, 119, 232–33, 258; lying during interrogation, 24, 107, 234, 237–38, 262; presumption of guilt, 20, 158–59, 232, 233, 234; styles of interrogation, 34, 103, 180, 278; training about juveniles, 27, 70, 76, 85, 110
Postadmission narratives, 235, 256, 265
Pretrial motions. *See* Suppression hearing
Privilege against self-incrimination. *See* Fifth Amendment; *Miranda v. Arizona*
Probable cause to interrogate, 10, 69, 229, 243, 244, 256–57, 258, 260
Progressive reformers, 1, 39, 282
Promises and threats, 14, 31, 123, 124, 125–26
Prompt presentment, 229, 260–61, 262
Prosecutors: adversary system, 12; confessions, use of, 94, 141, 166, 263, 278; view of youths who confess, 133;
Psychological interrogation, 8, 17, 24, 25–27, 34, 56, 76–77, 95, 104; closure, 138; establishing rapport, 76–78, 104; and guilt presumptive, 233; investigative interview, 28–29; manipulation, 104, 135, 234; maximization techniques, 25–26, 105–6, 110–26; minimization techniques, 25–26, 126–37; *Miranda* v. *Arizona*, 23–24; replacement of third degree, 17, 23–26; softening up, 76–78, 104;

training about, 24–25, 258. *See also* Phases of interrogation; Police interrogation

Questions, form of, 106–9, 140. *See also* Leading questions; Open-ended question

Race, 10, 40, 57, 60–61, 150, 209–12; and delinquents, 183, 184; and disproportionate minority confinement, 10, 178, 180–81, 210, 227–228; and geographic context, 10, 178, 180, 182, 210–11; impetus to get tough, 40

Race, juveniles interrogated: arrested, 214; attitude, 150, 211, 219–23, 227; confessions, 221; denial, 219, 221; detained, 214; and geographic locale, 212, 223–24, 272–73; length of interrogation, 222; location, 214–15; outcome and attitude, 220–22; and parental presence, 215, 226; police tactics, 218; present offense and prior record, 212–14, 226; responses, 219–23, 227; waive *Miranda*, 216–18, 223–24.

Reid, John, 23. *See also* Reid Method

Reid Method, 8, 23–27, 28, 31, 34, 64, 70, 104, 106, 109, 110, 128, 140, 156, 206–7, 232, 234, 243, 244, 257; alternative question, 132; Behavioral Analysis Interview (BAI), 26, 110; and false confessions, 234, 244; and juveniles, 27, 29, 70, 110, 202; and length of interrogation, 56, 156, 259; nine-step sequence, 26–27; and parents, 200–201, 202; themes and scenarios, 26, 128

Rhode Island v. Innis, 77, 160

Roper v. Simmons, 45–46, 48, 56

Schneckloth v. Bustamonte, 15

Scott, Elizabeth, 40

Secrecy in police interrogation, 14, 23, 60, 70, 247, 271. *See also* Isolation of suspects

Self-interest, 4, 12, 22

Sixth Amendment, 4, 5, 13, 17–18; right to counsel, 5, 17–18. *See also* Fifth Amendment; Fourteenth Amendment; Supreme Court

Slobogin, Christopher, 40

Snook, Bret, 31

State v. Burrell (Minnesota) 190, 196

State v. Scales (Minnesota), 11, 29, 71, 73, 74, 89, 90, 158, 166–70, 257, 266, 271–72, 279, 310n97; reduces suppression hearings, 167–70, 266–67

Stephan v. State (Alaska), 271, 272, 310n96

Suburban counties, 10, 66, 72; beer burglary, 186–87; demographic characteristics, 178–79, 181–82, 212, 272–73; delinquent

characteristics, 183–84; and parental presence, 72, 181, 182, 225; and police interrogators, 66

Suburban juveniles interrogated: arrested, 185; attitude, 209; confession, 209; detained, 185; location, 185; offense and prior record, 183–84; parental presence, 195–206; police tactics, 207; responses, 208–9; strength of evidence, 186; time until, 186; waive *Miranda*, 206. *See also* Parental presence; Race, juveniles interrogated

Suppression hearing, 7, 15, 16, 32, 33, 92, 101, 166–70, 238, 247, 256, 263, 264, 268; impact of electronic recording on, 166–70, 247, 263–66, 266–67

Supreme Court, 2, 4–5, 8, 12–23, 35–42, 57, 58, 244, 247; and decisions limiting impact of *Miranda*, 22, 247, 248, 249, 250; and efforts to regulate interrogation, 4–7, 13–18, 33, 247, 249–50, 251, 255–58, 260, 268; and Fifth Amendment, 18–23, 57, 58; and Fourteenth Amendment, 14–17; and interrogation of juveniles, 36–42, 248, 251–55; and juvenile court, 2, 35–42; and reduced culpability, 45–46; and Sixth Amendment, 17–18; and trickery during interrogation, 236. *See also* Fifth Amendment; Fourteenth amendment; *Miranda v. Arizona*; Sixth Amendment

Suspects: assert rights, 5–6, 19, 20, 22, 93–96; charges against, 94–95; establishing rapport with, 76–78, 104, 105, 138; invoke *Miranda*, 4, 19, 20, 97–100; isolation of, 5, 8, 23–24, 70, 234; juvenile, 1; *Miranda v. Arizona*, impact of, 30–31; softening up of, 76–78; "swearing contest" with police, 7, 17, 22–23, 247, 263, 271; waive rights, 30–31, 93–96; why they waive/confess, 95–96, 99

"Swearing contest" between police and suspect, 7, 17, 22–23, 247, 263, 271

Techniques of neutralization, 128–32

Television shows, 3, 81, 84, 157

Tell the truth, 3, 27, 76, 79, 80, 82, 95, 108, 119–20, 120, 133, 137; and Fifth Amendment, 3; interrogation tactic, 27, 76; parental urging, 44, 187–89, 203–5, 226, 257

Tell your story, 79, 80, 81, 106, 108, 121, 139

Terry v. Ohio, 258

Themes/scenarios, 104, 110, 126–37, 208, 218, 237, 257–58; adopted by juveniles, 129, 142, 143; and juvenile court treatment ideology, 137

Third degree, 14, 261, 262, 265; *Brown* v. *Mississippi*, 289n12, 289n13; era of, 14; Fourteenth Amendment, 14

ABOUT THE AUTHOR

Barry C. Feld is Centennial Professor of Law at the University of Minnesota and author or editor of many books, including *The Oxford Handbook of Juvenile Crime and Juvenile Justice, Cases and Materials on Juvenile Justice Administration*, and *Bad Kids: Race and the Transformation of the Juvenile Court.*